RADICAL CHAPTERS

Roy Kepler at Kepler's Books & Magazines, undated. Photographer unknown, courtesy of the Kepler family.

RADICAL CHAPTERS

*Pacifist Bookseller Roy Kepler
and the Paperback Revolution*

Michael Doyle

Syracuse University Press

∞ The paper used in this publication meets the minimum requirements
of the American National Standard for Information Sciences—Permanence
of Paper for Printed Library Materials, ANSI Z39.48-1992.

For a listing of books published and distributed by Syracuse University Press,
visit our website at SyracuseUniversityPress.syr.edu.

ISBN: 978-0-8156-1006-9

Library of Congress Cataloging-in-Publication Data

Doyle, Michael, 1956–
Radical chapters : pacifist bookseller Roy Kepler and the paperback revolution /
Michael Doyle. — First edition.
pages cm
Includes bibliographical references and index.
ISBN 978-0-8156-1006-9
1. Kepler, Roy C. 2. Kepler, Roy C.—Friends and associates—Biography.
3. Booksellers and bookselling—United States—Biography. 4. Pacifists—
United States—Biography. 5. Kepler's Books—History. 6. Paperbacks—
Publishing—History—20th century. 7. Bookstores—California—
Menlo Park—History. 8. Counterculture—United States—History—
20th century. I. Title.
Z473.K47D69 2012
381'.45002092—dc23
[B]   2012028712

Manufactured in the United States of America

To Beth, my bride

MICHAEL DOYLE is a reporter in the Washington, DC, bureau of the McClatchy newspaper chain. He is a graduate of Oberlin College. He earned a master's in government from The Johns Hopkins University and a master of studies in law from Yale Law School, where he was a Knight Journalism Fellow. His first book, *The Forestport Breaks: A Nineteenth-Century Conspiracy along the Black River Canal*, was also published by Syracuse University Press.

Contents

Illustrations

Acknowledgments

Honestly, I always figured I would write Roy Kepler's story, or try to. It was a feeling I had, for many years. But it was only after talking with Clark Kepler in January 2005 that I truly engaged.

Clark and his sister Dawn have been fantastically helpful, and they made this book possible. They opened their family records, shared their memories, and corrected the mistakes they saw. It can't be easy to let a reporter rummage around the attic, and I am grateful for their assistance and their tolerance.

Many people subjected themselves to interviews with me, and I appreciate every one. Some people, in particular, have gone above and beyond. Molly Black invited me to her home and has been kind throughout. Ira Sandperl is one of the world's great conversationalists, with a reservoir of stories and insights like you wouldn't believe. Historian Dennis McNally and Denise Kaufman put me in touch with assorted hip characters. Willy Legate and Alan Trist both wrote wonderfully detailed accounts of their Kepler's experiences. The late Ralph Kohn and his wife, Irene, provided hospitality and endless answers as they endured hours' worth of questions.

My turning-point meeting with Clark in January 2005 occurred while I was participating in the William and Barbara Edwards Media Fellow program at Stanford's Hoover Institution on War, Revolution and Peace. I especially thank executive assistant Mandy MacCalla for her help with this generous opportunity.

Historian Scott Bennett generously critiqued an early draft of the manuscript, and provided both encouragement and concrete advice. Eagle-eyed copy editor Jill Root polished the work.

Librarians and archivists—they are the best. Wendy Chmielewski, curator of the Swarthmore College Peace Collection, and her staff maintain a world-class resource and make it easy to use. The staffs at the Stanford University Archives in Green Library and the University of Maryland's Library of American Broadcasting were keenly professional.

Annelise Finegan, Mary Selden Evans, and Jennika Baines at Syracuse University Press have encouraged and accommodated me; they have made for this manuscript a wonderful home.

A project like this relies on good fortune, not all of which can be remembered. While working at the great *Palo Alto Weekly* in 1984, I drove to Grass Valley and interviewed Roy for several hours. Artist Ginny Mickelson carefully tended the tape recorder, which is something that wouldn't have occurred to me. The resulting tapes, rediscovered two decades later, proved invaluable. Attorney Jim Wolpman provided both sage counsel and documents relating to the Free U and the attacks that occurred in the late 1960s.

My employers at the McClatchy Company have been extremely helpful, more than they know, to tell the truth. Way, way back, the *Weekly* staff let me learn the journalism trade, in part by writing stories that decades later became the foundation for this book.

My parents, Joy and Bill Doyle, brought me to Kepler's the first time and then time and time again. They taught me to read, write, and question, lots and lots of questions.

My wife, Beth—well, words can hardly say. Except: thanks.

The errors, every single one of them, are my own.

Introduction

Closed.

Kepler's was closed. How could this be?

All morning, offerings and memories mounted outside the locked doors of Kepler's Books & Magazines in Menlo Park, California. Sunflowers and white roses were laid as at a bier. Mourners gathered in the nearby plaza, singly and then en masse. Cars slowed along El Camino Real, the Silicon Valley artery congesting more than usual. Kepler's hosted many demonstrations over the years: perhaps this was another. Drivers dawdled and then moved along, unsure of what they had just witnessed.

On the plaza, the first-arriving customers had gone through a common dumb show. They came, found the store doors locked, checked their watches, gave the handle a futile jiggle. They placed their hands to their eyebrows and peered through the windows. They could see the familiar stacks and shelves, but no human movement. They read the confounding sign: "Kepler's is Closed," and they looked around as if there might be an explanation.

It had started out such a lovely morning for bookstore browsing: August 31, 2005. The San Francisco Bay Area was in its glory, a monied, Mediterranean climate. Inside Kepler's, brightly colored banners still hung from the store's recently celebrated fiftieth anniversary. Some old-timers considered this latest cladding too sterile. Certainly the store was no longer revolutionary, the way it had been in May 1955 when Roy Kepler started selling paperbacks in his little Menlo Park . . . well, closet was what it was, back in the beginning. Still, as the gathering mourners told each other over and over: Kepler's was a *great* bookstore. If it was a book, Kepler's had it: 100,000 titles, at last count. It was the nation's best bookseller, *Publishers Weekly* had proclaimed several years earlier.

But books could be bought anywhere. Amazon.com or the big chains enticed with low prices, as the owners of independent bookstores like Kepler's knew all too well. Kepler's was, and here the gathering mourners searched for the right word and always found the same one: Kepler's was an *institution*. Its staff was famously free-spirited. "We fit," former Kepler's book buyer and poet Susan Mac-Donald once wrote, "like a badly knit sweater / all holes and space, but warm." The store itself was living history. Even casual customers could recite the chapter summaries; some were fortunate enough to know the principals.

"Roy Kepler. Dear Roy Kepler," singer Joan Baez had said, when asked about him by the *Palo Alto Weekly* in 1984. "Steady, solid, non-violent rock. Lovely man."

Roy Kepler was a World War II conscientious objector, educated and rendered more radical in a series of Civilian Public Service camps. He served as executive secretary of the War Resisters League. He founded myriad peace groups. He was a tax resister, a congressional witness, and a correspondent with the high and mighty. He helped promote the nation's first listener-supported radio station. He helped found one of the nation's first free universities. He survived a series of violent attacks. His store nurtured remarkable musicians when they were young and disreputable. He helped propel the paperback revolution and trained several generations of young booksellers.

"Roy," Grateful Dead lyricist and early Kepler's aficionado Robert Hunter said, "was an important man."

The plaza crowd swapped names like playing cards. Roy was Joan Baez's money manager, the man who helped guide her into tax resistance. His store welcomed a young Jerry Garcia, providing baklava and a place to hang. Roy debated pacifist tactics with the Chicago Seven's David Dellinger. Roy marched with Bayard Rustin, the immensely influential African American pacifist. When Ken Kesey needed someone to drive a bus, The Bus, he found his man abuzz at Kepler's.

When the young computer wiz Steve Wozniak needed an engineering book, he too went to Kepler's.

"It's almost certain that half of the books that bent my young mind, I got from there," said Stewart Brand, who begat the *Whole Earth Catalog* and its progeny.

Kepler's encounters changed lives. Take just one:

In the fall of 1959, Douglas Hofstadter was fourteen years old. His father was a Stanford University physicist, later to win the 1961 Nobel Prize, and the family had just returned from a sabbatical year in Switzerland. One evening Hofstadter and his father went to Kepler's Books & Magazines. The young teenager was drifting through the stacks when he spotted a thin paperback intriguingly titled *Gödel's Proof,* by Ernest Nagel and James R. Newman.

"I hadn't heard of Gödel," Hofstadter recalled, "but the idea of a book devoted solely to the detailed explanation of some proof, presumably some kind of mathematical proof, sounded extremely intriguing to me, so I flipped through the book, and soon I saw that it was all about how strict mathematical reasoning could be applied to derive rigorous results about the very process of mathematical reasoning itself. This was an absolutely mind-boggling idea to me, and I instantly knew I simply had to read this book and find out what it was all about."

Hofstadter ended up becoming fast friends with the sons of Nagel, then visiting Stanford, and *Gödel's Proof* exerted what Hofstadter called "an incredibly profound influence" on his own thinking. Years later, he says, the book he chanced upon at Kepler's and the thoughts it inspired led indirectly to his writing *Gödel, Escher, Bach: An Eternal Golden Braid,* which won the 1980 Pulitzer Prize.

Now, multiply that experience a millionfold. Every day Kepler's opened, for fifty years, it had braided together words and readers, ideas and people, men and women. Connections happened there, not all of them elevated but every one deeply human. Author Robert Stone, a Wallace Stegner Creative Writing Fellow at Stanford in the early 1960s, recalled Kepler's as both a very good bookstore and a happy hunting ground. So in his 2010 short story "From the Lowlands,"

Stone put into a Bay Area character's voice the recollection that one "could smoke dope and pick up chicks at Kepler's." It may not have been Gödel, but it was good.

Kepler's shaped my own life, for sure.

I grew up in the Bay Area. My parents tell me they first brought me to the original Kepler's when I was small, preliterate. That, I don't recall. But starting in about 1968, when I was twelve, I became a regular. I loved the books, of course. I bought them by the basket. Equally, I was drawn to the store's atmosphere. When I thought no one saw, I would hover over the newspaper rack and page avidly through the *Berkeley Barb,* the area's premier underground newspaper. Still later, when discombobulated, I would flake out on a store couch.

In the early 1980s, as a reporter for the *Palo Alto Weekly,* I began interviewing Roy and the people around him. The cultures that intersected through Kepler's fascinated me: The Ban-the-Bomb radicals, the Midpeninsula Free University, the rise of the sixties. What stories, what lives! One day a friend and I drove several hours out to Roy's home in the Sierra Nevada foothills to conduct a several-hour interview. It was for a newspaper article, but I kept the cassette tape for several decades, as if, I later fancied, it was a dormant seed awaiting its time. By January 2005, following conversations with Roy's son, Clark, I realized I needed to write the Kepler's story, A to Z. I began researching. By May 2005, on the occasion of the store's fiftieth anniversary, I was really starting to roll.

Yes, Kepler's Books & Magazines by August 2005 was an institution, though the term itself suggests its own twist. Once rebellious, the store had become cemented in place, and not just because Roy himself had died nearly eleven years before, on New Year's Day 1994. Some of what had made Kepler's, well, Kepler's had passed and was now legacy, framed pictures on the wall. Some of the stories on the plaza were being told wistfully: You should have been there, kid: Back when Roy sat down in front of the Oakland Induction Center, back when his store was unique in carrying both *Playboy* and *Paris Review,* back when going-nowhere Jerry Garcia nitpicked his guitar and a free spirit named Christie danced the flamenco down Kepler's tolerant aisles.

So much had changed by 2005. Paperbacks were passé, no longer part of a revolution. The famously weathered clerks, the World War II conscientious objector, the Socialist Labor Party candidate, the Stanford PhD were for the most part gone. The enchanting old pacifist Ira Sandperl still lingered, holding morning court next door at Café Borrone, but Ira was long past selling books. So much had changed, but still: Kepler's!

And then suddenly, in the midst of the anniversary year and my own initial research, the store shut down. By cell phone and Black-Berry, word spread: Kepler's is closed. The details slowly surfaced, how Clark Kepler had summoned his store's forty employees to a special meeting behind locked doors and drawn shades. There he had told the workers the store was insolvent and must close. Then he had handed out final paychecks, each with a modest bonus, and urged his employees to cash the checks quickly, before a bankruptcy filing froze the assets of Kepler's Books & Magazines.

Those details would become clear, in due course, as the Kepler's customers kept coming. Menlo Park City Councilwoman Kelly Fergusson came and left her business card, announcing her willingness to help reopen the store. Poster boards filled up with handwritten messages. "This is too traumatic for words," one wrote. Another writer summoned "Auden or someone who could try to express the profound sense of loss and disbelief." "Love," one wrote in large letters. Another declared, angrily, that Roy's "legacy deserved better."

The closing of Kepler's Books & Magazines became national news, invariably cast as a case study of the suffering independent bookstore. The *New York Times* paid attention. Clark Kepler read the obituaries and kept his emotions in check, as best he could. He hadn't really planned to go into the book business in the first place. He had other notions. Then, when the store's future was really on the line, Clark had taken the reins and done well with them. That had been in the early 1980s, and ever since Clark had moved with increasing confidence. But now, this. Inevitably, Clark thought of mistakes made, opportunities foregone. Had he driven his father's store off the tracks, misplayed his hand, or was Kepler's just an inevitable victim of business circumstance?

Clark began preparing the paperwork for entering the store into Chapter 7 bankruptcy. He was exhausted, wrung out. Debts loomed. Lawyers and accountants and creditors were all going to want a slice of Kepler's. There would be nothing left of the store, and something less of him. Then, from the energy that had gathered on the plaza outside Kepler's, the energy that the store had accumulated over five decades, the current shifted.

"Miracles started happening," Clark said.

Call it karma. The term fits as well as another.

Roy Kepler had sown much in his seventy-four years; more, perhaps, than he ever knew. He had lived by a strict moral code, shunning violence in all its forms. He could seem rigid and uncompromising, but he consistently tried to teach peace, love, and understanding. Through the words he spoke, the actions he undertook, and the books he sold, Roy had touched untold numbers of lives. Somehow, all of that came rushing back once word spread that Kepler's had closed.

Piece by piece, the little miracles came together. Silicon Valley mavens determined that Kepler's could be saved; *would* be saved. Public meetings were convened. City officials were engaged. Investors, large and small, put up their own money. And on Saturday, October 8, 2005, a different kind of rally brought hundreds of people to the plaza on which the shocked and grieving had gathered seven weeks before. Clark spoke, and then a few minutes before noon he led the way, opening the doors to the new Kepler's Books & Magazines.

It was an utterly fantastical turnaround, the stuff of fiction, but it all made sense. The reopening of Kepler's Books & Magazines was a belated offering to the store's founder, though the joyous moment itself would pass into a long grind. Even a beloved bookstore must pay its bills. Roy had known this. He knew: struggle never ended.

"Peace is not an end of war," Roy wrote. "Peace is not an end. Peace is not a goal. Peace is not absolute. Peace is not a thing. There is no such thing as peace. There is no way to peace. Rather, peace is a way. Peace is a way to live, struggle, behave here and now."

Peace is a way; that was Roy's unceasing message. Peace is a way to live. It is a life come together, a life very much like Roy Kepler's.

RADICAL CHAPTERS

1

Opening Chapters

War came calling, and the Kepler boys said no. One survived the whirlwind; the other did not.

On December 7, 1941, Roy Cecil Kepler reported for work as a surgical orderly at Denver Presbyterian Hospital. He was twenty-one years old, prime fighting age, but he had already vowed to do no fighting. He and his older brother, Earl, had declared themselves pacifists. They objected to war in any form, a belief that had already cost them and soon would cost them more. Roy had left his higher-paying previous job with a manufacturing firm after it started securing military contracts. Now the next test of conscience roared in with a wave of Japanese dive bombers mauling the U.S. battleship fleet at Pearl Harbor.

Not long after noon, Denver time, a young female coworker went looking for Roy amid the hospital's five floors. The first radio reports had aired, and the earnest young woman wanted to know what Roy was going to do now. Surely he would surrender his peacetime principles and march to his country's defense. Roy surprised her.

"My answer was, 'this is what I've been talking about,'" Roy recalled in an undated oral history. "'This is what I am against.'"

Roy stood firm, mentally and physically. He had been a high school wrestler and was hardened from ranch work during the summers. He was trimly built at 5 feet 8 inches tall and 155 pounds. He spoke well, having done a turn on the high school stage. An excellent student, forced by economic circumstances to work after high school, he was preparing after a several-year delay to enroll at the University of Colorado. His twenty-four-year-old brother, Earl, was a leader in his own right. Both would have been fine officer material, had they been so inclined.

Neither brother was particularly religious. The Kepler family did not belong to the Friends, Brethren, or Mennonites, the historic peace churches that upheld conscientious objection as a religious tenet. And yet, when push came to shove, both young men informed the Selective Service System that they rejected war in any form. Theirs was an absolute refusal. Earl would be given a chance to serve in a nonfighting capacity, and he chose prison instead. Roy advised Selective Service that he would not undertake alternative civilian work unless it had absolutely nothing do to with the national defense.

Even before Selective Service came calling, Roy withdrew from war-making. Before joining the Denver Presbyterian Hospital staff in May 1941 as a $50-a-month surgical orderly, he had been working for the Hendrie and Bolthoff Manufacturing and Supply Company. The venerable Denver-based firm made mining and woodworking equipment, and the imminence of war brought abundant military contracts. Roy could have had all the work he wanted. Instead, he quit. In joining the hospital staff, he took a $25-per-month pay cut.

But quitting one morally incompatible job was not sufficient to secure conscientious objector status. Selective Service insisted on stringent evidence of the sincerity of belief. The conscientious objector application had demanded the nature of the applicant's pacifist beliefs, the name and address of the individual relied upon for religious guidance, and the circumstances under which the applicant believed force might be necessary. The Kepler brothers had to list personal references and the names of various organizations they belonged to. Then they had to secure approval of the local draft board. This would be tough, as the young pacifists faced middle-aged men who wondered why anyone would avoid taking up arms when the country called. It was a question that had long vexed lawmakers, citizens, and soldiers alike.

War is a collective enterprise, but it takes an individual to pull a trigger. Every fighting generation confronts the resulting tension between common need and personal conscience.

During the American Revolution, some states including Pennsylvania and Rhode Island permitted objectors to avoid military service by paying a fine. Those who wouldn't pay faced imprisonment and the seizure of their property. Some objectors, setting precedent, fled to Canada. Following independence, the Founding Fathers debated whether to explicitly include protection for conscientious objectors in the Constitution. James Madison suggested phrasing that "no person religiously scrupulous of bearing arms shall be compelled to render military service in person." Ultimately the language was dropped and conscientious objection was left without explicit constitutional protection (Robinson 1990, 40).

During the Civil War, the Confederate government permitted members of the Friends, Mennonite, Nazarene, and Church of the Brethren to avoid service by paying a fine or providing for a substitute. The Union's initial draft law of 1863 did not address conscientious objectors at all. The next year, the revised Union draft law recognized the rights of those belonging to churches that were "conscientiously opposed to the bearing of arms." As an alternative, objectors could serve in hospitals, take care of freed slaves, pay a fee, or secure a substitute. Membership in a peace church was required (Robinson 1990, 44).

The Selective Service Act of 1917 likewise permitted exemptions for members of traditional peace churches. Unlike the Civil War draft, though, the ten million American men of draft age could not escape their obligation by paying a fine or hiring a substitute. Recognized pacifists could be assigned to noncombatant duty after being drafted, though they would still be in the army. "Association with soldiers might have a missionary effect on them and cause them to forget their base creed and rise to worthy levels in an atmosphere of self-sacrifice and of service and struggle for great ideals," declared the incessantly martial Theodore Roosevelt (Robinson 1990, 55).

Nearly 65,000 Americans filed conscientious objector claims during World War I, of whom 20,873 were eventually inducted. Most, though, eventually allowed themselves to be transformed into

soldiers. Others sought safety through routes that even some pacifists considered ignoble. Jessie Wallace Hughan, founder of the War
Resisters League, noted that "there were many methods of eluding
the trenches, especially for young men with money and influence: false
medical certificates, flight to Mexico, or safe and soft jobs with the
government" (Hughan 1942, 12). The pressure to submit could be
overwhelming, and the Espionage Act of 1917 further inhibited conscientious objection by making it a felony to interfere with enlistment
or conscription.

Only about 4,000 men persisted in claiming World War I conscientious objector status through their induction, a small fraction of
the 2.8 million men drafted into military service during the war. Of
the persistent objectors, 1,200 were sent to farms for alternative service, 1,300 were assigned noncombat duty, and 450 were sentenced
to prison. Absolutist objectors received terms of twenty to twenty-five
years, or more. More than one hundred war objectors were sentenced
to life in prison, where conditions were harsh beyond measure (Moroi
2008, 98). Conscientious objector Evan Thomas, a future War Resisters League chairman whose path would later cross with Roy's, was
among those with a life sentence who was thrown into a prison hole
and shackled to the cell bars for hours at a time (Cooney and Michalowski 1977, 45). It was only after the war ended that the sentences
were moderated, and by November 1920 all of the World War I conscientious objectors were out of prison.

The Selective Training and Service Act of 1940, signed by President Roosevelt on September 16, 1940, did not require objectors to
belong to a well-recognized sect. This liberalized the rules set in World
War I (Bennett 2003, 72). Lawmakers, though, retained a religious
requirement that disappointed those hoping for a more open-minded
law. Persons "by reason of religious training and belief" who were
"conscientiously opposed to participation in war in any form" would
be assigned to "work of national importance under civilian direction." A system of Civilian Public Service (CPS) camps was agreed
upon, with the peace churches coordinating their efforts through the
National Service Board for Religious Objectors. The camps would

congregate objectors, usually in rural areas that kept the pacifists conveniently remote from society at large. Still, many considered the CPS system a reasonable compromise that balanced individual conscience with collective obligation; it seemed the best deal possible at the time. This optimistic spirit would fade soon enough, through the experiences of young men like Roy Kepler.

Roy was not born into a pacifist household. He had, so far as is known, no single, life-changing revelation about nonviolence. He came to his beliefs by thinking, reading, and chance encounters along the way.

Roy was born in Denver on May 7, 1920. His father, Earl, was thirty-five at the time, a native of Kansas. His mother, LaClede, was twenty-seven, a native of Missouri. The story, as some heard it later, was that LaClede had been born shortly before the census enumerator came by. She was still unnamed when the census man asked her father for the names of all his children. The father ticked them off, one by one, until he came to the newborn. She had no name yet. But the government needed one, so the father looked about his room. His eyes fixed on the stove: a LaClede. That was it: the youngest daughter's name, the father reported, is LaClede.

Every family has its stories, not all of them subject to confirmation. However she came by her name, LaClede had been married to Earl for ten years at the time of Roy's birth. Earl was a traveling salesman. He trafficked in candy, cigarettes, beer. Earnings were intermittent. When he had a job, the Kepler family could keep an apartment and eat meat. When business soured, the family would move and it would be beans for dinner.

Earl and LaClede had lost one infant earlier in the marriage. They welcomed Earl Jr. on July 23, 1917, while they were living in Kansas City. They would not stay there, or anywhere, very long. The family was living on Denver's 10th Avenue when Roy was born three years later. LaClede took Roy and Earl to Arizona for about two years when the boys were young, so that the hot, dry climate might aid Earl's health, and even back in Denver the family kept moving about. Over the next twenty years, as Earl sold what he could and LaClede periodically worked as a cashier at the local Piggly Wiggly, the Keplers moved to at least five other Denver locations. For a time, seeking Roy's final year in high school, the Keplers uprooted to Boise. When that opportunity dried up, the family returned to Denver. The economic insecurity imprinted itself on Roy. When, in later years, he was painfully strict in managing Joan Baez's money or the bookstore's finances, his friends could trace it all back to his straitened Denver years.

"He was a tightwad," Joan Baez recalled, lovingly.

Roy's father had finished eighth grade and had somewhat of an independent spirit. He didn't believe in unions, a skepticism his son

1. Roy Kepler at age five, in Arizona. Photographer unknown, courtesy of the Kepler family.

would later share. LaClede was likewise limited in her schooling, but she was intelligent and urged books upon her children. From an early age, Roy remembered reading the likes of *Black Beauty* as well the now-forgotten Thomas Bailey Aldridge's autobiographical *The Story of a Bad Boy,* a title Roy would delight in, as if it foreshadowed his own radicalism.

The family was only moderately religious, though Roy's maternal grandfather was a deacon and his parents would periodically dispatch the children to assorted churches. Roy wasn't much taken with the ideology, and he would later say that he and his brother grew up not knowing the difference between Baptist and Presbyterian. Somehow, though, the Christian notion of turning the other cheek sunk in.

"I was influenced by the nonviolent message of Jesus in the church I was required to attend, though I was dismayed at the gap between the preachments and practices of the adult community," Roy wrote several decades later in a document he entitled "Testament of a Radical Pacifist."

A member of the high school wrestling team, Roy had further bulked up by working four summers at a ranch owned by a Dr. Herman Maul, a University of Pennsylvania graduate and the father of a friend. Roy rode horses, roped animals, dug fence posts. The hard work agreed with him. Years later, he would regale his children with tales of getting up early, gobbling the big ranch breakfasts, and working long hours with horses and cattle.

In junior high school, a seventh grade teacher opened Roy's eyes to the world around him. She "looked like a typical Hollywood version of a country teacher," Roy said, but she also held advanced ideas and knew the character of the city. Denver's population of about 256,000 had been swollen by German, English, Irish, Swedish, Scottish, and Italian immigrants. Once, making the point, Roy's teacher read aloud the name of each student in her class. As he heard one name pronounced after another, Roy began comprehending he was part of a wider world.

The public schools also gave Roy his introduction to peacemaking. He would later recall that a cosmopolitan curriculum had been developed in the years following World War I, not explicitly pacifist in orientation but antiwar in tenor. Teachers, Roy recalled, "would introduce the need for international amity." They would praise the 1928 Kellogg-Briand Pact in which Germany, the United States, France, and ultimately fifty-nine other countries renounced war as an instrument of national policy. Kellogg-Briand wasn't yet a synonym for diplomatic impotence. It reflected a deep-seated desire to avoid another global slaughter like World War I, and it was seriously considered enough to have been adopted by the U.S. Senate by an 85–1 vote.

Teachers communicated to their students that war was fruitless. Such antiwar sentiments were commonplace during the time. In May 1934, when Roy was an impressionable fourteen years old, an estimated 10,000 marchers participated in a No More War parade in New York City sponsored by the War Resisters League (Bennett 2003, 43). In April 1935, some 60,000 college students pledged never to participate in armed conflict, and *Time* magazine in 1939 put pacifist A. J. Muste on the cover. The former Dutch Reform Church minister–turned Trotskyist union organizer–turned Christian pacifist would in just a few years become one of Roy's regular marching partners.

Roy took his lessons seriously, though he also said of himself that at times he was "sometimes a bit too spirited" in school. He was tapped for a special program at Denver's North High School, dubbed the progressive education group. Chosen for their high intelligence test scores, the participants stuck together in common English and social science classes. Selected students were pressed harder, faced higher standards, and were exposed to the wider world through field trips. Roy garnered straight A's and joined the school's National Senior Honor Society. He also had a taste for the stage. He starred in one of the school's plays and later would take night classes in theater. Roy would never be thought of as theatrical, but as an adult activist he would be a showman of sorts, staging demonstrations and directing role-players.

In a more explicitly political vein, Roy joined the high school's Cosmopolitan Club. The Denver organization had been founded by a man Roy later described as "a Negro dentist," and the name

Cosmopolitan itself was a code word: it meant black students were welcome. One of Roy's teachers also told him about Kirby Page, who in 1936 spoke at a local junior high school. It was a propitious encounter. Page was a nationally known peace activist then in his exhortative prime. A Disciple of Christ minister in his mid-forties, Page edited *The World Tomorrow,* a publication of the Fellowship of Reconciliation. Page's 1931 book, *National Defense: A Study of the Origins, Results and Prevention of War,* had urged readers to repudiate war as a national tool. Hearing Page speak helped awaken Roy.

"It was my first contact with real pacifism, and I was surprised at finding myself in such complete agreement," Roy would note in a 1941 essay.

Roy and several friends began gathering in what he called a war and peace study group. They would recommend books to one another and convene at the home of the teacher who had first spoken of Kirby Page.

Sometimes their newly radical notions could conflict. A recruiter from the Abraham Lincoln Brigade attended one meeting, promoting the fight against fascism in Spain. Dominated by Communists, Socialists, and Anarchists since its formation in 1937, the Brigade was offering several hundred armed American volunteers in support of the Spanish Republican forces struggling against the Nazi-backed legions of Francisco Franco. This divided the Old Left activists against the pure pacifists, with whom Roy would come to more closely identify. Another time, the young Denver activists met a World War I veteran who had survived a gas attack in the trenches. He embodied war's wreckage. "His lungs were shot," Roy said in a June 1984 interview, and "he was very bitter over what had happened to him."

Step by step, Roy was moving away from his peers. North High School classmate Boyd McDonald, recounting conversations seventy years later, still recalled immediately that Roy was a "radical," and classmate Lola Edwards Clay admitted that Roy's pacifist convictions irritated her to no end. They did not comport with the conventional sentiments of the time, or of any time, really. McDonald would go on to military work, engineering ballistic missile systems. Sometime in the early 1970s, several decades after graduating from North High School, McDonald was leaving a Lockheed Missiles and Space facility in Palo Alto, California. Demonstrators were handing out flyers, and McDonald took one to see what the fuss was about. There, at the bottom, he saw the familiar name of his radical old classmate Roy Kepler.

"I thought, yes, that would be Roy," McDonald recalled.

After what he would later describe as the "traumatic experience" of being uprooted once more, Roy graduated from high school in Boise, Idaho, in June 1938. He prepared to enter the University of Colorado. Then, disaster. Three weeks before his fall enrollment, Roy's father again lost his job.

"The necessity of providing for the family," Roy wrote, "fell on me."

Roy went to work, for a time, at a gas station where cars rarely stopped. For Roy, shut out from college, the job had its compensations. At the age of eighteen, with time on his hands, Roy discovered George Bernard Shaw. Decades later, Roy still savored the writings of the Irish Socialist and Nobel Prize–winning playwright. For several months Roy tended the quiet gas station and continued his reading. He would long consider it one of the best jobs he ever had, simply for the opportunity to read the likes of Shaw, H. G. Wells's *The Outline of History,* and Erich Marie Remarque's *All Quiet on the Western Front.* Roy lacked money, but he could check books out from the library or, more and more, buy one of the cheap paperbacks starting to proliferate.

In 1939, Pocket Books entered the market with twenty-five-cent copies of James Hilton's *Lost Horizon,* Thornton Wilder's *The Bridge of San Luis Rey,* and Agatha Christie's *The Murder of Roger Ackroyd,* among other titles. The Pocket Books were an immediate sensation, an American follow-up to the British line of Penguin Books launched in 1935 (Davis 1984, 13). These affordable new paperbacks added to what was already available at Denver outlets like the Publication Book Store on 15th Street, which advertised "books of all kinds, new and used."

After leaving the gas station, Roy spent a year, between October 1938 and October 1939, as an assistant at the Hotchkiss Map

Company before joining Hendrie & Bolthoff. But really he and others of his generation were waiting for the draft and watching how others handled their martial obligations.

On October 11, 1940, twenty students at Union Theological Seminary in New York City released a signed statement declaring their refusal to "comply in any way" with the Selective Training and Service Act. The seminarians were not, in fact, subject to the draft. They had to register, but their religious studies exempted them from actual service. Nonetheless, citing their desire to "live in harmony with the will of God," the twenty young men said they would refuse even to register with the Selective Service. Conscription itself, they maintained, was part of the institution of war. "If we register under the act, even as conscientious objectors, we are becoming part of the act," the seminarians stated, as the *New York Times* reported on October 12, 1940. The seminarians added further their fear that the draft exemptions offered to ministers and theological students were a cynical maneuver designed to gain a religious sanction for war. They voiced their intentions to build "a group trained in the techniques of non-violent opposition to the encroachments of militarism and fascism."

The Union Theological Seminary students included twenty-four-year-old Yale graduate David Dellinger as well as Colorado native George Houser, the son of a locally prominent Methodist clergyman. Denver residents could closely follow Houser and the other seminarians, as the *Denver Post* and *Rocky Mountain News* carried front-page articles about the local draft resister. Many hoped Houser and his classmates would retreat from confrontation, having made their statement. Loved ones urged the men to capitulate. Seminary president Henry Sloane Coffin praised his students for their principles but then cautioned that no further purpose could be served by persisting all the way into prison. By November the original twenty seminarian resisters had shrunk to eight. A judge in mid-November then sentenced Dellinger, Houser, and the six other recalcitrant pacifists to one year and a day in federal prison. The sentence, one Selective Service administrator told the *New York Times* on November 15, 1940, was a "very salutary thing" (Gara and Gara 1999, 133).

The war preparations proceeded. By early May 1941, Denver residents were reading Ernie Pyle's accounts about how the locally bred 45th Infantry Division was training for combat. President Roosevelt was proclaiming the necessity of putting the defense industry on a war footing, cranking out ships and planes twenty-four hours a day, seven days a week. The Colorado draft quota was increasing. Even Hollywood was enlisting. Denver movie theaters were showing that spring Bob Hope's *Caught in the Draft,* giddily billed as a "gay comedy of the tribulations (not to mention the trials) of the rookies in America's new army." See, the movie said: war is fun! For those seeking more of a thrill, Denver's Denham Theater was showing the forthrightly propagandistic *I Wanted Wings,* which was said to portray "Uncle Sam's bravest airmen [and] squadron upon squadron of the newest fighters and bombers." Bombshell actress Veronica Lake added the *va-va-voom.* War could seem like a real kick, all right, but Roy wasn't buying it.

"The people of this country are being pushed into a war which they don't want, and which, if the United States enters, will divide the world into two hostile camps and ensure nothing except armed conflict and imperialism for years to come," Roy warned in a May 27, 1941, letter.

Just as Roy was writing, isolationist Senator Gerald Nye of North Dakota visited Denver to address several thousand participants in an antiwar rally downtown. University of Chicago President Robert Hutchins, whom Roy would later try to cultivate, was quoted in the *Rocky Mountain News* as saying that war would betray humanity itself. Peace still had its followers. Nonetheless, like the shrinking pool of pacifist seminarians, Roy's little high school war-and-peace study group grew ever smaller as the war drew nearer. By the time Roy formally registered for the draft on July 1, 1941, he was nearly all alone.

"Of the little group we had, my brother and I were the only ones to stick with it," Roy said in an interview. "When the cards were down, people went where the family pressure was."

War fever was irresistible, especially after Pearl Harbor. The Rev. John Haynes Holmes, a cofounder of the War Resisters League (WRL), sardonically observed of young idealists nationwide how, just as in Roy's Denver circle, "yesterday they were taking the Oxford oath; today they are rapturously taking the oath to King and Country" (Cooney and Michalowski 1977, 89). WRL founder and longtime leader Jessie Wallace Hughan likewise acknowledged that under the "smoke of propaganda," the avowed student pacifists of the 1930s rallied to the flag in the post–Pearl Harbor war fervor (Hughan 1942, 21). The wholesale concessions to convention further isolated Roy and Earl.

Roy's brother Earl had worked in a warehouse and as a hospital orderly after high school, and he had tried his hand as a commercial artist. But to Denver's Draft Board No. 4, the 5-foot 9-inch, 120-pound, self-proclaimed pacifist was an alien creature. The draft board members were American Legionnaires, Roy later recalled, and they seemed to believe that Earl simply needed some talking-to. One night the draft board members met for an hour with Earl, trying to dissuade him from his dangerously wrong-headed path, while he denounced what he called "the whole military machine." The discussion did not avail, and in September 1941 Earl was hit with his 1-A-O draft classification. It meant he could be called up for noncombatant military service, a reasonable compromise in the eyes of his draft board, but not good enough for Earl. He appealed.

"I am opposed to the whole of the military system, and not merely a part of it," Earl wrote the Selective Service on April 2, 1942, adding that "perhaps it seems futile and unrealistic for a man to say I don't believe in war when the world is in chaos and when humankind is suffering from an actual and terrible war."

Earl stood firm and refused to show up for his scheduled 7 a.m. induction on May 7, 1942. That Wednesday night, FBI agents showed up at the Keplers' home and arrested him. Earl came before U.S. District Judge John Foster Symes. The sixty-three-year-old former federal prosecutor was not inclined to be sympathetic. He was an American Legion member who had served as an army major during World War I. Judge Symes, his obituary writer would later recount in the *Rocky Mountain News* of April 6, 1951, ran his courtroom "with absolute dignity enforced by a discipline almost military."

Legally, moreover, Earl was particularly vulnerable. He did not claim membership in an organized religion. This put him in a minority of conscientious objectors. Of the some 12,000 men who would be assigned to Civilian Public Service camps, only 675 explicitly claimed no membership in a church. Rather, Earl considered faith a personal matter. He declared the core of religion to be "the spirit of Christianity, in the principles of love as taught by Jesus Christ."

"I take my stand as a pacifist in humility and without defiance, but with determination and the firm belief that war as a method of solving the world's problems is unjustifiable and an insult to the intelligence of man," Earl added in his statement.

Unmoved, Judge Symes sentenced Earl to thirty months in prison. It was harsh, but not unique. Throughout World War II, about 6,000 American war-resisters went to prison; still, the Denver draft board members had hoped they need not have gone that far with Earl. "They were . . . shocked when he refused induction and was sent to prison," Roy recalled. "They were quite disturbed, because they hadn't really wanted to feel responsible for sending a man of conscience to prison."

Earl was taken away on June 6. By then Roy too had been adjudicated, but with different results.

After a several-year wait compelled by his family's economic straits, Roy had finally entered the University of Colorado in January 1942. He threw himself into some meaningful extracurricular activities, helping establish an International House and serving on a student commission serving ethnic minorities. Meanwhile, the Selective Service system had ruled him physically, mentally, morally, and emotionally ready for duty. Roy's draft board members were "not well trained for the job and didn't know the law," according to Roy. Roy's, moreover, was a tough case, just like his brother Earl's, since he was not affiliated with a traditional peace church. Draft boards, Brigadier General Lewis Hershey, the Selective Service director, told a House of Representatives' subcommittee, really didn't know how to deal consistently with such men. "Some of our local boards go one way and some the other, because 'what is religion?' is a difficult thing to say," Hershey testified (Schlissel 1968, 228).

Roy lost his first bid. Meeting at its quarters at 810 14th Street, the Denver draft board in November 1941 had designated Roy as suitable for war. Roy's purely philosophical stance against war did not comport with the terms of the Selective Service Act. "They did not doubt my sincerity," Roy wrote in a later, undated account. "However, they felt it was their duty to classify me as 1-A because of the fact that I belonged to no religious organization." Roy appealed in December, another break from convention. Only about 10 percent of would-be objectors appealed their original draft board decisions. In his appeal, Roy sought to square his stance with the requirements of the law. He was frankly skeptical about the rituals and ceremonies of organized religion, which he likened to superstitious practices, but he found merit in the underlying principles.

"Religion to me," Roy explained in an undated paper, "is a philosophy of life that recognizes the need for faith in the ultimate good in men. My religion has made of me an idealist, but my ideals are also my guide."

Roy also cited a memo from the Selective Service System, in which officials clarified that membership in a religious organization was not necessary to claim conscientious objector status. Nor was formal church training necessary; a good home, or an influential teacher, might suffice. Still, the vast majority of conscientious objectors belonged to organized churches. More than 60 percent of all objectors were Jehovah's Witnesses. By contrast, fewer than 6 percent were unaffiliated and secular in their pacifism (Bennett 2003, 98). This absence of church identification meant the individual pacifist had a heavier burden to prove his case.

Roy was decades ahead of his time. It would take a 1965 Supreme Court case, rendered during another war, to establish the principle that a "sincere or meaningful belief" that was "parallel to that filled by God" might suffice for conscientious objection. Five years after that, the court would recognize that explicitly nonreligious moral or ethical beliefs would justify the pacifist position. All of that would come much too late to help Roy. He had to make his case on his own. Decades later, Roy recalled how an "old lawyer" on the appeals board pressed him with hypothetical queries. "He asked questions like, 'what would you do if a madman broke into the house and was going to hurt your sister?'" Roy said. "I asked, 'is it a big man or a small man?'"

"I said that if he broke down the door, then he was probably a big man and he would probably kill me," Roy recalled in a 1984 interview. "Then he asked what if I had a gun. I asked, 'Am I a good shot?' He said yes, and I said then I would shoot the gun out of his hand."

Roy was lucky. Even though Roy lacked an explicitly religious basis for his conscientious objection, the hearing officer agreed he was a genuine objector. Roy felt, as well, that he was given leeway because of his brother Earl's circumstances. The Kepler family had already paid a price for an act of conscience. Roy won his appeal and was designated a conscientious objector with the status 4-E. He was now where few were willing to go. Three days after the Pearl Harbor attack, only 2 percent opposed war against Japan. Even the War Resisters League would contort itself into a complicated posture once the homeland was attacked. Following Pearl Harbor, the League issued a statement condemning the "murderous" attack while also contending that "all nations must share responsibility for the causes leading up to the struggle." Pointedly, the League declared it would not obstruct the war effort; for a time, it even stopped conducting public demonstrations and soliciting memberships (Bennett 2003, 74).

On May 30, 1942, Roy was officially inducted into the noble and doomed experiment known as Civilian Public Service.

2

The Good War

Roy did well in war.

The provincial Denver kid grew up into the wider world. He would ally with America's future peace leaders, the men and women who carried the flame through World War II, Korea, the Cold War, and Vietnam. Hard experience would firm his convictions. He would learn the power and limits of radical resistance, and he would learn, too, how far men could go before they broke.

The lessons took time, for Roy as well as the 12,000 other conscientious objectors assigned to Civilian Public Service camps. These were camps envisioned idealistically, where pacifists were supposed to contribute meaningful national service. These were places, the *Christian Century* writer Wilma Ludlow enthused shortly before Roy reported for duty, that "have every chance of becoming that Third Order for which so many Christian leaders have been looking."

It was a shimmering vision; in truth, a mirage.

Roy took his farewells from his parents' East 17th Avenue home in early June 1942. CPS camp administrators had mailed him a one-way railroad ticket and provided generic packing advice: two pairs of pajamas, bed linens, two pairs of gloves, two pairs of long underwear, three pairs of denim work trousers, a mending kit, and more (Keim 1990, 38). Roy rustled his gear and got on his way.

On the westbound train, Roy found a seat next to another pacifist, a reserved-looking young Mexican American tenant farmer from nearby Greeley, Colorado, named John R. Lozans. Lozans belonged to the tiny Church of God in Christ sect. He was an earnestly devout soul, in precisely the way that Roy was not, but Roy recalled being thoroughly charmed by the hymns Lozans played on his twelve-string guitar. The music helped ease the ride, before the Colorado conscientious objectors and others collected along the way arrived June 3 in Southern California.

Roy and his new colleagues were hauled by pickup truck from Glendora to a mountain site called Tanbark Flats, a satellite of the Glendora Civilian Public Service camp. The camp served the Angeles National Forest, a 650,000-acre mountainous expanse east of Los Angeles. Glendora was one of the first CPS camps established, and it had a routine for newly arriving men. Roy and the other men would first report to the camp director. Glendora's manager was Oscar Marshburn, a Whittier College graduate later known, of all things, as Richard Nixon's uncle. The new men were then dispatched to the camp doctor. The doctor noted that Roy was in all-around good health, save for some acne. Roy stood a little over 5 feet 7 inches and weighed about 150 pounds. His eyesight was nearly perfect, his blood pressure was 120 over 66, and his pulse was 86. Roy received smallpox and typhoid vaccinations and briefings on safety rules and the types of jobs available in the camp.

Some 175 pacifists were stationed at the camp when Roy arrived. At Glendora, Roy and the other men worked six days a week. Some Glendora men would collect snow and water samples in the San Gabriel Mountains, take temperatures, and monitor various instruments scattered along the trails of the pine and fir forest. It seemed, for a time, to be an appropriately useful social contribution. Firefighting, too, could be diverting. Roy pitched in on about a dozen forest fires; at one point, Roy and his firefighting crew drove twelve hours in an open truck to help combat a 7,000-acre forest blaze near San Diego.

"An experience in itself," Roy recalled in a diary (Kepler n.d.).

The Sundays off could be diverting in their own way. Roy would escape on occasion to nearby San Bernardino, where he subsequently recalled in his diary "being entertained by the girls from a Baptist church." Other neighbors weren't so accommodating. The local postmaster, a Mr. J. A. Lee, had been communicating his distress in the several months before Roy's arrival. Conscientious objectors had refused to buy stamps emblazoned with war slogans. Some, Lee said, had even refused to contribute to the Boy Scouts or the Red Cross. He suggested bluntly that if the conscientious objectors didn't care to defend their country, then they might be better off in the internment camps with the Japs.

Roy's post–high school education began at Glendora, through endless discussions with literate and self-reflective men. Psychologists, after the war, reported that "conscientious objectors, like women, have more interests in musical, artistic and literary activities and in people than do non–conscientious objectors, who, as more representative men, prefer mechanical, scientific, physically strenuous and selling activities" (Tracy 1993, 20). In CPS camps run by the Society of Friends, 69 percent of the men had attended at least some college, compared to 10 percent of the nation's adult population. Fully one in five of the men in the Friends' CPS camps had advanced as far as graduate school (Wittner 1984, 49).

As far as the outside world was concerned, these principled, educated men were adapting well to the Civilian Public Service program. Selective Service officers were declaring that the system was 100 percent better than in previous wars. "There are throughout the camps a proportion of intellectuals, whose pacifism takes them into deep mental caverns," the *New York Times* observed on January 7, 1943. "But even these . . . are not so militant as to stimulate disorder."

The disorder would come, soon enough. CPS morale was, in fact, deteriorating by the month. Camp conditions were, naturally, austere, but under the right circumstances that might have been accepted, embraced even as the embodiment of virtuous simplicity. Circumstances, though, were not right. Most of the work was all wrong. Pacifists were being kept busy weeding, raking, mowing. For many, it began feeling like make-work. War Resisters League field director Frank Olmstead, with whom Roy would soon be corresponding, bluntly declared that "70 percent of the projects could be done by able-bodied morons" (Bennett 2003, 85).

The pacifists felt exploited. CPS men worked an eight-hour day, for which they in time received but $5 a month. Twice, the Selective Service officials sought to provide standard workmen's compensation for objectors. Congress wasn't interested. The conchies, as many called them, lacked political support. Food, clothing, and incidentals were being provided, not by the government but by the peace churches. The men were not receiving health insurance, nor were their dependents provided any support. The Selective Service System itself was emphatic about the relationship between the government and the objectors. Like draftees, the objectors had forfeited certain rights. They could be transferred, restricted, disciplined, and ordered about, all at the pleasure of the authorities (Keim 1990, 32).

Complaints accumulated. By November 1942, one-third of conscientious objectors surveyed admitted "considerable dissatisfaction" with the CPS system. Many, particularly those associated with the historic peace churches, stayed within the boundaries even if they seethed. Others took action. The first recorded protest occurred in December 1941, when four men at the Petersham CPS camp in central Massachusetts refused to work on an air raid tower they considered to be part of the war system. After a one-day strike, the protestors were assigned to other labor. In mid-February 1942, several months before Roy entered the system, a twenty-four-year-old Midwesterner named Alex Stach became the first man to simply walk away from a CPS camp. Others, in time, would follow him. In October 1942 three objectors walked out of a CPS camp at Big Flats, New York, declaring the camp system was simply another form of conscription.

Prisoners of conscience had it far worse. They weren't going anywhere.

Roy's brother Earl had been taken away to the Engelwood federal prison located in Littleton, Colorado, fifteen miles southwest from Denver. It was low security and close enough for family members to visit if they could manage, but still a world apart from any Earl had ever known. Assigned to work in the prison hospital, Earl conveyed his pain in poems, one of which would appear in the spring 1944 issue of *The Compass,* a magazine published by the Civilian Public Service camp in Waldport, Oregon. Wrote Earl:

> The screw comes by to take the last count
> Through the corridor dismal and drear
> While the big door clangs and the lights go out
> While about you creeps coldness and fear.

Prison wore on Earl, and he quickly sought parole to Civilian Public Service. In October 1942 his first parole request was turned down, but by mid-February 1943 Selective Service authorities had tentatively approved his application for release into public service. The final paperwork, though, kept getting delayed. The national pacifist leader A. J. Muste, mistakenly thinking Earl had already been released, sent a premature congratulatory note. Finally, on March 12, 1943, Earl exited prison and boarded a train for Los Angeles. He arrived on Sunday, March 14. Roy, who met him at the station, thought he looked pale, thin, and fidgety. Earl was clearly happy to be free, but prison had stuck with him; the ill-shaven young man was so jumpy, Roy later recounted, that he could barely control his hands enough to clip his fingernails while they sat talking in the station. The brothers caught up on all that had transpired over the previous ten months, filling in the blanks from their necessarily circumscribed letters to one another, before they walked to a nearby restaurant. Earl seemed to calm down a bit amid the restaurant's South Sea atmosphere and quiet background music, before the men returned together to the Glendora camp.

"I am happy to be here," Earl advised the War Resisters League's George Reeves on March 17, 1943. "However, my experience in prison is one which I do not regret."

For several precious weeks Roy and Earl caught up with each other. Earl shared his prison poems with Roy, who thought them quite good. In turn, Roy shared his growing disenchantment about the Civilian Public Service system. Together they watched the war from afar. In the Pacific, American bombers were attacking Japanese ships around the Solomon Islands. In North Africa, General George

Patton's armored forces were surging ahead. And on the afternoon of April 4, American Flying Fortresses were blasting factories in the Paris suburbs. "[There was] a whole mass of smoke and burning buildings," U.S. Army Air Corps Lt. E. J. Pollock declared, as the *Los Angeles Times* subsequently reported. "Gee, it was beautiful."

The Glendora men read also of faraway pacifist Mohandas Gandhi, who that April was reportedly planning a new fast. Closer to home, leaders of the fringe group Mankind United faced sedition charges in Los Angeles for various anticonscription efforts that included claims, as one witness put it in the *Times* of April 8, 1943, about "a mechanical device which could be suspended in the air to prohibit the firing of guns."

Earl helped Roy publish an edition of the camp newsletter, the *San Dimas Rattler,* on the weekend of April 3–4. That Sunday, the newspaper work finished, Roy and Earl settled in for a satisfyingly long bull session in which, Roy later recounted, they touched "on many subjects philosophical and otherwise." It would be the last time they could have such a conversation.

The next day, Earl and twenty-eight-year-old John Mills were assigned to a crew working in a side camp in the forest north of Glendora. Mills was a Quaker from Kansas, well liked for his sense of humor. The small Dry Lake side camp was thirteen miles from Tanbark Flat, the headquarters for what was called the San Dimas Experimental Forest. The San Gabriel Mountains were cold that day; the dreary rain at Tanbark Flat turned to snow up at Earl's side camp. Earl and Mills shared a two-man cabin, one of four in the side camp. They were relying on a wood-burning stove for warmth.

A wet snow continued to fall the next morning, April 6. Inside their twelve- by fourteen-foot cabin, Mills and Earl had packed the small stove with kindling. What happened next had to be pieced together, imperfectly, after the fact. Mills, it seems, was priming the stove with flammable liquid kept in an old one-gallon paint can. It was early; he had, perhaps, not yet fully awakened. Mills splashed the flammable liquid into the stove. He may have thought it was fuel oil, but he was wrong. It was gasoline.

The stove flared violently. Startled, Mills dropped the can, spreading the liquid across the cabin floor. Flames followed.

Alex Gozdiff was reclining in his own bunk in a nearby cabin, contemplating the new day. A twenty-three-year-old member of the Russian Molokan church, Gozdiff heard a dull explosion, followed by a roar and high-pitched screams. He leapt up and raced outside, still in his pajamas.

Flames licked from the door of Earl's cabin. Mills had already made it outside but Earl, apparently confused by the shock and the smoke, was trying to crawl through the cabin's broken window. He was on fire and bleeding badly from the neck where the window glass had cut him. Mills and Gozdiff braved their way back into the cabin to help maneuver Earl through the window, Gozdiff later recounted.

Once Earl was free, he rolled in the snow to quench the flames and then, panicked, he tried to run. Gozdiff calmed him and brought him to a cabin.

The phone lines were down, communication cut. A small first-aid kit was all the men had available. Gozdiff helped bundle Earl and Mills into the front seat of a truck, and the injured men were driven down the mountains to the Tanbark camp site. Roy was just finishing sweeping out a bunkhouse when the fire truck rumbled into the camp, its siren blasting. At first he thought the truck's arrival signaled a fire, but then he realized that was unlikely, given the prevailing rain and snow. The truck came to a stop near the camp office and mess hall, and suddenly Roy's heart dropped.

"I realized, for no reason at all, that something had happened to Earl," Roy late recounted in his diary.

Roy ran up to the truck. Earl and Mills were both sitting up, wrapped in blankets. They were in bad shape. Second- and third-degree burns covered 95 percent of Earl's body, even the bottom of his feet. He complained of being cold and numb. He was going into shock. A female camp nurse covered Earl and Mills to warm them and lay them down. Beyond that, there was little she could do. Roy offered such comfort as he was able.

"You're a good brother, Roy," Earl said, Roy later recounted.

Camp director Oscar Marshburn was called, and an ambulance was summoned from White Funeral Home in Azusa. After an excruciating wait of more than an hour, the ambulance arrived and took the two burned men to St. Luke's Hospital in Altadena, about twenty-two miles away at the base of the mountains. Marshburn and Roy started following the ambulance in a car, but it broke down and they had to run to a phone to catch another ride.

For over four hours Earl lay on the hospital operating table while doctors and nurses did what they could. They cleaned and debrided his wounds, doped him up on morphine, and pumped in as much plasma as he could take. Close by, a wing of soldiers endured their own struggles. In a room of hurting men, the pacifist was holding his own. "[He] impressed [the] scrub nurse, who later expressed amazement at their grit and uncomplaining courage [and] was impressed to find they were [holding their own]," Roy later recalled in his diary.

Roy sat by Earl's bedside, calming his brother by his presence and holding him upright while he sipped ginger ale. Earl had asked Roy not to contact their parents, but once Earl's prognosis became clear Roy had called them and urged them to come to California. LaClede and Earl Sr. did get on the first train they could from Denver. Roy returned to Earl's bedside and waited along with fellow Glendora camper Francis Duveneck, a pacifist whose prominent Palo Alto–area family would later play an enduring role in Roy's life. On Wednesday afternoon, Earl asked his brother, the former hospital orderly, for an assessment.

"Tell me the truth, Roy," Earl said, Roy later recounted. "How am I? You know enough about these things to tell me."

"It's serious," Roy replied, but then he assured his brother that he could make it. In fact, there was nothing to be done but wait and say some words. At about noon on April 8, while the parents were still en route from Denver, Earl Kepler died.

Earl's death wounded Roy, forever. Decades later, Roy's voice would still catch when he spoke of his brother. Sometimes Roy's words would fail altogether. Earl had been beloved, a protector and an inspiration. His pacifist principles had emboldened Roy. His imprisonment had apparently helped Roy slide into Civilian Public Service, as the Denver draft board members didn't want to send two brothers to prison. His death at twenty-five was all the crueler for coming so soon upon regaining his freedom. Roy's own children would come to wonder many things about Earl, the lost brother.

Citing "the condition of the parents and the serious physical condition of the grandmother," CPS officials on April 9 granted Roy an emergency furlough so he could accompany Earl's remains to Denver. While Roy was gone, Earl's cabin mate John Mills fell prey to infection and, on April 17, succumbed.

The funeral and a two-week leave caused Roy to miss a conscientious objectors convention he had been helping plan. Roy was one of about thirty listed "sponsors" for the Chicago Conference on Social Action, a week-long series of seminars and planning sessions. The April 19–25, 1943, conference was an outright act of rebellion. Selective Service officials explicitly directed the Civilian Public Service men not to attend. If they did, they would be considered AWOL and subject to camp discipline. More than sixty men nonetheless persisted, attending discussions on prison hunger strikes and civil liberties. Some of the session leaders, like Hungarian-born attorney Francis Heisler, would be working alongside Roy on peace and social justice matters for the next several decades.

Roy returned to Glendora, but he wanted out. His brother's ghost now haunted the place. Chopping brush and cutting fire trails no longer sufficed. Like many other CPS men, Roy craved meaningful work. His opportunity briefly arose with the Civilian Public Service's establishment of a relief and rehabilitation program. It seemed perfect. The pacifists would be trained and put to work rebuilding foreign lands broken by war. The idea had been floating around a while. In 1942 preliminary work had begun on a relief and rehabilitation program targeting China. The State Department killed the program—a cautionary note, in hindsight—but in mid-1943 Roy and other CPS men thought they would get their chance to rebuilt war-torn countries

(Eisan 1948, 313). The foreign possibilities intrigued Roy, who had briefly studied Chinese.

"Working with refugees and aliens would be a direct step toward my desire to better the world," Roy wrote in an essay.

Roy was accepted and traveled to Indiana's Earlham College for training that was supposed to start July 1, 1943. The shaded, 800-acre Earlham campus felt like home for the pacifists, an island of studied calm. Opened in the mid-nineteenth century as Friends Boarding School and still under the supervision of the Society of Friends, Earlham had declared it would abstain as an institution from participating in the war. Relief and reconstruction, though, was virtuous work, and it drew a remarkable student body. Roy's Earlham classmates included graduates of Berea, Grinnell, Swarthmore, Oberlin, and Haverford colleges. They included educators, engineers, businessmen, and journalists. One of the few noncollege graduates, Roy offset his educational disadvantage by a diligence that impressed camp administrators.

"He appears to have a well developed power of individual thought and good organizing ability," one camp official noted in camp documents maintained by the American Friends Service Committee. "He is well liked, a perfect gentleman and a willing and efficient worker, the outstanding non-college man of the unit."

Roy told camp officials that he planned to finish his college education after the war and then go into social work or politics. But even before the training began, it excited opposition. Critics complained the program would cost too much and unduly reward conscientious objectors. The *Atlanta Constitution* questioned whether the United States should "be represented to the peoples of ravaged Europe as a nation of Fanatics who refused to fight, either for the oppressed or their own skin" (Robinson 1990, 206).

Alabama congressman Joseph Starnes heard the fears. The forty-eight-year-old Democrat felt strongly about the honor of military service. As a young second lieutenant he had served overseas during World War I and had since risen to the rank of colonel in the Alabama National Guard. His son and three of his brothers were currently serving in the war. He thought America should be represented overseas by fighting men, not pacifist shirkers. Soon enough, he flexed his political muscles. In July 1943, Starnes pressed for a provision blocking conscientious objectors from serving overseas, a position he would hold for the rest of his time in Congress. Even the request of Office of Strategic Services director William Donovan, who thought German-speaking CPS men could aid with relief efforts in Europe, was to no avail. The pacifists were staying put.

Roy and his colleagues learned the relief and rehabilitation program was doomed as soon as they arrived at Earlham. It was a hard blow, though as a sop Selective Service allowed the men to partake in classes for the next two months. Despite the disappointment, Roy embraced the residential college life he had never experienced. He studied French, philosophy, and relief administration and, he recounted in his diary, he cultivated friendships with several coeds.

Even a brief taste of college was sweet, but the premature death of the overseas relief initiative soured men like Roy even more on the shortcomings of Civilian Public Service. The pacifists had already been fed up with unpaid, trivial work and subjugation to the will of the state. In the early spring of 1943, the War Resisters League had withdrawn from its advisory role with the National Service Board for Religious Objectors. The League did not want to participate in a charade. Selective Service officials, for their part, suggested it would be best simply to let the conscientious objectors languish in remote obscurity.

Obscurity was exactly where Roy ended up next. On September 1, 1943, Roy arrived at CPS Camp 32 in remote West Campton, New Hampshire. He came in a contingent of nineteen other CPS men, all recently withdrawn from the overseas training programs at Earlham and Haverford colleges. One of his fellow fresh-arrivals that day was a Midwesterner with a religious streak named Ralph Kohn, whose life would be entwined with Roy's for years to come. Like Roy, Kohn had been preparing for overseas service before Congressman Starnes stepped in. Decades later, Kohn would still recall the conservative Alabaman as "an asshole, a real fuckhead."

Campton was a Quaker-run camp north of Lake Winnipesaukee, centered in an isolated old Civilian Conservation Corps facility amid the Presidential Range of the White Mountains. Ostensibly the camp's chief work was timber stand improvement. In other words, it was the mindless shuffling of limbs and leaves that CPS men had come to loathe. The Harvard Nutrition Project was also utilizing camp residents, as scientists examined the effect of different diets on human health and performance. The scientists would deprive the CPS volunteers of Vitamin C, or of protein, and then test them on their physical abilities. The men grew weaker, their gums became softer, and the scientists would tally the data (Frazer and O'Sullivan 1996, 83).

The scientists considered their nutrition work significant, but civilian disdain otherwise surrounded Campton. One barber in nearby Plymouth posted a sign stating "No skunks allowed! So you conscientious objectors, keep the Hell out of this shop." Inside, too, the Campton camp seemed to be unraveling. The month Roy arrived, CPS inspectors identified potentially serious health and morale problems. Up to 10 percent of the camp's roughly 135 residents were on sick call at any one time. Inspectors worried it might reflect larger problems. Some odd ducks certainly tainted the Campton atmosphere. One Campton man who had entered the CPS system in December 1942, the future political gadfly Lyndon LaRouche, had already been expelled from his Massachusetts Friends Meeting for malicious gossiping. Inspectors found other signs of camp decline. The kitchen was dirty, with dust accumulated above the stove. The refrigerator stunk. Flies buzzed everywhere.

For Roy, New Hampshire proved relentlessly grim, "the low point," he would later say, of his entire Civilian Public Service experience. Gray skies mirrored the camp's rock-bottom morale. The wound of Earl's death was still raw; the strangling of the Earlham initiative still stung. The only positive development in New Hampshire was that Roy's time there ended quickly. By November, Forest Service officials had recognized the camp's timber work was too trivial to sustain. The camp was closed and Roy boarded a train to Gatlinburg, Tennessee, for an assignment at a National Park Service–affiliated facility dubbed Camp Rufus Jones.

In Gatlinburg CPS men were helping maintain Great Smoky Mountains National Park. Like Campton, the setting was beautiful and the camp was dreary. The dormitories were hot and stuffy. The recreation hall was run down. At night, bedeviling flies known as no-see-ums attacked. The social hall piano was, naturally, out of tune; the neighbors unwelcoming. One Saturday night, several months before Roy arrived, five Gatlinburg conchies were accosted at a town square dance. The taunts escalated. The pacifists retreated; nearly three dozen townies followed. One conchie was slugged, then another. One fell, and was kicked unconscious. The camp's newsletter, *The Calumet*, reported on August 16, 1943, that Gatlinburg camp administrators thought it might be best if the town were placed off limits for a while.

Roy worked in the Gatlinburg rock quarry, helping build a bridge and stone wall above a big creek. Gatlinburg also offered a liberal arts education of sorts. The camp had a relatively well-stocked library, professionally catalogued and freshened with forty newspaper and periodical subscriptions. Individual dormitories had smaller book collections. Discussion groups flourished with CPS men like Benjamin L. Reid, who would go on to win the Pulitzer Prize in 1969 for his biography of the New York lawyer and art collector John Quinn. Reid, like Roy, had earned his conscientious objector status the hard way, not through membership in a historic peace church but through a philosophical commitment to pacifism (Frazer and O'Sullivan 1996, 92).

In time, Reid and other Gatlinburg men grew uncomfortable at the thought that they were missing out on something crucial. Their generation was caught up in a war while they were building rock walls in the backwoods. The Gatlinburg men set their minds on the one remaining hope for meaningful CPS service. Conscientious objectors were being invited to work in mental hospitals, and in the asylums some thought they could yet find job satisfaction. A group of Gatlinburg men put in for transfer, hoping for assignment en masse. Reid and half a dozen others were sent to the Eastern State Hospital in Williamsburg, Virginia, a place once known more generally as the Eastern Lunatic Asylum. Roy in February 1944 went on to a camp at a training school in Laurel, Maryland. The place was still known, by some, under its brutal original name: the District Training School for the Feeble Minded.

↓

The American Legion thought it ridiculous, this idea of sending conscientious objectors into the hospitals. One local legion commander, on first hearing of the idea, proposed that instead the CPS men would be better deployed overseas, digging latrines for soldiers (Sareyan 1994, 59).

Crappers. That's what the conchies were good for. But finally, after overcoming the same kind of political resistance that had killed the overseas training program, the first CPS mental hospital unit had opened in June 1942 at Williamsburg. In time, sixty-one CPS units would open at mental hospitals and district training schools for the retarded. Some three thousand CPS men would serve in mental institutions through the war.

If the pacifists wanted to feel part of a struggle, the mental hospitals delivered in spades.

Undermanned in the best of times, the mental hospitals were stripped by wartime demands. What remained, Roy's friend Roy Finch said, were "unbelievable hell-holes," a rank assault on humane sensibilities (Bennett 2003, 85). They reeked of urine, waste, and despair, cut by an occasional futile swab of antiseptic. Emotionally calloused ward attendants enforced hospital discipline through beatings, isolation cells, and bread-and-water diets. The professional medical staff often appeared indifferent, opportunistic, or negligent. Brutality was a survival mechanism; indoctrination was a slap in the face. At Byberry, a particularly notorious hospital outside Philadelphia, a nurse equipped one newcomer with pillows and tongue depressors and then locked him into a room filled with naked epileptics, some cupping their own feces (Frazer and O'Sullivan 1996, 175).

The mental hospitals were horror shows, plain and simple. Once the CPS men recovered from their revulsion, they had to figure out how to cope. Faced with seemingly indifferent supervisors, they began collecting stories and observations: the Iowa hospital attendant who kicked a patient in the groin, the Ohio hospital attendant who hit a patient with a leather restraining strap, the New Jersey patients who were thrown handfuls of loose coleslaw to paw through for dinner, the Pennsylvania doctor evocatively dubbed The Butcher. CPS men at the Cleveland State Hospital in 1943 ultimately brought their grim stories to a reporter at the *Cleveland Press*. The series of articles that resulted, with headlines such as "Mental Patients Here Beaten and Shackled," helped spur institutional reform (Sareyan 1994, 65).

At Byberry the next year, staffers began publishing *The Attendant*, a monthly periodical of eight to twelve pages profiling the work within the mental hospitals. Four CPS men based at Byberry formed the cadre for what was first known as the Mental Hygiene Project, ultimately winning Selective Service approval to devote themselves full time to a nationwide mental hospital reform effort. They circulated ideas and techniques. The pacifists debated physical coercion, ultimately concluding that defensive physical manipulation of an intransigent patient was sometimes necessary. One view developed holding that force was appropriate if necessary to manage a ward, but not if used for strictly punitive purposes (Eisan 1948, 214). From their debate, reflection, and observations, the CPS published orientation manuals and set the stage for what evolved after the war into the National Mental Health Foundation and then the National Mental Health Association, endorsed by the likes of former First Lady Eleanor Roosevelt and theologian Reinhold Niebuhr.

Roy was heading to Laurel, originally built in the mid-1920s as the District Training Center for the Feeble Minded. The center had since shortened its name but not softened its rhetoric. The administrators spoke of working with the "mental defectives," the "mentally subnormal," or, most simply, "morons." Prophylactic practices could be irrevocable. Between 1933 and 1945, sixteen Laurel inmates were sterilized on the authority of relatives and hospital physicians.

Still, by some lights, the Laurel center was a relatively humane and modern place. Left on their own, administrators would say, the morons would be victimized, preyed upon by the unscrupulous.

Inside an institution, they would be happier, mingling with their own stunted kind.

The Laurel training center had long been overcrowded and understaffed. Academic and vocational classes were jammed into the basements of dormitories. A new hospital building was constructed in 1940, but the roadway leading to it was pocked by mud holes. The dozen red brick buildings were not unattractive, and several new dorms had been constructed, but landscaping was sparse on the one thousand acres. The area forests had been chopped like a bad prison haircut. The place, the *Washington Post* had reported on September 16, 1936, was threatening to become "merely an idiot colony."

The war aggravated every problem. The draft and higher-paying war-industry jobs stole away workers. Inmates kept escaping. Between September 1942 and August 1943, some three hundred Laurel inmates ran away or simply wandered off. The manpower shortage was so severe that, not long before Roy arrived, the Laurel administrators began raising publicly the notion of bringing in Japanese internees as staff. Roy was among the first cadre of CPS men to appear at Laurel, fifteen or so pacifists prepared for work that might actually mean something.

At Laurel, Roy was first assigned to Cottage 6, which he described in an April 21, 1944, diary entry as "a group of about 62 boys ranging in mental age from idiots, imbeciles through morons." In time Roy became recreation director. The job title fit the former high school wrestler. He joined forces with his new friend Ralph Kohn, the fellow alumnus of West Campton as well as the short-lived overseas relief program. Together they managed Laurel's baseball team and a bowling alley equipped with dwarfish bowling balls. It was tough work; resources could be scant at the District Training Schools. At one in Delaware, the terminally shortchanged youngsters relied on balls of twine for baseballs and a trusted rusty can for a football (Sareyan 1994, 129). The charges everywhere defied easy coaching. The children would eat their own feces, or splatter it on the walls. Their bodies were at war with themselves, limbs contorted, their eyes uncomprehending.

"These kids were just flotsam and jetsam," Kohn recalled in a 2005 interview. "They were at the end of the line."

Sixty years after the fact, Kohn tearfully recalled one child. His arms and legs were twisted, his head constantly shaking. He would never, ever get better no matter how much love was poured upon him. His name was Stanley, and one of Kohn's jobs was to feed him. Gently, insistently, Kohn would serve Stanley the porridge, one careful spoonful at a time pressed through the boy's meaningless grin.

"He would look up at me," Kohn said decades later, "with the most adoring eyes."

The work still meant something to Kohn, a devout young man born in 1918 in Chicago. While young, Kohn had fallen under the inspiration of Herman Will, one-time youth secretary of the Methodist Commission on World Peace. So it was that after graduating from high school in 1936, Kohn had gone to work in one factory until the company began making 75-millimeter artillery shells. Like Roy, Kohn was unwilling to be part of any war-making machine. He quit rather than make munitions.

Kohn's minister was a member of his draft board, easing his designation as a conscientious objector. Kohn began his own travels through the CPS camps in Indiana, where he did pick-and-shovel work for about six months. He then went to remote Trenton, North Dakota, a windswept camp about ten miles from the Canadian border. Learning of an opportunity to train for overseas relief work, Kohn signed up and began studies at Haverford College. This was similar training to what Roy had begun at Earlham, until Congress called a halt to it. Then Kohn went to New Hampshire, where he first encountered Roy during the grim winter. Finally, after a stop at Luray, Virginia, Kohn ended up at Laurel.

Roy really made an impression in Laurel, energetically undertaking the most mundane task. Kohn found him to be a real dynamo, like a "little Brigham Young," full of fervency and drive. Looking to improve himself, Roy was studying French through a local Berlitz school. He would take part in bull sessions that would sometimes last well past midnight, and he would constantly be inspired to learn more. After seeing a movie called *The Adventures of Mark Twain*, he vowed in his diary that he would "become more familiar with Twain's works, especially those published since his death." Roy was also going above and beyond for his charges, though sometimes with surprising results.

One Monday Roy took two mildly retarded teenage brothers from the training school to the home of a local activist. The three spent the night, and the next morning they made their way to a movie theater on Baltimore's Pennsylvania Avenue, the center of black culture in the segregated city. The theater ticket-taker informed Roy he could not enter, since he was white. She was polite and dignified, but insistent. As long as white people refuse to allow colored people in their theaters, she told him, the colored people will refuse to allow white people in theirs. Roy acquiesced. He bought the boys their tickets and then retreated to the nearby Druid Hill YMCA until the movie was over. It was, Roy later confided in his diary, a "most interesting experience."

"The experience of being discriminated against because of the color of my skin has enlarged my understanding of the evil of racial discrimination," Roy subsequently advised the NAACP.

Some encounters were more successful in their outcome. Decades later, Roy would tell his children about the short, stout woman who ran the Laurel kitchen. A teenage boy felt himself in love with one of the kitchen workers. One day, deeply impassioned, he barged into the kitchen and seized a butcher knife. He waved it around, threatening to kill his beloved and everyone else. The tiny kitchen supervisor, a stalwart woman, stepped up to the frenzied young man and called him by name.

"Give me that knife," the kitchen supervisor commanded, "right now!"

Immediately, or so Roy would later recount, the teenager complied. The supervisor reached up, grabbed him by the ear, and marched him out of the kitchen for a stern talking-to. It was proof, some thought, of how violence could be diverted without escalation.

At Laurel, though the work could feel meaningful, Roy continued growing more radically alienated from the underlying Civilian

Public Service system. He was increasingly convinced that religious groups had no business cooperating with the government in running the conscientious objector camps. Roy was not the only one. Acts of rebellion proliferated, and Selective Service authorities discerned certain patterns.

Four distinct types of objectors were present. Most were said to be cooperative in every respect; they worked hard and "led well-regulated lives from all angles during 'off-duty' hours." A smaller group was "prone to be influenced" in contrary ways. A small group of resisters advocated nonviolent passive resistance to the civilian work program, and there were those who "desired open and united rebellion, sabotage and violence" (Selective Service System 1950, 230).

Even the most establishment figures were growing dissatisfied. The best-known pacifist of the time, former *Time* magazine cover subject A. J. Muste, had initially been scorned by absolutist protestors like David Dellinger for collaborating too much with the government. Muste was initially willing to represent the Fellowship of Reconciliation on the National Service Board for Religious Objectors, which radical pacifists denounced for taking orders from the Selective Service director. By 1944, though, Muste had concluded there could be no meaningful cooperation with the government. Muste and the Fellowship of Reconciliation withdrew support for the Civilian Public Service system, joining the War Resisters League, which had likewise stepped away from the National Service Board for Religious Objectors.

In the spring of 1944, CPS men at the Big Flats camp in New York began organizing the Civilian Public Service Union. The new organization was described as a union for "drafted workers conscientiously opposed to war," and there was optimistic talk about becoming the unified voice pushing for wages and benefits. By the end of the year some five hundred men would be members. In June 1944 Roy traveled to New York City's Labor Temple to meet with Ralph Rudd, future Reagan administration ambassador Max Kampelman, and representatives of some twenty Civilian Public Service camps who were interested in forming the CPS union. The Selective Service System refused to recognize the group. It was absurd, officials thought, to consider granting bargaining rights to men fulfilling their national service obligation. Even with this, some home-front patriots thought Selective Service was being too conciliatory. In May 1944 the Verne O. Reed American Legion Post No. 78 in Bloomfield, Iowa, adopted unanimously a resolution urging that conscientious objectors be denied the right to own and acquire property.

Amid the souring atmosphere, Roy attended a Civilian Public Service camp conference at Earlham College in May 1944 that further propelled his own doubts about CPS. Over the course of several months, he came to realize it was time for a fundamental change. He could no longer participate in one of the traditional camps. The camp administrators were good men, by and large, but Roy felt the entire system had gone wrong. If the State conscripted him, then let the State control him directly. Other CPS radicals had reached the same conclusion. In response, the first government-run camp had opened at Mancos in southwest Colorado in July 1943. The Mancos men were put to work building the foundation for the Jackson Gulch Dam. It was honest work, but the Bureau of Reclamation supervisors came to regard their charges as uncooperative, contentious, and overeducated.

By September 1944 Roy had determined to transfer again. In November he requested placement in a new camp in Oregon. Instead, he was directed to a Michigan town memorably named Germfask. No one who knew it would ever forget it, no matter how hard they tried.

3

Germfask

Germfask opened May 12, 1944, as Civilian Public Service Camp No. 135. Or, as some preferred: the Alcatraz of CPS.

The place appeared placid enough. No metal bars or armed guards surrounded the rustic Civilian Conservation Corps outpost bordering the Seney National Wildlife Refuge in Michigan's Upper Peninsula. The 95,212-acre Seney refuge welcomed bald eagles, ospreys, and loons. The war could seem very remote. One moonlit night, CPS man Dan Dingman recalled decades later, several men out for a stroll came to a meadow's edge. They stopped, spotting deer. Something magical was happening. First one animal and then another stepped out from the herd and pranced briefly under the moon's spotlight before yielding the grassy stage for the next. Germfask was nature, beautifully raw (Dingman n.d.).

But rough, too. The once heavily timbered region had long bred lumberjacks, honored in the nearby town of Blaney Park with its looming statue of Paul Bunyan. The lumberjack's muscular ethos lingered. Residents hunted, fished, and trapped for sustenance. It was "he-man's country," whose brawny toughs were "always ready with their fists," a *Chicago Tribune* reporter approvingly noted. Saloons and their shadows abounded in the small Upper Peninsula towns: Manistique and Newberry, Munising and McLeod's Corner. Nominally speaking, Germfask was the strangest of them all. The town's name derived from the initials of the area's first eight settlers.

Near Germfask, a prisoner-of-war camp had been established for captured German soldiers. In time some local residents came to prefer even the Krauts to the pacifists. The Germans were appropriately subdued, having lost their war, while the Germfask conscientious objectors kept rebelling. They defied every convention. They broke the rules, and in time some broke themselves.

"These dormant talents were to be exercised in raising Hell instead of paying back to the nation the price of escaping military duty," a Germfask superintendent would lament. "No one who has not been closely associated with them for a substantial period of time could believe that such people could exist outside an insane asylum" (Selective Service System 1950, 237).

Roy saw just how disjointed Germfask would become. But he and other discerning pacifists also knew Germfask as more than a place. It would be a state of mind, the embodiment of radical resistance. In everything that followed, Roy would always retain a bit of Germfask in his heart.

At noon on May 12, 1944, several Fish and Wildlife Service employees joined the newly arrived conscientious objectors in the Germfask dining hall for a welcoming meal of roast pork, mashed potatoes, green peas, and pie. A general good cheer pervaded. Momentarily, camp administrators thought the new government-run experiment just might work.

Then Corbett Bishop arrived. A red-bearded John the Baptist, his blue eyes agleam, Bishop marched draped with clanking chains.

"This is slavery," Bishop proclaimed in a prophet's voice (Johnson 1945, 1).

Bishop's reputation preceded him. Once an oil company employee, he had gone into the secondhand book business without much success. His friends said he hated to part with the books. The Alabama native had been wrangling with CPS administrators ever since he entered the camp system in 1942. At the government-run Mancos camp in Colorado, Bishop would stand in the morning and deliver unto the congregation a word for the day. Once he urged the campers not to look outside, for the sight of so much natural beauty might spuriously raise the men's morale, an inappropriate state of mind for those consigned. Traveling to Germfask from Mancos, he had donned a ceremonial ball and chain.

"In our innocence," Germfask superintendent C. S. Johnson said, "we immediately concluded that Bishop was a screwball" (Johnson 1945, 135).

Undeniably, Bishop could rant, orating on tyranny and slavery. Alternatively, he could shut down completely. Eventually refusing to return to Germfask after a furlough in September 1944, he would go utterly limp and force officials to carry him away. He would not shave, bathe, or feed himself. He would lie still, despoiled and starving, rather than cooperate with authorities. One winter morning, his attorney Francis Heisler recalled in an oral history, hospital doctors discovered Bishop covered in snow. His window had blown open in the night, and he had simply lain there while the snow accumulated about him. Obdurate to the end, Bishop refused to lift his hand to sign his own parole papers (Tracy 1993, 103).

Bishop was extreme. He fit Germfask, though, which would become an extreme place. By the end of May, the camp held about forty residents. There were Christians, atheists, and Theosophists. There were engineers, artists, professors, and, well, weirdos.

"The outstanding peculiarity about them was the almost universal lack of expression in the eyes. Their laughter, if any, likewise had a vacant quality," one camp superintendent would report. "Some of these achieved a Christlike appearance, though as we were to learn the impression was to be dissipated of any inner saintliness of spirit" (Selective Service System 1950, 237).

Dan Dingman exemplified the Germfask rebellious spirit. Raised in the Congregational Church, Dingman no longer thought a church-run camp made sense. If the government insisted on conscripting young men for the war machine, then the government itself should do the holding. The twenty-year-old Dingman secured assignment to the Mancos camp in Colorado, where he committed himself to doing nothing at all. At Germfask, he deepened his noncooperative ways. One day he was placed on a crew assigned to repair a wire fence.

"I had difficulty comprehending the superintendent's detailed instructions on how to use a hammer and staples," Dingman recalled innocently. "Since he failed to clarify the final desired result, I had almost a hundred staples in that post before he redirected my efforts."

Passive-aggressiveness became a Germfask art form. Another Germfask man, ordered to clean a truck platform, spent all day sweeping two-thirds of it. Chopping one tree was a daylong joke. The supervisor had to order every blow, every withdrawal of the axe, every spot the axe was to fall. Foremen began quitting, one proclaiming his sheer relief at escaping the loony bin.

Outside the camp, this behavior rankled. The Upper Peninsula's Schoolcraft County had sent some one thousand men into military service. Mothers had lost their sons; children, their fathers; wives, their husbands. For civilians deprived of loved ones and luxuries, the Germfask conchies were at best an irritant and at times an abomination. One local newspaper editor claimed an enemy agent was keeping the camp riled up, a Fifth Column undermining U.S. domestic tranquility. Worse, a local American Legion leader warned that the camp was rank with gross sexual perversion.

"The non-fighters at Camp Germfask should realize that the general public does not, and will not, take to them with any kindness," the *Manistique Pioneer-Tribune* stated in an account republished in the *Germfask Newsletter* of February 3, 1945.

The Germfask men, Roy later summed up, were considered "perverts, irreligious, intellectuals with crackpot theories, drunkards and communists, who are lacking in humility, crazy, rejecting all discipline, threatening violence and practicing vandalism." Sixteen CPS campers, one weekend shortly after Germfask opened, ventured to the nearby town of Newberry for leave. Some went to the local movie theater. Others found one of the town's saloons. Townsmen gathered. There were glances, words, and warnings. The Germfask men backed out of the bar, retreating in the face of a mob. The conchies escaped intact, but were henceforth banned from Newberry for their own safety. In Manistique, swearing townsmen pelted the conchies with eggs. One Sunday the local parishioner who stoked the furnace for the town's Catholic church refused to heat the building if any of those damn conscientious objectors attended service.

Inside the camp, Germfask men escalated protests in their own fashion. Dr. Don DeVault, a research chemist, had done time in federal prison before being paroled to serve in the CPS camps. Mindless labor vexed him. Beginning at Mancos, on his own, he had started conducting modest but meaningful research examining antibiotics. Selective Service sent him to Germfask, where he was ordered to help build duck ponds. At that, he drew the line.

"I am done with this foolishness," DeVault declared on September 27, the *Germfask Newsletter* subsequently reported. "Henceforth, I shall be reported for work [only] on penicillin or related subjects."

DeVault eventually pled nolo contendere to charges related to non-cooperation on November 15 in Grand Rapids and was sentenced to another three and a half years in prison. DeVault's rebellion impressed many men. It came as Roy was setting in motion his transfer to Germfask, and as the camp grew more volatile.

Lust helped bring it all to a boil.

"There are," Schoolcraft County prosecutor W. J. Sheehan warned visiting minister Owen Krok, "a bunch of sex perverts in that camp."

Sheehan lacked direct evidence, but he abounded in ambition. In January 1945, the Upper Peninsula temperatures dropping to their wintry lows, Sheehan began stoking his case against the conscientious objector camp with the help of the Rev. W. A. Harrington. Harrington was pastor of Manistique's First Baptist Church, and though he was a good Christian man he had come to despise the Germfask conchies. Harrington reported that he, personally, knew of two married Germfask pacifists who were pressing young women for dates at the Baptist Young People's Society meetings. Harrington told authorities that three Manistique men had advised him they would personally "take care" of any Germfask man who chanced back into town.

"And they could do it, too," Harrington added approvingly.

This was all Sheehan needed, and on January 16 the prosecutor asked the Selective Service to place Manistique off limits. Pointedly he reported that Germfask men would "attempt to date girls in the high school library, in churches and on the street."

"Several have complained to the local ministers," Sheehan added, according to the February 3, 1945, *Germfask Newsletter*, "that the people of the community are anti-social as they fail to provide Victory Girls."

Victory Girls! It was a joke: farm maidens patriotically served up for lonely men. But with local sentiments aflame, the fanciful notion assumed a life of its own. It was bad enough that a soldier's gal might be wooed by some 4-F Johnny. It was pure poison to think the lucky stiff was a Gandhian zealot. To protect virtue, officials put the town of Manistique off limits. The local congressman, Representative Frederick Van Ness Bradley, quickly reinforced him. Bradley, a Michigan Republican, frankly despised most conscientious objectors. "They should be made work or fight," Bradley declared in the July 21, 1945, *Congressional Record*, adding that he could "conceive of no lower vermin in our nation."

A local American Legion man named Charles Gray shared the sentiment. In the last week of January, Gray visited Germfask and reported his dire findings in the *Escanaba Daily Press* of February 2, 1945. Germfask, he said, was the filthiest camp he had ever seen. Men were lingering in bed. The barracks floor had not been cleaned in weeks. Grime encrusted the walls and ceilings. Grease thickened the kitchen floor. Rubbish jammed the storage room; garbage cans were overflowing. "We actually took great pride," Dingman allowed, "in keeping [the barracks] as un-military as possible."

Dingman lived in a bunkhouse dubbed Tobacco Road. It was smoky and congested, more a joint than a barracks. Lights were strung up for nightly poker games. The men kept a coffeepot constantly warming, and offered visitors milk and bread liberated from the mess hall. The walls were covered, one visiting minister said, with a rather remarkable collection of nudes and pin-up girls. The men declared the spot *Toujours Gai:* Always Merry.

On Tuesday night, January 30, rebels snuck into the camp kitchen. The *Escanaba Daily Press* reported on February 3, 1945, that the raiders split a large, 100-pound bean bag and scattered the contents across the floor. They broke a three-gallon mustard jar and scattered that too. They broke seven quarts of orange and lemon extract and saturated thirty pounds of baking powder. In the kitchen cooler, steamed rice, stewed apricots, and prunes were glopped together. Light bulbs were smashed and the oven doors removed.

The kitchen raid was unleavened rage, a tantrum, but it wasn't the first assault on the camp. Germfask men had previously clogged latrines and hidden light bulbs. They had spread white flour an inch thick on the floor and used coffee grounds to write obscene epithets. Once some prankster stole the camp's knives and forks and buried them in a snowbank. Another day, doctors at the Germfask infirmary began noticing a peculiar pattern. Six men whose last names began with the letters B and C showed up sick, in alphabetical order. Then all four men whose last names began with the letter K fell ill. The Germfask men, doctors eventually realized, were systematically sick-calling their way through the alphabet.

The prank fit. The whole camp was one sick joke.

Roy arrived on the cold night of January 20. He found his way to the Tobacco Road dorm, where he later confided in his diary that he discovered a "Saturday-night atmosphere of beer and mixed singing that was somehow pathetic and strained, a put-on performance to convince themselves they were Bohemian." Roy, as ever, was both participant and observer. He took note of what was around him, the games and pretense. He could clinically critique the playacting, even among men who shared his pacifist ideology. Over the next few days, moreover, Roy discerned that, technically, the camp was superfluous. Seney refuge maintenance needs, the camp's ostensible reason for being, could not justify continued camp operations. The refuge required only about fifteen men, far fewer than the seventy-five or so confined at Germfask. The lack of meaningful work aggravated what Roy acknowledged as the boorish, and sometimes drunken, behavior of a few campers. At Germfask, Roy was surprised to find himself to be a conservative radical.

Roy communicated his observations to the War Resisters League headquarters in New York, and WRL leaders in turn asked Roy for some straight reporting on the Germfask disaster.

"Are they heroes, valiantly fighting a vicious set-up?" War Resisters League field director Frank Olmstead asked Roy in a February 13, 1945, letter. "Are they high-spirited pranksters, gaining a relief that keeps them sane? Are they psychopaths, revealing symptoms that need treatment?"

Roy described a pack of frustrated, bitter men who appeared "on the mental brink." Personalities were being warped and demoralized. "The main body of campers are divided and mostly inarticulate, carrying on the rather anarchistic practice of ignoring the acts of others," Roy reported to Olmstead in February. Nor did these pacifists always turn the other cheek. In late January, Roy reported, a camp truck had delivered campers into the town of Munising, on the shores of Lake Superior. When the men prepared to leave, though, the truck wouldn't start. Several pacifists, intent on extending their leave time, had removed a part of the motor.

"This group," Roy advised Olmstead, "passed the evening in some local taverns where they imbibed too freely and, during the course of the evening one of them invited a soldier outside where the C.O. then polished the soldier off."

The Germfask men had lost their way. Wrung out by confinement but convinced of their own virtue, they were both more radical and less tethered to any meaningful principle. Theirs was the freedom of incoherence. Twenty-five years later, amid the tumult of the sixties, Roy would lament a similar indiscipline among self-styled revolutionaries.

In Germfask, though he was new to the camp, Roy began asserting himself. He urged Olmstead to visit and see conditions for himself. He helped resurrect the camp newsletter, and barely a week into his Germfask tenure he joined four other Germfask men in writing Senator Arthur Vandenberg, the Michigan Republican who had recently formally abandoned his one-time isolationist tenets. The Germfask writers advised the senator of the case of Dr. DeVault, the research chemist sentenced to prison for refusing make-work. They noted the impossibility of supporting families on what amounted to sixteen cents a day; and, delicately, they rebutted charges that lust-filled Germfask men had been making moves on the innocent Manistique maidens.

No "aggressive or indiscreet" acts had been committed, Roy and the others wrote. Of course, they conceded, some harmless flirting might have taken place. A conscientious objector, Roy and his colleagues explained to the senator, "is a normal human being and, in judging his actions, you must expect him to behave as a normal human being."

Vandenberg apparently didn't care; he never wrote back. The Germfask frustrations, though, were heard by Roger Baldwin of the American Civil Liberties Union. Himself a former World War I conscientious objector, Baldwin requested a congressional investigation of camp conditions. Word spread, as well, to less sympathetic audiences. In the first week of February, the *Detroit Times* scornfully regarded the "intellectuals and college professors engaged in mutiny" at Germfask. Something had to be done. The local *Newberry News* was already urging appointment of a "hard boiled, two-fisted supervisor . . . with authority to maintain discipline in any way he sees fit. The conchies would go to work and they would keep their camp clean and sanitary, or there would be some sore jaws in the outfit." The *Shreveport Journal* heartily concurred, denouncing in a February 16 editorial the "coddling of these so-called conscientious objectors." *Time* magazine followed shortly afterward, observing on February 19, 1945, that the Germfask men "feigned sickness" while "with money supplied by relatives, they bought liquor" and "frequently they went AWOL and roamed the nearby towns, making ardent and often successful love to local girls."

Again with the lust. The specter of pacifist horndogs just wouldn't subside, no matter how often Roy or others tried to knock it down. *Time,* Roy wrote, "considerably overstates our abilities as Don Juans, or the amount of energy that has been expended courting local girls." Other visitors agreed. Carl Soule of the Methodist Church's Commission on World Peace visited in early March, and found what he termed a "distinct religious tone." One Sunday started with a Bible service in the morning, followed by a Church of Christ service in the afternoon and an Episcopal service at night. But the defenses hardly availed. The wider world cast judgment. In early March, *Chicago Tribune* reporter

Frank Hughes visited Germfask. He produced a week-long series of articles whose headlines pounded a drumbeat.

"Unruly Idlers Have Lark at U.S. Expense," the *Tribune* reported. "Objector Camp Inmates Vie at Work Shirking." "Idle Objectors Scoff at Whole Draft System." The stories elaborated. "[It] is the headquarters of the 'we-won't-work-or-fight club,'" Hughes wrote in the March 7, 1945, issue. "[It is] a camp of about 80 conscientious objectors clothed, fed and paid by the federal government to spend most of their time in idleness under discipline so lax nobody could touch them."

Camp manager Paul Voelker complained about the article as unfair to "boys of the finest integrity and cooperation," a rather striking characterization given Germfask's general reputation. Voelker, though, was himself a rather colorful character. A veteran and self-described "liberty-loving American," Voelker was a big talker whom Roy called, with some understatement, eccentric. Roy viewed him respectfully, though, telling his diary that "if the man is imbalanced, then the world needs more imbalance." In early March Voelker announced he could no longer continue. "I have found the Selective Service treatment of men in this CPS camp to be the re-establishment of slavery in our nation, and the punishment of men whose conscience does not permit their participation in war," Voelker wrote in his resignation letter, reprinted in the April 1945 *Germfask Newsletter.*

Roy shared the perspective, though he had his doubts about some of the Germfask tactics and personalities. Roy's radicalism had come into full flower. He suggested that meekly following orders in a Civilian Public Service camp was tantamount to serving as a Nazi concentration camp guard. "We must recognize," Roy wrote sternly in the third issue of the *Germfask Newsletter,* "that a majority of human beings are rapidly falling into two categories: those who resist, and those who collaborate."

Easter 1945 showed what resistance meant. Shortly before sunrise, Dan Dingman, Dick Lazarus, and Bent Andresen struck out on foot for the eight miles to catch the Greyhound bus to Manistique. Lazarus was the son of War Resisters League activist Frieda Lazarus and had grown up immersed in peace activism. In 1940 Frieda Lazarus helped found the Metropolitan Board for Conscientious Objectors to counsel young men in the New York area. Like Roy, she knew the power of publicity, and they would soon be regularly corresponding. Andresen was a thirty-seven-year-old native of Denmark who had spent several years as a union organizer. Prior to Germfask, he had participated in a cold-climate experiment at Cornell University whose primary effect was to leave him with a bad case of hemorrhoids (Frazer and O'Sullivan 1996, 116). He was an avid reader and spread his books around. Once Andresen sold Roy a ten-cent copy of a thirty-two-page screed entitled *The Truth about Pearl Harbor*, whose thesis was that President Roosevelt had been anticipating war with Japan well before the attack of December 7, 1941.

Police officers stopped Dingman, Lazarus, and Andresen as they exited the Manistique church following the Easter service. The three conchies were taken to the Manistique jail, where a phone call to Germfask administrators confirmed that they were absent without leave. Eventually a deal was struck for the charges to be dropped. A one-time Stanford student and former CPS man named Lew Hill, then with the American Civil Liberties Union's National Committee on Conscientious Objection, advised Roy on April 12 that the Justice Department really didn't want to get entangled in a freedom-of-religion fight. This was among the first communications between Hill and Roy, two equally energetic pacifists who would later both collaborate and clash.

Hill's assessment of the Justice Department's decision not to prosecute may have only captured part of the government's reasoning vis-à-vis Germfask. Confrontation had not quelled irksome resistance. The Michigan camp itself had become a hothouse; it needed uprooting, removal to some more distant place. Soon rumors were circulating within the camp that Germfask would be closing. Shortly the rumors proved true. On Monday, May 14, Roy and the other men learned they would be transferred to the newest Civilian Public Service outpost in far-off Minersville, California.

The Germfask men, objectors and administrators alike, tallied the pitiful score as they packed up for departure. By no conventional count could Germfask be called a success. More man-hours had been consumed by sick time, jail time, and refusals than by actual work on the camp's ostensible Seney refuge work project. Five different cooks had come and gone, as had five different camp managers. A steady stream of FBI agents, state police, parole officers, lawmakers, and reporters came and went, alternatively baffled and revolted by the Germfask goings-on.

"We hope now to forget the episode," Johnson sighed as Germfask closed for good (Selective Service System 1950, 241).

The Germfask men headed west by Northern Pacific train. In Portland, given three hours between transfers, several conchies fanned out to distribute a flyer entitled "Japan Is Trying to Surrender." It was not quite true. Five American divisions were even then fighting their way across the zealously defended island of Okinawa. Preparations were afoot for a planned November 1 invasion of the Japanese mainland. Peace still seemed a pacifist's pipe dream. Nonetheless, the Germfask men were able to hand out some five hundred copies of the flyer before returning to Portland's Union Station and continuing on their way to California.

Forest Service men met them on June 4 in the town of Redding at the northern edge of the Sacramento Valley. In a convoy, they were driven about fifty miles over several mountain ranges to tiny Minersville. From there the men passed on to Civilian Public Service Camp 148, nestled amid the Shasta-Trinity National Forest. Like many of the CPS camps, Minersville occupied an abandoned Civilian Conservation Corps facility. A stream ran alongside the campgrounds; the wind whispered in the Douglas fir trees. Roy thought it beautiful. Mere façade, though, would not deceive the CPS men. They figured they were still in Germfask, a name they would keep.

"As long as CPS exists we place value on the symbol of Germfask," Roy and his fellow Minersville newsletter editors explained in their inaugural June 15, 1945, issue. "It represents a strong opposition to governmental tyranny, and a healthy reaction against the moral bankruptcy of peace-church CPS administrators."

"The story of CPS is unchanged," the newsletter summed up. "At Camp Germfask, we begin again a chapter with which we are already fully acquainted."

While Roy was predicting that "antipathies of an insoluble nature" would eventually bring Minersville to a Germfask-like boil, Minersville camp director Bliss Haynes sought to convince his new charges otherwise. He'd treat them straight, give them respect. A Forest Service veteran, Haynes had previously impressed the men who knew him at another CPS camp. They considered him fair-minded and personable. He had their attention when he said they would be fighting forest fires, perhaps those set by fabled Japanese fire-setting balloons cast off into the Northwest woods. Germfask veteran Dan Dingman thought this task cleverly put; it sounded useful and hearty, a virtuous way to defend the country. At first the men accepted training in using axes, hoes, shovels, and forty-pound, water-filled backpacks to protect the surrounding Shasta-Trinity National Forest. For a time, it sufficed.

In mid-July a mission came. A fire had been spotted somewhere in the far reaches of the forest. Thirteen men including Roy, Bent Andresen, and Dan Dingman were driven to a jump-off point. There, led by

2. Roy Kepler (third from right) and fellow conscientious objectors in the Minersville Civilian Public Service camp, after their arrival from Germfask. Photographer unknown, courtesy of the Kepler family.

a guide the men called Injun Joe, the crew hoisted packs, tools, and two day's worth of rations and headed into the woods. They hiked for a day and found nothing. The next morning the Minersville men awoke to discover that Injun Joe had deserted them during the night. They were on their own. The abandoned team hiked on for a while, but they never reached the fire. Finally the bedraggled men dropped their tools, gave up the search, and began straggling back until they found a creek and splashed downstream in sodden boots. The Forest Service ranger flagged down a car and caught a ride to the nearest phone so the men could be picked up.

"We never heard from the guide again, but we did learn that the fire had been put out by a bunch of Boy Scouts on a camping trip. That was also the end of my forest fire–fighting experience," Dingman recalled.

The first months passed without dramatic confrontation. When a three-year-old child was reported missing in August, the Minersville men pitched in enthusiastically. A party of schoolgirls eventually found the child, but the Minersville men were pleased, the *Minersville Fortnightly Nugget* reported on August 28, 1945, to show "what even 'slow-downers' can do when really presented with a human problem."

Day by day, though, Roy and his fellow radicals were accumulating grievances. They still felt the squeeze of authority. On August 29, Roy was part of a crew called up to fight lightning-strike fires near the Hoopa Indian reservation. The men were ordered to load into the truck backpacks, Pulaski tools, saws, canteens, and other equipment. Roy reminded the Forest Service foreman of the safety rules prohibiting the transport of men and equipment in the same truck. The supervisor gruffly ordered the men into the truck anyway. Back at the camp, Roy complained to camp director Haynes, who told him to follow orders. Roy lodged a protest in a September 4 letter to the regional forester.

"How can conscript laborers, working under duress, be expected to obey regulations if the Forest Service's own representatives ignore them?" Roy asked.

Germfask-style resistance began resurfacing. One Minersville man, ordered to dig a small hole for the base of a flagstaff, commenced his work with a spoon. Another time, Haynes directed a conchie to throw leftover beans into the garbage. The man started, one bean scrupulously counted out after another. After the man had reached six hundred, give or take, Haynes impatiently ordered that all the beans be dumped at once.

Individual acts, though, offered only passing satisfaction. The system still stood. Roy and his campmates were talking more about unified action, perhaps through the Civilian Public Service Union that had been initiated in 1944 at the Big Flats CPS camp in New York. Roy had attended one of the early organizing sessions and had stayed in touch with union leaders. Their general idea was to expand communication across the camps and address, where possible, the systemic flaws and injustices of the Civilian Public Service. In the summer of 1945, Union members elected to the organization's General Executive Board four West Coast activists. Roy's friend from Minersville, John Lewis, was chosen along with two men who had been discharged from the CPS system, George Reeves and Denny Wilcher. Roy was the fourth man. The four pacifists would end up collaborating over the next three decades.

The West Coast men shared a distinctly radical perspective. They thought it senseless to refine an inherently flawed system. One might as well try to dress up slavery. Civilian public service, Roy and his allies believed, amounted to conscripted labor. The union's real purpose, they believed, should be the wholesale elimination of conscription and the CPS system itself. Other CPS Union men called this "revolutionary unionism" and contrasted it with a more traditionally accommodating "business unionism" designed to negotiate terms for benefits. Because of these conflicting perspectives, Roy and his allies wanted to know whether the rank-and-file would follow an avowedly radical leadership. The West Coast men tried surveying union membership, but were frustrated with the results. Many simply ignored the survey. Few of the CPS men who bothered responding shared the radicals' sentiments. With the war nearly done and the dissolution of CPS in sight, many conscientious objectors just wanted to get home. They'd leave revolution in another's hands.

Some simply dropped their shovels and walked away. By the summer of 1945, roughly two hundred CPS men had walked out of their camp assignments. They were fed up; they would take no more. These individual walkouts were a virtuous but essentially ineffective gesture, Roy and the radicals believed. Instead, the radicals envisioned a mass walkout that would strip the CPS camps of their population and their legitimacy. Quietly Roy and his allies looked ahead to March 2, 1946, as the potential date for a big, unified action. Others disagreed. Former CPS man Lew Hill, with the National Committee on Conscientious Objectors, thought a mass action was premature. Hill would ultimately win the argument. There would be no mass walkout. Nor would Roy and his three West Coast allies last long as CPS Union leaders; if the membership, such as it was, did not want to be led into radical territory, then Roy would not compel them. He resigned.

Then came the Bomb.

The August 6 atomic blast devastating Hiroshima and the August 9 atomic bombing of Nagasaki revolted CPS men. The mass slaughter was a diabolical apotheosis, summing up the whole bloody business. For Roy's friend Bent Andresen, in particular, the bombings clarified the necessity for direct, personal action. He would walk out, and then some. It was time for a definitive statement. Andresen had already gravitated to Roy back in Germfask, admiring what he called his general competence and intelligence. In Minersville, Andresen approached Roy and told him of his plans. Together they wrote an impassioned "Message to People of Good Will," in which they described the atomic bombing as "the most hideous of all atrocities," an abomination as bad as the war it ended.

Andresen exited Minersville three days before Japan's August 15 surrender and hit the road with hundreds of mimeographed copies of the leaflet. He hitchhiked across the United States, handing out along the way the leaflet Roy and he had written. In Denver Andresen spent a night on the Keplers' family porch. The next morning he inked a fresh sign reading "Cal to NJ" and hit the road again. Finally reaching New York, Andresen was picked up in Rochester and charged with distributing a brochure without a license. Shortly afterward, police again seized the bearded pacifist and charged him with vagrancy, a handy street-clearing device. Federal prosecutors in time transported him back West in the company of two U.S. deputy marshals. Eventually Andresen was packed off to federal prison for a two-year sentence.

Other CPS men awaited their release. Naturally it would not come easy. Even before Japan's surrender, Selective Service leaders had been struggling to draft a Civilian Public Service demobilization plan. A proposal released in late May resembled the scheme for shrinking the postwar military, assigning CPS men points for camp time as well as family circumstances. This equal treatment was too much for the Veterans of Foreign Wars and the ever-martial House Committee on Military Affairs, which opined that releasing conscientious objectors before members of the military "would adversely affect morale in the armed forces." Hershey, the Selective Service chief, dutifully slowed the CPS discharges. Fully 26 percent of men in uniform had been discharged by mid-fall, compared to 5 percent of men in Quaker-run CPS camps.

Anxieties rose among the pacifists as their detention seemed to stretch into the indefinite future, and on the night of September 28, Clifford Lang snapped. Lang had been in the CPS camps for two years, and he was desperate to return home to his family. The thirty-two-year-old Colorado native was a member of the Church of the First Born, a Mormon spin-off. Physically resembling a bearded Old Testament prophet, Lang would periodically summon the wrath of God upon the Minersville camp administrators. His denunciations grew more heated, until camp director Bliss Haynes and the camp's doctor declared he was dangerous. They summoned the Trinity County sheriff, who concluded the man was Bible crazy. Sheriff Bigelow and his deputies placed Lang into a straitjacket and prepared to remove him to jail. Other Minersville men gathered, outraged. The authorities had it all wrong. Lang was no crazier than the next man. Confinement had simply gotten to him. "Gestapo!" some men cried out, the Minersville camp newsletter subsequently reported. "Fascist!" Undeterred, Sheriff Bigelow took Lang to jail.

Shortly, apparently having soothed authorities, Lang won his release. Others were still boiling. Roy sent urgent dispatches to Frieda Lazarus, who chaired the War Resisters League's Problems Committee. She took these reports with her on October 9 when she met with General Hershey. He agreed that Minersville men with obvious problems could be discharged, though he admitted he feared reactions from the American Legion.

In the camps, rebellious acts kept occurring.

On Sunday, October 21, a deputy U.S. marshal arrested Minersville man Paul Crowder for refusing to work. Crowder was despondent over his inability to support his wife and ten children. His fellow Minersville campers sided with him. The deputy marshal assigned to retrieve Crowder reported that about twenty Minersville men "ganged up" and briefly threatened to stop the retrieval. The *Sacramento Bee* characterized the incident as "wild disorder," though Bliss Haynes, the camp director, stressed the camp was under control.

But not for long.

The Minersville men were finishing dinner on Monday night, November 26, when they first heard the shouting. The mess hall was on fire. Men rushed from their barracks and saw the flames. The building was already far gone. The men, besides, had only had three enfeebled garden hoses with which to contest the blaze. The men turned their attention to other buildings, stamping out sparks before they spread. By midnight a fire hose and pump had arrived from Weaverville, but the *Trinity Journal* of November 29, 1945, reported there was little to do save spraying water on the remaining embers of the destroyed buildings.

Roy made his way to the nearest outside phone two miles away and called newspapers to report what had happened. The fire, Roy told whoever would listen, was only the most dramatic problem. The laundry was iffy. The camp phone was off limits. The camp director had asked the area stores not to sell Minersville men necessities like kerosene or alcohol. The camp's water supply was brown with silt.

Cows trampled through the open ditch through which the camp's surface water flowed (Olmstead 1946, 2). Grievances and frustration had been building up; with the fire, and the FBI's subsequent suspicion about its cause, the whole camp turned a dark corner.

"Since the fire," Roy recorded in early January 1946, "any semblance of control or order by the administration has disintegrated."

Within days some seventy Minersville men began a slowdown strike. Work would happen in its own time, or not at all. Supervisors were powerless to move anyone along. The sullen Germfask spirit of aggressively passive resistance blanketed the camp. Into this fraught environment strolled two CPS men from the East Coast, Roy Finch and Richard Taylor. They had walked away from their own service in the Williamsburg, Virginia, mental hospital and made their way cross-country to Minersville, where Roy and others made them welcome. Finch and Taylor were particularly literate men with whom Roy could have fruitful conversations; after the war, Finch would go on to edit *Alternative* and *Liberation* magazines while Taylor would teach philosophy at Brown and the University of Rochester. They weren't supposed to be in Minersville, though, and after supervisors became aware of their presence Haynes summoned the sheriff on Friday, December 14. While deputies took Finch and Taylor into custody, Minersville men escalated their protests. Years of frustration seemed to boil over, as some pacifists eventually broke windows, battered doors, and hurled rocks. Reporters called it a "riot of major proportions," an inevitable exaggeration that further alienated Trinity County neighbors.

"Most everyone in Trinity County has sons and daughters in the armed services," the *Trinity Journal* editors fumed on December 20, 1945. "Under the same conditions, a service man would be court martialed and, if found guilty, would serve a term in a federal prison and lose his citizenship. Why does not the same condition apply here?"

Minersville was becoming Germfask, a worrisome development for the War Resisters League. Early in the new year, WRL field director Frank Olmstead arrived for a firsthand view. An experienced organizer and peace hand, formerly YMCA national secretary during the prewar years, Olmstead was like Roy in his ability to fairly appraise fellow pacifists. Minersville, he concluded, concentrated in one place "the most vigorous advocates" of those who were attempting to the "Gandhi-like policy of non-violent non-cooperation." Others, Olmstead reported, were "thoughtless, impulsive youngsters who have been brought up to reject war" but who also lacked a deeper understanding of principle. Approvingly, though, Olmstead noted the camp's bookshelves were liberally stocked with the likes of Shakespeare, the *Viking Book of Poetry,* and Catherine Drinker Bowen's biography of Oliver Wendell Holmes Jr., *Yankee From Olympus.* Books surrounded Roy and his fellow radicals (Olmstead 1946, 3).

Olmstead could observe, as well, how the Minersville men engaged in trivial rebellions, tiny acts of daily resistance. No one could predict which of these would escalate into full-blown confrontation, though it was inevitable that some would. Thus: the great Minersville blanket war.

Some Minersville men began hanging blankets around their bunks, carving out private space. The partitions offered respite, but they also flaunted Selective Service regulations. Blanket partitions were strictly verboten. On the morning of January 29, Haynes and his aides began their barracks inspection and saw what the men had erected. This must come down, Haynes said. John Lewis, Roy's close friend, told the director to stuff it. He would go to jail rather than take his blankets down. Haynes continued marching through the dorms, finally reaching a place where two men were sleeping. Haynes angrily stripped the bedding away and ordered removal of the blanket partition. One half-asleep pacifist swore at Haynes, who momentarily snapped. The Minersville conchies had tried his patience for many months. He had heard their complaints, nodded at their philosophizing, endured their foot-dragging and their ceaseless proselytizing. Haynes was fed up.

So he slugged the S.O.B.

Haynes's lieutenants quickly pulled the two men apart, but a blow had been struck that could not be retracted. Haynes called county deputy sheriffs to impose order, and on Friday, February 1, Lewis and eleven other Minersville men were arrested on charges of failing to follow orders. A U.S. deputy marshal transported them south to Sacramento. Bail was set for $500 and preparations mounted for a trial that promised to be quite a spectacle, the federal government versus pacifists who dared erect blanket partitions.

Roy was as close to Lewis as anyone he had met in his CPS service, and he took a lead role in rallying the Minersville legal defense team. The personal bonds would last. Years later, when Roy was a famous California bookseller, he would summon Lewis to help analyze the store for possible sale. The two men saw eye to eye on the business of pacifism. But Roy was also a short-timer in Civilian Public Service, and he was thinking beyond the Minersville blanket war. Through his position with the Minersville camp newsletter, he got some things off his chest.

"In an age of violence, in fact, in an age when we have the power to destroy ourselves and the world with it, each man has the moral duty of exercising his individual responsibility as a human personality," Roy wrote in his CPS valedictory, published in March 1946 in the camp newsletter.

Roy said the righteous individual would resist, in perhaps trivially small ways, the coercive power of the government. This could appear comically absurd—blanket partitions!—if not for the fundamental principles involved. A man must heed the inner conscience, regardless of social or political compulsions.

On March 1, 1946, after nearly four years in the Civilian Public Service camps, Roy regained his freedom. The Selective Service sent him on his way with a train ticket from Redding to Sacramento. He was one of 1,016 conscientious objectors released that month. It would take another year, until March 1947, before the CPS camps were completely empty. The closing of the camps allowed a reassessment of the entire CPS experiment.

The American Friends Service Committee lamented that so much good manpower had been wasted. More than half of the conscientious objectors had been shuffled off into forest-tending and land conservation work that could all have been deferred until after the war, while more pressing work waited. In particular, the committee noted the "desperate need for relief workers in war zones," but for which objectors were blocked. "Great waste and deterioration" resulted from the trivial work assignments: the physicist who cleared trails for a year, the statistician stuck in a weather shack, the public health engineer confined to the woods. With few exceptions, the conscientious objectors were denied jobs commensurate with their skills and experience. Morale further fell under the work conditions, with neither pay nor protections offered. Naturally the CPS men grew frustrated, and some cracked. In many respects, Civilian Public Service had failed to meet its promise.

The camps themselves would fade, and some disappear altogether. Minersville would be inundated when the Trinity River was dammed and the 16,000-acre Trinity Lake established in 1961. In the same year, as it happened, Germfask radical Corbett Bishop would die in a violent mishap in Alabama, an extreme end for an extreme man. And yet, for Roy and some others, camp lessons endured. Chain-shaking zealotry showed what commitment looked like. Relationships built in the camps would shape the future. Surely some good had been done.

"World War II was a very hard war not to fight," Roy said in a 1984 interview. "If ever there was a war to be fought, that was it. It was as close to a reasonably just war as you could get. [But] I had to take my stand."

4

Resisting the Next War

Roy reentered the free world ready for the fight of his life.

Civilian Public Service had toned him. Hefting tools and hauling stones had flattened his stomach, erected his posture. Bunkhouse discussions had sharpened his tongue. His brother Earl's death had seared him deep inside; neither authority nor convention would intimidate him. By bus, train, and thumb, he had crisscrossed Colorado, California, Indiana, New Hampshire, Tennessee, Maryland, Michigan, and back to California. He was a man, if not yet of the world, at least of his own country.

Roy had grown up. He was twenty-two when he entered the camps, a provincial young man. He was nearly twenty-six when he returned, prepared for national leadership. But where to begin?

He started in San Francisco. He was considering his options, including a job with the Brethren escorting war-relief cattle shipments to Europe, but he also had unfinished CPS business. Ten Minersville blanket protestors were awaiting a mid-April 1946 trial, and they needed help. Following his discharge in March, Roy began collecting contributions for the Minersville Defense Committee, aided by other CPS alumni including San Francisco poet Kenneth Rexroth. Attorney Francis Heisler, who had represented Germfask protestors during the war, was preparing to use the trial as a showcase.

"There will be a rather stiff cover charge accompanying the floor show that will be put on in the Sacramento Federal District Court," Roy wrote in one fundraising appeal (Lasar 1999, 19).

Roy was seeking to raise about $1,500 for the cause, and was preparing as well to be called as a defense witness. Behind the scenes, Roy and John Lewis spoke to a *San Francisco Chronicle* reporter, who they thought seemed sympathetic to their cause. Prosecuting pacifists over their blanket partitions seemed rank overkill, especially with the war over and the military rapidly demobilizing. Some pacifists feared that was the point. The Minersville prosecution, by this theory, was meant to demonstrate the subjugation of civilians to military authority. It was the test case for the permanent military state. Radical pacifists, in turn, intended to spin the spotlight and showcase the unjust world they had been forced to inhabit.

"What is being tried is the concentration camp system itself," one Minersville Defense Committee brochure stated.

The federal prosecutors started off strong. They declared that the Minersville men were not ordinary criminals, but saboteurs. They had willfully interfered with the orderly operations of a government camp. Soon enough, though, officials wearied of the case. They wanted to wash their hands of the whole conscientious objector business. Quietly the charges against the Minersville blanket rebels melted away.

Some wished the CPS camps would do the same. Six months after the war ended, thousands of conscientious objectors remained bound to Civilian Public Service. On April 27, 1946, shortly after Roy left Minersville, the *Los Angeles Times* reported that sixty-seven CPS men at the Glendora and San Joaquin camps went on strike to protest their treatment, including the forced transfer of two objectors to what they dubbed the government's "punishment camp" at Minersville.

Roy spent several months during the late spring and summer of 1946 reconnoitering the Bay Area's potential for a War Resisters League regional outpost. He had been introduced to the region earlier, during a week-long furlough to attend a Fellowship of Reconciliation conference in Berkeley in October 1942. There was much to like about the area, from its calm Mediterranean climate to its tolerance for the unconventional. Former conscientious objectors were burrowing in, making their postwar way, though Roy also found that with the war over, many preferred normalcy to activism.

"They were concerned with personal development and problems, picking up their marriages or marrying—that sort of thing," Roy recalled in a 1984 interview.

By the mid-summer, his Minersville work done, Roy returned to Denver. When the fall semester began, Roy enrolled again at the University of Colorado in Boulder, along with battalions of veterans served by the GI Bill. The 700-acre campus was crowded with some eight thousand students, many now matured well beyond their years. Roy began befriending ex-soldiers and reading the pragmatist philosopher John Dewey, himself an on-again, off-again pacifistic thinker. Roy became intrigued by the world federalist movement, then in its ascendancy. Perhaps, he considered, a single world government might move men beyond conflict. Outside the classroom, Roy joined a young sociology professor in forming a war-and-peace study group. They went beyond theory, putting their studies into practice by actively challenging the machinery of conscription.

Yes, the draft; always, it would be the draft. The world war was done, but the government still insisted on impressing men into service or at least having the means to do so. Roy and his fellow radical pacifists sought to rally resistance. They set February 12, 1947, as the date for national antidraft protests. In Colorado, Roy and the executive secretary of the Denver branch of the Fellowship of Reconciliation urged men to either publicly destroy their draft cards or mail them back to the president. In a January 28 open letter, Roy declared that "to further cooperate in any way with the socialized war system is to support directly man's move toward a suicidal destiny." This challenge carried risk. Though willful destruction of a draft card would not be a federal crime until the mid-1960s, one Colorado prosecutor warned he would go after anyone caught without a card. Undeterred, Roy followed with a letter to President Harry Truman on February 11, in which he enclosed his draft registration and classification documents.

"The stupidity and fallaciousness of the arguments presented for conscription are appalling," Roy advised the commander in chief.

President Truman never replied.

The mid-February demonstrations flared up in hot spots throughout the country. In Washington, DC, several young men placed draft cards inside a small pot in front of the White House and set them afire. In New York City, forty-two men burned their draft cards. A minister in St. Paul, Minnesota, burned his draft card following his service, and in Hebron, North Dakota, Pearl LaForce sent a telegram to Truman offering support for the draft protestors. Primly, Western Union refused to send it. The February demonstrations brought Roy further into the orbit of the War Resisters League, an organization with whose leaders he had been communicating while in Civilian Public Service.

The WRL was a stalwart. For several decades, founder Jessie Wallace Hughan and her right-hand man Abraham Kaufman had led the organization, which paradoxically flourished in wartime and faded with peace.

A longtime English teacher born in 1875, Hughan was an opera-loving, book-devouring, never-married true believer. She had helped organize in 1915 the Anti-Enlistment League, which gathered 3,500 commitments from young men pledging they would not join the military. In 1921, under Hughan's direction, the Fellowship of Reconciliation established a Committee for Enrollment Against War. That same year the War Resisters International was organized in the Netherlands under the declaration that "war is a crime against humanity." On March 15, 1923, Hughan hosted at her Manhattan apartment the meeting that established the War Resisters League, the U.S. branch of War Resisters International. Hughan conceived of the War Resisters League as a secular educational organization that could lure the public and not alienate it through radical demonstrations. Unlike the Fellowship of Reconciliation, a Christian fellowship founded in England in 1914 by two ministers, the new organization explicitly welcomed those with no religious affiliation.

Abraham Kaufman, a one-time high school student of Hughan's, started in October 1928 as the WRL's first paid staffer. Together they dominated the organization for years. The headquarters were in Hughan's own New York City apartment, until separate space was finally found. They set a certain staid tone; Kaufman believed war should be resisted with a certain amount of decorum. Civil disobedience and flamboyant confrontations were dangerous and counterproductive, tools of last resort (Bennett 2003, 134).

World War II swelled the organization's membership, but also splintered the tactical consensus. Conscientious objectors released from prison and the frustrations of Civilian Public Service were impatient and primed for confrontation. Roy belonged to this radical faction; he was a Germfask man, a Minersville man. He and his fellow radical activists were relatively young and highly energetic. They wanted more than the insulated silence of a Friends Meeting, and they would show their colors by steering the War Resisters League itself in a new direction. In June 1947 Roy and his fellow radicals won approval of a resolution declaring that the War Resisters League would henceforth promote "political, economic and social revolution by non-violent means" (Wittner 1984, 153).

Revolution, so blatantly put, was not everyone's cup of tea. Some old-timers were put off, but Roy and his fellow radicals pursued the idea. The "Conference on More Disciplined and Revolutionary Pacifism" convened April 2, 1948, at Chicago's Olivet Institute on the city's North Side. Roy joined some three hundred activists attending, an encouraging turnout that included a good number of newcomers participating in their first antiwar conference. Their discussions could ramble, some old-timers thought, but youthful fervor could also be harnessed. Radical activists saw an opportunity to coalesce the truly committed, the revolutionaries ready to take bold steps. These activists rallied around a name that captured their ambitions. They called themselves the Peacemakers.

The Peacemakers pulled their thoughts together into statements of principle. They emphasized authentic, grassroots action. Peacemakers believed in an economic system in which people cooperate and share rather than compete and exploit. The Peacemakers also believed there was more to the enlightened life than politics. Inner transformation was crucial. Peacemakers wanted to move from a self-centered to a God-centered, or at least a "for-the-good-of-all-men-centered" life. Bodies must be put on the line. Principles must be put into practice. Within the larger Olivet Institute peace conference, a relatively small core of pacifists signed up for the revolution. Forty-nine young men and women pledged they would work for peace on a subsistence basis for between six months and a year. Eighty-six delegates signed a pledge not to register for the draft and to actively resist conscription.

Some debated going further, into the dangerous world of tax resistance. The principle seemed straightforward. The government should conscript neither one's money nor one's body for war. Paying for the rifle was morally indistinguishable from actually shouldering arms. Indeed, there was an unearned smugness about a professed pacifist who paid another to do his fighting for him. Tax resistance, though, was also an outright felony, and it divided the activists. Not everyone was ready to face prison for the principle, and besides, some reasoned that taxes amounted to an obliged rendering unto Caesar. Ultimately, twenty-five conference participants signed a declaration that they would no longer pay at least that portion of the federal income tax devoted to preparation for war. Roy gave serious thought to the tax resistance question; in his own time, he would embrace the tactic and teach it to some famous pupils.

The Olivet conference marked Roy's ascension into the inner circle of American pacifism. As a member of the Peacemakers' original executive committee, Roy was now collaborating with the likes of David Dellinger, Dwight Macdonald, A. J. Muste, and Bayard Rustin. These were prominent men. Muste had been the very face of American pacifism since the prewar years, when *Time* magazine anointed him "The Number One U.S. Pacifist." Macdonald, formerly the editor of *Partisan Review,* was editor of a closely read magazine called *Politics.* Rustin was a charismatic African American pacifist and former Communist organizer who served twenty-eight months in prison during the war. He was a stirring public speaker, a gifted tenor, and a more-or-less openly gay man whose behavior would eventually undercut his influence (D'Emilio 2004). Dellinger had seized national attention as one of the Union Theological Seminary students who refused to cooperate with the World War II draft (Dellinger 1993).

Dellinger and Bent Andresen, Roy's friend from Germfask and Minersville, lived out their politics in the Glen Gardner Cooperative Community, a twenty-acre cooperative in New Jersey's hill region northwest of Trenton. Informally dubbed St. Francis Acres, Glen Gardner theoretically revolved around a cooperative business venture called Liberation Press (Frazer and O'Sullivan 1996, 185). Dellinger and his team produced the magazine *Direct Action,* an aggressive publication whose first edition included a call for "radical banditry" as well as "strikes, sabotage, and seizure of public property now being held by private owners." The combative rhetoric was not really Roy's style, but he joined Dellinger, Lew Hill, and eleven others in the Autumn 1945 issue endorsing "world-wide working class solidarity through the strengthening and extension of local socialist groups and . . . cooperation in a new Socialist International." In time, the magazine evolved into *Alternative.*

Roy spent some time at Glen Gardner and authored a May 1948 piece critiquing the U.S. occupation of Japan. It was the first of many articles Roy would pen for an assortment of small-circulation periodicals, none of them ever reaching the wider audience Roy sought. Roy would also be a member of the editorial board for the September–October 1950 issue of *Alternative,* which included an open call for readers to resist conscription. "Maybe draft-dodging isn't the most 'heroic' thing you can do," the unsigned piece stated, "but it certainly makes more sense than falling for the souped-up propaganda being passed out to justify the preparation for World War III." That caught someone's attention, for the January 1951 edition reported without further elaboration that "the last two issues of *Alternative* were confiscated and burned by the postal authorities for interfering with the enlistment and recruiting services of the United States." The four-page January issue proved to be the periodical's last.

The postal authorities weren't the only ones disconcerted by the radical rhetoric. Some peace traditionalists, too, wanted to keep a civil tone and a tight focus on opposing war. Radicals wanted revolution across a broader front, targeting policies from conscription to amnesty for the six thousand conscientious objectors imprisoned during the war. Traditionalists like Kaufman, Hughan, and Frieda Lazarus were skeptical about the uses of civil disobedience. They were still fundamentally law-abiders, yielding to the state's power (Bennett 2003, 134).

In some cases, moreover, personal relations were strained among the pacifists. Dellinger and Roy, though fellow radicals, would have a prickly relationship, as would Kaufman and Dellinger. Kaufman at times seemed to consider Roy an upstart, though he praised Roy in public and private. Kaufman advised War Resisters International leader Grace Beaton that Roy had a rare combination of qualities useful to the WRL, including a pleasing personality and an ability to work with diverse types of people. Kaufman did not, however, want Roy elevated to a War Resisters League leadership position that was just about to open up.

Kaufman in September 1947 announced he would be stepping down from his long-held War Resisters League post. After serving nineteen years as executive secretary, Kaufman had reached the end of his string. He seemed tired of the endless internal battles, the recurring sense of futility. He considered some of the most radical activists to be zealot ideologues who veered dangerously close to anarchy. Some, like Harvard dropout Jim Peck, Kaufman considered outright Soviet sympathizers. On a personal level, he resented his loss of influence amid the rise of the Young Turks. Dellinger, in particular, seemed to irritate him (Bennett 2003, 163). Kaufman suggested as his replacement Frances Rose Ransom, the League's membership secretary. WRL founder Jessie Hughan herself, though, cautioned that the general public would not respond to a woman leader. Hughan had declined over the years to be named executive secretary, citing this very reason. She didn't want war resistance typecast as a crank idea promoted by oddball women.

Kaufman left the executive secretary job by January 1948, though he remained on the board (Kaufman n.d.). Following some administrative drift, Dellinger suggested Roy as a good leadership candidate. In early May 1948, members of the WRL Executive Committee interviewed Roy. The remaining committee members agreed to hire Roy as field secretary on an experimental basis, to serve for the rest of the year. By late May, over Kaufman's objections, Roy was on the payroll at $45 a week. There was no time to wait. Another draft was coming, and the radical pacifists were mobilizing to fight it. Roy began considering several options, including finding ways to mobilize antiwar sentiment among military reservists. Perhaps, some thought, a mass resignation might be organized.

The end of World War II had left the future of conscription in limbo. The war's original draft authorization expired, and some lawmakers wanted to keep it that way. Some top military leaders, too, advocated a strictly volunteer military; in peacetime, opposition to the draft was no longer confined to the pacifist fringe. Farm, labor, and religious groups joined to oppose its renewal. Throughout early 1946, Congress had debated the merits of a renewed draft, finally passing a year-long extension that expired in March 1947. By early 1948, despite his earlier belief that the draft was a political headache, President Truman realized he needed to replenish depleted forces.

In June 1948, citing the Soviet threat, Congress approved a two-year draft extension that limited the allowances granted individual conscience. Conscientious objection would still be permitted if based on "religious training and belief." Lawmakers ruled out objections based on "essentially political, sociological or philosophical views, or a merely personal moral code." There would also have to be a relationship between that belief and "a Supreme Being involving duties superior to those arising from any human relations." Failure to register would subject a young man to five years in prison and a $10,000 fine.

This demanded action. Roy began contacting activists to prepare for June 5, 1948, antidraft demonstrations. The radical contrast with Kaufman's genteel approach was immediately apparent. Roy and his allies produced handbills emphatically urging young men to "refuse to be drafted." The explicit incitement prompted a resignation from attorney and WRL board member Julian Cornell, a Quaker and seasoned advocate who had represented numerous conscientious objectors during the war. Cornell explained that as a lawyer he could not encourage defiance of the law. Some of the confrontation-seeking radicals thought good riddance, but cooler heads agreed to rewrite the handbill. The important thing was to spread the word.

"We want to have the no-registration idea in the mind of every boy facing the law, and in the minds of his parents," Roy advised a friend (Bennett 2003, 374).

Spectacle could help, Roy knew. The one-time high school actor appreciated the power of theater to attract an audience and implant an idea. Though invariably serious himself, Roy could stage some entertaining demonstrations. On June 5, some seventy War Resisters League activists and sympathizers picketed the White House. The protestors showed radical flair and a knack for the bold public gesture. Several adorned themselves as Uncle Sam, with a slapstick twist. In tricolor trousers, swallowtail coats, and top hats, they marched as if they were Nazi storm troopers. "We don't want a goose-stepping U.S.A.," one sign read. Another, more restrained, urged "Gandhi's Way—Not Stalin's." Roy was seeking every available means to communicate peace.

Jim Peck shared Roy's radical notions, and then some. The FBI called Peck "one of the most enthusiastic pacifists in the New York area," but he was more than that. The thirty-four-year-old true believer was one of the most committed social activists of his generation. The son of a wealthy New York City family, Peck had abandoned fair Harvard after escorting one of his favorite black prostitutes to the school's freshman prom. He went off to sea, helped establish the National Maritime Union, and, in November 1942, a declared conscientious objector, Peck entered Danbury federal prison for the start of a three-year sentence. Peck and seventeen other Danbury objectors in August 1943 conducted a 135-day work strike to protest the prison's segregated dining room, finally winning their goal. He would always remember the lesson that a small number of protestors could gain wide publicity with a well-timed protest.

Peck could run himself ragged, but he and Roy were well matched and in their demonstrative prime on June 23, 1948, as they set out on an audacious plan. They were going to penetrate the White House itself.

Roy and Peck took the train down from New York City the morning of June 23. Nothing betrayed their purpose. They cast themselves as conventional commuters, organization men. Arriving at Washington's Union Station, they took a cab to the vicinity of 1600 Pennsylvania Avenue. Roy took the outside post. He waited by the White House's Pennsylvania Avenue gates, while Peck joined the other tourists passing through the East Entrance. Underneath his coat and tie, he carried a chain and padlock. Once inside, near a staircase, he stopped, removed his coat to reveal a "Veto the Draft" message, and affixed himself to the banister with the small chain.

Peck began thrusting antidraft leaflets at the startled families. Tourists, curious or simply polite, accepted the offerings. Several minutes passed before the Secret Service guards surrounded Peck and with a quick pull snapped off the cheap copper chain. The guards marched Peck out of the White House and across the street to Secret Service offices. There officers questioned Peck for several hours. They knew his type.

"Where's your card?" one demanded.

"What card do you mean?" Peck asked.

"Your Communist Party card," the officer said.

Peck had none; he was not a Communist. He was something else altogether. An officer called him a horse's ass. That, Peck replied, was a matter of opinion.

"You'd like us to put you in jail for this so that you can get in the papers again," one officer told Peck. "But we're not going to accommodate you. We are going to let you go" (Peck 1958, 183).

But the Secret Service hadn't accounted for Roy, the outside man. During Peck's interrogation, Roy was diligently alerting the press to this extraordinary protest, a man distributing antidraft leaflets inside the White House. The eccentric touch secured a place in the papers. Everybody won. The reporters got their story, and the activists got attention for their cause. Mission accomplished. Even stodgy Abe

Kaufman, the most traditional of War Resisters League men, publicly declared the demonstration a success.

The White House caper helped bind Roy and Peck. Roy that summer would host at his Brooklyn apartment a surprise party to celebrate the coming together of Peck and his beloved, Paula Zweier. Paula and Jim Peck were themselves quite the pair. They would marry and have two children, and Paula in 1961 would publish *The Art of Fine Baking*, an utterly apolitical work.

Roy tried to recruit Albert Einstein.

Allied with the Peacemakers and the ad hoc Resist Conscription Committee, Roy was working throughout the summer of 1948 on the anticonscription campaign. His message was both simple and severe: Do not register for the draft. Young men, Roy said, are fit for something nobler than slavery and training in the techniques of mass extermination. He presented his case at the War Resisters League's annual summer retreat in New Jersey, where old-timers and young radicals debated one another. Roy's sometime-ally David Dellinger summed up the radicals' message: We must not be cautious. The military madness must be resisted through acts of civil disobedience. The confrontational tactics and revolutionary rhetoric worried traditionalists such as Abraham Kaufman and Frieda Lazarus, but the radicals were gaining momentum (Bennett 2003, 160).

Though fully a member of the radicals' inner circle, Roy was always trying to reach out and attract new allies. He'd start with conversation, or a letter sent out of the blue. Neither rejection nor authority frightened him; he'd just give it a shot. So, one day, he sat down and wrote Einstein.

The famed physicist had electrified peace activists in the late 1920s when he declared the necessity of shunning arms. The War Resisters League distributed Einstein's pronouncements and invited him to become the organization's honorary chairman. Though Einstein subsequently resigned from War Resisters International as Nazis muscled their way to power in Germany, he had joined Bertrand Russell, author Pearl Buck, and theologian Reinhold Niebuhr in championing postwar amnesty for imprisoned conscientious objectors (Bennett 2003, 142).

Roy thought he could win Einstein back into the pacifist fold. One month after his White House adventure with Jim Peck, Roy wrote on July 28, 1948, to introduce himself and ask a favor. "I am a young man of the generation which is faced anew with whether it will acquiesce in the barbarism and regression of war and more wars, or which will face up to the problem of war and renounce it unequivocally," Roy declared. Roy then urged Einstein to declare himself unequivocally opposed to war. Pacifism, Roy explained, "lost greatly" when men of stature did not follow its precepts during times of war.

Remarkably, Einstein replied.

From his office at Princeton's Institute for Advanced Study, the 1921 Nobel Prize winner advised Roy that his own thinking had evolved after seeing the rise of Adolph Hitler and Benito Mussolini. Einstein advised Roy that it was no longer easy to calculate whether absolute conscientious objection was morally justified in the United States. Encouraged by the response, Roy quickly prepared a point-by-point analysis and enclosed leaflets for Einstein to peruse. Roy wanted an ongoing conversation. Einstein, though, did not, and the correspondence tailed off without resolution.

That was disappointing for Roy, though he had his hands full on other fronts.

Roy and his fellow radicals convened a three-day "Conference of Non-Violent Civil Disobedience to the Draft." Conference organizers were summoning activists, once more, to Chicago's familiar Olivet Institute. They planned sessions for July 30 through August 1, on topics such as organizing civil disobedience and assisting draft resisters. They were demanding that the U.S. "war policy" be "met with total rejection and all-out resistance," but it was not a propitious time for radical declarations. Chicago residents were reading, the morning of July 31, not about the Peacemakers but about the Vassar-educated spy Elizabeth Bentley. Avidly described by the *Chicago Tribune*'s man as "a curvesome and attractive woman in her thirties . . . garbed in a tight-fitting black gown which outlined a good figure," the sexpot spy had told a congressional committee that a Soviet espionage ring had been scooping up confidential government information.

With Elizabeth Bentley vamping, the earnest Peacemakers had a hard time gathering attention. The 1948 meeting, attended by about one hundred people, also lacked the springtime energy of the previous year's session. The Peacemakers essentially were talking among themselves, a perennial problem for Roy's peace groups. A. J. Muste in his keynote address denounced the draft as "part of the preparation for an atomic and bacterial war." Roy offered the prescription for action. He told the Peacemakers to remain adamant: men of draft age should neither register nor enlist. Men already in the military should quit. Men beyond draft age should actively agitate against Selective Service. Other peace activists considered civil disobedience to be counterproductive. Some organizations would founder on the divide.

For August 8, the anniversary of the Hiroshima bombing, Roy called for "A Day of Repentance and Mourning." He suggested that Selective Service registration offices be quietly picketed with appropriate signs as a witness against conscription and atomic war, and he prepared a pledge for activists to sign.

"We believe human beings are fit for something better, something nobler, than slavery and training in the mass extermination of their fellows," the pledge avowed, as readers of *Peace News* learned on July 23, 1948.

But somber pronouncements were easy compared to some of the tactical choices facing peace organizations. The day after the Hiroshima remembrance, the War Resisters League Executive Committee stopped short of urging outright defiance even as it passed a resolution condemning the draft. Jim Peck thought this ridiculous, a weasel copout on the all-important issue of state coercion. Not for the last time, Peck tendered his resignation from the committee and stomped out. Roy stayed, though he was philosophically aligned with Peck. He soon would have new stature to promote the radical pacifist perspective.

On September 1, 1948, Roy assumed the position of executive secretary of the War Resisters League. He was now strategist, tactician, fundraiser, and administrator. Essentially, he was the chief executive officer of the nation's most venerable peace organization.

At twenty-seven, Roy was twelve years younger and a world apart from Kaufman, his weary predecessor. Roy was taking over an organization struggling through a financial and identity crisis. The War Resisters League claimed three thousand members nationwide, but the members' commitment was scattershot. From dues, the WRL was collecting about $16,000 a year to pay for salaries, supplies, travel, and rental of the headquarters office at 5 Beekman Place. It was located conveniently enough, close to New York City Hall, but the dreary space was jammed with mimeograph machines, typewriters, postage meters, and stacks of literature.

Five days after Roy assumed his new position, twenty-five-year-old men began registering for the new draft. Roy and the WRL pacifists were ready. As draft registration centers opened, picketers circulated in Boston, Philadelphia, Lowell, Cincinnati, and other cities. Outside one New York City registration site, dampened by morning showers, the African American activist Bayard Rustin led picketers. Several miles away, at Washington Irving High School, other protestors carried signs stating "Refuse to be Drafted" and "The Draft is Hitler's and Stalin's Way." They distributed leaflets along with the *Catholic Worker* newspaper and the magazine *Resistance.* Unlike in Boston, where true-blue patriots hurled red-ripened tomatoes at the pacifist demonstrators, the *New York Times* of August 31, 1948, reported that New York protestors were unmolested and police made no arrests.

The draft law demonstrations continued. Shortly after noon on September 18, Roy joined ten other men and three women outside Washington Irving High School in Manhattan. They held their signs: "Refuse to Register," "Refuse to be Drafted," "This is the Hitler and Stalin Way," and an old faithful, "The Draft Means a Goose-Stepping United States." They began their circular march, neither singing nor shouting, but simply handing out leaflets to the young men going inside. Police officers eyeballed the placard-carrying pacifists and ordered them to disperse. Roy and his colleagues kept marching. Twenty minutes after the protest began, police had seen enough. The cops swarmed in and took the unresisting protestors off to a nearby paddy wagon. At the station, police charged the protestors with "willfully endangering public peace" while "advising resistance to the draft." That night, Roy and the others were released on $25 bail. Several weeks later, Roy and the others would be acquitted, but with a warning. The magistrate told them he didn't approve of their picketing, and he cautioned the pacifists that someday someone just might knock their blocks off.

Even with the public drama of an arrest, the protests could feel futile. Leaflets would be dropped on the street after a cursory glance. Young men would rush past without stopping; middle-aged men would sneer. But every now and then, something took hold.

On Wednesday morning, September 22, an eighteen-year-old budding actor named Stuart Zane Perkoff called upon the War Resisters League headquarters on Beekman Street. He apparently arrived unannounced, telling Roy he was refusing to register for the draft. It was the kind of moment Roy lived for, a new recruit for the cause.

An artistically precocious St. Louis native, Perkoff had drifted toward New York City's hipster underground after school, where he immersed himself in the theater. The short, rotund youth found firm purpose in resisting the draft. Conscription, he said, was simply another step leading toward totalitarianism. Roy told the teenager about the standard law enforcement procedures, and later that day Perkoff showed up at the FBI office to turn himself in.

"I feel sincerely," Perkoff said, according to the *New York Times* of September 24, 1948, "that all wars are unjust and immoral and that any steps leading up to war are consequently unjust and immoral."

The assistant U.S. attorney tried to talk him out of this rash step. Perkoff held his ground. All entreaties unavailing, Perkoff was arraigned before U.S. District Judge John C. Knox and charged with failure to register. Perkoff now faced five years in prison and a $10,000 fine. Knox urged Perkoff to think long and hard about what he was doing. The sixty-seven-year-old judge wanted young Perkoff to know there had to be limits to idealism. Be practical, that's the thing. Perkoff was adamant, and he had Roy in his corner. Roy told the judge he would take responsibility for Perkoff's later court appearances.

On Monday, October 11, Perkoff returned to court, accompanied by his father, a Midwestern tavern-keeper. Dad was at a loss about what to do with his son.

"I have talked to him for two solid weeks in an effort to get him to change [his mind], but he hasn't budged," Nat Perkoff said, the *New York Times* reported on October 12, 1948.

Authorities finally convinced Perkoff to spend a few days in jail before formally pleading guilty. He returned to the courthouse on October 15, resolute. He would not register. He pleaded guilty to the felony count, apparently becoming the first man in the New York City area to do so. Outside the courtroom, Roy and three dozen other protestors carried placards and handed out flyers, saying Perkoff was being imprisoned "for taking a stand against the militarization of America" and stating that the young pacifist's position had been endorsed by four hundred ministers.

Ultimately Perkoff was returned to St. Louis in the company of his father. He would, in time, find his way to the outlying Los Angeles community of Venice, and there settle in firmly to the Beat firmament. His first book of poetry, *The Suicide Room,* would appear in 1956, celebrating the free life:

Hey frankie, tony, let's get high
& dream our verse and dance to the purest sin . . .

And in 1959 Roy's Menlo Park, California, bookstore would be selling a book by author Lawrence Lipton called *The Holy Barbarians.* Lipton's reporting delved into the Los Angeles Beatnik *demimonde,* featuring a gifted hipster named Angel Dan Davies. It was, in cameo, Stuart Perkoff. The Perkoff/Angel character, amid some burning of the candle at both ends, elaborated on the end of his war resisters story. He had been in prison, he said, for six weeks.

"I decided to register," Perkoff/Angel said, "and they let me out. They stopped bothering me, that's all. They didn't want me . . . all

they wanted me to do was quietly register and get out of their hair"
(Lipton 1959, 113).

The circle coming fully around, Lipton would himself come to
speak at Kepler's Books & Magazines to promote his book about the
Beats.

↓

Other draft protests followed Perkoff's. Whenever a draft resister was
in the federal courthouse, Roy and David Dellinger and a dozen or
so other men would hand out flyers with enticing titles. "SEX is here
to stay," one flyer stated, "and so is opposition to war." Between mid-
November 1948 and mid-March 1949 Roy and his fellow activists
led, by one count, fourteen separate picket demonstrations at the New
York City courthouse. FBI agents watched each and every one.

For the night of October 2, 1948, the Peacemakers, the Fellowship of Reconciliation, and the War Resisters League were preparing a

3. Roy Kepler (left) in a 1949 protest. Photographer unknown, courtesy of
the Kepler family.

joint public meeting at New York's Community Church to commemorate Gandhi's birthday. Roy and the other organizers had placed an ad in the *New York Times* promoting the event. The *Times* accepted the ad, but excised a line announcing the appearance of "a conscientious objector who has refused to register for the draft." The upright *Times* didn't believe in encouraging lawbreakers, in this case one Robert Bone, a twenty-five-year-old automotive worker and Yale graduate. Bone, who would go on to earn his doctorate and teach for years at Columbia University's Teachers College, didn't hold back when he took the stage that night.

"I'll go on fighting against violence and regimentation in prison," Bone promised the audience, "if you will carry on the fight on the outside, helping to reach people who have never heard of non-violent direct action."

Nobel Prize–winning author Pearl Buck followed Bone to the stage and promised she would keep the pact he offered. Sixteen years after publication of her reputation-making book *The Good Earth*, Buck had become a fervent advocate for peace causes. Buck pressed the case for amnesty that night, to an audience that included an individual the FBI identified as Confidential Informant T-17. "The speeches," T-17 reported, according to an FBI memo, "were entirely uniform as to their trend, and appeared to be a strange blend of the gospels of Gandhi's philosophy, of pacifism, of war resistance, of anti-militarism and of anti-Churchill-ism."

With a famous author as a draw and Gandhi's birthday as a hook, the October 2 event was a success. More generally, though, the pacifist groups were struggling. The FBI reported about the same time that "the New York WRL is very low in funds and in the red." The Fellowship of Reconciliation, too, was struggling, having lost more than half of the four hundred chapters it claimed during World War II. Peace undermined the antiwar business. Roy kept traveling in hopes of expanding the WRL franchise, visiting that fall the Yale, Brown, Bennington, and Smith college campuses. He was constantly trying to build the base.

A typical event occurred January 25, 1949, when Roy and his allies summoned people to a meeting at the Community Church at

40 E. 35th Street. That night, at 8:30, sixty-three people showed up, one-third of them women and most middle-aged or elderly. One was an FBI operative. Roy spoke first. He quoted Gandhi, declaring that the Peacemakers advocated nonviolent civil disobedience so that prejudice, fear, and violence might be expunged. The Peacemakers, Roy added in closing, do not intend to hide. The Peacemakers will act in the open, knowing full well the consequences.

"I assure you," Roy accurately told the audience, in words captured in an FBI memo, "the FBI knows all about us and is developing thick brochures on us."

It was a fine night, the crowd responsive, but Roy felt sequestered. He was preaching to the choir. He knew he was out of touch with the country's sentiments, and he wanted to spread the word. So on Friday, March 4, 1949, Roy hit the road. He was going to reconnoiter, find out exactly what the postwar world had come to. Unmarried and socially unencumbered, Roy was well suited for the extended road trip.

It was, besides, the season for road trips. Two months earlier, the entirely unknown author Jack Kerouac, ne'er-do-well pal Neal Cassady, and Cassady's teenage wife, LuAnne Henderson, had embarked on their own two-month, cross-country jaunt that Kerouac would subsequently render into fiction as *On the Road*. In coming years, Roy would sell countless copies of Kerouac's fictional account of the 1949 trip, and Cassady would himself prowl Roy's bookstore. Like Roy, Kerouac had taken off from New York City. The pre-Beat trio, though, had headed directly west. Roy took a different direction.

For seven weeks Roy would travel 11,813 miles through twenty-five states. He would end up counting meetings with eighty-seven different groups. Starting from the Northeast, Roy found an experienced peace activist named Valerie Riggs in Cambridge distributing pacifist leaflets door-to-door. Riggs had been refusing to pay taxes since 1944. Her radical posture and shoe-leather work impressed Roy, and he learned from her what he could.

Roy then turned west, and on March 24 he reached West Lafayette, Indiana, a conservative college town, home to Purdue University. More comfortable with fraternities and engineers than radical pacifism, university administrators banned Roy's planned campus meeting with students. Roy moved it across the street to the Wesley Foundation, a Christian group affiliated with the United Methodist Church. Some sixty-five students joined a handful of professors to discuss war and peace. A sociology professor heatedly denounced war as a futile exercise, while Roy urged the young men not to register for the draft and not to work in a munitions plant. Two skeptical students subsequently reported back to Purdue's Student Affairs office, where officials alerted the FBI.

"They quoted Kepler as saying . . . 'the Democratic way of thinking is dangerous,'" the FBI reported.

Roy was never under any illusion. He knew his steps were being shadowed by the FBI or other security services. In early April, in the midst of his road trip, the Peacemakers returned to Chicago's Olivet Institute. The meeting included a session on tactical advice for handling FBI agents. Always have a witness, the Peacemakers counseled. Never sign a statement, and always be cautious in handing out information that might be distorted. The Peacemakers in Chicago mulled other tactical decisions as well. They considered the virtues and dangers of publicity. The assembled Peacemakers cautioned that exhibitionism was to be guarded against; publicity must emphasize the greater movement and not the individual.

At the Chicago conference, Roy was elected chairman of the Peacemakers board. While overlapping with the War Resisters League, this placed Roy in the middle of a far more comprehensively radical perspective. The Peacemakers went well beyond resisting conscription. Distinguishing themselves from those they called "orthodox capitalists," the Peacemakers pressed home the message of deep revolution. Live simply rather than luxuriously. Live communally, whether in cities or close to the soil and nature. Transform the inner self.

Roy finally reached the West Coast, where many of his Civilian Public Service comrades had been settling in. He found that John Lewis, one of the ten Minersville blanket-partition protestors, was now part of a Berkeley cadre behind the brand-spanking-new, listener-supported radio station KPFA. The high-ideals, low-wattage station had only been on the air a short while, starting April 15, and Roy was easily fit into the lineup for a half-hour evening interview, thereby becoming one of the station's first interview subjects. Admittedly, few people heard what he said. Most people still lacked the capacity to even receive the FM radio signal. Still, Lewis advised Roy that one World War II veteran subsequently showed up at the Berkeley studio and asked rather apologetically for the War Resisters League's address. Roy, in any event, would be returning to KPFA.

The Berkeley radio interview marked a highlight of Roy's cross-country reconnaissance. KPFA's founding showed that pacifists were actively engaged in making a better world. Roy likewise found pacifists embarking on experimental communities, farming groups, and shopping cooperatives. But Roy learned, as well, that pacifism, or even dissident thinking of any kind, had little purchase in the postwar United States. While students were "amazingly open to fresh analysis" and "highly uneasy" about Cold War propaganda, he feared they largely "parroted the newspapers, the radio and the liberal apologies, but without any real conviction." More broadly, Roy identified "a kind of creeping paralysis of defeatism and despair among pacifists which leads to inaction in other than little fellowship groups of mutual commiseration and fear." Ordinary working people seemed largely untouched by anything the pacifists did.

"Part of this, I suppose is necessary and healthy, for we can't live all of the time with great, complex problems of mankind and the world," Roy reported. "However, it is clear that the retreat into private lives is also a kind of waiting: waiting for the world to explode, for the bottom to drop out" (Kepler 1949).

Roy returned to New York City and his office duties, though he was always prepared for taking his beliefs out on the road where people could see them. In early October this brought him to Washington, DC, in support of self-identified "world citizen" Garry Davis.

Davis was a former World War II bomber pilot who had conceived a soaring passion for world government. At the U.S. embassy in Paris in May 1948, he had renounced his American citizenship. Henceforth he would be a citizen of the world. Davis established a World Citizen

Registry in January 1949, which soon gathered half a million signatories. Some true believers began carrying an "international identity card" concocted by Davis to cross European borders. In a world tired of war and wary of nuclear annihilation, the notion of global unity had widespread appeal. The U.S.-based United World Federalists claimed nearly 47,000 members by mid-1949, when ninety-one members of the House of Representatives endorsed legislation identifying world federation as a "fundamental objective" of U.S. foreign policy (Bennett 2003, 182). State legislatures were passing resolutions urging support. University of Chicago President Robert Hutchins spoke seriously of drafting a world constitution.

Roy was entranced. Davis showed, Roy believed, what one committed man could do. Roy praised the notion of world citizenship in an *Alternative* article, declaring that "we are held in thralldom by the nation-state and its creed of violence." The French government was less impressed. That fall of 1949, Davis was demonstrating in front of a French military prison to protest the treatment of a conscientious objector. On October 4, a French court had sentenced Davis to eight days in jail for lacking a foreigner's residency permit. Roy and others wanted to stand in solidarity with him.

At about 1 p.m. on October 4, after the news of Davis's sentence had come across the Atlantic, Roy and eleven other demonstrators convened at the French Embassy on Belmont Road in Washington, DC.

The men wore ties and jackets; they appeared entirely respectable. While some demonstrators remained outside, a bespectacled Quaker poet in her forties named Winifred Kate Rawlins and four others rang the embassy's doorbell. They carried a letter expressing support for Davis. While a bemused embassy official regarded the missive, the protestors announced they would be sitting down and occupying the embassy for the next twenty-four hours. An embassy spokesman gave them five minutes to leave. The five demonstrators went limp so that they might be hauled back outside. It was all quite continental and civilized; Rawlins described her carriers as "extremely gentle."

David Dellinger proved more adamant. He lay down on the embassy's driveway and refused to budge. Roy, A. J. Muste, Bayard

Rustin, and the others were solemnly parading outside the embassy. Police officers arrested all of them and charged them with picketing within five hundred feet of an embassy, the *Washington Post* reported on October 5, 1949.

Muste posted the $100 bond. Roy and the others, though, remained behind bars at the DC jail. The next day, pleading guilty, most agreed to pay $25 fines rather than spend an additional thirty days in jail. Rawlins, wed to her conscience, accepted the jail term out of what her lawyer described as sympathy for "the many unfortunate people who can't pay fines when they are convicted." The demonstration impressed World Citizen No. 1 himself. After reading about it while in France, Garry Davis subsequently urged Dellinger to declare Dellinger's Glen Gardner cooperative in New Jersey as an American "world community" (Bennett 2003, 184). Glen Gardner would do so in June 1950, days before the Korean War broke out.

Taxes divided the pacifists. James and Paula Peck had picketed outside of the New York City IRS office in March 1949, carrying signs urging passersby to "Refuse to Pay Income Taxes for War Progress." But the question was more than an individual one, as peace organizations with payrolls had to determine whether to withhold taxes for their employees.

The Fellowship of Reconciliation, following extended study, had concluded that federal taxes would continue to be withheld from salaries. When Roy took the WRL job, he asked whether it was possible for his paycheck to be provided without withholding, so that he might then refuse to pay the defense share of his tax. He figured it made no sense for a pacifist organization to funnel money into the war machine. Kaufman, though no longer executive secretary, argued vehemently that the organization's future should not be mortgaged to a radical policy promoted by a minority of members. The Executive Committee of the War Resisters League formed a tax committee in October 1949 to tackle the problem.

Roy, Bayard Rustin, and two veterans of the Civilian Public Service health experiments named Nat Hoffman and Charles Bloomstein together formed the WRL's "Subcommittee on Tax Withholding." After some study and discussion, they concluded the government always held the whip hand when it came to property. Refuse to pay taxes and the government would simply seize assets. Organizational resistance would be worse than futile, because the government would take everything in the end. Despite his philosophical belief in tax resistance, which he would later put into practice, Roy endorsed the committee's conclusion that refusing to withhold taxes as an organization would be imprudent. It could threaten the organization's very survival. It would be better, Roy reasoned, to send a letter of protest and then render unto Caesar. To ease message-sending, the War Resisters League sold stickers that could be affixed to tax returns. "This tax goes chiefly for war purposes, as a pacifist I pay under protest," the sticker stated (Bennett 2003, 152).

Roy returned to Washington in late January for a January 30, 1950, hearing of the House Armed Services Committee, which was examining conscription. Roy faced an extremely skeptical audience. The committee was chaired by Carl Vinson, a conservative Georgia Democrat. He *was* Mr. Armed Services. Vinson had been in Congress before the World War I draft started. No pacifist testimony was going to change his mind about the necessity of maintaining the country's martial stature.

Roy, nonetheless, would try.

"Conscription," Roy told Vinson's committee, "means not just the rigid control of the lives of young men for a period of military training, but the general control of population and natural resources, of what people say and even what they think."

Roy further asserted a "foreboding similarity, in kind if not in degree," between the concentration camps of Nazi Germany and the imprisonment of Americans who refused draft registration. "In the process of organizing fear and violence," Roy stated, "we tend to succumb to that which we would prevent, we begin to imitate that which we are preparing to defend ourselves against."

The House committee members let Roy expound up to the point where he began quoting Gandhi. Then Vinson began pressing back. The chairman asked how many members the War Resisters League had. He asked for the names of the officers. He asked how the group was financed. Roy was answering the questions so quickly that the sixty-seven-year-old Vinson said he had a hard time following the answers. But the chairman also persisted; how, he asked, did the War Resisters League plan to oppose the draft?

"We are advising [men] to follow their conscience and to do whatever they think is the right thing for them to do," Roy said.

"And in that way," Vinson pressed, "you are carrying on a campaign to resist conscription?"

Vinson was not given to random observations. If the War Resisters League was undertaking a campaign to impede the draft, the chairman of the House Armed Services Committee wanted incriminating details. Vinson asked for a copy of the organization's financial statements. One week later, Roy mailed one. Following the hearing, Roy also unleashed a five-page, single-spaced letter filled with pacifist aphorisms and a return to the theme that "our society knows what it means by war but not what it means by peace," Roy wrote, adding that "We are now our brothers' keepers for sure. Our survival is indivisible."

Shortly after Roy returned from his Capitol Hill appearance, a small New York newspaper named the *Putnam County News* offhandedly denounced the War Resisters League as a Communist organization. Even from such a relatively obscure publication, the charges stung. Roy and his allies were determinedly unattached to any party apparatus. They were, in fact, acutely aware of the Communist exploitation of some front groups. The year before, Roy and the Peacemakers had held themselves apart from a "Cultural and Scientific Conference for World Peace" conducted at New York City's Waldorf Hotel. The event, Dwight Macdonald had warned in the *Peace News* of April 14, 1949, was in actuality one more effort by Communists and fellow-travelers to use the peace movement for their own purposes.

Ideologically, Roy and like-minded War Resisters League members rejected Soviet military aggression. War was war, no matter who waged it. Tactically, too, the pacifists wanted to protect their organizational credibility by steering clear of the Communist crowd. Arm's length was the bare minimum distance. War Resisters League directors would even reject use of a dove on a peace calendar for fear the bird was too closely identified with the international Communist movement (Bennett 2003, 198).

Given all this, some WRL members thought they should sue the Putnam County newspaper for defamation. In April Roy took the seventy-mile trip north along the Hudson River to visit the *Putnam County News* newsroom. He would converse with the paper's editors, hear them out, and say his piece. The newspaper staff's position was that some reputable lawmakers had suggested the Communist Party had its hooks into the War Resisters League. Roy could only come away with the editor's commitment that if the WRL could present proof to the contrary, then that would be published as well.

The Putnam paper's casual slur touched a nerve, precisely because some of the pacifists themselves feared being drawn into the Communist orbit. In November 1950 Abraham Kaufman retired altogether from the War Resisters League following a dispute over whether a representative should attend the second World Congress of Defenders of Peace. Kaufman thought the gathering in Sheffield, England, would be dominated by Communists. Wanting no part of it, nor of the War Resisters League's own political shift, he walked away.

Longtime pacifist leader Evan Thomas, brother of onetime Socialist Party presidential candidate Norman Thomas, likewise left the League along with Frieda Lazarus. Lazarus had been serving with the League's Executive Committee since 1935 and had corresponded regularly with Roy during the war. Their departure might have been interpreted as the triumph of the radicals, a chance for the organization to remake itself in the spirit of the absolutists.

Roy, though, had come to the end of his own string. He was ready to return to college.

By May 1950 Roy had made clear his plans to leave the job as War Resisters League executive secretary. The reasons were almost certainly complicated. Kaufman suggested years later that Roy had a series of problems with the League's Executive Committee. Roy, at times, apparently felt second-guessed on certain administrative decisions. But Roy had personal plans as well, especially plans to finish the college education interrupted by World War II.

The leadership baton was passed to Sidney Aberman, a commercial artist from the Bronx who had spent World War II in two East Coast CPS camps. On June 14, 1950, Roy bid a formal, written farewell to the War Resisters League headquarters, asserting that he felt "gratified by what I felt to be a growing attitude of understanding and cooperative effort" among the often-fractious pacifists. The WRL Executive Committee, in turn, presented Roy with a suitcase, which he would use on his journey west to his new life.

5

College

Roy was ready. Ready: To return home to the West and secure at last his college degree. Ready: To escape the burdens and bickering attendant upon keeping the peace at the War Resisters League. Ready: To catch up with his life. He was turning thirty, and still single. His cohort, the wave of World War II veterans and Civilian Public Service alumni, had largely swept through college and moved on. Now it was Roy's turn.

Carrying his new suitcase, the parting gift from the War Resisters League, Roy traveled west seasoned and a bit singed from his experiences. Beyond college, his future intentions remained unclear. Graduate school and a life in academia appealed to him. So did activism. He could sort out the possibilities in Boulder, a cozy, mile-high university town braced by the Rocky Mountain air. Boulder had but twenty thousand full-time residents when Roy arrived in June 1950, some nine years after his brief initial foray into college. The mountain air, he declared, was "free of both recriminations and humidity." He worked construction during the summer while he shook off the East Coast weight from his shoulders.

"In such a climate and area, all men are brothers, and we can lick any so-and-so who says they aren't," Roy wrote Vivien Roodenko on June 10, 1950.

Vivien was the younger sister of Igal Roodenko, a radical pacifist who had done prison time during and after the war before globetrotting for the War Resisters League. Vivien was a twenty-eight-year-old former secretary of the Committee for Amnesty for All Objectors to War and Conscription. Vivien and Roy enjoyed a joshing epistolary relationship. The petite Vivien told Roy of her ventures into modern dance with Merce Cunningham while Roy, the former high school wrestler, said he was starting to lose his urban flab at the university gym. Roy further advised his friend that he intended to "infiltrate into the sororities in order to bring sex appeal into the pacifist movement." "My approach is to make clear from the start that I admire Gandhi but I find myself in disagreement on the matters of cow worship and celibacy," Roy alerted Vivien in his June 10 letter.

Vivien seemed to nudge Roy socially: date, date! Roy sought to reassure her.

"You'll be encouraged to learn that I have not neglected cultivating the acquaintance of several young ladies in these parts," Roy wrote Vivien on November 24, 1950. "So far, it has availed me little, for none of them is prepared to support me. I have my eye on one with a shiny new convertible, but so far I haven't been able to catch her on foot."

In a more serious vein, Roy confided that he thought Abraham Kaufman's departure from the War Resisters League would allow the organizational wheels to turn more smoothly. He was also stepping up his campus activism. North Korea had invaded South Korea in June 1950, and U.S. war mobilization was again clanking into place. Through a letter in the University of Colorado's student newspaper, the *Silver and Gold,* Roy invited potential conscientious objectors to contact him at his dorm room. On October 10, a man of serious intent followed up Roy's offer.

He was not a student, though, but an FBI special agent.

The 1948 draft law was explicit. Anyone who "knowingly counsels, aids, or abets another to refuse or evade registration or service in the armed forces Selective Service System" was subject to a five-year prison term and a $10,000 fine. This was serious business. War Resisters League member Larry Gara, while a history professor at Bluffton College in Ohio, had been sentenced in 1949 to eighteen months in prison for having "counseled, aided and abetted" a student draft resister (Bennett 2003, 179). Roy knew the rules when the FBI agent asked whether his draft counseling service amounted to aiding and abetting. It did not, Roy replied, not least because only two students had ended up approaching him. Both had been referred to Roy by the Central Committee for Conscientious Objectors.

"Kepler pointed out that he never at any time counseled anyone to refuse or evade registration or services with the Armed Forces," the FBI agent subsequently recorded. "He stated that it was not his intention to make converts of people who were not already conscientious objectors, but that he desired only to be of assistance to bona fide conscientious objectors."

Roy was not acting surreptitiously. Far from it; he sought attention. He and several others formed the University of Colorado's Peace Action Committee, having first submitted to university officials a list of organization officers and charter members, complete with their grade point averages. The *Denver Post* saw fit to note that Roy's Peace Action group on campus was part of a national campaign that "has received the open blessings of the Communist Party's *Daily Worker*." The newspaper further observed that one of the backers of the Peace Action group sounded suspiciously radical, as a "top leader in the Texas 'Wallace for President' organization who had picketed a segregated Houston store, while yet other student members were active in Leftist causes."

Roy tried spreading the word beyond the small audiences who would show up for Peace Action meetings. He wrote to the university's *Silver and Gold* student newspaper regularly—incessantly even. He would opine on Korean War developments, delve into pacifist theory, advise his fellow students that war was the chief enemy. Roy would pound out a two-page, single-spaced letter citing everyone from Gandhi to Supreme Court Associate Justice Robert Jackson. Roy's letters could be thorough, crisp, and impeccably argued. He could also be painfully wordy, trying the patience of readers with densely abstract paragraphs. In his more intentionally philosophical work, he could go on at even greater length. It could make for painful reading.

To wit: "We shall argue that if one actually examines human experience, that is, actually refers to real, historical experiment and experiences, that one finds a great body of evidence to support the view that it does not necessarily follow that if Nation A were to disarm unilaterally Nation B's power would be augmented by a factor of infinity or even that Nation B would necessarily want to, or be able to, tyrannize and exploit Nation A," Roy wrote several years after college, in a sixty-one-page, single-spaced assessment of nonviolent defense (Kepler 1964).

A. J. Muste had once put his finger on the problem with Roy's writing, in an August 15, 1949, note. Muste respected Roy's energy and intelligence, but he questioned whether Roy's terminology would put his message beyond a popular audience. He urged Roy to sharpen his writing considerably. Otherwise, Muste warned, the crucial message of peace would remain confined to a select few. But if Roy could be abstruse in his writing style, he could also slice away with great verve. He might practice nonviolence, but he debated aggressively, as when he challenged the *Silver and Gold's* editorial criticism of the Peace Action Committee.

"But let [the editor] have no care," Roy wrote on January 7, 1951. "This war-making world will find a spot for him, at a desk in the OWI [Office of War Information] no doubt. Bright young men from the upper half of their class and who can write will be needed to issue inspiring communiqués to the embattled population."

The *Silver and Gold's* callow young opinion-slingers were child's play for Roy, but he and his fellow activists faced more serious adult challenges as well. In December 1950 the House Un-American Activities Committee (HUAC) had summoned to the congressional inquisition a University of Colorado philosopher of science named David Hawkins. Hawkins had served in the Manhattan Project as Robert Oppenheimer's assistant during World War II. He had helped found the Federation of American Scientists. Between 1938 and 1943, he had also been a member of the Communist Party.

Hawkins's HUAC testimony, published verbatim by the *Denver Post,* alarmed state and university officials. They needed to protect themselves and their institution by rooting out the Reds before Congress did it for them. In February 1951 the University of Colorado's board of regents approved hiring two former FBI agents to investigate. Under pressure from Governor Daniel Thornton, the university's loyalty oath was revived and the purges began. Having separated from the Communist Party, Hawkins survived. Others did not.

Irving Goodman, an assistant professor of chemistry, was dismissed in June 1951 on the grounds that he had lied about his past membership in the Communist Party while conducting military research. An informant, identified as "Source 'E'," advised investigators that philosophy professor Joseph Cohen was certainly a Marxist, because, as Source E observed, "the philosophy of Hegel as advanced by Marx and Engels would appeal" to him. Curiosity was suspect. An informant reported that a history professor had "borrowed some maps of Europe" for a lecture in which he supposedly articulated "an unusual apology for Russia's international activities since World War II" (Hafer and Hutchinson 1951). Even square dance instructors were put under the microscope. Paul Kermiet was a Civilian Public Service alumnus and part-time instructor in the university's Denver extension center. He believed in the egalitarian power of the square dance and he rejected the loyalty oath as designed to force conformity. The university cast him out.

Roy fought the loyalty oaths through a new organization he established called the Student Committee for Academic Freedom. The important point to remember, Roy advised in a February 26, 1951, statement, was not the specific oath itself but the democratic right of an individual to inquire and believe as he wishes without being restrained. In late March, having heard of what Roy was up to, the American Civil Liberties Union wrote him about forming a Boulder-based civil liberties organization. But by and large, allies were few. Most faculty members were submitting to the state, ducking their heads into the library or the lab.

In May 1951 the investigators called upon Morris Judd, a young navy veteran and philosophy instructor who had run a Boulder bookstore before being hired by the university. Judd, the investigators determined, had attended Communist Party meetings back in 1945 or 1946. An unnamed student advised the detectives that Judd was "90 percent or better a probable Communist." It was considered suspicious that Judd and his wife in April 1947 had hosted a reception for African American singer Paul Robeson, when Robeson came to campus at the invitation of a group called American Youth for Democracy.

The ex-FBI men pressed Judd about his political affiliations. Judd rejected the questions as a violation of his constitutional as well as academic rights.

Three weeks later Judd was summoned by university president Robert Stearns and advised that teaching was a privilege and not a right. It would be best to answer all questions. Judd, still hopeful of retaining his teaching job, compromised and said he was not at present a member of the Party. It didn't suffice. Summer arrived, and the untenured Judd lost his teaching position.

The academic purges soured Roy on graduate school. He had come to see how political contingency swept away intellectual principle. When the Colorado American Legion passed a 1952 resolution denouncing the state university for harboring Reds, Stearns dutifully recounted all of the true-blue loyalty steps the university had taken. Faculty members had been fired, Stearns reminded the veterans. Allegiance oaths had been adhered to and charters revoked for questionable student organizations like the suspiciously named American Youth for Democracy. Stearns assured the Legion he would be vigilant in dealing with communism, according to news accounts.

Until then Roy had been laying the foundation for an academic career, taking the Graduate Record Examination in April 1951. He scored a perfect 800 on the social studies section and scored in the 99th percentile in the vocabulary, arts, and literature sections. His 480 score on the math portion of the GRE, ranking him in the 38th percentile, might have hurt him in some graduate school admissions circles, but he was, more to the point, reconsidering the very idea of academia. His History Department chairman told Roy he would have to choose between being an activist and being a scholar.

It proved a simple choice.

"I informed the History Department if they hired me, I would have to embarrass them because I wouldn't sign the loyalty oath," Roy recalled in a 1984 interview. "I left the history profession and they didn't miss me, and I didn't miss them."

Besides, Roy was distracted. In 1951 he had met a Denver-area native and fellow student named Patricia Ellen Petersen. Patricia had been raised in Wyoming and Colorado, the only child of poor parents. Patricia's mother's parents had come from Russia when they were young adults; their past, Roy's daughter Dawn said, "was always somewhat mysterious." Dawn, as she grew older, would wonder if her own grandmother and grandfather had been raised Jewish. It seemed a distinct possibility to her; as an adult, Dawn would herself convert to Judaism.

When Patricia's mother, Clara Ann, was in her early twenties, she married an older man named John Petersen. Throughout the Great Depression, living in Wyoming, John Petersen took a variety of odd jobs, including work as a bartender and as a horse jockey. The story was that he had a heart attack while hunting at the age of sixty, forcing Clara Ann and young Patricia to move to Colorado. As an adult, Dawn Kepler grew curious. Evidence mounted that maybe there was more to John Petersen than family lore let on. John Petersen, she learned, was not actually her grandfather's real name. From Patricia, Clark Kepler once received a collection of their grandfather's belongings.

"He looked them over, and told her that what she had given him were the tools for loading dice," Dawn Kepler recalled in a 2008 interview. "He asked, 'Was Grandpa Johnny a gambler?' She burst into tears and left the room."

After Patricia's father died, Clara Ann went to work for the telephone company in Colorado. Patricia worked hard, and entered the University of Colorado to study English and child development. She worked part-time to pay the bills and, like Roy, she was assigned as the switchboard operator, in her case at one of the women's dormitories. Roy was working eighteen hours a week at the switchboard at one of the men's dormitories. Patching through calls, they grew familiar with each other's voices and, in time, with each other before they ever met.

"Someday," Roy told Patricia, "I'm going to come over and see you. And when I do, you'll know me just by the sound of my voice."

One Saturday night not long after, Roy showed up at Pat's dormitory. Without identifying himself, he began chatting away even as she juggled the calls and wires. Impatient, she advised him she was very busy right that moment.

"Don't you know me?" Roy asked.

"Of course I don't know you," Pat said.

"I'm Roy Kepler," he said (Ong and Walker n.d.).

Roy, as he would explain years later, had been postponing both marriage and serious personal attachments for years because of his interest in social change. He had been able to strike out for New York City to run the War Resisters League, and then to leave the WRL and return to school, without familial entanglements. But in meeting Patricia, Roy's heart was finally being drawn out.

"He said he liked the look of my legs," Patricia recalled in a May 2005 conversation. "It would have been a lot nicer if he had said he liked the look of my face."

In the classroom, Roy wrapped up his final papers. One, in particular, captured his fancy. It was an essay entitled "The Function of the Terror in the French Revolution" (Kepler 1951). The paper was imperfect, except as a reflection of Roy's own thinking at the time. Roy himself admitted he had undertaken only "meager research" for his paper, which was padded with long excerpts from other writers. There was throughout, though, Roy's enduring belief that means and ends could not be separated. One could not build a society of liberty, equality, and fraternity through immoral means, Roy argued. The revolutionary means chosen must be consistent with the ends being sought. Self-delusion was a systematic danger among those participating in the French Revolution. A true revolutionary must see clearly, and recognize the inseparability of means and ends.

Peace was a process, not an end. This was the heart of the matter for Roy. In the quiescent early 1950s, this was a somewhat abstract notion. It would take another fifteen years or so for Roy's bedrock beliefs to be fully tested in the fire of street demonstrations. Roy would also need time to more clearly articulate his views. As telling as Roy's paper might have been with regard to his own views and priorities, and he would be citing the Terror for some time, he earned only a B+. The writing was overly abstract and the sourcing was thin.

"You are in some danger of using history only as an illustration of your own philosophical or ethical ideas," the teacher wrote in pencil.

"If carried too far, [this] results in an inability to learn new things; i.e., to grow."

Nonetheless, Roy's examination of the French Revolution occurred at an opportune time. He was nearing graduation, uncertain of his next steps, when he chanced upon a notice inviting Fulbright scholar applications for students wishing to study independently abroad. The Fulbright program had only been established in 1946 and wasn't yet widely known, but its stated purpose of promoting international peace and understanding seemed aligned with Roy's own interests.

"I thought, 'what do I have to lose?'" Roy recalled in a 1984 interview.

He applied for the Fulbright, proposing to expand on his initial examination of the Terror and the French Revolution. Roy was a superb candidate by strictly apolitical measurement: a summa cum laude graduate, elected to Phi Beta Kappa. His most serious obstacle turned out to be his political beliefs. He later recalled that at least one community leader didn't feel that a pacifist should be awarded a Fulbright fellowship. After all, the Fulbright scholar while overseas would be seen as speaking for the U.S. government. Roy refused to sign a loyalty oath, and it reportedly took the president of the university to intercede on Roy's behalf. In June 1951, all obstacles overcome, Roy learned he had won the fellowship. That summer he brushed up on his French, and in September 1951 he departed for the University of Bordeaux.

Roy arrived in Europe on October 1 and spent the first month in Paris along with about 230 other Fulbright scholars. During this orientation period, the weather gray and damp, Roy practiced his French in small classes and recounted to his friends how he was making his way through the city's restaurants. He was then assigned to the University of Bordeaux, arriving on October 27 to spend the next two months. His French skills slowly improved and, one conversation at a time, he began, as he recorded in his diary on November 18, 1951, "to pick up French viewpoints." One older gentleman, for instance, assured Roy that the French people were utterly incapable of democracy.

Another night, Roy went to dinner at a friend's house in Bordeaux. He was the only American present. Through books like Richard

Wright's *Black Boy,* his French hosts had learned of the racism rampant through the United States. They considered themselves above such coarse sentiments. Then one of the French sophisticates asked Roy why there were so many black men in the United States army. Roy explained that it only seemed that way because an army engineering unit was stationed nearby. The engineering units, Roy noted, tended to be heavily populated with black soldiers.

"Why do you bring up this question?" Roy asked.

"Well," the Frenchwoman replied, "doesn't your government know that many of them go with our girls?"

Yes, of course: the black man had come for the young French girls. There it was, coming from a worldly Frenchwoman: the same fear and fascination about race-mingling that curdled many American households.

"What difference does that make," Roy asked the woman, "if, as I was told earlier this evening, you bear no feeling of racial prejudice?"

After a moment, a man confessed to Roy the abrupt realization: if France had a black population like the United States, then it probably would have a racial problem as well.

Roy returned to Paris in January to use the *Bibliothèque Natio-nale,* after spending two sunny weeks in Spain during the Christmas holiday, traveling with two young female American teachers. Roy was realizing that he was not cut out for purely academic research. He wanted to be in the world, not simply back in the books. Still, the French national library founded in 1368 and opened to the public in 1692 impressed itself on him. It was so capacious, holding what might seem to be all the world's volumes. Roy would remember that, the endless stacks.

Roy was thinking big. He advised his friends in a January 16, 1952, letter that while abroad he was getting a chance to delve into "some problems I had been trying to solve." Perhaps inspired by his own travels, Roy urged his friends to use the new year as a time for "testing new paths, new thinking." Roy reported that he had been contemplating whether being "against war and for peace" really solved anything. He noted that the American Federation of Labor was reversing traditional resistance to conscription. The labor union was only the latest organization to accept the draft, Roy said, even though pacifists had kept agitating against it. Perhaps, he mused, it would make no sense to urge an eighteen-year-old American boy to refuse to register for the draft.

"There is an area," Roy observed in his January 16 letter, "in which pacifism grows or declines, is relevant or irrelevant, to the degree that its practitioners are not just holy but also intelligent and sensitive to problems as they appear to non-pacifist eyes."

Roy was keeping his eyes open, as he had in his 1949 cross-country trip or throughout his time in the CPS camps. In late January he advised WRL headquarters that "pacifist efforts are, for the most part, non-existent or at best almost entirely submerged" in postwar France. Still optimistic, though, Roy felt that Europeans were ready to listen to pacifist ideas.

Germany had promise, Roy thought. He met with a German leader in War Resisters International and was encouraged to learn that the pacifist organization's Hamburg chapter alone claimed some one thousand members. The WRL should step in immediately, Roy urged, to start organizing against the country's rearmament. Spending $1,000 on organizing in Germany would be more fruitful than $50,000 scattered about the complacent United States, Roy advised Sidney Aberman in a June 25, 1952, letter. In time the WRL would fund posters, pamphlets, and half a million leaflets promoting the German resistance to rearmament and membership in the North Atlantic Treaty Organization (NATO) (Bennett 2003, 177). The campaign would fail, as would so many others; in 1955, West Germany would join NATO.

Roy was being torn in several directions. Even after the loyalty oath business back in Boulder, he still lingered over the idea of going to graduate school. And even after meeting Patricia, he may still have had other romantic notions. Here the record becomes ambiguous. In Paris Roy tracked down a young woman he had known in the United States. Her name was Margaret Reed. She informed him, he reported, that "she would prefer not to see me further." And with that, Roy told his diary on January 27, 1952, somewhat enigmatically, "so ends the matter."

Romantic disenchantments aside, Roy's Fulbright experience, he subsequently said, was "a dream year." He was able to observe Europe's postwar recovery and meet, as he put it, "some of the world's most beautiful women, and ugliest men." The experience opened his mind to other dynamics as well. His year in Europe enabled him to see problems from new angles.

"We are outmanned, outshouted, outpublicized and outmaneuvered on many occasions," Roy wrote Sidney Aberman on January 22, 1952. Therefore, "while our principles may be steady, our tactics should be flexible. Too often, we confuse one with the other."

After departing France, Roy spent some time in London with the staff of the periodical *Peace News,* published since 1936 by War Resisters International. It was a flimsy-feeling publication, dense with words and short on space, but it covered the global peace movement diligently and Roy saw its possibilities. He began writing occasional items for *Peace News,* and when he returned to New York City following his London sojourn he urged other WRL leaders to consider taking over the publication.

From New York City, the War Resisters League directors were feeling out his interest in performing more fieldwork. Roy, though, had developed other plans.

"It so happens," Roy advised Sidney Aberman on May 9, 1952, "[that] I have made a commitment beginning in September in California, a dangerously personal and selfish one, at least on the surface, but which may, I hope, make it possible for me to follow up my pacifist concerns with more energy."

Patricia Petersen, the attractive young woman Roy had met in Boulder, was about that time moving out to the San Francisco Bay Area. Roy did not mention her name to Aberman in May, instead promising to provide full details about the mysterious California allure at a later time.

Roy set sail from Southampton on the RMS *Mauretania* in late June, landing on the East Coast and eventually reaching his family's

4. Roy Kepler on board ship, returning from France, 1952. Photographer unknown, courtesy of the Kepler family.

Denver home at 1312 Lafayette Street. Home was exactly the same, and yet entirely different following his continental sojourn. The Denver grocery stores overwhelmed him with their abundance. The western U.S. history was callow, nothing like the ancient feel of the Bibliothèque Nationale. Political discussions took smug, self-indulgent turns.

Shortly after he arrived in Denver, several friends invited Roy to a dinner sponsored by the local chapter of the Fellowship of Reconciliation. Their hearts were in the right places, and the guests spent the dinner complaining about the repression of civil liberties. Roy, freshly returned from a country not long free from Nazi occupation, asked what would happen if they spoke out to a broader audience. There must have been a pause, as Roy abruptly realized that none of the well-meaning activists had really spoken their minds where it really mattered. They were only presuming what would happen. In private, they could unburden themselves. In public, they were reticent, fearful. They could blame Joseph McCarthy, but Roy began thinking that for these dinner party radicals, McCarthy was a convenient excuse. Perhaps, he thought, the activists were silencing themselves. Perhaps there were places where ideas might yet be freed from both chains and excuses.

6

KPFA

Lew Hill burned hot.

His eyes pierced. He was pale and spectral thin, painfully arthritic and usually wreathed in cigarette smoke. He spoke mellifluously in complicated paragraphs that could sound either brilliant or utterly incomprehensible. Some people, he enchanted. Eleanor McKinney, one of his chief allies, said Hill "brought together in one man the radical ideals of a visionary and a poet with the practicality of a man of action" (McKinney 1966, 9). Others, like Roy, resisted his spell.

"He drew to himself," Roy once wrote, "a strange assemblage of disciples who were little more than rubber stamps."

Roy was Hill's unequal partner in a great venture, for a time. The two men worked side by side at KPFA, the nation's first noncommercial, listener-supported radio station unaffiliated with a church or university. The station was really Hill's baby, but Roy helped nurture it. Together they liberated part of the broadcast spectrum. People's lives changed by listening to KPFA. Careers were turned, thoughts inspired. Roy's own life reset as a result of his work as the station's promotions and marketing director, as he honed his business skills and cultivated a broad Bay Area network.

Hill and Roy worked together well, until they did not. Their relationship ended badly. In some ways they summoned the best and the worst in each other. Both men believed in radical direct action. Effective pacifism, they thought, must go beyond mere protest. Principles must be lived. And enemies, it turned out, must be fought.

↓

The son of a well-to-do lawyer who served in the Missouri state leg-
islature, Hill was a military school alumnus who went on to Stanford
in the late 1930s. While there, the tennis-playing teenager repudiated
his military school past by declaring himself a pacifist and registering
as a conscientious objector. In September 1942 Hill was assigned to
the Coleville Civilian Public Service camp located on the eastern edge
of the Sierra Nevada mountains abutting the Nevada border. Like Roy
and many others, Hill soon enough lost patience with the trivial work
that he likened to moving rocks from one side of the road to the other.

Medically discharged in October 1943, Hill served for a time with
the American Civil Liberties Union's National Committee on Conscientious Objectors, advocating on behalf of pacifists who had walked
out of their camps or stopped cooperating. More generally, he was a
fount of notions. As U.S. troops drove closer to Japan in 1945, Hill
characteristically began plotting a dramatic gesture that would end
the war once and for all. A dozen pacifists would sail across the Pacific
Ocean and carry a peace message to the Japanese people on behalf of
the American people.

"The plans, very extensive and detailed, included bombarding the
major cities with [peace] leaflets," Hill advised Roy in a March 6,
1948, letter (Tracy 1993, 176).

Even Hill's friends dismissed the notion as harebrained. But it
was a big idea, no one could deny. It was just the ambitious kind of
idea Lew Hill specialized in. He kept hatching others, often circling
around the general theme of direct communication. People talking
to people, that was the key. While in Coleville, Hill had discussed
with fellow CPS man Roy Finch the idea of creating a different kind
of radio station. It could help spread the message of pacifism, yes,
but more broadly such a station would bind people in conversation.
It would neither condescend nor incessantly sell, sell, sell. It would
bring progressive political action into the twentieth century, updating the street-corner soapboxes and pamphleteering of yore. The
Coleville conversations would spread as the CPS men scattered. After

Hill left, Finch would eventually move on to Minersville, where he would join Roy.

That radio could be a force for social change was not, in itself, a radical thought. During the initial radio boom of the 1920s, the new medium was envisioned as a potent resource for educational and political discourse. It would enable conversation across vast distances, uniting society. It was not, at first, regarded strictly as a commercial medium. Commerce Secretary Herbert Hoover, at the dawn of the industry, had declared it inconceivable that advertising chatter might drown such potential for public service. Instead of ad revenues, many thought some type of public support would be required. From the time the station KDKA took to the Pittsburgh airwaves in 1920, through the growth of four hundred stations over the next two years, advertising wasn't really part of the picture. Fully one quarter of the radio licenses granted between 1920 and 1925 were for noncommercial stations; some, like the labor-oriented WCFL in Chicago, were explicitly aligned with ideological perspectives (Land 1999, ix).

By the 1930s, the tune changed. Radio ads soared and the number of educational stations plummeted following passage of the 1927 Radio Act, as the new Federal Radio Commission began redistributing licenses to commercial outfits. Reformers began worrying that commercial interests were overpowering the public interest. There was talk of government-supported stations, free of commercial enterprise, so that the public's interest might be better served (Engelman 1996, 18–23).

Hill knew the commercial radio scene from a brief, unsatisfying stint as a news announcer on WINX radio in Washington, DC. The experience helped propel his thinking. Roy, following his discharge from Minersville, recalled meeting with Hill and Hill's wife, Joy, along with George Reeves, John Lewis, and several others to discuss radio's potential. Hill was having many such conversations. One memorable evening in particular, in San Francisco in March 1946, Hill and several pacifist friends and sympathizers talked for hours about the quest for peace, the shortcomings of traditional media, and the possibility of creating an alternative. Perhaps radio could be the answer, if only the money could be found.

Hill elaborated on his beliefs in a July 1946 prospectus for what was to become the Pacifica Foundation. The proposed station, he explained, would undertake activities that would contribute to "a lasting understanding between nations and between individuals of all nations, races, creeds and colors" and would "gather and disseminate information on the causes of conflict between any and all of such groups" (Lasar 1999, 44).

Matthew Lasar, in his detailed history *Pacifica Radio: The Rise of an Alternative Network,* notes that copies of the 1946 Pacifica prospectus were carried about the country by pacifist Denny Wilcher, a Yale man and Coleville CPS alumnus who had also passed briefly through Minersville. It's not clear whether Roy got his hands on the prospectus or when he heard about it, though the ideas it conveyed appealed to him and the pacifists involved with it were part of his circle.

Hill's original thought was to have both an AM and an FM station, but that proved infeasible. Hill then applied for an AM radio license, the proposed 1,000-watt facility to be operated out of Berkeley's blue-collar neighboring town of Richmond. By 1947, following an assessment of the political landscape, Hill shifted gears. In a pamphlet called *The Promise of Radio,* the case was made for fairness and public service. Pacifism was downplayed, as were the pacifist backgrounds of the Pacifica founders. Neither was the proposed station billed as being entirely noncommercial. Instead, it would "eliminate the most objectionable features of today's radio advertising" through self-imposed limits such as banning commercials during news broadcasts and resisting ads that employed "irritative or excessively repetitious use of names, slogans or catch-phrases, singing, music or sound effects" (Lasar 1999, 52).

Denny Wilcher and others ferreted out contributions from prosperous Quakers and well-heeled liberals, bringing the Pacifica Foundation's bankroll to $32,000 by the spring of 1947. Hill made his formal pitch to the Federal Communications Commission in March 1947. That June the FCC denied the application, citing the proximity of existing commercial stations. The AM atmosphere was jammed.

Consequently, Hill concluded, the Pacifica Foundation would make a foray into the sparser regions of FM.

FM was fresh territory, a frontier. It stood for "frequency modulation," different from the "amplitude modulation" of AM. FM offered superior sound quality and less interference, though the FCC had also shoved FM into the left-hand ghetto of the wavelength scale between 88 and 108 million cycles per second. This would become a problem, because the common radios of the time couldn't pull in those signals. To reach listeners, an FM station would have to get new radios into the hands of their audience. In time, this would become a big part of Roy's job.

In January 1949 Hill met with Roy's old Minersville ally John Lewis and other members of the Pacifica circle. They agreed that they would make a stab at a 550-watt start-up station. The KPFA crew only had enough money for about six months; it would be a big gamble to start operating without more. Hill urged all to press on. He kept saying: In a crisis, take risks and expand. Using volunteer labor and donated equipment, the crew set up on the sixth floor of a building on Berkeley's University Avenue.

On the afternoon of April 15, 1949, still bleary from the night before, Hill went on the air and began talking about the Pacifica Foundation. When he was done, KPFA's first music show commenced: "Anglo-American Folk Ballads." Staff and volunteers grinned at each other in the control room, wiped away tears, and tipped back a celebratory bottle of hootch (Lasar 1999, 64).

The new station's organizers hoped to find between four thousand and five thousand subscribers willing to pay $10, but it was a hard slog. The feeble signal fell short, the programming was hit or miss, and in any event there weren't many FM radios in the Bay Area. People didn't even know to look for the new station. Sometimes it felt like broadcasting into the void. Still, the like-minded were starting to find it. The station had barely gotten on the air when Roy appeared at the makeshift studio one Sunday afternoon in late April during his 1949 War Resisters League cross-country field trip. An intellectually aggressive U.C. Berkeley economics graduate student named Robert Schutz, with whom Roy would later sometimes clash, hosted a program entitled "Men and Issues." Schutz asked Roy questions about pacifism and war resistance. It may well have been Roy's own first radio appearance.

A little more than a year later, with barely three hundred subscribers lined up, KPFA went off the air in August 1950. The little station just wasn't making it. Surprisingly, though, the radio silence brought an outcry. In its short life KPFA had attracted an audience whose loyalty wasn't yet reflected in the subscription list. In a public outpouring similar to what would happen with Roy's own bookstore a half-century later, fans rallied together to save what they now missed. New dues were collected, contributions gathered, and in the summer of 1951 the station returned with the help of one thousand dues-paying subscribers.

An early Ford Foundation grant in November 1951 enabled the fledgling station to buy new equipment and office space. Even with the grant, though, the station retained its shoestring feel and egalitarian notions. KPFA's was an honest sound. The station's announcers and personalities spoke directly to listeners, dispensing with the commercial conventions that larded up standard radio fare. There were no orchestral fanfares to swell a mood, no catchy theme songs to shape a sentiment. The hackneyed professional radio phrase "Well, our time's just about up" was all but banned, a sign that programs might well break out of their conventional schedule. A program was done when it was done (Whiting 1992). Programming gaps were honestly ornamented as if they were Shaker furniture, with but a touch of poetry or music. A conversational tone replaced the sonorous baritone of commercial radio. The programs respected the listener's intelligence.

Roy had come west, though not apparently with any particular employment commitments. He sold Kirby vacuum cleaners in Marin County, and then moved to Berkeley in the winter of 1952. There, it seems, he remembered Patricia, his friend and fellow dormitory telephone operator from the University of Colorado. He sent an Easter card to her mother in 1953 and learned that Patricia was likewise living in Berkeley, only several blocks away, and working as a secretary at the University of California. Roy and Patricia renewed the relationship they had begun in Boulder, and on July 12, 1953, they would marry in a civil ceremony; later, they repeated their vows in a Colorado church (Ong and Walker, n.d.).

Roy at the time was serving the War Resisters League as one of two "field men." That meant prospecting, looking for potential members, affiliations, and projects. He was looking out, as well, for himself. He could see at KPFA a natural home. Roy and Lew Hill had sometimes disputed over wartime tactics, such as on the timing and wisdom of a general walkout from CPS camps, but they were more or less as one on the overall principle of pacifism. Besides, there weren't many other organizations in which pacifists played such an essential role.

In January 1953 Roy formally joined the KPFA staff as promotions director and subscriptions chief. It was a congenial fit, at first, and the goals sounded reachable. The KPFA subscriptions were cheap, only $10 for a year. Hill cast the payment not as a charitable donation or as a membership due but as a subscription, as if for a newspaper. Hill called it the 2 percent solution. If 2 percent of an audience paid the subscription price, the station could meet its budget (Hill 1968). It sound reasonable in theory, but it was frustrating in practice. Fewer than one in four Bay Area homes even had FM radios in 1952. A January 1953 assessment found that at least one thousand new subscribers would be needed in just the first three months of the year.

Roy found direct mail solicitations and newspaper ads essentially useless as promotional tools. One early direct-mailing campaign targeted San Francisco physicians, but barely 1 percent of those contacted responded. An ad in a Bay Area cultural magazine called *Audience* came and went without leaving any trace behind. Roy tried circulating free copies of the station's biweekly programming newsletter, *Folio*, to Bay Area public libraries, radio stores, and the like. It did little good. On-air announcements several times a day touted the station, as did occasional ads in the *Daily Californian*. Roy put up displays in Bay

Area bookstores like the popular Cottage Bookshop in downtown San Rafael, north of San Francisco.

Big campaigns flopped. Informality worked better, consistent with the station's personality. Roy and his KPFA colleagues tried inculcating a sense of relationship between listeners and station. Open houses every two months invited the audience to visit the modest facilities. Roy also sought out group sponsorships, talking with a San Francisco lawyers association about supporting a legal affairs show. He drafted a promotional brochure and worked to encourage feature stories about this new listener-supported station. Slowly the efforts began paying off. By October 1953 the station would claim some 2,700 subscribers and was setting a goal of 3,900 by November 1954.

But the promotion and subscription drive confronted a structural problem: There simply weren't enough FM radios in Bay Area homes. What really worked was the distribution of at-cost FM radios direct from the factory. A company called Pederson Electronics developed a cheap FM set dubbed "The Subscriber," which was sold for $40 plus the $10 KPFA subscription. The Emporium and other popular Bay Area stores began distributing inexpensive Zenith FM radio sets. Potential subscribers could even obtain a free radio for a week. A budding San Francisco poet named Lawrence Ferlinghetti, for one, began his long association with KPFA as a subscriber initially lured in by the low-cost FM radio. He had company. Between May 1953 and January 1954, nearly four hundred Subscriber FM sets were sold.

Roy proselytized. He wrote some well-to-do KPFA subscribers and asked for contributions of several thousand dollars to finance the manufacturing of additional Subscriber sets. Roy would contact KPFA subscribers and ask them to set up a meeting, a house party where he could explain the merits of the public radio station. Then he would sweeten the deal with the cheap radio. He circulated throughout the Bay Area, sometimes venturing over the Santa Cruz Mountains to remote, redwood-shaded communities like Scotts Valley. He attended one open house in Sausalito, accompanied by a flamenco guitarist. In homes and elementary schools, introduced by allies and flanked by a radio provided by local appliance stores, Roy would expound on the power of FM. The KPFA station, Roy declared, was not simply a place for pacifists. The really important part of KPFA was that it would make available every conceivable viewpoint.

Certainly the KPFA voices stood out.

Alan Watts, a former Episcopal priest avid for both enlightenment and the high life, delivered commentaries on Zen Buddhism. Annihilation, Watts characteristically told KPFA listeners in January 1953, is funny stuff. But do not worry, he added, for death is actually quite marvelous, necessary to clean the slate every now and then. Poet and former conscientious objector Kenneth Rexroth would hold forth omnisciently on a show called "Books," though the title hardly did justice. Rexroth knew all and everything; just ask him. Starting in 1953, a single mother and former University of California at Berkeley debater named Pauline Kael would sally forth into the world of cinema. When a local newspaper columnist in early 1953 complained about the "Alpine intellectual level" assumed by all the KPFA brains, Roy countered in a February 2, 1953, letter to the *San Francisco Chronicle* that "ordinary listeners both understand and prefer intelligent public affairs programs."

Roy secured his own microphone time as well. Starting in October 1952, even before he joined the station's full-time staff, Roy held forth on a show he called "Perspectives Abroad." Roy used foreign newspaper clippings to showcase weekly how the United States was perceived in other countries. For one typical program, Roy used French newspaper accounts to show how the French people considered the U.S. Army to be occupiers of their country. He could be scathing. Europeans, he proclaimed, were attracted by America's notions of liberty and democracy but they were repelled by the country's witch hunts, self-righteousness, and reliance on military might.

"The common man is now free; he has the vote, a job and can even get a college education," Roy proclaimed in one typical commentary in October 1953. "So what does he do with it all? He buys a shiny car, a shiny refrigerator, a TV set and indulges himself in pop culture." American society, Roy believed, was vulgarian and anti-intellectual. The mass media, Roy said, was dominated by "Bob Hope, soap operas, singing commercials, Mickey Spillane, Dagmar and Marilyn Monroe."

Roy could really wind himself up. One day he was starting to roll on one of his weekly commentary shows. He would play a taped excerpt from an earlier appearance by a member of the conservative Daughters of the American Revolution, and then he would comment bluntly on the woman's obvious mental deficiencies. Hill dashed into the studio when Roy was done and made a quick on-air apology to the DAR woman. He reproached Roy afterward. The woman had been a guest of the radio station, Hill noted, and she deserved better than to be cruelly repudiated by her hosts. Roy's denunciations seemed to be outright defamation, Hill feared. At the least, he thought it shockingly discourteous to a woman who in good faith had accepted an invitation from the station. Roy disagreed, just as fervently. He had simply told the truth as he saw it (Lasar 1999, 139).

There were more and more such disagreements between Roy and Hill. Roy was chatting another day with Anthony Boucher about the complicated KPFA dynamics. Boucher was a lively companion, an intellectual omnivore born under the name William Anthony Parker White. He was then in his early forties, an opera-loving man of pronounced opinions. He reviewed mysteries for newspapers and was a founding editor of the *Magazine of Fantasy and Science Fiction;* he had gotten his start in radio during the 1940s with *The Adventures of Ellery Queen.* Boucher shared Roy's scorn for Lew Hill's shortcomings. KPFA, the two men concluded, resembled a Rosicrucian Order, a strange and demandingly mystical place with Lew Hill at the bleeding center of it all. Hill was a big talker who spun a lot of malarkey but couldn't administer worth a darn, while he was worshipped by an inner circle that Roy witheringly referred to as the Triumvirate.

"He drew to himself a strange assemblage of disciples, who were little more than rubber stamps," Roy concluded in an undated account that he tellingly entitled "The Terror During the KPFA Revolution."

For raw interpersonal politics, nothing in Roy's life would ever exceed his experiences at KPFA. That's saying something, given what Roy went through with the likes of the War Resisters League and, later, the Midpeninsula Free University. The Pacifica Foundation's memos and minutes, stored in part at the University of Maryland's National Public Broadcasting Archives, depict warring factions, angry denunciations, and parliamentary maneuverings. One side and then another would deploy Robert's Rules of Order to press their points or shut down the opposition. At one meeting Roy asked for a chance to speak. Robert Schutz, who in 1949 had welcomed Roy to the KPFA studios for an early on-air discussion of pacifism, objected. He didn't even want Roy to talk.

Hill did not help. He kept coming and going.

In October 1952 Hill and his allies had backed a notion to consolidate decision-making. Amid resentment over Hill's seeming power grab, the station's executive membership rejected the management proposal. On October 10, Hill had offered his resignation (Lasar 1999, 142). By December, amid various machinations, Hill was restored to his position. In July 1953 Hill again announced he would resign effective the end of the month. A crowded meeting on July 9 put the question to the station's executive membership: Would Hill's ally Richard Moore, Eleanor McKinney's husband, continue as acting administrator and bring Hill back, or would the station try to hold on to the notions of cooperative decision-making? Moore felt that KPFA without Lew Hill was a contradiction in terms. One was nothing without the other.

Moore wanted, as well, to streamline the staff. He sought approval to fire three KPFA employees and to get two others, including Roy, to resign. The reasons were not simply economic. Moore was part of one faction, and Roy was part of another. Moore lost the leadership vote, and he promptly resigned. Alan Watts announced the news on air, locking in the decision (Lasar 1999, 148).

As promotions director and member of the anti-Hill faction, Roy drafted a letter formally announcing Hill's departure. He also joined station manager Wallace Hamilton and five of their allies in signing a declaration that it would be "untenable" for Hill and Moore to return to management positions at the station. Without them, Roy and his allies said, the station would be a far more productive medium. And if Hill and Moore were to return, Roy and his allies pledged that they would resign. In time, circumstances would compel them to ratify their pledge.

↓

The KPFA schedule for April 22, 1954, promised a discussion of "Various Conceptions of Freedom." The station's subscribers were given a slightly more specific guidance. The show would deal with "Marijuana: Some Notes and Comments on the Use of the Narcotic." It sounded quite abstract, and the show itself began discordantly. Some strange music, straight from a viper's nest, snaked about before mellow jazz guitar softened the mood. The half-hour conversation began drifting over the airwaves. Four characters introduced themselves as Red, Lola, Louie, and Sam. Their topic was pot.

"There's nothing harmful in it," one said.

"It's relaxing," said another.

Marijuana, the four panelists agreed, heightened the senses, rendered entertainment vivid, and enlivened music. Someone audibly puffed on a pipe. The four-way conversation fractured as the program wore on. The voices thickened, grew drowsy, languid. Red said he was thirty-four years old and had been smoking marijuana since he was seventeen. He never had any problems with the stuff. That's right, the others agreed. Everyone laughed. An inspiration struck, an historical hypothetical.

"Now take the case of good Queen Bess," one of the panelists said, as the *San Francisco Examiner* recounted on April 25. "Suppose Walter Raleigh had brought her a few leafs of the stuff. It would have changed the entire course of civilization! There wouldn't have been the fights with the Spanish, because everybody would have been too relaxed to fight."

The dime dropped. Red, Lola, Louie, and Sam were stoned out of their collective gourds, live on KPFA.

For Raymond Pierce, the dopers' public show was a final provocation. The *San Francisco Call-Bulletin* reporter had been monitoring KPFA for some time. He knew all about the station's radical ways, the leftist politics and subversion. Now it was promoting drugs. Pierce called California narcotics officers to bring their attention to the marijuana show. Agents subsequently showed up at the Berkeley studio and demanded a tape of the show. The state authorities had neither a search warrant nor a court order, but Assistant Attorney General Leo Vander Lans said he had the power to "borrow" the tape as a public nuisance.

"Until we check further into it," the lawman said, as the *San Francisco Chronicle* reported on April 23, 1954, "we'd rather that it not be broadcast."

This was an extraordinary request, tantamount to police acting without a court's authority to suggest that a newspaper withhold from publishing its next edition. But the times, too, were extraordinarily fraught. Subversives, or at least their shadows, were everywhere. The clash between Senator Joseph McCarthy and the U.S. Army was capturing the stage in televised Senate hearings. California Governor Goodwin Knight was proclaiming the upcoming May 1 to be "Loyalty Day," when all good Americans could renounce atheistic communism. Nor was communism the only wolf at the door. Marijuana, too, was spooking straight America. Only days before Red and Lola toked up on air, the attorney general's Citizen's Advisory Committee warned of pot's dangers, calling the herb an outright threat to the social and moral order.

California Attorney General Edmund "Pat" Brown denounced the KPFA show, while state chief of narcotics enforcement Walter Creighton complained that after hearing the potheads rave about their elixir, "any one on the fence about the stuff might go overboard and start using it." Authorities copied the tape, sending it to the Federal Communications Commission. The station issued a public statement declaring the program "an important social document of interest to all who seek a sincere and enlightened understanding of the narcotics problem." The statement did not mollify very many. As subscription director, Roy had helped attract six hundred new paying subscribers between October 1953 and May 1954. By the time of the marijuana show, the station had 3,300 subscribers, and some of them were very displeased. Roy's job was to mollify and explain.

"The basic question was one of the right of a radio station to free expression on any of a number of controversial subjects," Roy advised one unhappy subscriber. "Unfortunately, when one's right to free expression is challenged, the challenge comes not upon the issues one would choose but upon the bad issues."

Attorney General Brown conceded that his narcotics officers had no right to unilaterally seize the tape, and on April 24 he ordered that the tape be returned to KPFA. Still, Brown urged the station not to rebroadcast the pot program at any time when impressionable children might be listening. Public affairs director Wallace Hamilton complied. A cum laude graduate of Harvard, Hamilton had served, like Roy, first in the Campton Civilian Public Service camp in New Hampshire's bitterly cold White Mountains and then as an orderly in a hospital. The *San Francisco Chronicle* reported on April 27, 1954, that Hamilton declared the controversial program would not air again, even as narcotics officer Creighton said his men were still going to track down the speakers to determine if they were addicts or could be booked on a possession charge.

For KPFA the controversy came at a particularly sensitive time. Though Lew Hill had resigned in the summer of 1953, he and his allies had undertaken what historian Lasar called a government in exile. Hill was waiting for his opportunity, and the marijuana show provided it. His close ally Eleanor McKinney wrote the *Chronicle* on May 13, 1954, proclaiming herself "shocked at the human indifference which would expose users of an illegal drug to possible prosecution for the sake of satisfying sociological curiosity." Behind the scenes, McKinney was passing along word about how Roy had seemed to ramble on for hours when discussing the show and its implications for KPFA.

By early May two dozen members of KPFA's outside advisory committee had resigned in protest. The marijuana incident "further confirms our lack of confidence" in the station management, the advisory committee members declared. One advisory committee member, former University of California–Berkeley School of Education dean Frank Freeman, filed a complaint with the Federal Communications Commission. The Ford Foundation, whose timely three-year grant had enabled the station to grow, announced it would withhold the final year's payment until the station settled down (Lasar 1999, 154).

Roy thought McKinney and Hill's other allies were fanning the flames, using the controversy to smoke out the competition. Even before the pot show, Roy wrote, "the Hill group kept predicting KPFA's financial collapse publicly and then worked privately to bring it about." Management conflict was a private affair that should be handled discretely, he thought. The high-profile resignation of Freeman and other advisory board members further "succeeded in making my job more difficult," Roy advised a friend.

He was already fending off other threats. Republican Senator Alexander Wiley of Wisconsin, who a decade earlier had survived a primary challenge by a young Joe McCarthy, was now talking about imposing loyalty oath requirements on radio license holders. Roy acknowledged to one friend that "of all the radio stations in this free land, most will probably cooperate," but in July and early August he was nonetheless coordinating opposition with the Friends Committee on National Legislation and others. The dangerous loyalty oath idea had to be killed quickly before it gained momentum, Roy thought.

Roy wrote Senator Wiley himself on August 3, stating that the loyalty oath proposals seriously threatened basic American freedoms. It would be one of Roy's last acts as a paid KPFA employee. Energized by the marijuana show controversy, the rival KPFA alliances had been maneuvering all summer, and on August 4, 1954, a new KPFA board dominated by Lew Hill enthusiasts was elected. The new board members said they would create a new position of president of the Pacifica Foundation and of the KPFA radio station. Hill, of course, would take the job.

That was it. Roy, station manager Wallace Hamilton, William Triest, and two others gave two weeks' notice. They were quitting, effective August 6.

"We don't believe . . . that Hill is the 'greatest ethical teacher since Christ,'" Roy wrote, dismissing one of the airier enthusiasms heard around the station. In fact, Roy added, "we don't care to work under his authoritarian direction."

Good riddance, Hill thought. He had come to consider Roy as nothing more than a troublesome subscription clerk. The restored KPFA leadership accepted Roy's resignation and granted him his remaining salary, as well as pay for two weeks' vacation. Beyond that, Hill offered him the back of his hand. After Roy left the station, Hill directed that Roy's mail not be forwarded. The mail, Hill reasoned, belonged to the station and not to the former employee. The Berkeley postmaster wrote Roy on September 7 to advise that since the ownership of the mail was officially in dispute, it would be held at the post office until the matter could be resolved.

Roy, in turn, deployed his knowledge of the French Revolution to heatedly critique Hill and his allies. In his account "The Terror During KPFA's Revolution: A Chronicle of Division and Dissent," Roy likened the pacifist radio pioneers to the ruthless leaders of 1789. "Hill," Roy wrote, "was forever seeking to hold all of the strings of authority or [was] unilaterally carrying out actions and commitments in the name of the organization for which he did not have the support of the majority."

Lew Hill did not long enjoy his triumphal return to KPFA. The work itself was draining. By December 1954 Roy was noting with some grim satisfaction that, "in true Hill fashion, [KPFA's] costs have gone up," adding that he still lacked any faith in Hill's "management or his integrity." Roy showed no particular sympathy for Hill's physical state, which was deteriorating. Diagnosed with spinal arthritis, Hill at times needed help in simply arising from his chair. He was increasingly reliant on pain medication, but even huge jolts of cortisone couldn't always muffle the agony. In time it would all became too much. In August 1957 Hill would attach a garden hose to the exhaust pipe of his green 1953 Dodge and with a dose of redirected carbon monoxide retire from his misery. He left behind a note, explaining or not: "not for anger or despair / but for peace and a kind of home" (Land 1999, 60).

The public radio station notion that Hill pioneered would spread out from Berkeley, with Pacifica's KPFK starting in Los Angeles in July 1959, followed by WBAI in New York City in January 1960.

Roy's own severance from KPFA would not last forever. He would pay attention when the Red-hunters of the Senate Internal Security Subcommittee convened in January 1963 for extended hearings into the Pacifica Foundation's supposedly radical ties, even though he was not an investigative target. In 1965 he would appear in the KPFA studios with pacifist allies for a series of extended on-air discussions about war and peace, and he would offer solo commentaries during the most heated moments of the Vietnam War protests of the late 1960s.

But as a salaried employee, Roy was out for good with his 1954 resignation. He needed to find something new. Patricia was pregnant, preparing for natural childbirth, and money was scarce. Along with the other KPFA expatriates, he briefly considered exploring commercial radio possibilities, but they seemed slim and, frankly, not all that interesting. Roy considered a six-month stint with the American Friends Service Committee's latest antidraft campaign. A Unitarian church in Berkeley needed help with fundraising. A KPFA subscriber in Monterey discussed with Roy a rather vague job that would only require about fifty hours a month, This would leave Roy time to write; perhaps, he thought, it would be his chance to write a book about French Revolution Terror.

The vague Monterey job prospects evaporated like coastal fog. Roy thought briefly of newspaper work, but that went nowhere. Roy wrote Henry Geiger, an ex-CPS character living in Los Angeles, and suggested coming to work in Southern California to manage Geiger's printing operation. Geiger had gotten his publishing start in the Glendora CPS camp, where he edited the intellectually provocative *Pacifica Views* newspaper. Once back in civilian life, Geiger started *MANAS*, a little magazine of ideas closely read by fellow pacifists.

The *MANAS* job didn't work out, though Roy would periodically write for the periodical starting in December 1953. Instead, Roy established himself as the "director" of Pacifica Research Associates. It was a fancy name for a one-man operation operating from the Kepler home. Citing the "unmanageable mass of material" flowing through newspapers, magazines, and more, Roy noted that "the pacifist, world government . . . civil liberties and reform groups" had become unable to muster research resources "comparable to those available to the forces with which they are competing." Roy's four-page solicitation letter advised potential clients that "the professional services of Pacifica Associates" would be more efficient information-gatherers. Roy offered a "review and purview" of newspapers and periodicals. Subscribers could order clippings in any of fifteen areas, from "H-bomb" to "race relations."

Roy did not limit himself to the research proposal. In an August 1954 letter to Robert Smith of the Palo Alto Co-Op, Roy explained that he was "beginning to scout the field to learn what the possibilities are for the kind of work I would like to do (first priority) and the work I may have to do (second priority)." In an August 13, 1954, letter, he asked Trevor Thomas of the Friends Committee on Legislation about "any openings in the field of general social betterment."

Roy spent the fall of 1954 stringing together pitches and letters, in between which he conducted a constant dialogue with the world. An early October article in the *Oakland Tribune* about civil defense planning spurred Roy to write denouncing "the whole farce of so-called civil defense from H-bombs." It would make much more sense, Roy urged *Oakland Tribune* readers on October 5, 1954, for Americans to put their energies into preventing war. Roy believed the main effect of Civil Defense planning was to condition the public to think that something could actually be done about a nuclear war. That simply made nuclear war more likely. Roy put it bluntly: It would be better to build a fence at the edge of the cliff to prevent war, rather than run an ambulance below the cliff for the benefit of any survivors.

City officials didn't share Roy's radical perspective. But in their own way, some were coming to question the air raid exercises. City managers in Oakland and Piedmont, among others, wondered whether the monthly alarms were wearing out their welcome. "Many of us feel that any further tests would be much like the proverbial boy crying wolf," Oakland City Manager Wayne E. Thompson cautioned in the *Oakland Tribune* on November 27, 1954.

On November 25, two days before Thompson's declaration, Patricia had given birth to a daughter, the Keplers' first. She was Dawn, a healthy child. Roy and Patricia had every reason to be happy, except for the fact that Roy still didn't know exactly how he would be making a living over the long term. But though he didn't know it, at the age of thirty-four Roy was on the verge of finding his right livelihood.

7

Kepler's Books & Magazines

Paperbacks were a problem child.

They were coarse, cheap, and morally soft. Proper books were hard clad, a firm handshake between High Culture and Dear Reader. Downtown Palo Alto, a fundamentally conservative university town in the mid-1950s, had several booksellers that maintained strict hardcover standards. The Stanford Bookstore buyer, content with her campus textbook monopoly, shunned the paperbound slop as unworthy. "She thought they weren't really books," Roy recalled in a 1984 interview. This sentiment prevailed among gentlemanly purveyors of serious literature, "the sherry and biscuit boys," as author Kenneth C. Davis called them. When a Penguin Books salesman first approached the venerable Old Corner Bookstore in Boston, shortly before World War II, the owner assured him that paperbacks would "be dead and gone in five years" (Davis 1984, 54).

But the revolution had already begun.

Penguin Books arrived with its first ten offerings in July 1935. Penguin was an immediate hit, inviting Pelican Books to follow. It was likely a Pelican Book that introduced Roy to George Bernard Shaw's two-volume *Intelligent Woman's Guide to Socialism, Capitalism and Sovietism*. One success bred another. The patrician publisher Robert de Graff had used Pearl Buck's popular novel *The Good Earth* to test the concept of an inexpensive paperback service, an idea formalized in 1939 that was made formal with Pocket Books (Davis 1984, 31). Pocket Books announced itself in a June 13, 1939, *New York Times* advertisement, proclaiming that the new paperback editions were "handy as a pencil, as modern and convenient as a portable radio, and as good looking."

War propelled the business. The mass mobilization of World War II expanded the market, as the Red Cross and the military began buying millions of books for a captive audience. Business boomed for Pocket Books and the British-based Penguin Books. When paper shortages and overseas distribution impediments proved troublesome, civilian and military officials combined to produce, starting in June 1943, the Armed Services Editions. A mix of fiction and nonfiction, each volume vetted by army and navy officials, the Armed Services Edition line produced upwards of forty books a month. By war's end, the Armed Services Edition had published 1,324 titles and circulated some 123 million paperback copies (Bonn 1982, 48). These were stapled, cheaply printed, and precious beyond measure to men far from home and fighting for their lives. The captain could pass the paperback to the sergeant who would pass it to the private who would send it around the barracks, the cover avulsing a little more with each handoff.

"The books are read until they're so dirty you can't see the print," one soldier reported gratefully. "To heave one in the garbage can would be tantamount to striking your grandmother" (Tebbell 1987, 345).

In the Civilian Public Service world too, books were a precious commodity. Some of Roy's camps, like Gatlinburg, had reasonably good little libraries. The men would also swap books among themselves and occasionally sell them for a pittance. In Germfask, Roy had once paid a dime to get an evening's worth of reading. The pacifists and the soldiers were alike in discovering books during World War II, and an industry had found a market. In 1939 some 3 million copies of paperback books were published. By 1951 the paperback population had reached an estimated 214 million. New publishing houses seemed to arise annually, each finding their respective niches.

Avon Books was begun by the hard men of the American News Company, the muscle behind magazine distribution. Avon catered to the popular market with blood-and-guts titles like Rex Stout's *Over My Dead Body*. Dell Books began in 1943, offering the equally morbid likes of *See You at the Morgue*. In 1945 Bantam Books entered the field, favoring Westerns (Davis 1984, 126). The new business was a natural fit for magazine publishers, with their existing distribution

channels and their fingers on the pulse of the mass market. The Fawcett family, for one, had gotten its under-the-counter publishing start
when World War I veteran Wilford H. Fawcett returned from Europe
with a footlocker full of randy French jokes. Fawcett published *True,*
for male readers, and *True Confessions,* for women, and then in 1950
the company launched a succession of original Westerns, mysteries,
and thrillers under the Gold Medal Books name.

Checkbooks began opening up. Norman Mailer's World War
II novel *The Naked and the Dead* secured a record $35,000 for its
paperback publishing rights in 1949. It was an opening shot in what
would ultimately become a literary arms race. Instead of the traditional twenty-five-cent paperback, New American Library declared
it would sell longer books for thirty-five cents, starting with Richard Wright's *Native Son.* Bantam and Pocket Books soon jumped in,
and in 1952 Ballantine and Ace arrived. Prices rose to fifty cents,
as meatier hardcover books were reprinted and sold as paperbacks.
Doubleday's Anchor Books, starting in 1952, and Alfred A. Knopf's
Vintage Books further raised the standards with serious-minded trade
paperbacks targeting the academic and literary set. David Dempsey
summed up the mixed bag in January 1953, writing in the *Atlantic
Monthly* that with some twenty paperback publishing houses, paperbacks had become "a highly competitive mélange of serious literature and trash, of self-help and pseudo-science, of sex and inspiration"
(Dempsey 1953).

Sex especially.

Sex was pimping sales for even the most exalted of classics. Critic
Bernard DeVoto, in an October 1954 *Harper's* essay that dismissed
paperback publishers as "tripe merchants," described "the covers [that]
showed next year's Miss America hurrying out of her brassiere or slid-
ing out of her nightshirt, and the blurb [saying] 'She LONGED to be
raped! Read Longfellow's *Evangeline,* a torrid story of unnatural lusts
that omits no details.'" He was hardly exaggerating. Popular Library
offered a buxom babe adorning the 1948 edition of John Erskine's
The Private Life of Helen of Troy. "Her lust," the cover explained,
"caused the Trojan War."

Violence beckoned as well, Mars wed to Venus.

Mickey Spillane was Roy's particular bête noire, the sick, dark beast of popular culture. Spillane's Mike Hammer embodied the crude, vengeance-seeking violence that Roy abhorred. "A scream [was] starting to come up out of his throat," Mike Hammer recounted, characteristically, in *The Big Kill*, "only to get cut off in the middle as I pounded his teeth back into his mouth with the end of the barrel." The reading public ate this stuff up (Server 1994). By 1951, the year *The Big Kill* muscled it way onto bookshelves, more than five million copies of Spillane's Mike Hammer novels had been sold. In his writings and KPFA commentaries, Roy repeatedly cited Spillane as an example of what he called the vulgarian culture.

The House Select Committee on Current Pornographic Materials had warned in 1952 that paperbacks had "largely degenerated into media for the dissemination of artful appeals to sensuality, immorality, filth, perversion and degeneracy." Honestly, the politicians had a point. They also had cast a troublingly wide net. Urged on by the National Organization for Decent Literature, the House committee drafted a list of objectionable books that included the literary likes of James T. Farrell's *Young Lonigan* and John Steinbeck's *The Wayward Bus* (Davis 1984, 221). More than one monitor of the nation's moral fiber agreed with Newark's public safety director John B. Keenan, who made the connection between the international Communist conspiracy and the torrent of filth undermining America's bedrock values. The nation was under assault, from within and without.

It took courage to enter this paperback jungle. In the San Francisco Bay Area, three outposts arose within a few years of each other. They would be three points of a magic triangle. Between them, Roy Kepler, Lawrence Ferlinghetti, and the team of Pat and Fred Cody would build the stores in which a generation would find itself.

Lawrence Ferlinghetti arrived first.

Born in 1919, one year before Roy, Ferlinghetti had an unconventional upbringing. When his Italian immigrant father died and his middle-aged mother was committed to a hospital following a nervous breakdown, Ferlinghetti shipped off to France to live with an aunt and uncle. A New England boarding school further groomed him, and he studied at the University of North Carolina before enlisting in the navy for World War II service. He rose to command a 110-foot wooden submarine chaser, a compact warship for whose crew he ordered a complete set of Modern Library volumes. He stashed the books in every nook and cranny.

Shortly after Japan surrendered, while Roy was still encamped in Minersville, Ferlinghetti and his ship arrived at the Japanese port town of Sasebo. On a day off, Ferlinghetti and some shipmates took a train about thirty miles to Nagasaki. The blistered city, Ferlinghetti later recalled in the *San Francisco Chronicle* of June 8, 2003, "was like three square miles of nothing but mulch." The experience, he said, made him an "instant pacifist."

Ferlinghetti, like Roy, found his postwar way back to France, where he earned his doctorate from the Sorbonne. Puckishly, Ferlinghetti spread the word in later years that his thesis concerned the bidet. In reality, the dissertation was a conventional enough academic work entitled "The City as Symbol in Modern Poetry: In Search of the Metropolitan Tradition." His thesis done, Ferlinghetti came back to San Francisco in January 1951. The City, as some fashioned it, seemed open to all and anything. It was politically tolerant and ethnically diverse. For those equipped with the right radio, KPFA offered an intelligent soundtrack. For those seeking opportunity, it offered chance encounters.

"I was driving up Columbus Avenue," Ferlinghetti recounted. "It was just when I was discovering North Beach. And I saw this guy putting up a sign . . . and it said, Pocket Book Shop. So I got out of the car and I went over, and I said, 'what are you doing?'" (Sileski 1990, 56).

Peter Martin introduced himself. A San Francisco State sociology professor and publisher of a short-lived pop culture magazine called *City Lights,* Martin told Ferlinghetti that he intended to sell pocket books as a way to fund the magazine. It sounded good to Ferlinghetti. In June 1953 he and Martin each put up $500 and opened the City

Lights Pocket Book Shop at the corner of Broadway and Columbus in San Francisco's North Beach. City Lights offered paperbacks and attitude. Ferlinghetti and Martin stocked the shelves with books from New Directions Press and the likes of William Carlos Williams, Albert Camus, and Ezra Pound. The poet and intellectual omnivore Kenneth Rexroth, by then a KPFA personality, became a regular. The store expanded beyond one room. In 1955 Martin divested his interest in the store for $1,000 and moved back to New York, where in time he started the New Yorker Bookstore in Manhattan.

Since leaving KPFA, Roy had been casting about professionally. "My hope," he explained in a December 28, 1954, letter, "had been to have a basic job and basic income with enough time and freedom of action left over to seek out particular freelance radio and public relations jobs."

He dabbled, getting hired at one point to help pull a small Bay Area business away from the brink of bankruptcy. Roy reported that he worked out a plan with the chief creditors to save the business. The creditors set up a three-man committee to oversee the business, and then they fired Roy as being too expensive. "I succeeded so well that I eliminated myself from the picture," Roy advised Bayard Rustin in a December 20, 1954, letter. It was a lesson Roy took to heart. He told friends that December that before he would work for another boss, he would give self-employment a serious try. But doing what?

There was always peace work, of course. Rustin had sent Roy a veiled inquiry about his availability to help the War Resisters League, and Roy offered to prepare a fundraising campaign. Roy feared the League was frittering away its focus, devoting resources to side projects like sending books and clothing to Africa when all attention should be paid to the primary goal of fighting conscription. A WRL and Peacemakers member named Bill Sutherland had been dispatched to Africa on a peace mission. Roy confided to Rustin on December 20 that this was "worthy perhaps for getting rid of Sutherland," but that Sutherland had accomplished little except to "marry an African poetess." The sardonic assessment captured Roy's edge. For a pacifist, he could cut to the quick.

Roy declared himself "willing to be designated" as the WRL's West Coast secretary, perhaps on a six-month trial basis. He could handle all of the League's mailings, thereby relieving burdens on the League's New York City headquarters. The League certainly needed the help. Its membership had dwindled to below one thousand and its budget was bare bones at about $9,000 a year. This pitch didn't go far, but Roy had other ideas. He conceived of a research and documentation service, providing information to peace and civil libertarian organizations. He floated the idea to the National Council for the Prevention of War. Roy and a friend then conceived a new plan, prompted by an article Roy read in *Collier's* magazine about Western oral histories. Roy and his friend would conduct oral histories of their own, interviewing old-time Californians for their reminiscences. Roy wrote the National Association of Educational Broadcasters and the California Historical Society, requesting modest grants.

"When properly woven together, it would be of interest to anybody who has ever been fascinated by the West, its development and its symbol[ism]," Roy explained in a February 16, 1955, letter.

The broadcasters association was sympathetic but could offer little money. Roy kept looking, while he squeezed in side activities like attending War Resisters League meetings. He delighted in talking again with old friends, but he felt glum. The pacifist organization, as ever, was struggling, seeking relevance. Membership meetings were ill-attended. In peacetime, people grew indifferent. Roy said the WRL needed to work on the fundamentals: more field trips, and faster reports to the members. He noted that his own three-month trip in 1949 cost the League only $200 in expenses, because he lived frugally and accepted the hospitality of others whenever he could. He urged that the League's limited staff avoid purely local and ephemeral matters.

More broadly, Roy was applying business lessons honed at KPFA over the past two years. Make personal contacts. Meet face to face. Ask for what is wanted. Follow up requests. Be creative. Perhaps, Roy suggested, the War Resisters League could hold a contest with "prizes substantial enough to attract good writers."

Roy persevered in his own writing. With fellow Civilian Public Service alumnus Henry Geiger, he found an outlet. Geiger was a self-educated, self-made character who had learned about many corners of the world as a journalist, as a commercial printer, and, improbably, as a Broadway chorus boy. At Glendora, after Roy had left the camp, Geiger had founded the weekly newspaper *Pacifica Views.* Like Roy, he combined business savvy with idealism. Postwar, Geiger was making money by doing fine art printing. In January 1948 he started an eight-page newsletter called *MANAS,* styled a "weekly journal of independent inquiry." The official circulation never rose above three thousand, but Geiger was able to attract contributors ranging from Henry Miller and Marc Chagall to death row inmate Caryl Chessman and former University of Chicago president Robert Hutchins. It was not explicitly a pacifist periodical, though that was the tendency.

Starting in 1953, Roy began contributing thought pieces.

"Let us begin," Roy expounded in his inaugural December 2, 1953, essay, "by considering for a moment the matter of American cultural mediocrity . . . certainly it requires no great effort to make a devastating case against it. American society is vulgarian, and often anti-intellectual."

There it was, that term again: "vulgarian." Roy had seized upon it. It was his fundamental diagnosis of mid-century America, Mickey Spillane's country. But Roy was not just sardonic; he was also idealistic. He insisted the "common man" could still free himself from the onslaught of commerce and government propaganda. Gandhi, with his path of abstinence and asceticism, provided one of the "roads to freedom," Roy advised. Relatively few Americans would shed entirely their material comforts, Roy conceded, but they could learn. Abundance need not be inevitably destructive to the soul. There was hope. Men could learn.

Publication was gratifying, and *MANAS* reached an interesting if small audience, but Roy still confronted the practical question of how he would make a living. Reading newspapers and clipping articles would not pay all the bills. He was circulating a résumé in which he described himself as "seeking connection in the field of public relations." He trumpeted his experience in direct mail and promoting subscriptions. He was willing to relocate.

In February and March 1955 Roy began traveling through the Bay Area on behalf of the Eastern News Company. Eastern News distributed books and magazines to roughly 850 outlets nationwide. Roy was checking out the region's available bookstores and newsstands, seeking likely outlets for books and magazines. He had mixed success. The University of California's bookstore manager told Roy he would try to free up more magazine space. The book buyer at nearby Mills College, too, seemed amenable to Roy's push; the small women's college increased an existing order. But Oakland, overall, was a cultural desert, nearly devoid of decent newsstands. Roy talked to the manager of Capwell's, the city's leading downtown department store, and came away unimpressed.

"The stand carries no trashy stuff," Roy advised Jack Zucker of Eastern News on March 24, 1955, "but, on the other hand, it is mostly the usual women's mediocrities: *McCall's, Better Homes,* etc."

Roy's scouting work for the Eastern News Company paid the bills. It was also a bookselling boot camp. He learned how distribution companies serviced newsstands throughout the country. He learned the Bay Area's cultural geography, the gross and subtle differences that separated, say, shaded Menlo Park from the grittier Redwood City. He confronted those he called "the hard-boiled magazine men" who ran stands along San Francisco's Market Street. Liquor stores in Contra Costa County, east of San Francisco, were better than newsstands, but in Alameda County, home of Oakland, Roy found that liquor store owners had no interest in magazines. One Monday near the end of March, Roy was peddling magazines to Oakland outlets like the ABC Cigar Stores, The Bottle Shop, and Barrett's Smoke Shop.

"Tough country," Roy sighed in a March 30, 1955, letter to Zucker.

Still, the more Roy looked, the more possibilities he saw for initiating a regional distribution scheme. By March 31 he was advising

Zucker that he could envision a "step-by-step plan of moving into local book distribution, starting very modestly in San Francisco, reaching out to Oakland and Berkeley, and perhaps later a shot down the Peninsula toward Palo Alto." Palo Alto definitely had promise. It was Stanford University country, populated with literate professionals. Palo Alto was not large, with a population of only 41,000, but it and the surrounding communities of Menlo Park and Los Altos abounded with readers.

In mid-April Roy pitched Eastern News with a proposal for permanently taking over the distribution firm's West Coast accounts. It made sense, Roy believed, to establish a central distribution center to handle the region's business. The idea fizzled. Jack Zucker advised Roy that his company had barely been skimming by in recent years, and it could not afford Roy's vision of a new West Coast distribution center. Zucker added that he was willing to consider other ways for Roy to make money on a temporary basis. Perhaps, he suggested, Eastern might pay $5 for every magazine account that Roy signed up. Roy, though, had conceived another notion.

"Despite the fact that we seem unable to work out an arrangement at this time, you have gotten me interested in magazines and books," Roy told Zucker on April 18.

As he traveled about, Roy had observed that bookstores were, actually, relatively scarce. Though drugstores and variety stores carried the vulgarian paperback slop that Roy despised, devoted readers might travel a long way to find a stand-alone bookseller. Nationwide, there were fewer than 8,360 bookstores in the mid-1950s, and this for a country of 165 million (Miller 2006, 30). The vast majority of stores confined themselves to hardcover books: Real books, that is. Roy found the Stanford and Palo Alto area to be one such underserved region. There were traditional bookstores and there were newsstands, but no good paperback outlet.

"The region could easily, in my opinion, support a U.C. Corner," Roy observed in an April 18, 1955, letter to Zucker, referring to a venerable Berkeley bookstand. "Therefore, I am tempted, on extremely limited capital, to try to be the guy who tries it out."

This was it: Roy's first avowed interest in bookselling. As it happened, the epiphany occurred shortly after the April 10 death of War Resisters League founder Jessie Wallace Hughan at the age of seventy-nine. Hughan had been the grande dame of pacifism, an inspirational figure whom Roy respected even when he differed with her on tactics. Roy could but note her passing as he zeroed in on the details of his current life. He began asking Zucker on April 18 what advice might be offered on shelving, discounts, payment arrangement, and the like.

"Who knows?" Roy mused to Zucker. "If something like this got going, we might build such a store into a kind of depository . . ."

In less than a month, it would be done.

Roy had a modest vision. He wasn't contemplating a major book emporium, but rather a solid little place that offered periodicals, newspapers, and quality paperback books. Roy asked Zucker for advice on setting up the business, as well as for special price breaks. Roy and Patricia looked further into the possibilities and into their own limited finances. There were many obstacles, not least the competition from existing bookstores already serving Stanford and its leafy environs. Three, in particular, stood out.

Bell's College Books on Emerson Street in downtown Palo Alto was an elegant establishment, run by the multitalented Herbert Bell. A sometimes tart Alabama native, the kind of man who would build his own harpsichord for fun, Bell had first arrived in Palo Alto in 1935 bearing a load of textbooks stashed in the backseat of his car. He opened his College Book Store in 1936, moving to a new location under the Bell's name in 1953. Shirley Cobb's Books was also in downtown. Shirley Cobb, the daughter of fiery baseball great Ty Cobb, was a strong-willed woman who in 1940 had opened her bookstore on downtown's University Avenue. Like Herbert Bell, Cobb ran a good bookstore but could wound those who crossed her.

"She yelled at everybody," Ira Sandperl recalled in an interview, "because Ty yelled at her."

Then there was the Stanford Bookstore itself, which essentially printed its own money. Each year, like clockwork, the university bookstore would render a $10,000 contribution to the university and a 10 to 12 percent rebate to customers. The Stanford Bookstore was a self-satisfied establishment, doing business as it always had. Although some university leaders were beginning to think that at 5,900 square feet the store was too small, and its stock too stodgy with texts and trinkets, it would not change quickly.

In the space between these existing stores, Roy saw a niche. The question that dogged him since leaving KPFA now had an answer. He could both support his family and do a world of good by selling books. It made perfect sense. He knew books well. He was an experienced organizer. He knew marketing and promotions. Selling books wouldn't scour his soul. He could make the bottom line. Bookselling, some said at the time, was a very interesting way to make very little money. Roy could live with that.

In short order Roy and Patricia pulled together about $4,000 from their meager savings. They scrounged fixtures, and Roy ordered the books he liked or thought would sell. The San Francisco Bay Area bestseller lists that spring were topped by Françoise Sagan's *Bonjour Tristesse* and Norman Vincent Peale's *The Power of Positive Thinking*. Less conventionally, Grove Press offered Roy the likes of Herman Melville's *The Confidence Man* and Erich Fromm's *The Forgotten Language*. Anchor Books and Vintage Books made available high-quality lit like Thomas Mann's *Death in Venice*.

It was mid-May 1955, the very solstice of the fifties. Bay Area radio listeners were tuning in to Red Skelton and the Cisco Kid. Television viewers comforted themselves with Tennessee Ernie Ford. A visiting air force colonel was reassuring the Stanford Mothers' Club that month about the virtues of military training, and no one disputed him. When, amid Roy's store preparations, the American Friends Service Committee convened a meeting to discuss military enlistment legislation, only four Stanford students showed up. And few noticed when, on a mild, sunny Sunday, May 15, 1955, barely a month after

Roy had first floated the notion, Kepler's Books & Magazines opened at 939 El Camino Real in Menlo Park.

El Camino Real is a commercial drag, connecting San Jose in the south to San Francisco in the north. It encourages neither dawdling nor window-shopping, and the passing traffic could easily miss the new Kepler's Books & Magazines. Even pedestrians could pass unknowingly by the store that more closely resembled a walk-in closet. Kepler's was a narrow, unadorned, single room, a row of eight shelves along both sides and another row down the middle. Fine art posters hung rather haphazardly on the walls. The staff was, more or less, Roy himself. To make change, Roy sometimes fished out coins from his own pocket.

But the store had its advantages, starting with Roy's work ethic. Kepler's stayed open from 10 a.m. until 11 p.m. six days a week, and between 5 p.m. and 10 p.m. on Sundays. Late-night book browsers, a special breed, started spreading the word. The location, too, proved felicitous. The Guild Theater next door, Patricia Kepler recalled, "always had lines and lines of people" waiting for a movie. During Kepler's opening week, couples arrived to see the British comedy *Doctor in the House* and then, curious, some popped their heads into the little book nook. The next date night, some would arrive earlier or stay later.

The movie *Diabolique* was showing at the Guild in 1956. One night a Palo Alto–area high school student and budding word-slinger named Robert Hunter went to see the French flick with its famously twisted ending. It was raining when the movie concluded, and Hunter ducked into the little book joint next door. He liked what he saw. He could browse poetry, philosophy, religion. Every idea in the world beckoned, at paperback prices or no price at all, just the investment of standing at the shelves and thumbing through the books for free. Hunter would keep returning. In several years, he and his newfound pal Jerry Garcia would be hanging out at a larger and relocated Kepler's. And a half-century later, Hunter would still fondly recall the vivid first impression made by his initial entry into the little bookstore next to the Menlo Park movie theater.

5. The early Kepler's Books & Magazines, circa 1956. Photographer unknown, courtesy of the Kepler family.

The Guild was likewise what first brought Kentucky writer Ed McClanahan into the Kepler's orbit. McClanahan says he was "trying and failing" to be a Stanford graduate student between September 1955 and April 1956 when, one night, he went with a friend to see a movie at the Guild. Afterward, they drifted into the plain-looking little bookstore.

"I was immediately struck by the fact that he had all these literary quarterlies that you couldn't get anywhere else," McClanahan said.

Kepler's offerings *were* uncommonly literate. Roy would carry the year's popular paperbacks, the likes of Leon Uris's *Battle Cry,* but browsers could find more offbeat publications as well. In October 1955 Roy urged customers not to be "half-red, be well-read" as he promoted David Reisman's newly published *Individualism Reconsidered* as well as out-of-left-field selections such as Friedrich von Gentz's *French and American Revolutions Compared*. The seemingly oddball choice of books to promote was telling, on several fronts. Roy, with his past Fulbright studies of the Terror, was surely playing to his own interests with Herr Gentz's early nineteenth-century work. A popular best-seller it was not. But that was Roy, an undying individualist, heedless of the crowd. He was also an egalitarian. He credited his customers with having an intellectual curiosity equal to his own. And, he was an effective marketer, signaling his store's unique, nonvulgarian character. Readers could find in Roy's little store fresh provocations from publishers such as New Directions, Thinkers Library, and Evergreen, as well as the work of authors unlikely to be found in more conventional stores.

"We were probably the only bookstore on the Peninsula with books by and about Marx," Roy recalled. "I remember people asking, 'isn't it illegal to have that book?'"

Marx, in fact, was legal. Others, for a time, were dicey.

In November 1956 Lawrence Ferlinghetti's City Lights published Allen Ginsberg's *Howl and Other Poems*. The publication had its roots in the spirited night of October 7, 1955, when Ginsberg joined poets Gary Snyder, Michael McClure, Philip Lamantia, and Philip Whalen in declaiming their poems at the Six Gallery, an old auto repair shop turned artists' cooperative on San Francisco's Fillmore Street. Theirs was poetry as performance, words become flesh. "Go!" an enraptured Jack Kerouac had shouted while he passed round the red wine jugs. "Go!"

Kerouac would later enshrine the experience in his novel *The Dharma Bums*, and Beat Generation historians and acolytes would count it as a pivotal historical event. Roy missed it. Poetry jams and cheap California burgundy were not his scene. Ferlinghetti, though, caught the moment. He approached Ginsburg, and hence came the November 1956 publication of *Howl and Other Poems*.

"I saw the best minds of my generation destroyed by madness," Ginsburg wrote, and then descended to the nitty-gritty in his nearly three-thousand-word poem.

Dismayed by what Ginsburg's saintly motorcyclists were doing in the poem, and to whom, U.S. Customs Service officials seized copies of the book from entering the United States after it was printed in England. San Francisco police charged both Ferlinghetti and coworker Shig Murao in San Francisco Municipal Court. The American Civil Liberties Union took up the defense, and in October 1957 Judge Clayton Horn ruled that *Howl* couldn't be judged obscene if it had redeeming social importance. Throughout the legal fight Kepler's carried *Howl* and other City Lights' publications shunned by the straitlaced.

This took courage. Police officers through the mid-1950s had a habit of cleansing bookshelves they found filthy. The Jersey City police chief in 1953 had strongly encouraged local bookstores to rid themselves of James Jones's *From Here to Eternity,* and Detroit officials ordered John O'Hara's *Ten North Frederick* off local shelves in 1957 (Davis 1984, 241). Once, in later years, the Menlo Park chief of police personally directed a Kepler's clerk to remove *Playboy* from public display. The clerk complied.

"When I returned from San Francisco and was told of the incident, I put the issues back on the stand," Roy recounted, explaining to the clerk that "my store is not operated on the basis of allowing the police to select which books or periodicals shall appear."

With the new store demanding all his time, Roy had less opportunity for radical activism, though he could appreciate the demonstrations being staged by his old War Resisters League colleagues. He could admire the audacity of Bayard Rustin, Jim Peck, and David Dellinger when they were among twenty-eight individuals arrested in New York City on June 15, 1955, for refusing to cooperate with a civil defense drill called Operation Alert. Instead of seeking shelter as ordered, the protestors remained aboveground and defiant in a city park (Bennett 2003). The civil defense protests would grow in coming years, until the drills themselves collapsed altogether.

The bookselling business, too, was growing. Kepler's was also gaining company. The third of the San Francisco Bay Area's paperback triumvirate was about to be planted with Roy's help.

Fred Cody, a World War II Army Air Corps veteran, had been attending Columbia University on the GI Bill in the fall of 1945 when he met a young economics graduate student named Pat. They married in 1946, moving to Mexico City for several years, where Fred worked on his master's degree in history and Pat wrote for a small tourist newspaper. They then moved to London, where Fred finished his PhD in Latin American history. From a chance encounter with another couple while crossing the English Channel during the winter of 1951, Pat and Fred set their minds next on sunny California. Arriving by train with their accumulated savings of $854, the couple settled into Berkeley. Pat kept writing economics reports, and Fred landed a job promoting the Paper Editions Book Club in Palo Alto (Cody and Cody 1992, xxi).

The book club capsized in the spring of 1956, costing Fred his job. Like Roy when he left KPFA, Pat and Fred were cast out. Like Roy, they gravitated to the idea of a bookstore. Pat, with her economics degree and eye for the bottom line, could handle the finances. Fred had picked up a serviceable knowledge of the publishing industry through his work with the paperback book club. The idea of being their own bosses appealed to them. A bookstore it would be.

With Roy's assistance, Fred and Pat began pulling together the threads. They researched different locations before settling on Berkeley. The existing Berkeley university bookstore, like Stanford's, concentrated on textbooks and hardcovers. The Codys saw a niche. In addition to paperbacks and best-selling hardcovers, they would follow the lead of City Lights and Kepler's and feature abundant foreign books and periodicals. Theirs would be a cosmopolitan place. Scraping together $5,000, Fred and Pat found a compact site on the north side of the campus. On July 9, 1956, Cody's Books opened with about seven hundred books on the shelves. They had no office, no stockroom, and no bathroom. They had no heat. To keep warm, Fred wore thermal underwear the year round.

The Bay Area now had its triumvirate of paperback bookstores: City Lights in San Francisco, Kepler's in Menlo Park, and Cody's in Berkeley. The stores' owners were natural collaborators.

Roy, whose counsel had guided Pat and Fred Cody through the start-up, enabled the Berkeley couple to obtain books at a favorable discount rate. On Sunday mornings, Fred would drive the forty-five minutes down the Peninsula to pick up from Roy his books for the week. One time, as well, Pat and Fred Cody had visited Menlo Park to observe Roy's book inventory system in action. Individual cards were inserted in each book and collected as the books were sold. The cards were then placed in the appropriate publisher's stack, and once a week hand counted for orders to publishers. The inventory cards slid within the pages was a Kepler's stamp on every book.

Within a year the Codys secured their own deal with a distributor offering a 25 percent discount. Fred no longer had to make the weekly trip to Menlo Park, but the men stayed in touch in other ways. Kepler's, Cody's, and City Lights ran joint spots on San Francisco's classical FM station KSFR, whose cultured announcers would periodically urge listeners to "Bow toward Salzburg and hum something from Mozart." Cody, Roy, and Ferlinghetti would also share in newspaper ads, though putting them together could be a trial. Publishers financed part of the ads, promoting certain books. The three men then had to design the ads, an exercise in creative tension.

Ferlinghetti, the poet, was an advertising minimalist. He preferred a simple listing of book titles, shorn of fluff or visual adornment. Roy and Fred, each with a marketing background, wanted a little more flash. Once the three booksellers wrangled for what seemed like hours over a two-page advertising spread planned for the *San Francisco Chronicle*. "Kepler, Ferlinghetti and I sat down together and tried to work out the copy of the ad," Fred Cody wrote at the time. "I only wish I could have taped it. It would make even Mort Sahl cry for mercy" (Cody and Cody 1992, 25).

A typical full-page ad displayed three small boxes across the top, identifying Kepler's, City Lights, and Cody's. Thick with small-type text, the ad would showcase books published by the likes of New Directions, Evergreen, and the University of California Press. For prices starting at fifty cents, readers were offered Erich Fromm's *The Forgotten Language*, Clarence Darrow's *The Story of My Life*, Wallace

Stegner's *Big Rock Candy Mountain,* and Ferlinghetti's own *Pictures of the Gone World*. Roy would also run spots on his own. In May 1956, marking his store's first anniversary, Roy took out a compact ad in the small *Menlo Park Recorder* newspaper announcing his latest promotion. Spend more than $5, Roy's ad promised, and the store would toss in another book for free. Customers could pick up the likes of *Catcher in the Rye, The Loved One,* or William Inge's smoldering *Picnic*. Grace Metalious's soap opera *Peyton Place* was burning up the paperback bestseller list that year, and Kepler's offered that too. Roy was always commercially accommodating. His more distinctive tastes, though, were earning him a unique reputation. *The God That Failed,* for one, was a series of essays by *Darkness at Noon* author Arthur Koestler and other disenchanted ex-Communists. It had made a splash upon initial publication in 1949, before going into paperback. Sales had dwindled by the mid-1950s, except at Kepler's. Roy once told his son, Clark, that a Curtis News distributor asked "who this Roy Kepler was, because Kepler's had sold more of that book than the entire rest of the country."

In his solo store promotions, Roy often favored a sardonic tone. In one characteristic *Stanford Daily* ad of the time, Roy offered the books that would help students "fulfill the spring quarter requirements of the education that will make you a National Resource in the Cold War."

"Even if you aren't a physics or math major, and hence won't easily fit into Lockheed's or GE's electronics space-production line, don't hang your head," Roy's ad teased bitingly. "Perhaps training in the humanities will handicap you a bit, but you can always hope to become a 'psychological warrior' or a public relations officer for the AEC."

Roy's activism extended beyond taking a dig at the Atomic Energy Commission in a bookstore ad. In April 1956 he ventured into dangerous new territory. No longer would he render unto Caesar his share for Caesar's army.

Tax protesting put both individuals and organizations in a bind. One way or another, the state would claim its pound of flesh.

Individuals risked their freedom. Henry David Thoreau had spent a night in jail for refusing to pay a Massachusetts poll tax in protest of the Mexican-American War. During World War II, Methodist minister Ernest Bromley refused to spend $2.09 for a defense tax stamp. He was incarcerated for sixty days and lost his church. Chicago social worker Eroseanna "Sis" Robinson stopped paying taxes in the early 1950s and would likewise serve time in jail. Cincinnati-based Presbyterian minister Maurice McCrackin would serve a six-month prison sentence in the late 1950s after several years of refusing to pay income taxes.

The potentially fearsome penalties kept the number of known tax protestors to no more than one hundred a year through the 1950s. Roy knew a number of them.

The Peacemakers, from their beginnings at the 1948 conference in Chicago, had established a Tax Refusal Committee. George Houser, the pioneering conscientious objector from Roy's hometown of Denver, refused to pay his 1949 taxes. So did A. J. Muste. Through 1952, Muste wouldn't even file a return. His money, he declared publicly, would not go toward the government's construction of more hydrogen bombs. In lieu of a check, he once sent the Treasury Department a copy of Thoreau's *Essay on Civil Disobedience.* Fyke Farmer, a Nashville attorney and active civil libertarian, earned more money than Muste but likewise declined to pay his 1950 taxes, saying that to do so would make him guilty as an accomplice in the crime of war preparation. Farmer would later represent condemned spy suspects Jules and Ethel Rosenberg, and during the Vietnam War he would help the new generation of conscientious objectors challenge the draft.

Peace organizations, too, faced the tax question. By 1948 some radical pacifists were arguing that organizations including the Fellowship of Reconciliation and the War Resisters League were aiding the war-making state by withholding federal taxes from employees' paychecks. The WRL leadership established a subcommittee to address the issue, with Bayard Rustin and Roy among the members. Philosophically, Roy believed in the absolutist position. Pacifists should not be collecting taxes for the Pentagon. When he first took his paid position with the War Resisters League, Roy had asked whether the organization could stop withholding from his paycheck so that he might properly resist paying taxes. That never happened. But for the organization, pragmatically speaking, Roy recognized that tax resistance could be lethal. Roy and his colleagues warned that the absolutist position on tax withholding could be maintained only at the risk of destroying the organization itself. As an employer, the War Resisters League continued submitting to the government's tax withholding requirements (Bennett 1998, 372).

But once he was his own boss, Roy could put his IRS Form 1040 on the line. He would neither soldier nor pay for others to soldier on his behalf. In April 1956, as his store approached its first anniversary, Roy advised the Internal Revenue Service that he would be paying only 40 percent of the tax he owed. That was the amount going for peaceful government purposes, he figured. As for the rest, Roy advised the tax-collectors that there was "no human choice" other than refuse to cooperate with the frantic arms race fueled by taxpayer dollars.

Silent protest wasn't enough. Like other forms of direct action, Roy's tax resistance was meant to summon attention and rouse the public. He needed the press to spread the word. Roy alerted local newspapers and was rewarded with several stories. The *Palo Alto Times* was impressed enough that it put Roy on the front page, though it misidentified the still-obscure bookseller as "Paul" Kepler. Roy seemed to be among the very first Bay Area residents to refuse to pay his taxes on ideological grounds. He was certainly the most assertive about it. With his penchant for no-quarters rhetoric, Roy likened IRS officials to concentration camp directors, or to pilots who heedlessly dropped bombs on cities.

The tax collectors went about their business, unperturbed.

"If he doesn't pay the bill, we'll send someone to see him," the aptly named Richard Nickell, assistant director of the IRS, said in the *Palo Alto Times* of April 16, 1956. "If that fails, we'll file a lien and sell his property . . . Everybody has to pay taxes, no matter what they think."

The May–June 1956 issue of the *WRL News,* edited by Roy's old compatriot Jim Peck, praised Roy's tax protest as a publicity jackpot.

Kepler's Books & Magazines   ◆   141

That still left, though, the question of how Roy's IRS obligation would be resolved. In Henry David Thoreau's case, a well-meaning sympathizer had satisfied the debt and thereby sprung the disobedient tax resister. In Roy's case, it was the IRS itself that acted. In August 1956 Roy and Patricia returned from a three-day vacation in Los Angeles to find a notice that the IRS had simply tapped into the Keplers' bank account and taken what was owed.

As an attention-getter, Roy's protest succeeded. The newspaper stories and radio reports provided a platform to articulate his pacifist views. Several dozen people telephoned Roy or stopped by to congratulate him on his fortitude. Others were less enthusiastic.

"Civilized people who prize their good citizenship should make an example of weak-livered crackpots trying to escape their just taxes," one anonymous individual wrote Roy in an April 17, 1956, postcard. Another, three days later, questioned, "How much tax does one pay on the income from an egghead bookstore, anyway?"

The resistance delighted Roy. Friction causes sparks, which when sufficient can both heat and illuminate. In time, it might erupt into a signal fire.

8

Paperback Revolutionary

Word spread.

Roy knew how to draw a crowd and get the message out. His War Resisters League flyers had once lured young men with headlines about sex. He had been the outside man for Jim Peck's audacious White House staircase protest, calling reporters with the latest. He had marketed KPFA with cheap radios. Now he had his own business to pitch. Roy's 1956 tax protest served that purpose. He wasn't just a local man fighting the IRS, he was a local *bookseller*. He was a man, maybe, with just the book for you.

Like-minded souls began finding the store on El Camino Real. Shortly, one in particular would show up and become Roy's essential partner. He would be the missing brother: a wounded, big-hearted man, a meditating sensualist, a brave pacifist, a flirt, a showman, a gossip, and a brilliant teacher, all in one.

This was Ira Sandperl.

Ira and Roy would plot together, march together, and survive incarceration together. Theirs was a decades-long conversation about war, peace, and the individual conscience. On the fundamental principle of nonviolence, Roy and Ira were as one: brothers disarmed. But as individuals, they were night and day. Roy was tight-fisted. Economical in gesture and restrained in emotion, he was the adult who kept the books and made the payroll. Ira lived with larger gestures, wine sloshing in the glass. He embraced the pleasures of the world, thoroughly amused by them all. He partook.

6. Ira Sandperl, undated. Photographer unknown, courtesy of Ira Sandperl and Molly Black.

Unlike many of Roy's closest allies, Ira had not been seared in the World War II Civilian Public Service camps, or federal prisons, or military service, or even the impoverishments of the Great Depression.

He was born in comfortable circumstances on March 11, 1923, the second child of a Jewish doctor and his younger wife. Ira's father, Dr. Harry Sandperl, was a first-generation American then advancing toward prominence in St. Louis. He had married Ione when he was thirty-one and she was eighteen. In time, Ione had mature opinions of her own concerning pacifism. She was a Norman Thomas aficionado, albeit with a social flair. Ira called her a parlor room Socialist, a woman at home in St. Louis's University City and other fine places of the world. Growing up, Ira and his older sister, Betty, were tended by serving girls. He became accustomed to the habit. Once, on a West Coast family jaunt, the Sandperls stayed at San Francisco's luxurious Mark Hopkins Hotel.

"My mother said, 'this is how I want everybody to be able to live,'" Ira recalled in an interview decades later.

Ira took after his mother. As an adult activist, he would embrace dichotomy, wearing a silk Christian Dior dressing gown while he slept on a cabin floor with migrant farmworkers. He spoke admiringly of Gandhi as a young law student, adorned in Bond Street's best (Sandperl 1974, 83). Ira graduated from a posh prep school and entered Stanford in the fall of 1941, a member of the class of '45. In his first days on campus, the European war still rumbling closer, one of Ira's roommates asked him what he thought about Hitler.

"I'll tell you,'" Ira told filmmaker Alex Beckstead. "I'm a Jew and a pacifist. He makes me very nervous."

Ira tried to live in style. He sent his shirts home to St. Louis for laundering, draped himself in Brooks Brothers suits, and dallied with attractive married women (Sandperl 1974, ix). Initially, Ira had thought he might put himself on track to earn a doctorate in history or English, but he grew disenchanted with the academic world and was not a particularly dedicated student. For a time he took a retreat in Carmel, a charming coastal place to which he would repair periodically, returning to campus for the occasional exam.

Ira was draft-exempt because of a game leg. Though never formally diagnosed with polio, his right arm and leg had not fully developed, and he had worn a leg brace through childhood. He compensated by developing strength and endurance, but he was not military material. Following the December 7, 1941, Japanese attack on Pearl Harbor, as his classmates rushed to enlist or prepared for conscription, he briefly considered service as an ambulance attendant with the British. It was an apt choice, tending the war-wounded while foregoing the gun, and it had a decent legacy. The literary likes of Malcolm Cowley, Ernest Hemingway, and Edmund Wilson had all famously served as ambulance attendants during World War I. Ira, though martially incapacitated, could still stand up for what he thought was right. He recalled protesting the forced relocation of Japanese Americans to internment camps. For his pains, Ira said, FBI agents visited his father in St. Louis to ask what was going on. The ambulance service, though, never materialized, and after about three meandering undergraduate years, Ira left Stanford without a degree. He would later polish the line that the university was interfering with his education, though he sometimes acknowledged he also wanted to have a good time.

Footloose, Ira crossed the southern border and landed in Mexico City. There he met a young woman from Palo Alto named Merle, who was in the import-export business. They married, in Acapulco, and then after a time they moved to Europe. He hung about, always reading. Tolstoy was a favorite. Like Gandhi, Ira was indelibly stamped by Tolstoy's "The Kingdom of God Is Within You." More modern books, too, shaped Ira's course, such as *The Perennial Philosophy* by Aldous Huxley.

Huxley was one of a kind.

Living in Hollywood, he had been denied U.S. citizenship because he refused to certify he would take up arms to defend his new homeland. It was a statement of pure principle, considering that Huxley was legally blind. But Huxley could *see,* much farther than the broadside of the barn that he could not hit. Amid the wreckage of the postwar world, Huxley found the thread, what he called "an essentially indescribable Fact" expressed variously in the Gospel of St. John, in the Bhagavad Gita, in the Persian Sufis and the Christian mystics. Published in 1945, *The Perennial Philosophy* explored the essential unity of disparate religions. There is, Huxley discerned, a Divine Ground permeating the phenomenal world. In man, there is both individual ego and the eternal Self, the spark of the divine. Through acts of charity and self-abnegation, simplification and right action, one dissolves the impediments to the inner Self. And if the Divine truly runs through all, then how can violence be done to another? Surely it cannot.

Huxley gripped Ira by the lapel and compelled him to attend. An observation attributed to the Englishman, that "at the end, one has no more to offer by way of advice than 'try to be a little kinder,'" provided Ira with the phrase for his own modest 1974 book *A Little Kinder.* They even met once, almost certainly more memorably for Ira than for Huxley, while the Englishman was visiting at Stanford. Other chance encounters moved Ira even further along the way.

Walking past a bookstore one day, he noticed through the window a volume on Gandhi, sitting at a spinning wheel. Ira finagled a copy of the book. By 1947 or so, Ira had declared himself a pacifist, citing Huxley. With Gandhi's autobiography, *The Story of My Experiments with Truth,* he would realize that personal self-perfection was not sufficient. Gandhi's lesson was that pacifists must directly engage in the world (Gandhi 1993).

Roy and Ira apparently first met in 1954 at the Hidden Villa Ranch of Los Altos Hills. Heaven on earth, Hidden Villa Ranch was a serene, thousand-acre oasis that Frank and Josephine Duveneck had been cultivating since they bought the property in 1924. The Radcliffe-educated Josephine and her engineer husband Frank had initially envisioned Hidden Villa Ranch as a family getaway. It was a place, she would later recall, in which she was "overwhelmed by the sense of past lives lived in serenity and harmonious fulfillment" (Duveneck 1978, 146).

But Josephine also embraced bigger ideas. Inspired by philosopher John Dewey, also one of Roy's favorites, and by the thinking of Maria Montessori, Josephine in 1925 had helped open the Peninsula School in Menlo Park. In 1937, the same year that Josephine joined the Palo Alto Friends Meeting, the Duvenecks established at Hidden Villa Ranch a youth hostel. The family's disarming sentiments had settled upon the children, and son Francis Duveneck would serve at the Glendora Civilian Public Service camp during World War II. He was with Roy the day Roy's brother, Earl, died. Francis would later take his CPS campmates to Hidden Villa for furloughs, enjoying the opportunity for some unsupervised relaxation at the place some dubbed "The CPS Country Club" (Duveneck 1978, 209).

Postwar, Hidden Villa Ranch was a natural location for potential KPFA audiences to meet. In June 1954 Roy and KPFA station manager Wallace Hamilton talked to the Duvenecks about the possibility of bringing the KPFA signal into the folds and foothills of the ranch. It was apparently about this time that Roy arrived at the ranch to make a KPFA pitch, offering as part of the promotion a low-cost FM radio. Ira was not impressed.

"I got so bored, I walked out," Ira said in a 2005 interview.

But Roy and Ira were moving in similar circles, and their paths were bound to cross again. Ira taught at the Peninsula School for a while and, for about six years, at First Day School for the Palo Alto Friends Meeting. He had also meandered through various Palo Alto area bookstores. Bell's Books owner Herbert Bell took a shine to Ira and hired him to manage a newly opened store in Redwood City, a few miles north of Palo Alto. Ira would hitchhike up El Camino Real to work and manage the store after his own fashion. When he wanted to chat with the fascinating man next door, he would lock the door and post a sign promising to return in fifteen minutes. It was a congenial way to spend the day, though a lousy way to sell books. Soon enough, the Redwood City shop shut down (Sandperl 1974, 35).

Ira's wife, Merle, would sometimes work as a secretary, but she was also raising daughter Nicole, born in 1950, and son Mark, born in 1953. Though Ira could seem distracted from mundane family responsibilities, he needed to find a job; something suitable. Naturally he had seen this new Kepler's Books & Magazines on El Camino Real, and one Saturday he walked into the small store. Ira told Roy that he needed a part-time job. He knew something about the business from his misadventures with Bell's Books, and he certainly shared Roy's interest in pacifism. He was a compatible soul, and Roy needed help. Patricia was pregnant at the time and would soon be needing replacement. Ira's timing, though, seemed off. Unfortunately, Roy said, he had just hired a clerk who was scheduled to start the next day. Roy said if another opening occurred, he'd call.

The next day, Ira's phone rang. It was Roy, asking him if he still wanted the job. The clerk Roy had hired never showed up to work that Sunday. The job was Ira's for the asking.

"And I didn't get out of there for twenty-five years," Ira said.

With Ira in place, Kepler's ran true. The store now had its maître d', a defining personality and a real performer. At the cash register, Ira could converse with anybody about anything. One author would remind him of another. Bookselling was less a commercial transaction than an ongoing seminar. Among themselves, too, Roy and Ira could talk about everything from tactics to Tolstoy.

"It was my luck," Ira said of the twist that brought him into Roy's orbit, "and to be perfectly immodest, it was his luck, too."

The work itself was only barely remunerative, but Ira was not raised to worry about money; quite the opposite. Roy, the quintessential Depression kid, thought Ira worked with the peculiar disinterest of a man who never had to earn a living. That was putting it mildly. Ira did not make a big thing out of salary. Raises would come in their own time.

"He gave them to me when I asked," Ira said, "but I had to ask."

A fundamental attitude toward money was not the only difference between Roy and Ira, those two great friends. While both embraced pacifism, read voraciously, and excelled at debate, they were distinct personalities. Ira was more overtly sensual, an embracer. Roy seemed clinical and cerebral. Ira attracted young women and held each one dear. Roy did not flirt. Ira gossiped and could be withering in his wit. Roy, Ira said, "was much kinder than me." Sartorially, Roy could be rather dapper in jacket and hat. Ira was more explicitly bohemian. He favored Levis and sandals, at a time when most others took after the title of Sloan Wilson's 1955 book *The Man in the Gray Flannel Suit*. And while Roy seemed to attract universal regard, Ira invited conflicting opinions. Many adored him. Decades later, Grateful Dead lyricist Robert Hunter still recalled Ira's "big, beautiful, sad brown eyes" and the sense of "peace and love and sadness" he radiated, and the way he would call everyone friend.

"He was fabulous, one of the great teachers," Lee Swenson, a longtime peace activist who met Ira in 1959, recalled in an interview. "He was charming; he had a great way with children, although not necessarily with his own children."

Ira seemed, in fact, a bit of a distant character to the two young children he had from a marriage that lingered through the 1950s. But then, if he wanted, he could cite Gandhi himself. Asked once about his children, Gandhi had declared grandly that all of India was his family—which was fine for the great cause of peace, but not so good for particular flesh-and-blood sons (Fisher 1962). Ira was less attuned to other aspects of Gandhi's personal life, in particular his *brahmacharya* vow of sexual continence. Not everyone could be a perfect saint.

Others were even more skeptical. Longtime Kepler's manager Ralph Kohn confessed he "always thought [Ira] was a bit of a four-flusher, actually." Patricia Kepler, Ira himself recalled, didn't much like him at all. She blamed him for leading Roy into too many peace protests. But it was author Joan Didion who would really pin Ira down, a butterfly in her collection, in an essay written in the mid-1960s. Observing Ira in his guru role at Joan Baez's school for peace, the Institute for the Study of Nonviolence, Didion mercilessly summed him up.

"Ira Sandperl," Didion wrote, "has, besides the beard, a shaved head, a large nuclear disarmament emblem on his corduroy jacket, glittering and slightly messianic eyes, a high cracked laugh and the general appearance of a man who has, all his life, followed some imperceptibly but fatally askew rainbow" (Didion 1990, 51).

Ira gave Roy the helping hand he needed, and he enriched the character of Kepler's Books & Magazines. He was a devoted browser, who had merrily tossed away his careerist timecard so he might meander among books and ideas and people. The bookstore, too, seemed to be off the clock. Browsers were welcomed. Consumption was not compulsory. Meandering paid off, in its own sweet time. One might end up someplace interesting. The store's shelves offered every available idea, each awaiting a ride like a hitchhiker on a country road: Go ahead, pick it up. Or, maybe it was the other way around: The book was the ride. It transported.

Slowly, slowly, Kepler's was becoming known as an intellectually tolerant place. It was highbrow, middlebrow, and occasionally low-brow all at the same time. The store pandered with the likes of *Peyton Place,* reprinted as a Dell paperback in 1957, even as it provoked with more elevating fare such as Herman Hesse's *Siddartha* and Nathaniel West's apocalyptic *The Day of the Locust.* Copies of Lawrence

Ferlinghetti's *A Tentative Description of a Dinner Given to Promote the Impeachment of President Eisenhower,* published by Ferlinghetti's own City Light Books, were selling for sixteen cents. Customers could pick up copies of the *Manchester Guardian, Paris Match,* or the German-language weekly *Der Spiegel.* Roy delighted in offering the intellectual antithesis of the domestic magazines he dismissed as "the usual women's mediocrities." As one small Bay Area newspaper put it in a September 1958 headline, "Palo Alto Bookman-Pacifist Individualistic, So Is Shop." The reporter identified Kepler's customers as "mostly university and professional persons, artists, jazz musicians, and some Stanford Research [Institute] employees."

The freewheeling aspect helped set Kepler's apart from other stores, but certain competitors had their own enticements. Price, in particular, was a problem. From the very beginning, the painfully familiar plot would bedevil Kepler's and other independent bookstores for decades. Before the behemoth chains of the 1990s and the online sellers of the twenty-first century, independents had to deal with dominant stores offloading books at a discount. In the Palo Alto of the late 1950s, this was the work of the Stanford University Bookstore.

The Stanford Bookstore sat fat and happy on campus, about a mile from Kepler's. It was not, at the time, entirely well regarded. Some professors and students thought the store was overtaken by decorative plates, mugs, gifts, and assorted other Joe College geegaws. Outside of the obligatory classroom texts, books qua books sometimes seemed a secondary consideration. Student David Egger, writing for the *Stanford Daily* on October 7, 1957, called the store's general book selection "a table of cartoon books, the left-over selections from the current quarter's humanities courses [and] a smattering of the Modern Library." Only Kepler's, Egger added, offered a reasonable selection locally.

Accustomed to monopoly, the Stanford Bookstore could even fall short in its core responsibility of handling texts. In 1958 German Department chair Friedrich W. Strothmann would complain that he had ordered seventeen copies of Jules Supervielle's short-story volume *L'Enfant de la Haute Mer* from the university bookstore. The books had never arrived, the latest in a series of frustrations. As a result, Strothmann made what he called the "heroic decision" to use Kepler's for certain textbook needs. The more nimble Kepler's could do in a few weeks what the Stanford Bookstore needed months for.

"Kepler's is smaller and can devote more time to obtaining those books," Strothmann explained to the *Stanford Daily*.

But for all its aesthetic and professional shortcomings, the Stanford Bookstore offered customers one great, bottom-line advantage: dollar savings. The store provided rebates of as much as 20 percent to anyone affiliated with the university. The rebate was so significant that some technical and scholarly texts were essentially being sold at their wholesale price. Precisely foreshadowing what would later happen with chain stores and online purveyors, Roy in May 1957 observed that customers would peruse independent stores like Kepler's, Bell's Books, and Shirley Cobb's but then gravitate to the Stanford Bookstore for the rebate when it came time to buy. In Berkeley, Roy's friends Fred and Pat Cody unhappily discovered about the same time that potential customers were window-shopping at Cody's new Grove Press display but then purchasing their books at the university bookstore with its superior discounts. Foreshadowing later conflicts, Fred Cody recognized that "if discounting really gets going in books it will just wipe out a lot of small outlets like us" (Cody and Cody 1992, 27).

Roy resisted as best he could. Ever the organizer, he had become chairman of the rather grandly named Palo Alto Area Booksellers Association. The association could claim only half a dozen members and a letterhead, but it would have to do. On its behalf, Roy wrote the Stanford Bookstore on May 2, 1957, voicing concerns about Stanford's plans to expand its bookstore. Independent stores, Roy explained to the Stanford Bookstore, were different from the "vast impersonality" of the big stores. The independents brought to their work the "concern, interest and flexibility" of someone "carrying out a work of love." Roy suggested that Stanford reduce the rebate. At the least, the rebate should only be limited in its application.

Stanford officials shrugged it off. This Kepler fellow was little known, and his five-page, single-spaced letter rambled on a bit crankily.

The university administrators noted that local bookstores that had closed on University Avenue suffered from their poor location, and that in recent years half a dozen new bookstores had opened locally.

"Any business difficulties which the members of your bookstore association now encounter should not be attributed to the Stanford Bookstore," the president of the university bookstore's board advised Roy on May 16, 1957, further dryly noting that Roy's missive was "quite long."

The brush-off bothered Roy. He was not pursuing a radical agenda this time. He was a businessman representing other business owners who held legitimate complaints. Roy wrote the *Daily* denouncing the "monopolistic development of one overall bookstore" and stressing the benefits of "friendly cooperation." Roy cast his store as not simply a competitor but rather as a complement to the university bookstore, part of what he liked to think of as a fraternal book community. He met with business professor Arthur Kroeger, a sales and marketing specialist, and Harold Bacon, a veteran mathematics professor, for a civil discussion about ways to cooperate in getting books ordered. But the university bookstore's rebate continued to be a problem, prompting Roy to complain again in a 1960 letter about what he considered unfair discount. Roy's complaints did not go far. They flew in the face of the Stanford Bookstore's own commercial imperatives, and Roy himself still lacked local stature.

Roy's concerns did, however, strikingly foreshadow what would happen again four decades later with the rise of Internet bookselling.

"Your [rebate] places local retail stores in the embarrassing position of furnishing sample stock for your customers to examine before buying or ordering through your store," Roy would write Stanford officials in 1960.

By then the Palo Alto Area Booksellers Association was claiming thirteen members. They were a diverse lot. They included the likes of Mac's Smoke Shop in Palo Alto, a tobacco joint that incongruously prided itself on an extensive periodical section, as well as the more upscale Emporium, where ladies could buy the latest best-seller. Roy scorned department stores and their middlebrow tastes, but they had been in the book business a long time. By the early 1950s, by some estimates, department stores accounted for between 40 and 60 percent of all retail trade book sales (Miller 2006, 35).

The independent Palo Alto–area stores had more to contend with when, in March 1960, a newly refurbished Stanford Bookstore opened to good reviews. It was spacious, airy, and well lit. Its shelves had space galore for ten thousand texts and trade books; and, not least, it still offered customers the rebate. Within a few months Roy and other members of the expanded Northern California Booksellers Association complained yet again about the Stanford Bookstore's price-cutting policy. It was the same old complaint, but this time with some teeth. If Stanford didn't change its ways, the independent booksellers warned they would contact every single publisher and demand that Stanford Bookstore be cut off.

The independents never carried out their threat, but they were on to something in their belief that the big booksellers were getting a break. In November 1959 the Federal Trade Commission charged that New American Library, Dell, Bantam, and Pocket Books were granting special promotional allowances to certain chain retailers. The complaint, though eventually settled with a 1962 Federal Trade Commission requirement that every bookstore get the same sales terms, foreshadowed the debilitating competition that would later undermine Kepler's and other stores in the 1980s and 1990s (Davis 1984, 266). In the Bay Area, the Stanford Bookstore finally calmed the waters by limiting the discounts to students and faculty members.

Kepler's and the other independents could never compete on price alone. They had to stand out, show flair and personality. In Berkeley, Pat and Fred Cody decked their store with German art calendars. Roy put on classical music tapes and promoted avant-garde publishing houses like Evergreen Press. In the *Stanford Daily,* Roy ran ads touting Kepler's Kwik Kourse: The History of Western Civilization. The ads provided a seven-hundred-word summary before the punch line: Outline of Western Civ for only $1.50.

"Stanford welcomes you," Roy wrote in a September 23, 1957, *Daily* ad, "but Kepler needs you! He needs your TV-warped personality, your commercial smile and your Candidean optimism. But most of all, he needs your jangling dollars."

Kepler's had a voice, and it was getting noticed. While Roy was running his Kepler's Kwik Kourse ads, a Midwesterner named Philip Levine arrived at Stanford to take up a poetry fellowship. Levine spent the 1957 school year at the university, developing the craft that would in time win him the Pulitzer Prize, the National Book Award, and, in 2011, the title of poet laureate of the United States. Well before that, during his Stanford fellowship year, Levine discovered Kepler's. It seemed to him a uniquely California store, unlike what he was accustomed to in the Midwest or East Coast; Roy's imprint was all over the place.

"What surprised me was the range of material that was there, especially the political material," Levine recalled in a 2011 interview.

About the same time as Philip Levine was browsing the Kepler's shelves, a College of San Mateo student named Roy Seburn chanced upon the store as well. The 1955 graduate of Redwood High School in nearby Redwood City was a budding artist, and perhaps just a little bit lost. Searching, at any rate. In the fullness of time, he would become the most accomplished decorator of the Merry Prankster's Bus immortalized in Tom Wolfe's *The Electric Kool-Aid Acid Test*. In the pre-psychedelia days of the late fifties, though, Seburn was just starting to expand his horizons into the realms of religion and philosophy. He had grown up knowing books as expensive, straitlaced, and bound between hard covers. But now, here was an alternative at Kepler's Books & Magazines. Seburn took in the narrow aisles, the shelves lined with paperbacks. They weren't pulp mysteries or Mickey Spillane's gunplay, either; these were serious works. Seburn bought a book or two on Zen Buddhism, his mind's eye opening to new possibilities. The place seemed to him a hub, with spokes radiating outward.

Seburn would return, one more Kepler's customer caught by chance. Others were hearing of the store because of Roy's activism. Roy estimated his 1956 tax protest had prompted queries or comments from hundreds of people, every one a potential buyer of books. It was encouraging, and in 1957 Roy declared he and Patricia would again refuse to pay part of their federal income tax. The global menace of militarism and atomic weaponry had not diminished, Roy told the *Stanford Daily*. One must take a stand. In April 1957 the Keplers sent the IRS a check covering 40 percent of their due taxes. They also sent a letter to every Bay Area newspaper, declaring their latest act of conscience.

"My wife and I, and we hope an increasing number of our fellow human beings, are determined not to support any government in the preparation of genocidal weapons which can destroy a whole city by blast and fire," Roy wrote.

The IRS could have crushed him, as it had others. In September 1958 federal officials would arrest a Cincinnati clergyman named Maurice McCrackin on charges of tax resistance. McCrackin was an absolute resister, refusing even to talk to the judge. For the purity of his principles, he received a six-month jail sentence and $250 fine. With Roy, the IRS responded more placidly. If Roy wouldn't surrender the money, the government would simply take it.

"I guess they can grab things," Roy acknowledged on April 15, 1957, "but I won't give them my taxes voluntarily. I don't pretend to be all-powerful, if they will grab for the taxes."

Roy's 1957 tax protest would be resolved unilaterally, on IRS terms. It succeeded, though, in drawing attention. Year after year, he would engage in the same conversation with the tax collectors. Each go-around would burnish his activist reputation and, by extension, his store's repute. The curious would show up and find Roy, trim and youthful looking but his hair already white, always ready to talk about his refusal to prepare for future annihilation. Roy kept up the tax dialogue, onstage and behind it. The IRS would write him concerning his tax liability. Roy would write back elaborating on his reasons for refusing to pay, just as if he expected someone to listen to his arguments.

One of the curious who found their way to Kepler's in 1958 was a student at Menlo-Atherton High School named Kathryn Lawson.

Aided by her discussions with Roy, Kathryn crafted an essay for her American Institutions class. Kathryn earned an A for her brief summary of Gandhi's work and her suggestion that the United States might consider preparing a civil disobedience campaign in anticipation of a potential Russian invasion. Establishing a "strong, national, coordinated civil disobedience campaign" would be the best response to a Russian occupation, Kathryn argued; all Russian orders would be universally but peacefully disobeyed. And thus, the high school student concluded, "we would remain independent and invincible."

Kathryn had clearly learned from Roy; her ideas mirrored his own. Her notion of a peaceful civilian response in the face of an enemy occupation echoed, as well, ideas articulated earlier by War Resisters League founder Jessie Hughan in a 1939 pamphlet entitled *If We Should Be Invaded: Facing a Fantastic Hypothesis*. Through Roy's devices, Kathryn's essay found its way to *MANAS*, the little journal of big ideas published in Southern California by pacifist Henry Geiger. *MANAS*, as Ira Sandperl put it, was "one of the most interesting, varied and curious encyclopedic magazines in America," and it was perfect for young Kathryn's essay (Sandperl 1974, 65). The essay was then picked up again and republished, along with her name and a picture, by Roy's colleagues at *Peace News*.

Enter George Sokolsky.

A Hearst newspaper man of unusual provenance, Sokolsky had been denouncing Red dupes, fronts, and causes since the 1930s. His fervency was all the more remarkable for his background, as the Russian-speaking, Utica, New York, native had once cheered on the early stages of the Russian Revolution while a reporter for the English-language *Russian Daily News*. He returned from fourteen years in China committed to the market causes of the National Association of Manufacturers and the service of FBI director J. Edgar Hoover. Hoover would use Sokolsky for selected tips, and in turn the columnist would funnel information about Hollywood Leftists.

So Sokolsky, the high priest of militant U.S. anticommunism, knew all about the workings of the world. He could tell Kathryn Lawson was a patsy. She might seem innocent enough, with her plans to study theology at San Jose State, but Sokolsky saw in Kathryn's brief essay a dangerous exercise in liberal thinking by a naïve young girl. The nonviolence she preached would quickly collapse in the face of the brutal Russian enemy. Sokolsky knew all about it. "This young lady," Sokolsky said in a November 1958 column, "has of course never been in a war in which no prisoners are taken because they are too expensive to feed." Practically speaking, Sokolsky explained, the posited U.S. civil disobedience campaign would be simply thwarted by the "50 million Chinese [who] could be conveyed to our country" and put to work. More fundamentally, this Miss Lawson was too naïve and, apparently, too beholden to some crackpot idealist.

"She has never seen prisoners of war stuck on poles," Sokolsky wrote with grim satisfaction. "She has never met human beings who are brainwashed. She has read *Walden* and has listened to someone called Roy Kepler."

Someone called Roy Kepler.

Some shadowy obscurity, that is. A character of no weight; a nobody, really. But also, perhaps, there is a hint this is a name to be checked against the government's lists. For, who was this man who had so bent the thinking of a high school girl? Sokolsky's diatribe came to the attention of a Menlo Park parent, a Mr. Oliver Dibble Jr., who demanded some accountability from the school. Just what kind of pacifist prattle and nonsense were they teaching there anyway? Seizing the moment, Roy spun off a detailed exegesis to the local newspaper. He noted that the ancestors of several recent U.S. political leaders, including then–vice president Richard Nixon, had come from the historic peace churches, and he stressed that young Kathryn's teachers deserved praise and not censure. The teachers, he said, should be proud that their school allows original thinking untrammeled by fears of official disapproval.

Sokolsky would move on to fresh fulminations. Young Kathryn Lawson, too, would move on, her mind and life both shaped by exposure to Roy. Other youngsters, though, were on the way.

9

Joan

The lovebirds met over music, at a Drew University dance.

One fine fall evening in 1934, twenty-year-old Joan Chandos Bridge was enduring the company of a clod. A trim Scottish-born beauty, the daughter of an Episcopal minister, Joan let her mind drift as she shuffled about the dance floor with her ill-matched date. When she saw her chance, she stepped outside for a breather, and she saw *him* then: Al Baez. This young man was exotic, dark, and handsome. He was laughing, boisterously, as he entertained an audience with hand gestures and the sounds of airplanes taking off. Joan took him all in.

"Nothing boring about this cookie," she thought (Baez Sr. 1996, 112).

And that, for all intents and purposes, was that.

Born in Puebla, Mexico, Albert Vinicio Baez had moved to the United States when he was two. He was adept in math and music. At Drew, he took a degree, and the heart of Joan Chandos Bridge. Together they went off to Syracuse University, where Al earned a master's in physics. Their family began to grow. Then the couple moved with their two young daughters Pauline and Joan Jr. to the San Francisco Bay Area for Al's doctoral work at Stanford. The third daughter, Mimi, was born at Stanford Hospital in 1945. Al made his mark at Stanford, coinventing in 1948 the X-ray reflection microscope. And with his expanding professional reputation, Al faced a fork in the road.

The military industrial complex beckoned, with compelling physics problems and powerfully high stakes. Curious, Al spent three stomach-churning weeks aboard an aircraft carrier during an amphibious exercise in 1950 called Operation Portrex. But Al was being pulled in another direction as well. At his wife's urging, the Baez family had begun attending Friends Meeting while in upstate New York. The silence soaked in, and Al over time embraced pacifism. It informed his career, as he hauled his family to Iraq for the 1951–52 school year so he could teach at the University of Baghdad. The family returned to the United States, where Al had a job teaching at the University of Redlands in Southern California. There young Joan Jr. felt herself an outsider: olive-skinned, skinny, and physically awkward. She could charm, though, with her smile, her voice, and her craving for the spotlight.

"I love to be the center of attention, and pardon the conceit, I usually am," young Joan wrote in 1955. "I like to show off" (Baez 1987, 33).

Young Joan craved her father's regard in particular. He broke her heart sometimes. He seemed incapable of telling her anything nice to her face. He gave her much, though, including the love of music that was often playing in the Baez household. Back in Palo Alto in the spring of 1954, while Joan was thirteen and her younger sister Mimi was nine, the Baez sisters attended a Pete Seeger concert at the Palo Alto High School gym. It was a fundraising event for the California Democratic Party, at the end of which Seeger sold copies of his booklet entitled *How to Play the 5-String Banjo*. Another member of the audience who bought Seeger's book, a Stanford sophomore named Dave Guard, went on to form the Kingston Trio in 1957.

By the time Joan was in eleventh grade, she was attending Palo Alto High School as well as the Quakers' weekly First Day School on Sunday. It was so, so dull and serious, all those terminally earnest Friends and the time just ticking slowly along, one second after another, until the morning Ira Sandperl showed up as teacher. Ira was working at Kepler's for money, such as it was, but he was teaching for love. Funny, erudite, and looking not at all like the conventional Joe, Ira held forth on Leo Tolstoy, Aldous Huxley, the Bhagavad-Gita, and more. In his corduroys and sweatshirts, baggy coat, and beat-up alpine hat, he was cut from an altogether different cloth. Ira and his students would sit on the sidewalk outside the Palo Alto Friends

Meeting House, chattering away and then occasionally falling into eloquent silence.

"We, who sat in that circle, all loved Ira," Joan's mother recalled. "Perhaps it was the bard-like beard that belonged to his thin face, his electric eyes that focused on a questioner. Perhaps it was the limp he had lived with all his life" (Baez Sr. 1994, 13).

The style touches helped, but Joan's mom recognized that Ira's appeal was more fundamental. He listened to the young, he took them seriously, and he kept a light heart. Good humor was key to the pacific life. Laughter, Ira always said, put military uniforms in their place: comical costumes in an opéra bouffe. He could turn his humor on himself and his own posturing, simultaneously dismissing any notion that he had all the answers even as he held forth omnisciently. Whether standing at the Kepler's cash register or lounging about, Ira would enumerate exactly what books must be read. *Anna Karenina* was an absolute imperative. Photographer Margaret Bourke-White was a remarkable woman, see her *Portrait of Myself.* Pascal's *Provincial Letters* was a must, dear girl.

Ira, though himself not a model family man, could also offer sage answers to some pressing familial questions. Once Joan asked how she could stop fighting with her sister Mimi.

"Ira said to pretend that it was the last hour of her life as, he pointed out, it might well be," Joan recalled. "So I tried out his plan. Mimi reacted strangely at first, the way anyone does when a blueprint is switched without his being consulted. [But] I learned to look at her, and as a result, to see her for the first time. I began to love her" (Sandperl 1974, vii).

Al, during about this same time, was collaborating with Roy and Ira in a new peace effort. In the spring of 1957, Roy had invited Ira, Al, and others to his Los Altos home to discuss the need for a local, grassroots organization dedicated to opposing nuclear weapons. The topic weighed heavily, everywhere. That April, opponents of nuclear weapons testing met in New York City and set the foundation for what would become known as the Committee for a Sane Nuclear Policy (SANE) testing. *Saturday Review* editor Norman Cousins helped promote the cause when he published "Call to Conscience," a lengthy denunciation of nuclear testing authored by eighty-two-year-old Nobel Peace Prize laureate Albert Schweitzer. SANE styled itself as the pragmatic side of the peace movement, emphasizing civil discourse toward the goal of ending nuclear weapons tests and the international control of missiles and outer-space satellites. More radical pacifists, insistent upon direct action, turned toward the Nonviolent Action Against Nuclear Weapons, which within a year would change its name to the Committee for Nonviolent Action (Milton Katz 1973, 84).

In the San Francisco Bay Area, the Peninsula Committee for the Abolition of Nuclear Tests exemplified the flourishing of activism under the H-bomb's shadow. Besides Roy, Ira, and Al, the committee's members included businessmen, realtors, engineers, and professors. They were not fringe characters. One, future Palo Alto school board member Aggie Robinson, had gotten her own start in social activism with the Addison Elementary School PTA. Committee members convened meetings and distributed blue flyers averring that "continued tests of [nuclear] weapons may increase, rather than decrease, the probability of their use in war." More vividly, the committee's flyers described how a nuclear blast fills the sky "with the bluish white incandescence whose heat approaches that of the center of the sun itself."

The various Ban-the-Bomb committees incited reactions ranging from fear to contempt to a patronizing pat on the head. The *New York Daily News* denounced SANE as "nutty as so many fruit cases," while *Time* warned that the disarmament advocates were aligning themselves with "the sworn enemies of religion, liberty and peace itself." At the reliably conventional *Palo Alto Times,* editorial writers in July 1957 faintly praised the Peninsula Committee for the Abolition of Nuclear Tests' "idealism" before stressing its dangers. It might be comforting to imagine the "happy time" when weapons disappeared, the *Palo Alto Times* said in its most adult voice, but "if we halt the testing of our most effective weapon, we would be putting ourselves at the mercy of the Communists."

"We would be baring our throats to the wolves of the world," the paper added ominously on July 19, 1957.

Russia had sharp teeth, no doubt. The Soviet Union conducted forty-nine nuclear weapons tests between its first on August 29, 1949, and December 31, 1957. Not to be outdone, the United States conducted thirty nuclear weapons blasts just between May and October 1957, as part of what was called Operation Plumbob.

Kepler exploded on July 24.

This was the code name for a test shot, part of Plumbob's aboveground series of nuclear weapons tests that had also included names like Galileo and Newton. Kepler was the test of an 11-kiloton warhead placed atop a 500-foot tower in the remote Nevada Test Site. The next month, activists gathered near a military testing ground in Nevada. Roy was still bound to his bookstore and did not make it to the Nevada desert that August, but he would later learn from his old ally Jim Peck of how the demonstrators camped the night of August 5 at Lee's Canyon, northwest of Las Vegas. The activists conveyed their message with three large placards.

"Will you act for peace without fear?" one sign asked.

The morning of August 6, 1957, the activists confronted some fifty armed men from the Atomic Energy Commission and local police and sheriffs' agencies. At 10 a.m., with newspaper and television reporters recording the action, Peck and two other demonstrators approached the security line. The guard told them they could not enter. The demonstrators explained their opposition to nuclear weapons. The guard held firm.

"Don't you, yourself, have any feelings regarding the Bomb?" asked Lawrence Scott, the forty-eight-year-old ordained Baptist minister who had earlier convened the influential Philadelphia meeting of Ban-the-Bomb activists.

"No, none," the guard dutifully replied (Neil Katz 1974, 44).

After several minutes, the conversation going nowhere, eleven protestors stepped a symbolic step or two past the guard. They were arrested and subsequently given suspended sentences. The next morning, before sunrise, Los Alamos National Laboratory scientists set off a 19-kiloton warhead hung from a balloon hovering at 1,500 feet.

Some considered the August 1957 Nevada Test Site demonstration a success. The desert protest gained national attention and showed the power of individual witness. The austere conditions certainly stamped the individual participants. They had passed through the fire and they had, some thought, made a real difference. Roy, though, thought the event fell short. It had been confined to Nevada, when it should have been made part of a national day of action. It left behind no coherent organization or game plan for follow-up (Neil Katz 1974, 49).

Roy's critiques were unsentimental and frequently unforgiving. He unerringly found the bottom line. Sometimes, as in his pragmatic critique of the Lee's Canyon protest, this could be a bracing tonic against surplus self-satisfaction. Sometimes it could be coldly unsympathetic. The same month as the Lee's Canyon protest, KPFA founder Lew Hill killed himself at the age of thirty-eight. Hill had been wracked by arthritic pain for years, and his death for some was a time to reflect on both his contributions and the travails of his life. Roy, though, focused on what the suicide said about KPFA's larger travails. There is something terribly wrong if the radio station could attract as many as five thousand subscribers and yet still not be self-supporting, Roy told friends. Perhaps, Roy speculated in the *San Francisco Chronicle* of August 25, 1957, Hill's death might have something to do with KPFA's unraveling financial and management crisis.

Roy, in any event, had his own priorities to worry about. Though a May 1957 survey found 63 percent of Americans agreed that the United States should stop nuclear tests if other countries did likewise, this fell short of what pacifists sought. Roy wanted disarmament. It was time to push harder. It was time to go to Livermore (Neil Katz 1974, 64).

Livermore was still the countryside, a cow town east of the Bay Area. It was an adventure just to get there and back, traveling over sunbaked mountain passes that strained car radiators to the limit. But on these outskirts, some of the nation's finest minds were preparing for war. In 1952 officials had established the University of California Radiation Laboratory on the one-square-mile site of a former navy air training station. Ernest Lawrence and Edward Teller had successfully argued for the second weapons lab to complement the Los Alamos facility in New Mexico. By 1957 the Livermore Radiation Laboratory was coming into its own. Livermore's bomb designers were already making their mark through the test shots of Operation Plumbob and the early design of the Polaris missile, and they spoke firmly of their adult responsibilities to protect the nation.

"We must not let ourselves be mesmerized by the specter of nuclear war; we must not give way to hysteria, we must defend our ideals and, I believe, we must be prepared to face the risks of limited war," Mark Mills, associate director of the Livermore Radiation Laboratory, declared to the American Association of Newspaper Editors on July 13, 1957.

Within a year of his self-confident presentation, while preparing for the Eniwetok Atoll atomic bomb tests, Mills would die in a 1958 helicopter crash. That misfortune, though, was still untold when, on November 24, 1957, caravans began forming throughout Northern California and the San Joaquin Valley. A Modesto-area activist named Samuel R. Tyson had called Roy about bringing the Ban-the-Bomb protests right into Livermore: The belly of the beast, Tyson called it. The conversation bore fruit, and now the caravans were forming. Some cars bore signs pleading "Save Humanity." Some had but one or two passengers. Others were station wagons, packed to capacity. They all converged on Foresters Hall, a one-time fraternal lodge near downtown Livermore. Some five hundred activists filled the two-story building, the overflow spilling out onto the sidewalk. Roy took the stage, the master of ceremonies, and saw in the overcrowded room vindication. The public was finally waking up.

"This is a test of whether the people are really interested in stopping deadly nuclear experiments," Roy said, the *San Francisco Chronicle* reported on November 25, 1957. "And from a look at the crowd, we've proved that point."

Roy and Ira and Al Baez had done yeomen's work drawing the Sunday crowd. They had worked all their contacts, played every card, but their success ultimately stemmed from the celebrity of the headline speaker: Linus Pauling. The Nobel Prize–winning chemist was the nation's highest-profile crusader against nuclear weaponry. By 1955, when he joined Albert Einstein and nine other Nobel laureates to sign a manifesto warning of the danger of nuclear weapons, he was spending at least half of his time focusing on disarmament. He was throwing himself into the work that would earn him in 1962 his second Nobel Prize, for peace. He was just the man to excite the Livermore crowd that Roy had helped convene.

The fifty-six-year-old Pauling was, perhaps, the nation's leading peace celebrity at that moment, and the audience was with him before he spoke a word. Repeatedly interrupted by applause, Pauling declaimed his message. War is no longer an option. There is no such thing as a safe level of radiation. Nuclear tests would inevitably poison thousands. International law must curtail their toxic spread.

The audience ate it up.

Pauling's Livermore speech was a great hit, and it gave Roy hope. He was perpetually on the lookout for high-profile champions, headliners for the cause. Pauling's worldwide reputation legitimized the disarmament argument. The nuclear weapons debate could no longer be cast simply as kooks and grannies versus scientists and soldiers. Indeed, public skepticism about nuclear weapons and civil defense was growing more pervasive. Several months after Pauling's Livermore speech, in early February 1958, San Francisco's civil defense leaders admitted that most civilians seemed to have a "what's the use?" attitude toward postapocalypse preparations. Few believed the Bomb would leave anything civil standing. Duck and cover served no purpose. The city's volunteer civil defense organization had not met in the past two years, the *San Francisco Chronicle* reported on February 6, 1958.

That month Palo Alto school officials planned a customary civil defense and disaster preparedness drill. The script was clear. Upon the ringing of the bells, students would retire to their homes, where they could ride out the hypothetical atomic holocaust in the company of their family. Al Baez thought it ridiculous. For Joan's benefit, he calculated the travel time for a Russian ICBM missile to reach Palo Alto High School. Mere minutes elapsed between launch and obliteration. As Roy and Ira had before her, Joan realized there was neither time nor place to hide. So, in the alternative, she would stand in place.

Joan agreed with several friends that they would protest by refusing to participate in the civil defense exercise. In the end, though, only Joan held out. Rather than retreat to her family's home near the Stanford campus, Joan simply remained at Palo Alto High School until the standard adjournment time of 3 p.m. Her sole compromise, at the request of her teachers, was to wait in the principal's office rather than sit alone in a classroom.

"I don't see any sense in having an air raid drill," Joan explained, the *Palo Alto Times* reported on February 7, 1958. "Our only defense is peace."

Our only defense is peace. The seventeen-year-old high school student had heard this often from Roy and Ira and her own father, Al. Joan, though, declared that the high school civil defense protest was entirely her own idea. She had been reflecting on these things. She was a conscientious objector, she informed a Palo Alto reporter. It was her duty to stand up for what was right. It was the duty of other students, as well, and their apathy upset Joan. Some of her high school peers, Joan reported sternly, were even so frivolous as to use the civil defense drill simply as an excuse to throw an impromptu Thursday party at their homes. Joan herself confessed that she had been "expecting more of a reaction" to her protest. Most people were much too placid, unshaken by outrage.

Still, quietly, the protest had some effect. One of Joan's teachers tearfully told Roy afterward that she was stuck in the position of having to enforce the rules she didn't believe in. Joan's solo stance also further endeared her to Ira. They began spending hours together, strolling the Stanford campus and neighborhoods, delighting in each other's company. He was the wise one, garbed in a British tweed hat and wielding a gnarled walking stick. She was the acolyte, her long hair tangling down her back.

Ira's wife, Merle, had seen all this before. Once, she uncorked her pent-up feelings to Joan. All these women thought Ira was such a saint, but they didn't *know* him. The man was impossible to live with, constantly going off to attend meetings and save the world while he was barely a father to his own children, Mark and Nicole. And now, along came the most beautiful and talented muse of them all to entrance Ira once more (Baez 1966, 74). Joan's father, too, wasn't keen about the bond developing between the middle-aged man and his teenage daughter. Some of her mother's elderly friends added their own concerns. Young Joan was so fresh and beautiful, an unplucked flower, and Ira was a bearded, older man of a bohemian aspect, goatish even, some thought. Joan's mother was not worried, but she mentioned the friends' anxieties to her daughter, who merely laughed and informed her mother she was learning about the world. Sex was not part of the relationship.

It never would be for Joan and Ira, though in other respects theirs was a love affair through and through, complete with soul-sharing and jealousy, bitter rending and reconciliation.

Edward Teller was making the case for nuclear weapons. After Pauling in January 1958 had presented to United Nations Secretary-General Dag Hammarskjöld an anti-Bomb petition signed by some nine thousand scientists, Teller prepared a *Life* magazine screed entitled "The Compelling Need for Nuclear Tests." Clean bombs, the Hungarian-born weapons designer explained, were essential to fend off Communist advances. Renouncing nuclear weapons, he argued, would simply open the door to aggression. The magazine's declarative cover headline, explaining that "Dr. Teller refutes 9,000 Scientists," conveyed the message that Dr. Teller was single-handedly demolishing the fuzzy-minded musings of the Ban-the-Bomb crowd.

"I said to Roy, 'how can we compete with this bastard Teller?'" Ira recalled in an interview. "And the next thing I knew, he was calling Cal Tech."

Roy, never hesitant to approach men of stature, telephoned Pauling and insisted that he was the only man who could debate Teller.

Pauling demurred. He said he had a cold. Roy insisted. Pauling had a responsibility. Teller had to be confronted head-on. Pauling finally agreed, and Roy and the Peninsula Committee for the Abolition of Nuclear Tests invited Teller to debate. The weapons designer replied that a mass meeting wasn't the proper venue for such a discussion. Nonetheless, in February 1958, Pauling took Teller on in an hour-long debate televised by the San Francisco public station KQED. By all accounts, Teller prevailed. In his rumbling Hungarian accent, Teller assured listeners that, of course, everyone preferred peace. The real question was over how to reach it. The friendly atom, Teller said reassuringly, was man's ally, useful for domestic purposes as well as for defending the nation. Teller effectively cast a broad and comforting blanket over the controversy. Pauling sounded shrill, hung up on minute details. It was the last time Pauling would agree to debate Teller.

Nonetheless, the Teller versus Pauling confrontation lived on at Kepler's Books & Magazines, as the debate transcript was published in a fifty-cent booklet entitled *Fallout and Disarmament*. Roy advertised it in the *San Francisco Chronicle,* where he would describe Kepler's as "the Peninsula's largest anti-missile bookstore" and would pledge to "be here until the first ICBM grounds in." For *Fallout and Disarmament,* Roy wrote that paperbound books have traveled like a shock wave from coast to coast. But there, he stated, the similarity ends. "For the paperbounds are proving a boon to man, while A and H bombs bring only BOOM to man, and perhaps DOOM to man," Roy wrote.

Roy advertised with a distinctive voice, alternating between seriousness and sarcasm. "It's hard to say which is growing faster, the Peninsula's war industries or Kepler's Books," another ad stated. Sometimes Roy's wording worked. Sometimes it fell flat, or overreached, or the humor was too broad. It was like a protest demonstration in that respect. Roy used outrage, a touch of theater, to command attention to an underlying cause. Plenty of demonstrations failed; they were of only passing moment. Some succeeded beyond anyone's expectations.

The *Golden Rule* succeeded. It was not one of Roy's concoctions, but he learned from it.

The *Golden Rule*'s captain, Albert Bigelow, was a man willing to fight. During World War II the Harvard graduate commanded a submarine chaser around the Solomon Islands and, later, a destroyer escort bound for the invasion of Japan. Bigelow was on the bridge of his destroyer escort, the *Dale W. Peterson,* when word arrived of the atomic bomb leveling Hiroshima. His world began turning. By 1955 Bigelow had resigned his commission in the Navy Reserve and had along with his wife, Sylvia, joined the Society of Friends. He joined Jim Peck and others at the August 1957 protests outside the Nevada Test Site. With the United States charging ahead with weapons testing in the far reaches of the Pacific Ocean, Bigelow had an opportunity for even more creative protests.

Starting out from Los Angeles on February 10, 1958, several days after Joan's solo Palo Alto protest, the four-man crew of the *Golden Rule* attempted to sail the thirty-foot ketch into the nuclear test area of the South Pacific. The *Golden Rule* made it about seven hundred miles off the California coast before turning back amid bad weather. The Atomic Energy Commission rapidly announced regulations making it a crime to enter the 50,000-square-mile weapons testing area (Lynd 1966, 341).

The *Golden Rule* set sail once more on March 25, arriving in Honolulu to find that the federal government had obtained a restraining order. The *Golden Rule* sailed on, making it a mile out of port before the Coast Guard tracked it down, boarded the ketch, and towed it back to Hawaii. The crew was charged with contempt for violating the judge's order. The federal judge rejected the pacifists' plea of moral necessity, found them guilty, and sentenced each to sixty days in jail, suspended. On the mainland, demonstrators rallied in San Francisco and more than four hundred Bay Area residents petitioned the U.S. attorney in solidarity with the *Golden Rule.*

In Hawaii, the *Golden Rule* crew, joined by veteran troublemaker Jim Peck, once again tried on June 4 to sail for the Pacific testing grounds. The ship made it about five miles out of Hawaii before again being stopped, seized, and returned to shore. Three crew members received sixty-day sentences. Peck received a suspended sentence, which meant he was free to arrange picket lines outside of the jail where his compatriots were being held. Ultimately, in December 1960, an appellate court would strike down as invalid the Atomic Energy Commission's hastily concocted rules banning public entrance into the Pacific test area.

Peck, after being released from Hawaii, returned to Northern California and spent a night at Roy's Bay Area home. He was on the way to Livermore, to speak at a "Nagasaki Day" protest at Livermore, but for the one night Peck simply settled into the Keplers' home to swap yarns with Roy and Pat and play with the children.

The month after the *Golden Rule*'s final aborted protest voyage, another World War II veteran named Robert Pickus in July 1958 circulated his notion for yet another peace group. The one-time Office of Strategic Services officer had served during the mid-1950s as an organizer with the American Friends Service Committee. He insisted he didn't want to impinge on the work being done by others. Instead he envisioned a coordinating group, something that could bring together the Bay Area's radical and conventional peace activists.

Pickus met with Roy, who saw the benefit in what Pickus was proposing. For years Roy had been making much the same criticism. The War Resisters League and the Fellowship of Reconciliation had never sustained their reach outside of New York City. Pickus and Roy also shared a willingness to take on the fellow traveler problem. They considered communism a fatally jealous master, demanding ultimate fealty. They knew, as well, that the credibility of a peace campaign would wither if it could be credibly labeled a Communist front.

The War Resisters League donated several thousand dollars and Pickus succeeded in rallying a dozen different peace organizations to create Acts for Peace. The Berkeley-based coordinating group, as it was originally envisioned, would in time change its name to Turn Toward Peace. His voice carried, though Bob Pickus was not everyone's cup of tea. For this peace group and others, success, sometimes, could be as troublesome as failure. When President Eisenhower on October 31, 1958, announced that the United States would enter into a one-year nuclear weapons testing moratorium, following the

Soviet Union's earlier offer to do the same, Ban-the-Bomb activists lost one of their best recruiting tools: the pictures of rising mushroom clouds.

Roy was balancing his activism with his business, which kept growing. In September 1959, having again outgrown his space, he moved his store to a larger, 3,800-square-foot space at 825 El Camino Real. His profile was bigger than ever on the Stanford campus, where students were starting to discover the world beyond frat parties and the homework grind. "It was a place where hours could be spent," Stewart Brand, a Phillips Andover graduate who entered Stanford in 1956, recalled of Kepler's in an interview. Kepler's, Brand could tell, was a "bookstore run by somebody who wasn't in it for the money." It was certainly a bookstore run by someone who scrimped on decorations. Aesthetically, the store remained largely unadorned, low-rent even. Its bookshelves were hammered together from the cheapest lumber around.

The readers who found it, though, were enraptured. They were growing in number, and they were also finding more like-minded places to hang, especially after St. Michael's Alley opened on April Fool's Day 1959, about a half-mile from Roy's store.

St. Michael's Alley was a coffeehouse, both a throwback and a cast-forward. Vernon Gates, an army veteran and an independent cuss, named his new place after a seventeenth-century English establishment. He drew his inspiration from his continental exposure. Like Roy, Gates had found his way to Europe after college, in Gates's case at the University of Innsbruck in Austria. Gates had then come back to the United States to earn a Stanford master's degree in communications, which he put to work doing consumer surveys. After he insisted on a raise, he found himself out of a job. Casting about, he struck on the idea of mimicking the coffeehouses he had enjoyed in Europe. Space was cheap and plentiful. There were, Gates recalled, plenty of empty buildings along Palo Alto's University Avenue. He chose one, at 436 University Avenue, and on the cusp of turning thirty years old

Gates opened up the newest thing in town. The lighting was subdued, with exposed beams and a dark, rustic look. Gates offered live music, an open piano, and the crackle of caffeinated conversation.

"I was the first one," Gates recalled in an interview, "to have an espresso machine south of San Francisco."

Soon enough Roy would also get his own espresso machine. It was not the only overlap between Kepler's Books & Magazines and St. Michael's Alley. They complemented each other. Although Roy and Gates did not socialize much with each other, their customers would move from one place to another as if completing a circuit. Hang at Kepler's, buy a book, drift over to the Alley, have some coffee. Joan, for one, would come in with Ira for lunch; invariably, she would be the one to buy.

"She would start singing at a table, and she would never stop," Gates said. "I couldn't sell anything, because the tables wouldn't turn over."

Kepler's and St. Michael's Alley stood out because Stanford, at the time, was still a stiflingly conservative and self-satisfied place. The dutiful children of California's middling rich dominated the university. The Farm, it was called, and politically it was, in fact, rather vegetative. Dress codes imposed order. Fraternities ruled. Controversial political speakers were all but banned. In 1958 a nontenured associate history professor named Richard W. Lyman had arrived on campus and was quickly set straight on what to expect. "One colleague told me that anyone in search of intellectual excitement would have to journey fifty miles to Berkeley," Lyman recalled (Lyman 2009, 5).

But the tectonic plates were shifting. One could see the signs, in the growth of Kepler's and the birth of St. Michael's Alley. In books, too, what once was revolutionary or subterranean was coming to the surface. By the end of 1959, for the first time, the dollar value of paperback sales exceeded that of hardcover books. Bookstore owners who once resisted the paperback upstarts now saw them as an economic boon. Paperbacks increased foot traffic for bookstores, attracting new customers. More people wanted to get into the business.

In late 1959 a former sociology professor of Roy's from the University of Colorado wrote to seek suggestions about starting a good paperback bookstore. Roy, characteristically, was both helpful and unsparing.

"You will be unable to use my store as a model," Roy wrote the professor, Howard Higman, on December 2, 1959, "since it is based upon values, truth and nonviolence, which you reject as useless and even positively harmful. In short, you wouldn't understand how to accomplish this kind of bookstore."

The sally seemed hardly fair. Higman was, in fact, an accomplished and complicated man. An enterprising liberal who had challenged Senator Joseph McCarthy in 1953, Higman was a prominent academic impresario whose long-running Conference on World Affairs had been bringing leading lights to Boulder since 1948. A bookstore along Kepler's lines might have fit in nicely, and Roy did soften his rebuke with specific observations about his own store's operation. He said he was obtaining most of his quality paperbacks from the San Francisco–based Paper Editions Corporation. He recommended specific distributors for French, German, and Spanish books. He was getting his quarterly magazines from a New Jersey supplier, his Russian periodicals from New York, and his French paperbacks from Paris. Stylistically, Roy favored what he termed "asymmetrical bookcases rather than long, unbroken rows glistening with chrome." Self-service worked well. Displaying the books face-out helped grab the browser's attention, and sprinkling throughout the store "unusual books not easily found elsewhere in [the] usual homogenized bookstore" captured customers.

"We try to supply as wide a range of paperback books, diverse magazines and quarterlies covering most varieties of political, social and literary viewpoints, and inexpensive art prints as possible," Roy explained.

But that was just the business, a set of techniques. The *place* was something more, a living entity that Roy described as "a personal store, [whose] owner is a human being with an identity in the community and with opinions of his own." Put another way, the place had a third dimension. It had breath, which expanded every time someone new discovered it.

In late 1959 nineteen-year-old Stanford philosophy major Lee Swenson had found his way to this Kepler's place. There he found Ira one day, leaning against the counter by the cash register and looking ready to talk. So they conversed, and when Ira learned of Swenson's interests he invited the Stanford student over to the Peninsula School, where Ira was teaching. With that, Swenson began hanging at Kepler's in his free time. Nowhere else but there could he discover books like *A Field of Broken Stones,* Lowell Naeve and David Thoreau Weick's 1950 account, published by David Dellinger's small Libertarian Press, of World War II conscientious objectors in prison. Kepler's, inevitably, was also where Swenson chanced to be in mid-October 1959 when word came down about what was happening in Berkeley.

A University of California–Berkeley student named Frederick Lawrence Moore Jr. was conducting a one-man fast and sit-in on the steps of Sproul Hall to protest the university's compulsory ROTC. Swenson was intrigued. He left Kepler's, told the Palo Alto Recreation Department he wouldn't be able to work that day, and drove up the Peninsula to Berkeley, where he found Moore in the middle of a rolling debate. Starting at midnight on Sunday, October 18, Moore had held fast, and in the process collected well over one thousand signatures urging the end of the ROTC requirement. Moore would stay put for fifty-nine hours before calling it quits. Pale and weak, eight pounds lighter than when he started, the eighteen-year-old student told reporters that the one-man protest had "accomplished my purpose." His father, an air force colonel, showed up to bring him home; he was proud of his son, though frankly worried about his predilection for deep philosophy.

"Sometimes, I wish he had read some comics or something lighter once in a while," Colonel Moore said, the *San Francisco Chronicle* reported on October 22, 1959.

The encounter with Fred Moore inspired Swenson, who would in later years pull duty both as a builder of Kepler's bookshelves and as a director of the Institute for the Study of Nonviolence. For the University of California, too, the one-man protest left a lasting mark. Two days after Moore stopped fasting, the University of California's Board of Regents announced it had begun a review of the ROTC program. The review, University of California President Clark Kerr revealed, had actually been ordered, quietly, a month before Moore's protest began. Still, Moore's protest was acutely timed, a foreshadowing.

10

The Sixties Begin

Ken Kesey needs his bus driver. Naturally, he turns to Kepler's.

And so begins the sixties qua sixties.

It's a June day in 1964. Kesey and his clan cavort on the farthest side of the Santa Cruz Mountains. The former Stanford writing fellow's first novel, *One Flew Over the Cuckoo's Nest,* had been a favorite of Roy's, who appreciated the antiauthoritarian sentiments as well as its commercial popularity. With his book earnings, Kesey has removed himself from the Bay Area to La Honda. It's hardly a town, more a deeply shaded place seventeen miles from Menlo Park. Kesey and crowd are burrowing in. They also have a bus, a 1939 International Harvester, and they have divined a new destination. Kesey et al. will be traveling east, bound for the 1964 World's Fair and publication of his latest book, *Sometimes a Great Notion* (Perry 1990). On this particular June day, Kesey and his best friend Ken Babbs, another former Stanford writing fellow, need a steady hand at the wheel.

"Kesey asked if anyone had seen Neal Cassady," Babbs recalled in an interview. "Ron Bevirt said he just came from Kepler's, and Neal was there."

Kepler's: Of course!

The entire circus had been drawn to the store. Kesey himself would pal around with Ira, the ex–college wrestler periodically challenging the slender pacifist to an arm-wrestling match that would have set a world record for brevity. Writer Robert Stone, a Stegner Writing Fellow who ran with the Kesey crowd, recalled that most of the Stegner Fellows would spend some time at Kepler's, because it was the best bookstore around. Stone saw in Kepler's reminders of

New York City's legendary Gotham Book Mart and the 8th Street Bookshop.

Even after Kesey moved over the mountains to La Honda, some of the crew would continue frequenting Kepler's. Certainly it would be a fertile spot for Neal Cassady, the muscular motor-mouth known to Beat aspirants as the inspiration for Dean Moriarty in Jack Kerouac's *On the Road*. Kepler's had sold many copies of the paperback. The store abounded with the books and magazines and, well, the girls that were purest nectar for Neal Cassady and his acolytes.

Bevirt says he does not remember the episode, but Babbs has recalled it several times. So it could have gone: Bevirt exits Kesey's La Honda homestead and heads east up Highway 84, winds his way over the crest at Skyline Drive, and then rolls down through the mountains until he's at El Camino Real. In Kepler's familiar environs, Cassady must be easy to find: a restless man in his late thirties, his raw energy throbbing. A while later, Babbs recalls, a smoking Buick, radio blaring "Love Potion Number Nine," pulls into La Honda headquarters. His jeans hanging below his belly, a Camel cigarette from his lips, Cassady is reporting for duty.

Kesey astounds him. The crew is traveling across country and needs a driver. Cassady is that man.

"You mean we'd be making movies? I'd be a film star in my declining years?" Cassady says, in Babbs's 2005 recollection.

"There's nothing I'd rather do for you," Kesey says, according to Babbs.

And with one or two more adjustments, the 1939 International Harvester known more popularly as Furthur or The Bus was on its way across the country, in a journey subsequently enshrined in 1968 by Tom Wolfe's *The Electric Kool-Aid Acid Test*. Which, in turn, like *On the Road* before it, would be sold abundantly at Kepler's Books & Magazines, the place where characters sometimes came to life.

Maybe it happened, just like that. Maybe, more probably, some key facts are missing or have been somehow compressed. The point is,

Kepler's was right there at the beginning. Right there, when the two distinct themes that defined the sixties arose. Call them, with gross exaggeration, the political and the psychedelic. The political is the world of protests and peace activism, culminating in but not limited to the mass demonstrations against the Vietnam War. The psychedelic is the world of mind enhancement and artistic expression, epitomized by Ken Kesey's acid tests and all that sprang from them.

Both classic expressions of the decade found root at Kepler's Books & Magazines. Roy himself was a political animal, the straight-arrow radical. Kesey's frolicsome world was beyond his ken. But Roy was also tolerant when it counted, when conformity still wore a gray suit.

Sixties skin magazines exemplified Roy's tolerance. Roy was as far from a nudist as there could be possibly be, but he allowed his store to carry magazines featuring butt-naked women. In June 1960, when Barry Goldwater's *The Conscience of a Conservative* was among the Top 10 nonfiction sellers, Roy was advising Lawrence

7. Roy Kepler at Kepler's Books & Magazines, undated. Photographer unknown, courtesy of the Kepler family.

Ferlinghetti of City Lights Books about the best place to find distributors for sunbathers' magazines such as *Helios* and *Sunshine and Health,* the latter being billed as the "official journal of the National Nudist Council." It was at Kepler's, one-time Stanford Writing Fellow Ed McClanahan said approvingly, that the curious could find, not far from the foreign newspapers and literary quarterlies, some alluring nudie magazines.

"I would stand there and read them," McClanahan said in an interview. "Well, not read them; I would look at them."

The skin magazines could be risky. Roy's wife, Patricia, definitely didn't approve of them. Roy's mother, LaClede, would toss them out if she could. Ira wasn't opposed to the idea of them, but he thought the models were rather ugly. Righteous lawmen disapproved altogether. Once, Ira recalled, a law enforcement officer told him to remove the magazines or face arrest.

"So I called up Roy, and I said, 'am I going to get arrested [for the] goddamn nudist magazines which I hate anyway?'" Ira told filmmaker Alex Beckstead. "He said, 'Ira, we can't always be arrested for things we want to be [arrested for.]'"

As it happened, Roy and Ira would both be arrested multiple times during the sixties. This was the price paid for their engagement in the cause of peace, the decade's political facet. They would lead others, too, into jail. But in the same way as Roy offered space for nudists' magazines, even though he was not himself a sun worshipper, he provided crucial space for the unconventional young. Freaks and protofreaks, in other words, could find their way at Kepler's when no one else would have them. Throughout the first years of the sixties, in particular, the political and the psychedelic threads were woven together at Kepler's.

If Kesey's 1964 bus trip kicked off the decade's psychedelic side, the political roots started earlier, when the House Un-American Activities Committee announced in early 1960 that it would be exposing California's Communist cesspool. Though past its McCarthy-era prime, the panel could still be fearsome. Ira heard he might be summoned as a witness at the San Francisco hearing. It made sense that

Ira or Roy could be targeted. Both were well known to those who monitored the Left.

In the end, neither Ira nor Roy received subpoenas. Even so, Ira was always up for a good show, and he certainly wouldn't want to miss the scene when the House committee convened its first hearing on May 12, 1960, at San Francisco City Hall. By lunchtime, nearly one thousand people had rallied at nearby Union Square. After lunch, about two hundred students surged into City Hall, chanting and singing in the corridors. San Francisco County Sheriff Matthew Carberry finally worked out a deal to permit the movement of students into the hearing room as seats became available. The day ended in a truce.

The next day, May 13, students and activists gathered across the street from City Hall and some entered the building. The chants began: "Abolish the committee." "We shall not be moved." The volume rose, until judges couldn't hear conversations in their own third-floor courtrooms. Police officers warned demonstrators to be quiet. The demonstrators jeered.

Tensions rose. At noon, police began trying to dislodge the protestors. When words and muscle failed, the officers deployed a fire hose and opened it up. The blasting water drove students back to the top of the City Hall stairway. They slipped, fell, struggled against the blasting water. Some protestors sat down, their backs to the fire hoses, their arms linked. Some began singing the national anthem. Policemen surged toward them. The grand staircase became a tumult. Police officers disentangled the protestors and hauled each in turn down the grand stairway to the paddy wagons below. Limp students allowed themselves to be dragged down the stairs. A *San Francisco Chronicle* reporter saw one writhing student carried away by two husky officers.

"Then from nowhere appeared a third officer," the reporter recounted. "He ran up to the slender boy firmly held by the other two officers and clubbed him three times on the head. The boy went limp and was carried out."

It took police half an hour to clear the building. The noise infiltrated the hearing room, where Chairman Edwin Willis of Louisiana was gaveling the afternoon session to order. Willis welcomed informer

Karl Prussion, a metallurgical engineer with a story to tell about Communist infiltration of the San Francisco Bay Area. Prussion had joined the Communist Party in 1933. By 1947, he had found God and signed on as an FBI informer. Prussion had joined the Mountain View–Los Altos cell of the Northern California Communist Party. By 1956 he had become attached to the Palo Alto cell.

"Probably the most vicious and the most conspiratorial, the most fraudulent work done by the Communist Party in Palo Alto was done through the Palo Alto Peace Club," Prussion testified ominously.

Claiming about sixty-four members at its peak, the Palo Alto Peace Club published a newsletter called *The Flashlight* that Prussion described as "the megaphone of the voice from the Kremlin." In February 1954 the Justice Department had formally designated the club a subversive organization. The designation was Orwellian, as the club had neither the right to see the evidence nor to challenge the ruling, but Ira later acknowledged that the Palo Alto Peace Club members were, in fact, "unmitigatedly pro-Soviet." The club's flavor was suggested in its June 1956 newsletter, which pronounced that "the history of Palo Alto is a history of imperialist domination."

Prussion would go on, in 1961, to cut a record entitled *Inside a Communist Cell,* serving up tales of life among the Reds. The House committee itself would later report that while "a few trained Communist agents" were among the arrested at the City Hall demonstration, many others were "the unwitting dupes of the party who had, in their demonstrations against the committee, performed like puppets, with the trained Communists manipulating their strings." Roy and Ira knew the assessment was absurd, but they closely followed the San Francisco hearings. The episode was an object lesson in protest tactics. Roy could appreciate the essentially nonviolent posture of the demonstrators, their absorbing of blows.

Several months after HUAC had returned to its Capitol lair, Roy returned to the parched Livermore Valley east of San Francisco. Marking the fifteenth anniversary of the atomic bomb blasts at Hiroshima and Nagasaki, Roy and his fellow activists had ambitious August plans. Livermore had been their target for several years, from the Linus Pauling speech in 1957 to several subsequent protest walks and Easter vigils. Now, for five days, activists gathered at the lakeside Del Valle Campground five miles from the Livermore lab. They picketed and distributed literature during the day, and met for communal meals at night. Livermore lab director Harold Brown, a future defense secretary, declined several invitations to meet with them, though Roy had tried calling him at home.

Security officers monitored the Livermore action, recording license plate numbers and filming the demonstrators. All-out security measures were being maintained at the lab in view of reports that Communists might try to turn the large peaceful demonstrations into riots, one Bay Area newspaper reported. By August 9, the fifteenth anniversary of the 1945 bombing of Nagasaki, about seventy-five adults and twenty-five children were on hand. As it happened, the State of California had also set August 9 as the date for the execution of a prisoner in San Quentin Prison. The coincidental timing struck activist Samuel Tyson as intriguing. California was preparing to execute one man even as the University of California was researching how to achieve the deaths of millions (Tyson 1960, 1).

Rising early that anniversary morning, Roy led the way to the Livermore parking compound, arriving about 6:30 a.m. Joining Roy was Tyson, a forty-one-year-old farmer and father of five, from the tiny San Joaquin Valley town of Waterford. Raised as a Quaker, Tyson had been booted from UCLA when he refused to participate in mandatory ROTC training. He subsequently served four years in Civilian Public Service, including time at the Glendora camp, where Roy had started his own CPS journey. With them was Hal Stallings, a strapping, twenty-nine-year-old father of four from Altadena, and Jerry Wheeler, a navy veteran and unemployed twenty-nine-year-old Berkeley resident.

A chain-link fence topped with barbed wire surrounded the lab parking compound. Shortly before 8 a.m., as the lab workers began arriving for their day shift, Roy and his three associates stood, for several minutes, face to face with guards. Roy looked natty in his jacket, white T-shirt, and hat. He said the demonstrators wanted to speak with lab workers. The guards said no. Roy asked again. No, guards told him.

"Then," Roy recalled, "we just sort of sidled past them."

Roy stepped inside the gate. The police officers shifted over, creating a hole on the left. Tyson walked in. Police advised both men they were now under arrest. They were handcuffed, bundled into cars with Wheeler and Stallings, and conveyed in a caravan to Alameda County's Santa Rita Rehabilitation Center, a grim human sink many activists would come to know in the coming decade. Roy and the three other arrested men were gently defiant. They would not submit their hands for fingerprinting, nor would they sign for their property. Three refused the offer of $500 bail. Roy explained, according to the *Hayward Daily Review* of August 10, 1960, that bail was fundamentally unfair because it means that "those with money can go free, while those without funds cannot."

Three days later, on August 12, U.S. Commissioner Harold Jewett oversaw a hearing attended by reporters, law enforcement officials, and some fifty friends of the arrested men. The federal prosecutor advised Jewett that Roy and the others were "not the usual type of criminal; they had no interest to do harm or to gain personal advantage." He recommended only nominal punishment. Roy, Tyson, and Stallings having pled guilty, after their initial bid for a nolo contendere plea was rejected, Jewett declared that the three days already spent in jail were sufficient. He imposed a one-year probation, though in a further act of resistance none of the men would sign the probation papers.

Roy did have something to say, though. Remember the Nuremberg trials, Roy declared. Citizens had a duty to resist a wrong-doing government. One must stand up for what was right notwithstanding the dictates of those in authority. Roy said his piece and then was let go. Potentially, he was still at risk. Ira recalled that following Livermore, it was suggested that Roy might be sentenced to a full six months if he were rearrested within a year. That would devastate the store.

"I said, 'what the hell are you going to do, if they really give . . . the six months?'" Ira told filmmaker Alex Beckstead. "Well, he said, 'Ira, I'll start something else again.' And he said, 'It doesn't matter.' He said, 'this is more important to me than the bookstore.'"

Tyson, for one, thought the Livermore action cost-effective. The activists had spent about $150 for postage, mimeographing, and other administrative services, in addition to the food costs for the campers. But in return, Tyson noted that the demonstrators secured attention in the *Oakland Tribune, San Jose Mercury,* and half a dozen other newspapers, as well as on local television. Media coverage might only scratch the surface of how a demonstration can change people's hearts and minds, Tyson knew; but, still, the attention was welcome (Tyson 1960, 4).

Certain books foreshadowed the coming decade and its dualities, the tension between mind and politics. For those of a political bent, sociologist Paul Goodman's *Growing Up Absurd: Problems of Youth in the Organized Society* critiqued the Establishment against which the disaffected would rebel. The apolitical, mind-expanding perspective was captured in Robert De Ropp's *Drugs and the Mind.* Either perspective might be found on Kepler's shelves.

Roy would carry anyone: lowbrow, highbrow, and no-brow whatsoever. He carried pacifist poet Kenneth Patchen's collections like the 1946 volume *An Astonished Eye Looks Out of the Air,* and he carried the antithesis, Herman Kahn's 1960 provocation *On Thermonuclear War.* "Be sure to read what James R. Newman calls 'this evil book,'" one Kepler's ad stated. Roy carried the 1960 paperback edition of *The Ugly American,* Eugene Burdick's and William Lederer's barely veiled account of U.S. government actions in still-obscure Vietnam. El Camino Real passersby might also see through the front window notices for Harold Robbins' steamy trash *The Carpetbaggers* and, for those who preferred their titillation a little classier, Henry Miller's *Tropic of Cancer.*

At one point Roy conceived an interest in the John Birch Society, which after its founding by Robert Welch in 1958 had begun publishing tracts denouncing one-worldism, communism, and collectivism. Welch's 1961 book *The Politician,* also known as the *Black Book,* denounced former Secretary of State George Marshall as a Soviet agent and asserted that Dwight Eisenhower had served the worldwide Communist conspiracy. It sounded nuts, but Roy made inquiries. Roy figured people could decide for themselves what was right. Besides, the books might sell. A John Birch Society member eventually came around to check out the store, Roy later recalled. Apparently, though, Kepler's Books & Magazines didn't pass muster, and the John Birch Society's oeuvre was not made available to Roy or his customers.

Even fringe ideas deserved serious consideration. Roy wanted his store to be a place for intellectual engagement, the articulation of ideas. Increasingly he was bringing in authors and speakers to make their points and sell their books directly. In the fall of 1960 the British writer C. P. Snow had alighted in Berkeley for a visiting professorship. Snow was at the height of his fame. He had been knighted three years before, and in 1959 had published his thoughts on the gap between the "two cultures" of science and the humanities. For the year, Sir Charles was savoring life as a Regents Professor at the University of California. From Cody's, he had been gathering up *Classics Illustrated,* which he considered thoroughly delightful (Cody and Cody 1992, 37).

In early October Roy and Fred Cody brought Sir Charles down to Menlo Park for a luncheon and book signing. This was a sign of Kepler's growing stature. In the five years since opening, and through moving to larger quarters, Roy had turned Kepler's into a destination point for authors. Snow drew a standing-room-only bookstore audience, for whom he delivered a dry run for his upcoming Godkin Lecture at Harvard and then signed copies of the Anchor paperback of *The Masters* and the Cambridge hardcover of *The Two Cultures.* Afterward, Roy organized a dinner for Snow, and some of Ira's acolytes were about. They were California girls, Ira would recall later, darling and idealistic. The girls were impressed with Snow, and Snow, who turned fifty-seven that month, was said by Ira to have been impressed by them as well.

The demonstrations in San Francisco and Livermore were part of an accelerating season of protest. College students were taking off to swell the civil rights movement. "Planning a vacation trip thru the South?" Roy asked dryly in one 1960 ad. For these idealists and others, Roy offered books including *The History of Bigotry* and *Stride Toward Freedom*. Roy appreciated how nonviolent tactics served the civil rights movement. Still, disarmament and not desegregation remained his personal focus. On December 1, 1960, eleven pacifists affiliated with the Committee for Nonviolent Action set out from San Francisco on a Walk for Peace. About two hundred peace sympathizers gathered in San Francisco's Union Square to send off the nine men and two women, dressed as if for a Sunday stroll.

Their goal: Russia.

The marchers strolled south from San Francisco, down El Camino Real and through Roy's Menlo Park neighborhood before proceeding down to Los Angeles. The peace marchers would continue on, facing daily adventures for ten months and six thousand miles, until they entered Russian territory on September 15, 1961.

The San Francisco-to-Moscow march inspired burgeoning Bay Area activists like Theodore Roszak, who yearned for more than simply the ivory tower. A graduate of UCLA, with a freshly minted Princeton doctorate, Roszak had arrived at Stanford to teach in the fall of 1960. He wanted to be involved in the peace movement, and someone suggested that he talk with Roy. So the twenty-seven-year-old Roszak made his way to Kepler's, where he found Roy buzzing with energy. There was a world to save and work to be done.

"As soon as you showed up, he was trying to recruit you to do something," Roszak said in an interview.

Roszak became a regular in the Peninsula Committee for the Abolition of Nuclear Tests. Members would meet in each other's homes, talking tactics and strategy, but they also wanted to circulate their ideas more broadly. They wanted a clubhouse, to which the world might be invited. By the fall of 1960 Roy and Ira and the others had established the Peninsula Peace Center, a rented two-story house on the southern edge of the Stanford campus and about a mile south of the bookstore. Renting out the bedrooms paid for the place while groups like the local Fair Play for Cuba Committee, Methodist Peace Committee, and American Friends Service Committee met downstairs.

Several nights a week, students and others might gather at the Peace Center for discussions or talks by visitors like Committee for Nonviolent Action activist George Willoughby. The Peninsula Peace Center attracted a diverse crowd. There were young searchers, under-grad idealists, and an occasional dropout needing a place to crash. The center itself was essentially maintained for a while by Stanford Law School student Howard Richards, who had known the Baez family in Redlands. Richards came to live at the Peninsula Peace Center while he attended law school, sat in on philosophy classes, and tried his hand at writing. On the side, he split his time between Stanford's International Club and Kepler's.

"It was the place to get *Liberation* magazine, which we all read," Richards, who would go on to found Earlham College's Peace and Global Studies Program, said in an interview.

Through Kepler's, Richards also discovered the poetry of Kenneth Patchen, a pacifist who had befriended everyone from E. E. Cummings to Allen Ginsburg. "Wars will only end," Patchen poetically maintained, "when the present murderous forms of society are allowed to die and all men are at last permitted to live together as brothers." A spinal injury had by then confined Patchen to bed in his modest Palo Alto home, while his wife, Miriam, worked and tended the Patchen reputation. At one point Richards organized a benefit for the ill poet, even as he began publishing his own notions through a modest journal of ideas called *Utopian Papers*. Kepler's was about the only bookstore that would carry it, Richards recalled.

Academically credentialed, Howard Richards and Theodore Roszak represented one facet of Roy's world: the Stanford crowd, the

Quakers and Unitarians, the well-meaning liberals and occasional political radicals. But Kepler's was drawing another crowd as well: hangers-on, dilettantes, autodidacts, and streetwise meanderers, the new avant-garde.

Willy Legate was a curious soul. While attending Redlands High School in Southern California circa 1956, he had met a young Joan Baez. Legate lasted several years at the University of Redlands, but he was beginning to draw outside the lines. In February 1959 Legate had sat in his college dorm room with some friends, truly hearing Bach's aural architecture and agog at how the new drug LSD bent the walls. By May 1960, he recalled in a 2005 letter, Legate was out of school and living in Palo Alto. For a place to hang out, Kepler's Books & Magazines presented itself.

Kepler's reminded Legate of a library, with its seemingly endless shelves of paperback books and racks of magazines and newspapers. The store carried everything from the ephemeral to the enduring. But there were other, more social touches: the coffee machine and trays filled with sweet baklava. The reading room, or what passed for one, offered round tables and cheap, scattered chairs. It was open space for open minds.

"I did think of a visit there as an intellectual adventure," Legate explained. "Or, at least, a chance to sit and talk about whatever."

A talented wordsmith who could spend a lot of time at the typewriter, Legate nonetheless was slapdash about certain things. He didn't always fit in at his digs at the Peace Center, where for a time he rented one of the three upstairs rooms. Once Roy berated him for leaving junk scattered on the Peace Center's stairs. Neatness mattered, to Roy. Willy would rather do as he pleased. The serious men, Roy and Howard Richards among them, thought that for public relations purposes outer appearances mattered. Willy thought otherwise: The important thing was to express oneself freely. He did so during a brief stint as a Kepler's clerk.

"One evening at [the] store, I was popping pills, either Benzedrine or probably Dexedrine, and lost track of what I was doing at the cash register," Willy recalled.

So that didn't work out too well. There were other crazed episodes too, that hinted at generational fissures to come, the conflict between carnival and commitment. In a 2010 memoir, *The Things We Do for Love,* writer Ruhama Veltfort recalled her rambunctious seventeenth birthday party held in March 1961 at the Peninsula Peace Center. Legate was her boyfriend at the time and the wild affair would have gotten him evicted from the Peace Center, Veltfort recalled, "if the people who ran it hadn't been Quakers and willing to talk about it" (Veltfort 2010, 45).

Born Danya Veltfort, she had grown up with her sister, Suzie, in a politically engaged Palo Alto household. Their parents were part of the old Palo Alto Peace Club, and Danya was raised to respect rebellion. One summer day, when she was sixteen and soon to start her last year in high school, Danya bicycled past the kempt places of her youth, all the suburban tracts, until she ended up at the Peninsula Peace Center. She was there to volunteer. Willy Legate and the other tenants happened to be painting that day, sprucing the place up. Danya dismounted, and there she was: talking to this curious, articulate guy, a twenty-one-year-old college dropout with a flaming red beard and a Camel cigarette in his hand. He was a definite character, Willy was.

Danya and Willy began seeing each other. When they weren't holed up in Willy's second-floor Peace Center room, with its teetering stacks of books and its walls painted purple, they might end up over at Kepler's. It was becoming quite the scene.

In November 1960 Alan Trist arrived from England. The son of a visiting scholar at the Center for Advanced Studies in Behavioral Sciences, cozily located next to the Stanford campus, Trist was taking leave before returning to start university life at Cambridge. In time, a friend advised him there was a lively bookstore he should check out; Kepler's, Trist recalled being told, "not only was a more interesting bookstore, in terms of selection, than the Stanford University Bookstore which I had been going to, but there were also more interesting people who were congregating there." Curious, Trist made his way to Kepler's. Its narrow aisles stretched back, Trist recalled forty-five years later, "into dusty depths . . . jammed with crisp volumes of perfect-bound editions." Christie Bourne, a flamenco-dancing high school student, was serving coffee and some shaggy local character was playing his guitar. Roy and Ira appeared as tolerant proprietors.

"Right before arriving in Palo Alto, I had spent the summer hanging with Beats and sundry other bohemians on the Left Bank in Paris, where the Shakespeare and Company Bookstore had a similar open-door policy to Kepler's," Trist recalled. "Now, an ocean and a continent away, it was exciting and joyous to run into these freethinkers, students, ex-students, bohemians, and musicians, all of whom had an entirely positive, non-Establishment, nonjudgmental, and open attitude to life, just at the beginning of our adult lives."

"Never looked back," Trist added.

Exactly so. Trist, in fact, would eventually come to work starting in 1970 for the Grateful Dead, and as of 2011 he was still managing the band's music publishing company. That shaggy guitar player Trist found at Kepler's, you see, was Jerry Garcia. He and his pal Robert Hunter, Trist soon learned, were Kepler's regulars. "Jerry," Trist recalled, "was always there. He was always playing his guitar, practicing, singing, talking, laughing, and others in our scene would drop by." Hunter had been coming to Kepler's since discovering it while in high school, in 1956. The place stuck with him. He would end up finishing his high school career in Connecticut, leaving college, joining the National Guard, and ending up back in Palo Alto. Hunter was there, living at the Palo Alto Hotel, when he met the prematurely charismatic Garcia. A Peninsula kid ejected from the army in December 1960, Garcia stayed with a Palo Alto couple before he and Hunter lived for a while out of their cars parked in gritty East Palo Alto. Kepler's was the convenient place to hang during the day. In March 1961 Garcia met Willy Legate at the St. Michael's Alley coffeehouse in downtown Palo Alto. Legate told his newfound friends about his place and so, between April and June 1961, Garcia and Hunter came to crash at Roy's Peninsula Peace Center.

"The . . . peace center was a great place for social trips," Garcia recalled. "The peace center was the place where the sons and daughters of the Stanford professors would hang out and discuss things. And we, the opportunist wolf pack, the beatnik crowds, would be there preying on their young minds and their refrigerators" (Jackson 1999, 30).

They were keeping bohemian hours. Garcia, who might sleep until noon if he had a chance, wouldn't show up at Kepler's until the afternoon or later. "We would be sitting around . . . and Jerry would say, 'I have a feeling something is happening at Kepler's,'" Hunter said in an interview, "and so, we would pop down there." Books were part of the store's appeal. Grateful Dead historian Dennis McNally noted that Garcia was reading James Joyce's *Finnegan's Wake,* Kenneth Patchen's poetry, science fiction, "and lots of other things that fell off Kepler's shelves" (McNally 2002, 31).

Books were only part of the scene. At Kepler's, Garcia would fix a cigarette in his guitar's fret board and play. It wasn't necessarily a performance per se. He and Hunter or whoever would simply play over and over folk songs made popular by the likes of the Kingston Trio, the Weavers, and Pete Seeger. Garcia commanded a repertoire of Appalachian ballads, folk songs, and the likes of "Long Black Veil." Then, after Kepler's and St. Michael's Alley closed at night, Garcia, Hunter, Legate, and Alan Trist might meander down El Camino Real to the all-night Stickney's restaurant. They would sip mediocre coffee and eat donuts and talk, Legate said, "about the arts and a lot of profound nonsense."

Into this burgeoning Kepler's scene, in the late spring of 1961, came a one-time school acquaintance of Garcia's named Marshall Leicester. Leicester was a Yale undergraduate who had known Garcia slightly from Menlo Park's Menlo Oaks Middle School.

"Jerry was sitting there playing a twelve-string guitar and singing tunes like 'Everyone Loves Saturday Night,' which was one of those kind of Pete Seeger 'love-your-worldwide-neighbors' songs in which the verses are the words 'everybody loves Saturday night' in about 15 different languages," Leicester recalled (Jackson 1999, 38).

He asked Garcia if he could borrow the guitar and play something else; and there, amid the Kepler's bookshelves, the Yalie and the army dropout resumed an unlikely friendship. Leicester began teaching Garcia finger-picking tricks.

Kepler's was also where another young musician named Phil Lesh encountered Garcia in 1961. Lesh was, at the time, a regular at KPFA. Gertrude Chiarito was striking a chord with her show *Midnight Special,* and Lesh advised her that he had encountered some promising new talent down at Kepler's. Lesh subsequently recorded Garcia for Chiarito's show, on which the guitarist would appear multiple times. Kepler's was a fork in the road for Garcia, more than once. One summer's evening in 1961, Garcia was sitting in Kepler's and playing the old standard "Railroad Bill" when budding music entrepreneur Rodney Albin walked in, accompanied by brother Peter Albin and aspiring musician David Nelson. In time Nelson would help found the country rock group New Riders of the Purple Sage and Peter Albin would play in Janis Joplin's group Big Brother and the Holding Company.

"So we were peeking through the books . . . into the area where the tables were," Nelson recalled, "and I see this hairy, swarthy guy with an open Levi's shirt and a real brooding look and an olive wreath in his hair, playing a Stella twelve-string. There was something scary about him; something awesome, some invisible quality" (Jackson 1999, 39).

They listened, and they were impressed. Rodney Albin asked Garcia if he wanted to appear at Albin's club in San Carlos, called the Boar's Head Inn.

Between bouts of song, the young hangers-out would goof, talk about whatever. Characters kept shuffling into Kepler's. Bobby Peterson, a budding writer who was going to team up with Phil Lesh on Grateful Dead songs, arrived along with Willy Legate. Joe Novakovich, an autoharp player who hung out with Neal Cassady, was there. Kepler's had become a place for kicks. At least once, indelibly for all who were there, Palo Alto High School student Christie Bourne joined a school chum in an impromptu flamenco dance. They struck the posture and off they went, suburban gypsies dancing the aisles of Kepler's Books & Magazines.

The Kepler's kids gave each other nicknames: John the Poet. David X. Phony Dave. Party John. John the Cool. Some had a loose notion of property. They weren't stealing, exactly, just borrowing. Alan Trist said, "We could take the books home overnight, and did, and sometimes they were not returned, though we meant to." Sometimes Ira himself would tell a kid to take a book home and read it. At least once, though, Ira called Roy and asked, plaintively, whether he could throw the ruffians out of the store. They were such a distraction, with their loud talk and their endless guitar noodling that sounded, to Ira, like one note played over and over.

"Roy said, 'they're not hurting anyone,'" Ira said.

Hank Harrison, known in later years as the father of rock singer Courtney Love, was a Kepler's guy too. He used to marvel that Roy seemed so tolerant about the gaggle, seemingly unconcerned about whether the daylong coffee drinkers might stain the books. But actually, Roy was not nearly as casual as the young crowd thought. Theodore Roszak recalled Roy's having to "dash out there and wipe down the tables" after the coffee slurpers left. Some wished they would never come back.

Kepler's clerk Nick Simon, for one, thought the hangers-on were bad for business. Simon was a hardcore Leftist, having run for governor of Connecticut in 1946 on the Socialist Labor Party ticket. A former teacher and Kepler's employee since February 1960, Simon had a severe aspect. He didn't much like Ira, he didn't think Roy went far enough in his politics, and he thought the hangers-on were simply taking up space. Some of the animus was justified.

"It wasn't just goofing around," Veltfort said in an interview. "Some of those guys were petty criminals."

Others were just plain sweet, including the sorority that one Kepler's denizen described as "Sara and the bicycle girls." These were high school and Stanford students, riding their Schwinns to Kepler's.

They came for the books, and the slightly older boys, and they came for Ira, who was magnetic and spoke with such unabashed gentleness.

"It's my joy," Ira would tell his girls, "it's my joy."

Barbara "Brigid" Meier heard him. In 1960 she was a fifteen-year-old Menlo-Atherton High School student, the daughter of a one-time Stegner Writing Fellow. She looked like a young model, simply gorgeous, but she had also been nurtured in a musical, literate atmosphere. "I'm in junior high school, and I read *On the Road*," Brigid recalled in an interview, "and suddenly, a big world opens up."

Brigid had begun riding her bike to Kepler's. Roy intimidated her, but Ira was something else. Ira would counsel Brigid, suggesting books she absolutely *must* read. He would call her darling. Her parents could be unsettling, Brigid said, and she was in a hurtful world with them, but when they would call the store in search of her, Ira would assure them she was safe. It was only partly true. In fact, while Meier was doing her homework, she was also drinking coffee and smoking cigarettes and dallying with some edgy characters.

"Roy erected an oasis for us, an alternative to the Eisenhower life," Brigid said.

Ira had many like-minded acolytes. When Willy Legate's girlfriend Danya Veltfort graduated from high school in 1961 and prepared to go off to Barnard College, Ira gave her a copy of Leo Tolstoy's "The Kingdom of God Is Within You." The late-nineteenth-century essay summed up Roy's and Ira's philosophy. It denounced compulsory military service and stressed the importance of avoiding force in the act of resisting evil. Danya's younger sister Suzie, too, had been impressed by Ira, one of her teachers at the local Peninsula School. For Suzie's 1961 Peninsula School graduation, Danya arranged for Jerry Garcia and Bob Hunter to play at the graduation, a gig for which they earned $50 (Jackson 1999, 36).

Roy wasn't really paying that much attention to the Kepler's crew. He just let them be. That may have been all they needed. Roy had, besides, other priorities to attend. In the last week of October 1961, General Maxwell Taylor was hinting that President Kennedy might have to send U.S. forces to aid South Vietnam. The Soviet Union, that same week, detonated the largest thermonuclear bomb to date, a 30-megaton atmospheric blast. A 100-mile-wide fallout cloud rolled across the Soviet Union, traveling toward North America at an estimated eighty miles per hour.

The timing was perfect for Roy to head up the Peninsula into the heart of San Francisco.

The state senate Fact-Finding Committee on Local Government had arrived in the swank Fairmont Hotel for a hearing on planning for nuclear war. Californians were dangerously exposed, state and local officials warned; only about 15 percent of the state's 15 million residents could be protected in existing shelters. One senator, echoing the common view, declared the only answer was to build more shelters. Roy was at the Fairmont Hotel to say No. Identified as a steering committee member of the Peninsula Peace Center and the Berkeley-based Acts for Peace, Roy told the committee that accepting the concept of nuclear war meant writing off cities as doomed. Sardonically, he pictured one civil defense scenario.

"The general population would be moved into the countryside, where deep, several hundred feet at least, underground caverns, cities in themselves, with all of the paraphernalia necessary to sustain life and a community, including the ability to grow food, would afford some credence to the claim of giving protection," Roy testified.

Plainly, the whole idea was absurd. Roy said civil defense plans were "self-defeating, since the present push for a crash shelter program is likely to make a nuclear war seem acceptable, and therefore to make it more probable." Roy's, though, was the token voice in the wilderness. The senators heard him out and ushered him on his way. He left the hearing itching to increase his activism. The world was going mad, and he needed to be heard.

Roy and Ted Roszak brainstormed that winter and during the spring of 1962, floating one radical idea after another. Roszak thought about helicopters and other modern contrivances; might they be deployed for peace in some fashion? Roy, in turn, mused to his friend in a June 16, 1962, letter that airborne sedatives might be conjured to calm conflict. When armies mobilize, spray them until the fighting subsides.

Airborne sedatives: obviously absurd, a joke on the order of Germfask conscientious objectors demanding their Victory Girls. Except that, starting in about 1955, the U.S. Army itself had undertaken secret research into the potential use of LSD and other drugs as tools to render enemy soldiers hilariously incapacitated. Maybe there was something to the idea after all. Roy was willing to consider any notion in the cause of ending war. He advised A. J. Muste on March 20, 1962, that he was "working to free myself somewhat from the time and effort required to run a business as well as father a family . . . to be more free to work on peace." Even as Kepler's Books & Magazines was taking off, Roy was looking sideways. He was always of two minds in that way. He needed to make money by selling books, and he needed to pursue peace. As the sixties unfolded further, Roy would feel the potential tension between these two imperatives, particularly, perhaps, when he saw certain radical actions catch fire.

In late May 1962 Harold Stallings, Roy's protest ally from the Livermore demonstrations of 1960, sought to sail a boat called the *Everyman* into the atomic testing waters of the Pacific. Scientists planned to test the effect of nuclear blasts on the earth's magnetic field, and military planners sought to know what would happen to radio communications. The *Everyman's* crew members were curious too. They wanted to know what would happen if they sailed 2,500 miles into the testing waters. Stallings, red-bearded and audacious, was the skipper. A thirty-year-old Quaker, Stallings was director of Pacific High School in Palo Alto. He was accompanied by crewmen Ed Lazar and Evan Yoes. Yoes was a navy veteran, but Stallings was reckoned to be captain "because of his dignified whiskers," Yoes told *Chronicle* columnist Art Hoppe.

On Friday evening, May 25, U.S. Attorney Cecil Poole obtained a restraining order blocking the crew from sailing into federal nuclear testing waters. Moving quickly, Poole's men reached the Sausalito dock, north of San Francisco, but Lazar refused to accept the legal papers. They were placed on the dock, where the wind scattered them. About seven in the morning the next day, the *Everyman* set out. The goal: Christmas Island.

At 2:20 p.m. the necessary court papers finally obtained, Poole and other law enforcement landlubbers boarded a ninety-five-foot patrol boat and set out in chase. Nine miles off the coast, U.S. Marshal Edward Heslep steadied himself amid gusty winds and boarded the *Everyman*. Stallings and Yoes surrendered quietly. Lazar lay down on the *Everyman's* deck and did nothing.

Two Coast Guardsmen took the helm and steered the *Everyman* back to port. Neither the contempt citation nor the Coast Guard, though, could ring down the curtain. While prosecutors brought their case against the crew members, demonstrators began gathering at the main post office at the corner of Seventh and Mission streets. One of the protestors slipped into the courtroom, unfolding a banner that read "Freedom Cannot Survive Nuclear War." Bailiffs quickly led the former San Francisco City College student, Jefferson Poland, out of the courtroom and into the hallway. Poland, who shortly thrust his way back into notoriety as champion of the Sexual Freedom League, went limp. Bailiffs carried the nineteen-year-old protestor outside.

For the next week demonstrators, led much of the time by Ira, rallied daily in support of the *Everyman* crew. Roy had the bookstore to run, but such nine-to-five obligations were of secondary importance for Ira. He and nearly three dozen others spent June 1 sitting in the corridors of the main post office, announcing they would remain until Lazar was freed from jail and the *Everyman* released from government custody.

"Whenever people confront brutality and violence, it does good," Ira said, as the *San Francisco Chronicle* reported on June 2, 1962.

Federal officials decided they would let the demonstrators remain inside the building so long as it was open. Early the next morning, a dozen returned and settled in for the long haul. It became a scene. One demonstrator exhibited her Greek dancing technique. Others studied for exams. Ira ran a rolling seminar on nonviolence, the *Chronicle* reported on June 3, 1962. That day forty demonstrators returned to the post office. Some announced they would begin fasting, consuming only fruit juices, vitamins, and water. The fasting, Ira explained, would deepen everyone's commitment to ending all organized violence.

By Thursday, June 7, Ira brought Joan with him. As Ira sat close by, Joan entertained the demonstrators with old-time ballads. This was a magic moment, a sidewalk-level performance by a young woman right on the verge of mainstream stardom. In just a few months, *Time* magazine would be putting Joan on the cover: Sibyl with Guitar, as the November 23, 1962, headline would put it. "Palpably nubile," the love-struck *Time* writer would add.

On Friday, June 8, the judge sentenced the *Everyman* crew to thirty days in jail for contempt of court. Ira and some three dozen demonstrators entered the federal building and refused to leave. Ordered to go, Ira and the demonstrators went limp. Guards carried them outside and informed them they would be arrested if they returned. Ira led the demonstrators back in. They sang "We Shall Overcome" as they were hauled to jail.

"You did it, kids," Ira cheered on his young acolytes, according to the *Washington Post* of June 10, 1962. "You're under arrest."

In October 1962 nuclear confrontation seemed suddenly nigh. A U.S. reconnaissance plane on October 15 had snapped photographs of Cuban missile bases, barely ninety miles from American shores. A week later President Kennedy announced a naval quarantine around Cuba. Legally, it was an act of war. Kennedy warned a "full retaliatory response upon the Soviet Union" was part of the U.S. arsenal. The U.S. Strategic Air Command raised its nuclear forces alert to DEFCON 2, its highest ever. In London, philosopher Bertrand Russell gloomily declared that "it seems likely that within a week we shall all be dead." Those that could stocked their civil defense shelters. Others went for long walks.

One afternoon late in the crisis, Jerry Garcia and his girlfriend Brigid Meier, one of Ira's girls, tried escaping the terror. They made their way up Menlo Park's Sand Hill Road, seeking elevation. They found the right hill to climb and then they settled in. The sun was setting, and they regarded the cities spread below them. Out there, beyond the Bay Area, the end of days might be at hand. The twenty-year-old Garcia cradled his guitar and played "Go Down Old Hannah," an old Leadbelly song. There was a sense, Brigid said, that "if we made it through the day, then we would make it."

The moment stuck with Brigid, while the crisis ignited Roy, who saw U.S. culpability. The naval quarantine, Roy reasoned, was a natural consequence of an earlier series of errors and decisions, some of them by the United States. "Whole populations of human beings look on helplessly as they are made hostage twice over in the international game of 'chicken' being conducted by leaders on all sides in the sacred name of national honor," Roy wrote in the *San Francisco Chronicle* of October 23, 1962.

Shortly after, the crisis subsided, thanks to luck and deft diplomacy. Soviet Premier Nikita Khrushchev announced on October 28 that the Cuban missiles would be removed, though neither Soviet nor U.S. officials made public a behind-the-scenes agreement by which the White House had agreed to remove missiles in Turkey.

Roy was at that very time taking on even more bookstore responsibilities. He opened a second Kepler's Books & Magazines in south Palo Alto on November 20, 1962. Expansion made sense. The year was a good one for paperbacks, some of them generation-defining. The Dell edition of Joseph Heller's *Catch-22* was a huge seller, as was the Signet edition of *One Flew Over the Cuckoo's Nest*. Two years later, the second bookstore moved south to a small shopping center in Los Altos.

About the same time, Brigid Meier's unhappy father forced a breakup with that shaggy dropout who had taken his daughter's heart. He was just no good, that Jerry Garcia guy. By the time Barbara figured out she knew better than her father, it was too late. Garcia had met his next paramour. Once again, his lucky stars had aligned at Kepler's.

One evening, in February 1963, Garcia was hanging out at the bookstore with his musician friends David Nelson and Robert Hunter. After they had finished playing, Garcia wandered back toward the store's coffee machine, where he saw nineteen-year-old Stanford student Sara Ruppenthal eating a tangerine. She offered him a slice. They looked into each other's eyes, and that was that. They were together (Greenfield 1996, 27). Sara Ruppenthal had first fallen into Ira's circle back in her days as a Palo Alto High School student. She considered Ira her mentor, and sometimes would help run the store's coffee machine. Meeting Jerry Garcia, though, put her in a different orbit.

Sara Ruppenthal and Jerry Garcia seemed the oddest of fits. Stanford student Gerry Masteller, another Ira acolyte, had recruited Sara to silkscreen peace caucus banners for his Stanford crusades. He thought she deserved better than the guitar-slinging high school dropout. Her parents agreed. But within a few weeks of meeting Garcia at Kepler's, Sara was pregnant. They would get married April 25, 1963, at the Palo Alto Unitarian Church, a favorite worship place for freethinkers of the Kepler's ilk. As for Barbara Meier, she would graduate from high school and move to San Francisco. She would find Buddhism, move to Taos, and a generation later would reconnect with Garcia for a middle-aged reawakening of romance.

↓

Fallout shelters were all the rage.

They helped indoctrinate civilians for World War III, whenever that might come. The 1955 Operation Alert, for instance, had anticipated a nuclear attack on fifty U.S. cities. Survivors could ride out the blast in shelters. Plan on it, officials said. Pacifists like Roy considered this insane. Starting with a few War Resisters League demonstrators in 1955, who sat on benches outside New York City's City Hall rather than take spurious shelter, radical activists had been inviting arrest by publicly refusing to participate in the civil defense drills. Their cause was gaining momentum. The New York City protests that had begun with twenty-eight sit-in participants in 1955 had grown by 1960 to a high-profile media event that included authors Norman Mailer and Kay Boyle among more than one thousand demonstrators (Bennett 2003, 211). Beset by an even larger demonstration in 1961, civil defense authorities canceled the 1962 Operation Alert.

The fallout shelters, though, remained dug in, along with underlying assumptions about the prospects for survivability in a nuclear holocaust. Nobel Prize–winning chemist and Manhattan Project veteran Willard Libby captured the can-do spirit with a fifteen-part newspaper series penned in late 1961, optimistically entitled "You Can Survive Atomic Attack." The more comfortable and elaborate the shelter the better, Dr. Libby explained. On the Stanford campus, eighteen basement shelters marked with black-and-yellow signs were stocked with first aid equipment, water, and "survival biscuits." The Stanford shelters could accommodate some 6,800 people, and they sent a muscular message. The shelters, a *Stanford Daily* editorial writer firmly opined on April 5, 1963, demonstrate "that the American people are determined to survive a nuclear war and are not defeatists or pessimists."

Look on the bright side, some satirists suggested. In the "radically simplified post-strike environment," one visiting history professor suggested, fewer associate deans might be required. As for students, perhaps a B average should be required for shelter admission. Let only the academically deserving survive. In a more serious vein, Ira in mid-April debated a conservative political science graduate student who argued that the fallout shelters demonstrated resolve and thereby deterred attack.

"In order to carry out a policy of Christian love, we must fight communism by being prepared to fight a war," graduate student Richard Weinig declared.

"There is a way of love," Ira replied, as the *Stanford Daily* reported April 16, 1963, "and it's not through burning 200,000 people, as we did in Hiroshima."

Ted Roszak, still straddling academia and activism, added at another spring debate that bomb shelters were worse than futile. They would so give the illusion of safety that U.S. military leaders might be tempted into war. For more information, Roszak urged listeners to purchase Arthur Waskow's book *America in Hiding* and Seymour Melman's *No Place to Hide*. Both were conveniently available at Kepler's for a total of only $1.35, an April 4, 1963, *Stanford Daily* ad stated.

The next month, on May 12, Ira led a demonstration of some two hundred people at San Francisco's Civic Center Plaza. By confronting the shelter program, Ira said, the demonstrators could show there's another way: a way of nonviolence, truth, and the way of love. Following a five-minute period of silence, amid the city's whoosh and clang, the demonstrators paraded to a nearby fallout shelter sign. Police warned against interference with the civil defense program. Everyone understood what was going to happen next. A ladder was readied. Ira climbed it and placed an "Our Only Shelter is Peace" sticker straight across the fallout shelter sign. Police politely arrested Ira the minute he climbed back down, and a civil defense worker climbed back up the ladder to scrape away the peace sticker.

Ira pled guilty, was placed on six-month probation, and then promptly resumed his proselytizing. The Stanford freshman dorms were among his favorite trolling grounds. A bearded esoteric, tooling around the Stanford campus on his bike, Ira wasn't everyone's cup of tea. The wealthy frat rats preferred Ayn Rand. But there were always some for whom Ira's words resonated, like Holly Chenery, a member of Ira's Student Action for Peace.

Holly was the brainy daughter of economist Hollis Chenery, an Army Air Corps veteran with a Harvard doctorate. Born in Arkansas, Holly had been moved about as her father took on various consulting and academic jobs. In 1953 the family moved to Stanford when Holly's father joined the economics faculty and later got involved with the Stanford Bookstore. Holly responded well to good teachers. One day in 1959, her English teacher at Palo Alto High School had introduced to the students a guest speaker: Ira. Holly listened attentively, her life's path opening up to her. She joined the adults in demonstrations, first at San Quentin prison to protest the May 1960 execution of author and convicted rapist Caryl Chessman, and then on other fronts.

By 1963 Holly was a committed activist. With her casual tennis shoes, thick glasses, and long, frizzy hair, she seemed indifferent to style. She shunned meat. She didn't really date. Life was serious. Fellow activist Melinda Sumrall called her a "peace nun," which in time became literally true. During that summer Holly and her young allies would confer with Ira and then picket outside Palo Alto area churches. Their signs urged Christians to resist war taxes, military service, and defense contract work. They weren't trying to stop anyone from entering the churches. They simply wanted a conversation with congregants. Nonetheless, Ira's acolytes with the radical Christian message did not pass ministerial muster. "If a few members had bothered to dress more neatly, then they might have made a greater appeal to churchgoers," one Congregational minister told the *Palo Alto Times.*

And then someone shot President Kennedy.

Kepler's Books & Magazines had barely opened the morning of November 22, 1963, when the first national radio bulletin went out from Dallas. By 11 a.m. television networks were reporting the catastrophe full-time. Writer Robert Stone and psychologist Vic Lovell, the man who had turned on Ken Kesey, heard the news and began driving around the Peninsula, taking the temperature of the day. Inevitably the Perry Lane pals ended up at Kepler's.

In the bookstore Stone and Lovell learned that Lee Harvey Oswald was a member of the Fair Play for Cuba Committee. Endorsed by the likes of Allen Ginsburg and Lawrence Ferlinghetti, with local haunts at Roy's Peninsula Peace Center, the Fair Play for Cuba Committee was opposed to the United States' ongoing hostility toward Fidel Castro. Kepler's clerks, naturally, had the inside dope about this organization seeking to subvert U.S. policy. It was a brief shock, though, for Stone and Lovell, to find such a connection.

"A clerk laughed at our dismay," Stone recalled (Stone 2007, 85).

Kennedy's assassination cast Roy off track. For several weeks he was inattentive to business. Truly, the world was crazed. Violence was everywhere. Even Kennedy's memorial services, with their military paraphernalia and martial ritual, seemed to Roy a celebration of war. Roy tried to make sense of the killing, not just of Kennedy but of Oswald. He saw in it a kind of karma, citing Kennedy's tacit go-ahead to the November 1, 1963, Vietnamese coup that ended in the killing of Ngo Dinh Diem. "Hatred, anger, revenge, all the dark underside of human nature, seem to have been released in this violent and tragic sequence," Roy wrote not long after Kennedy's death. Presciently, Roy cited South Vietnam several times. He saw American muscle running amok there.

By January 1964 Roy was ready to reenter the fray. His two bookstores were doing upwards of a quarter of a million dollars a year in sales. The paperback season had fully arrived. There were now about five thousand paperback bookstores nationwide, nearly double the number identified in 1958. Paperback book sales, too, had doubled to $90 million during roughly the same period. The very idea of a paperback bookstore had taken form, iconic enough to be affectionately represented on a *New Yorker* magazine cover (Gross and Steckler 1963, 1).

Roy wanted to do more than just sell books, though; he also wanted to write them. He approached Ballantine Books with his latest manuscript pitch for a peace project. The editors saw little market potential in a pacifist screed, and Roy remained confined to the world of little journals, newsletters, and *Peace News,* the house organ of War Resisters International. Kepler's was one of the few bookstores to carry the small-circulation newsletter, which had an opening in 1964 for an editor in London. Roy helped Roszak land a job at the newsletter, where Roszak would serve a two-year stint before gaining fame through *The Making of a Counter Culture.*

Roszak's departure for *Peace News* occurred just as Roy and his allies were turning more concertedly toward Vietnam. Joan, Roy, and Ira all took the same tack. Ira was Joan's spiritual and ideological mentor, and Roy was handling her finances. Under their guidance, she advised the IRS in April 1964 that "modern war is impractical and stupid" and that she was "no longer supporting my portion of the arms race." She said she would not pay the 60 percent of her tax that she calculated served the military. Ira issued the press release trumpeting Joan's tax protest, and was happy to talk to any reporter who called.

The IRS bided its time for several months, until November 6 when an agent went to the Monterey County courthouse and filed a $50,182 lien against Joan's property. Then the IRS summoned her to a meeting.

"Surely, Miss Joan, you don't want to be a bad citizen, do you?" the agent asked.

"The way I see it," Joan recalls replying, "you can either be a good citizen or a good person. If being a good citizen means paying to make napalm to dump on little children, then I guess I'd rather be a good person and refuse" (Baez 1987, 121).

11

Grindstone

Grindstone was a do-gooders' getaway.

An eleven-acre island in Ontario's Big Rideau Lake, Grindstone also provided the name for an institute that hosted intensive training programs for nonviolent civil rights activists. The first week-long session in August 1963, sponsored by the Fellowship of Reconciliation and the Canadian Friends Service Committee, brought in thirty-five men and women who participated in workshops, lectures, and role-playing exercises.

Roy heard good things about the Grindstone training, and he wanted to participate. His bookstore nearly ran itself, and Patricia was accustomed to handling the kids, and so in August 1964 Roy joined four other Americans in Grindstone's second annual Training Institute in Nonviolence. The timing was more apt than anyone could know. On August 2, just as Roy was embarking for Grindstone, U.S. officials spuriously reported that North Vietnamese patrol boats had fired on an American destroyer. In an August 5 speech, President Lyndon Johnson sought from Congress the authority to respond militarily. Congress saluted, approving on August 7 the Tonkin Gulf Resolution by a 416–0 vote in the House and an 88–2 vote in the Senate.

The Tonkin Gulf resolution began the U.S. commitment to South Vietnam in earnest, though Roy had already been paying attention. As early as 1962, Roy was clipping articles about U.S. military forces in Vietnam. It takes a guerrilla to kill a guerrilla, one 1962 article about Green Berets noted approvingly. In this shadow, as Congress was writing Johnson a blank check payable to quagmire, the Grindstone trainees began going through their paces.

The participants were a diverse lot. They were community work-ers, nurses, artists, craftsmen, students, and one bookseller. From six in the morning through ten at night, the Grindstone students studied, practiced, and meditated. In the afternoons they would work, clear-ing paths through woods, digging garbage pits, hauling firewood. The Grindstone theoreticians cited Erich Fromm in speaking of how the manual labor would help overcome modern man's alienation from nature, though not everyone bought the theory. Sometimes it just seemed like drudgery.

At night, inside a lodge originally designed for the first admiral of the Canadian navy, the participants would rap about peace. Johns Hopkins University psychiatrist Jerome Frank explained hostility. Humans, Frank asserted, are naturally inhibited against committing violence against someone similar. Wartime indoctrination therefore establishes the enemy as someone other: the Jap, the Kraut, the Chink, the Gook. The task of a nonviolent movement was to recognize a sense of common humanity with the enemy. Roy talked about the necessity for new approaches toward practicing nonviolence. Turn the famous American ingenuity to solving the problems of war and peace. Invad-ers, for instance, could be explicitly welcomed. Greet them, house them, feed them. Fundamentally, Roy urged, communicate with the enemy as human.

For a day and a half the Grindstone participants put their ide-als into practice with a scripted scenario involving nonviolent Island-ers being invaded by a military force called the Southern Alliance for Peace. The Islanders prevailed, in part due to persistent bickering among the invading force members. That, too, was a lesson. Person-ality clashes, egotistical assertions, and tactical disagreements could drive a wedge into any alliance.

A week after returning to California from the training, Roy had finished a sixty-one-page, single-spaced paper summing up his thoughts. The session invigorated Roy, reminding him of where his life's work was meant to be. Roy himself had a lot to offer the Grind-stone program. He was level-headed, rational, and seasoned as an activist. Alluringly, he also had some attractive contacts. One of the

Grindstone organizers subsequently wrote Roy and asked whether he would attend a future session scheduled for the summer of 1965. And, by the way, was it possible to bring Joan Baez?

As it happened, neither Roy nor Joan would attend the August 1965 Grindstone session. Joan, though, was listening to both Roy and Ira. Roy helped handle her finances. He could tend the bottom line. The money was rolling in, and temptations were everywhere: No one who saw it ever forgot young Joan's new Jaguar sedan. Ira was more the intellectual advisor, the one to accompany Joan on her political outings. He was with her on November 20, 1964, when she sang on the steps of Berkeley's Sproul Hall for several thousand students participating in the Free Speech Movement (Goines 1993). On December 2, Joan again marched along with demonstrators at Sproul Hall, singing "The Times They Are A-Changin'" and led the students in "We Shall Overcome" as they entered the university hall. She and Ira shared peanut butter sandwiches with the protestors, but left before the arrests that came later that night.

Nationwide, other activists were gathering force, propelled by the swelling U.S. commitment to Vietnam. On December 19, 1964, an estimated 1,500 protestors bundled in the New York City cold to hear speeches by A. J. Muste and others. In San Francisco that same day, some one hundred people gathered at the Federal Building and then marched four blocks to Union Square. Straitlaced reporters observed that male demonstrators sported beards while young women had adopted Joan's look: straight hair and no makeup. Roy, beardless and dapper, was the master of ceremonies. He greeted the San Francisco demonstrators at Union Square and introduced speakers. Ira, Roy said, was "one of the great nonviolent souls of our time." Joan sang a calypso version of The Lord's Prayer and spoke briefly.

"Get out of Vietnam," she said, the *San Francisco Chronicle* reported on December 20, 1964, "because all we're doing is murdering people."

Joan, Roy, and Ira next brought their antiwar campaign back to the Stanford campus. On January 18, 1965, they explained the moral and practical intricacies of war tax refusal to a large audience gathered in the university's Memorial Auditorium. Joan kept her remarks simple, as always, saying succinctly she had decided to stop contributing to the war effort. Roy was more audacious, accusing the United States of violating the principles laid down in Nuremberg.

"Refusing to pay 60 percent of your income tax is not the final answer to today's problems," Roy said, as the *Stanford Daily* reported on January 19, 1965. "It is only a personal response."

One skeptic asked Roy how he could call the U.S. military effort immoral at the same time as he kept "an abundance of pornography" in his store.

"Whereas I am opposed to war and violence," Roy said, "I'm in favor of sex."

Roy scored with that line, though usually it was Ira with the mot juste. Ira was the entertainer in public appearances, while Roy pressed home his points with incessant reason. Both were finding more platforms from which to speak, as the American presence grew in Vietnam. Through 1965 Roy returned to KPFA's Berkeley studio for a series of programs on nonviolence. It had been ten years since he left the station, and the bitter aftertaste from past palace intrigue had long since evaporated. KPFA's audience was also larger, and Roy could settle in along with Ira and Ed Keating, founder of the liberal Catholic magazine *Ramparts,* for a rolling, multipart discussion entitled "Nonviolence in a Violent World." Nonviolence was not the same as passivity, the three men agreed. Nonviolence was love; *love.*

The hour-long KPFA talks touched far-flung listeners, in ways the speakers couldn't always know. One listener was a poet named Helene Mullins. Mullins had been around unconventional scenes since she discovered Greenwich Village in the 1920s; her first collection of poems, *Earthbound,* had been published in 1929. She heard, really and truly heard, Roy's January 5, 1965, KPFA program on nonviolence. The words inspired her to write a painfully earnest poem entitled "Peace on Earth" and send it on to Roy in appreciation.

Roy intended his KPFA conversations to incite as well as inform. One must act, not just talk about acting. On a breezy Tuesday afternoon, March 22, 1965, some five hundred demonstrators gathered around Berkeley's Sproul Hall. David Krech, an eighteen-year-old Oakland City College student, proclaimed it was time for a dramatic step. He took out his draft card and tried to light it. The wind whiffed the flame. Krech tried again. Again the flame died. Repeatedly Krech tried to burn his draft card. The wind prevailed every time, the *San Francisco Chronicle* reported on March 23, 1965. Finally Krech simply tore his card into pieces.

The next day Holly Chenery and other activists followed up. Since her Palo Alto High School days, Holly had come into the West Coast vanguard of the War Resisters League and the Committee for Non-Violent Action. After high school, she had lasted a year at Swarthmore College before the cause of peace pulled her away. With Roy's help, Holly had interned at the War Resisters League headquarters in New York City. Now, back in the Bay Area, she would demonstrate her convictions. Holly was joined at Sproul Plaza by Stanford history graduate student Garrett Lambrev and high school senior Melinda Sumrall from Palo Alto's Cubberley High School. With guidance from Roy and Ira, they had determined to get themselves arrested as a form of protest. They had practiced going limp, letting the muscles go, and in a Bay Area schoolyard they had practiced climbing chain-link fences.

Then Holly asked Melinda for something even more difficult. She wanted the younger girl to give a speech before her fellow demonstrators.

"I was mortified with fear," Melinda said in an interview decades later.

Melinda was too young to get entangled in this protest, some believed. She was just a kid; it was irresponsible for the adults to let her endanger herself. But ever since Melinda had first gravitated toward Kepler's and the Peninsula Peace Center in 1962, she had been moving deeper into the mix. Her parents' divorce had shaken her badly, and Melinda found some respite in Ira's peace salons, where students would jam into Ira's small apartment, sitting cross-legged or with arms wrapped around knees for serious talk.

Melinda accepted Holly's challenge and prepared her brief speech. She delivered it earnestly, telling her fellow demonstrators about the importance of making a commitment, taking a stand. We can no longer blindly follow the laws of the military simply because they are established, Melinda said. We must assume personal responsibility for each action or policy we follow. She might have been channeling Ira; he had taught her well.

Then they marched, from the Berkeley campus several miles to the Oakland Army Terminal. Their purpose was simple, the demonstrators told Major Richard Giacomazzi about 11 a.m. They wanted to enter the army facility and discuss the Vietnam War with the workers loading munitions ships.

"No," the army major said, the *San Francisco Chronicle* reported on March 24, 1965, "you're not going inside."

But they were. Peace demanded it.

Holly and her companions gathered themselves for their next step. The young women, who were wearing dresses, began to climb the eight-foot fence. The protestors who made it over the fence scattered, the men moving fast. One got as far as the gangplank of the cargo ship *Korea Bear* before guards seized him. One protestor was shoved into the Bay by an unsympathetic forklift operator and had to be fished out by a patrol boat. All of the protestors, once captured, went limp just as they had practiced. The soldiers hauled them to the provost marshal's office. He warned them to stay out, and then released them.

Soon protestors were again climbing over the fences. Again military police grabbed them. Giacomazzi warned them to stay off the base. The demonstrators were taken back outside the gates, where they split up and in their several smaller groups once more began climbing. The army and police had lost patience. Holly, Melinda, and ten other demonstrators were arrested on various charges including maintaining a public nuisance, failure to disperse, and resisting arrest. Resisting arrest was the funny part, as the young protestors didn't resist at all. They simply went limp in the hands of uniformed authority. Noncooperation was one lesson they had learned from Roy and their other teachers. Another was the importance of using spectacle to send a coherent message.

"I went to lend my individual weight to try to stop the killing, the terrible division of men from each other, being done in my name as an inhabitant of the U.S," Holly declared in a written statement.

Authorities delivered Melinda, a minor, to the Alameda County juvenile detention center. Her eyes opened wide. The guards were coarse, the clothes they gave her ratty. A stained mattress lay on the floor. The place was altogether foul, and Melinda was out of her element. The streetwise girls in Oakland Juvie didn't know what to make of this Palo Alto white girl, an idealist whose mother, Betty, showed up bearing books by Daphne du Maurier and W. Somerset Maugham. There Melinda was, jailed with a bunch of juvenile delinquents, and her mother was bringing her books from Kepler's. It was sweet and clueless all at the same time; but after all, Betty Sumrall said later, what did she know? Melinda was the first of her kids to make it into juvenile hall.

In the middle of what turned out to be a three-day stay, authorities summoned Melinda to an office. Two men had come to the detention center and asked to see her, she was told. They weren't relatives, so they weren't admitted, but she was given their names: Roy Kepler and Ira Sandperl. The two experienced activists, learning of Melinda's arrest, had driven up from the Peninsula in hopes of giving succor. The news enlivened Sumrall's spirits: She wasn't alone after all.

"I remember dancing all the way back to the cell," she said in an interview.

After three days, a judge brusquely advised Melinda she would be released if she agreed not to repeat such foolhardy behavior. Melinda had made her statement and she was willing to move on; she had no desire to return to her cell. Holly was different. She would not promise to steer clear of the Oakland Army Terminal grounds, and the impatient judge sentenced her to ten days in Santa Rita. He counseled Holly that her actions, however idealistic, appeared a bit anarchic, and he warned her she would get an even stiffer sentence if she continued her protests.

"I hope to see you again," Holly said.

With that, Holly went off to Santa Rita Rehabilitation Center, the former navy brig where Roy had spent some time following Livermore laboratory demonstrations. She found the experience enlightening. Holly had traveled the world with her family. Living in Chile when she was thirteen, she had seen the jarring juxtaposition of wealth and poverty. Santa Rita, though, was different. Holly was even more fully immersed in an alien environment: a big room with eighty different women, each with an exotic story to tell. Holly survived intact and emboldened for antiwar protests that were growing ever bigger.

With nearly 50,000 U.S. troops in South Vietnam and plans brewing for more, activists rallied for a May 21, 1965, "Vietnam Teach-In" at a softball field on the U.C. Berkeley campus. Upwards of five thousand students and activists heard speakers like journalists I. F. Stone and Robert Scheer denounce the war. Folk singers and comics kept the audience loose. A San Francisco–based satirical troupe called The Committee offered their interpretation of a sales pitch for a brand-new robot demonstrator, the perfect pacifistic liberal machine that can sit-in for hours and go limp on command. People roared. Peace didn't have to be so serious all the time. Still, the range of speakers at the Berkeley Teach-In hinted at what was both a strength and a weakness of the peace movement. It teetered perpetually on the verge of incoherence. The Vietnam War unified activists only on the surface, as Roy advised A. J. Muste that June.

"Our readiness to work with liberals open to nonviolence is not based on their gentle dispositions, but on our pragmatic experience," Roy wrote A. J. Muste on June 8, 1965. "I have urged radical pacifists not to merge themselves into liberal organizations, not to forward the liberal's program, not to engage in the traditional liberal's politics."

At the same time Roy, Ira, and Holly had issued a mid-1965 memo warning it would be a "tragic error" for pacifists to work closely with Marxist groups, not least because of the latter's unwillingness to see the Soviet Union's depredations clearly. Roy opposed totalitarianism in all forms. Roy, then and always, identified himself with the radical pacifists, those willing to undertake blatant civil disobedience in the service of the great cause. He respected young men like David J. Miller, a twenty-two-year-old Catholic Worker Movement activist. A veteran of antinuclear protests, Miller made rhetoric real on October 15 outside the Army Induction Center on Whitehall Street in Manhattan.

"I believe the napalming of villages is an immoral act," Miller declared. "I hope this will be a significant political act, so here goes" (Ferber and Lynd 1971, 23).

Then he lit his card on fire, much as the demonstrators organized in the late 1940s by Roy and Jim Peck had done. The difference was that just about two months before Miller acted, a provoked Congress had passed a bill making the willful destruction of a draft card a felony.

"Beatniks and so-called 'campus cults' have been publicly burning their draft cards to demonstrate their contempt for the United States and our resistance to Communist takeovers," Representative William Bray, an Indiana Republican who won a Silver Star leading tanks in World War II, had explained on August 10, 1965. "If these revolutionaries are permitted to deface and destroy their draft cards, our entire Selective Service System is dealt a serious blow."

David Miller's draft-card defiance would take on greater importance over the next few years, confronting courts with a fundamental question about when the punishment of a meaningful act violates First Amendment protections. Roy could appreciate it, and he could see that with the Vietnam War growing there would be more opportunities for similar confrontations. Certainly there would be more recruits for the cause.

It was time to expand. In mid-December 1965, the War Resisters League formally opened its Western branch at 584 Page Street in San Francisco. War Resisters League Field Secretary David McReynolds chose for the West Coast work a Bronx native, then in his mid-twenties, named Bert Kanegson. Kanegson had grown up in a lower-middle-class Jewish family. Bohemia attracted him, and after high school he moved to Greenwich Village. He took up with the War Resisters

League, finding in Bayard Rustin an early mentor. Bert was ready for a move after visiting San Francisco in the late summer of 1963. He found it a congenial place, he recalled in a 2007 interview.

The national organization put up about half of the money, and Roy, as cochairman of the new WRL/West, helped Bert raise the rest in contributions from various conscientious objectors and peace benefactors.

"Roy probably put up a good chunk himself," Bert, who later changed his name to Sat Santokh, said in an interview.

From the money raised, Bert drew an annual salary of $6,500, making him, he said, "one of the best-paid young activists on the West Coast." He conjured some fresh ideas about direct action as a means to peace. He had the notion of carrying out a Gandhian-style project. The initial strategy was to approach company executives politely and ask them to cease making weapons of war. He identified a small Bay Area manufacturing firm that made spraying equipment used in defoliating the South Vietnamese jungles. The company, presumably, would refuse to give up its Pentagon dollars. Then the activists would target the company with a relentless series of sit-ins, picketing demonstrations, letter-writing, and what the young activists called "hauntings."

Roy thought the Building Peace project had some potential, but he was skeptical about making it the centerpiece of War Resisters League/West. He wanted the organization to grow into something substantial. From New York City, Bert's one-time mentor Bayard Rustin likewise raised cautionary notes. Rustin warned the project would be a difficult one so long as people were concerned primarily about economic stability. He urged the younger activist to hold off on the Building Peace project until he could secure more unified support from Roy and other WRL old-timers.

This was hard-won experience speaking. Since his 1949 arrest with Roy while picketing the French Embassy, Rustin had seen his own influence ebb and flow. He had played what scholar Scott Bennett termed the "critical role" in moving Martin Luther King Jr. to embrace Gandhian pacifism in 1956. He cofounded the Southern

Christian Leadership Conference in 1957 and had helped organize the famed 1963 March on Washington for Jobs and Freedom (Bennett 2003, 217). But he had also served a sixty-day jail sentence in 1953 following arrest on a morals charge in Southern California, and some feared his open homosexuality and Young Communist League past made him a politically dangerous associate. By 1965 Rustin had also shifted his allegiance away from street protests and toward coalition-building politics. In a word, he had become more moderate. It was in this vein that he urged Kanegson to first build a foundation of organizational and public support before embarking on the Building Peace project.

Roy's advice was sound, and it went unheeded. Soon enough, Building Peace fizzled.

"It turned out to be, for some psychological reasons, one of the slowest preparations ever known," Roy said later. "Some periods they were meeting as often as once a week training themselves . . . [but] they had difficulty actually doing it."

Eventually Building Peace activists did approach a small company or two, but nothing much came of it. The project's failure lingered over War Resisters League/West, although WRL was not alone as a West Coast peace organization. Vietnam War conscription demands, in particular, were starting to provoke new efforts. The Mid-Peninsula Draft Counseling Service had arisen by 1965, started by peace veteran and future Kepler's Books & Magazines clerk Hank Maiden. Maiden had rejected ROTC in Washington and then dropped out of Antioch College in the late 1940s to work with the American Friends Service Committee, he recalled in a 2007 interview. In time, Maiden had earned his undergraduate degree from U.C. Berkeley before establishing the Mid-Peninsula Draft Counseling Service with some friends. Other draft counseling efforts were likewise arising, prompting sharp questions about how they might be better coordinated.

One Sunday afternoon in late 1965, activists convened at the San Francisco Friends Meeting House to discuss a proposed West Coast office of the Central Committee for Conscientious Objectors (CCCO). Bert Kanegson and George Reeves from the War Resisters League were present, as were Roy and other seasoned pacifists. Paul Seaver had championed the West Coast outpost for the Philadelphia-based Central Committee for Conscientious Objectors. George Willoughby had spent World War II at Civilian Public Service camps in Trenton and Chicago. Roy argued against the new office. He said there was no need for it. There might have been more to Roy's argument as well; some present thought Roy didn't think there was a big enough market to support competing draft counseling offices.

"I experienced a churlish undertone in his delivery," Maiden recalled.

Roy lost the argument, and the Central Committee opened an office on San Francisco's gritty Mission Street. Alan Strain, a World War II conscientious objector who would go on to serve as an associate dean of students at Stanford, joined the CCCO office. He and Roy would work closely together in coming years.

The new draft counseling services, evolving peace organizations, and developing antiwar tactics were still works in progress. There was still room for new ventures. One, ambitiously envisioned, would be called the Institute for the Study of Nonviolence.

12

The Institute

Some schools taught war. Now, one would teach Gandhian nonviolence.

The idea of a peace institute had been circulating for years. Bob Pickus, founder of the Berkeley-based Acts for Peace, had suggested to Roy as early as 1962 that they establish a West Coast Peace Study Center. Pickus thought of seeking contributions from some of the pacifists' Hollywood friends, like singer John Raitt or actor Don Murray, a Korean War conscientious objector. A peace-oriented research center might publish reports, provide research fellowships, and illuminate pacifist ideas. More directly, people would live the ideals they were studying. They would move, meditate, and embrace. They would crack the shell, find the love within.

Peace, the concept, was a fringe idea in 1964, partly because war, the shadow, hadn't yet come into its new own. The Tonkin Gulf Resolution had empowered President Lyndon Johnson to start building up U.S. forces in South Vietnam. But with only 23,000 U.S. troops yet in the country, and conscription not yet omnivorous, the world's attention was not riveted. At Kepler's Books & Magazines, Roy and Ira could see the distant jungle slowly coming into focus. Both in their early forties, seasoned from years of engaged debate, they were in their activist prime. They were ready to lead. Joan was two decades younger but ready to do what she could. She had blossomed personally and professionally. She had money, fame, and a safe retreat in the calming Carmel Valley. Over the Santa Cruz Mountains from the Bay Area, soothed by the sea air, the Carmel Valley was a green and pacifying place. Republican retirees loved it.

So did Ira, who had misspent some of his Stanford undergraduate career in the area.

The relationship between Joan and Ira was still in its original proportions: Ira the mentor, Joan the student. For all her worldly achievements, Joan had come to realize her limitations. Her brief Boston University sojourn following her 1958 Palo Alto High School graduation hadn't prepared her for the skeptical world. She was gifted in certain ways, but lacking in others. "One day," Joan recounted, "I told Ira I did not want to remain an ignoramus forever and asked if he would consider tutoring me more formally" (Baez 1987, 124).

She didn't have to ask twice. This was what Ira lived for. After Joan in the summer of 1964 built her own home in Carmel Valley, she and Ira convened regularly for what amounted to tutoring sessions. Joan, in turn, passed the lessons along. When she toured with Bob Dylan between late February and late March 1965, she devoted stage time each night to discussing human rights and pacifism. Coming off the road and returning to the Carmel Valley by mid-1965 brought Joan back into Ira's orbit. They had corresponded throughout her various East Coast and road adventures, but nothing matched Ira in person. Not everyone appreciated that fact.

"Joanie was always susceptible to simplistic thinking," her father, Albert, said. "Simple, overarching solutions appealed to her, and I suspect that's why she fell prey to that man" (Hajdu 2001, 199).

That man. Al and Roy had a mutually respectful relationship since their time together in the Peninsula Committee for the Abolition of Nuclear Tests. Ira, though, was a more complicated matter. He was moved by Joan, and she by him. When she was only sixteen, he would ride his battered bicycle by the Baez home in Palo Alto so they could visit before high school started. Some feared Ira was the Rasputin character, the glinty-eyed seducer. At times, it seemed Al Baez, the innocent's father, couldn't stand Ira.

But what other adults didn't always appreciate was that Ira was also a superb teacher, funny, flirty, and, yes, wise. From the one-on-one tutoring, Ira and Joan both recognized a bigger and better idea could grow. Joan thought people learn more in a group than one-on-one, and so a school seemed a natural progression. "I agreed to take a year of my precious time to be her tutor," Ira explained in the *Los Angeles Times* on October 23, 1966. "[But] setting up the school, inviting other people to sit at my feet, that was Joan's idea."

The peace institute began taking shape. Ira was designated president, a rather grand title for a Kepler's bookstore clerk. Joan was vice president. Holly Chenery, the young woman that Joan considered "possibly the brightest woman I'd ever met in my life," was secretary-treasurer (Baez 1987, 125). Roy had no formal title, but he was a presence, not least because he was bankrolling the nascent school's personnel. Holly and Ira both still worked at Kepler's, Holly keeping the books in the back and Ira holding forth in front. Their modest paychecks enabled them to devote their hearts and minds to the greater cause. On the side, Roy was handling Joan's finances.

Roy didn't have Ira's special relationship with Joan, but he had deep experience from which both could learn. Roy was also equally committed to the cause. In the summer of 1965, with little fanfare, he took out two small ads in the *Wall Street Journal*. The ads announced the availability of his two paperback bookstores, declared to be "among largest in U.S." with combined gross sales of some $300,000 a year. His stores were profitable, but Roy explained that he had other priorities. He was ready to go back to full-time peacemaking.

"I am selling," Roy explained in a letter to a potential buyer on September 8, 1965, "to join a newly organized institute in Carmel."

This was the peace school. For help in selling the store, Roy turned to his Minersville and KPFA friend John Lewis, then with Massachusetts Mutual Life Insurance Company. Lewis liked what he saw in Roy's accounts. The store's 8 percent pretax profit margin was double that of the average bookstore. The store had a splendid inventory. The numbers were strong. But Lewis did have some concerns. He warned that Roy was being ill served by his current bookkeeper, a disorganized man, Lewis said, who couldn't seem to see beyond his lead pencil. It wasn't just Roy's problem. Lewis, the professional money manager, warned Roy that Joan's business affairs, too, might be harmed as a result of Roy's bookkeeper's being beyond his depth. This needed watching.

As it developed, Roy would not sell the stores. It is not clear whether the potential buyers backed out or whether Roy himself found reason not to give up his livelihood. The institute, in any event, had its first cadre. Ira and Joan were the stars. Roy was backstage. Holly Chenery was the indispensable woman who simply got things done. She was easily overlooked, a plain shadow next to the dazzling stars, but those in the know appreciated that Holly was taking care of business. She ran the mimeograph machine, kept the books, and filed the paperwork. She saw through pretense and sentiment. She admired Ira, but knew he didn't have a practical bone in his body. Roy, she truly respected. He showed concrete application of pacifist ideals while running a business and holding a family together.

Holly ran off a leaflet describing the school's plans. Seminars would start with twenty minutes of silence. Each day between 3 p.m. and 4 p.m. would be "hour alone" time, when no books, cigarettes, or other distractions would be allowed. A half-hour would be devoted to physical fitness daily: walking, swimming, or perhaps folk-dancing, the people's social exercise. One day each week would be given over to silence. Students would pay from $75 to $100 for the entire course. The institute would combine idealism with practicality. Students, the initial leaflets promised, would learn "basic office skills" and practice the "writing of press releases."

"Our goal," the founders declared, "is to root out violence in ourselves and make it at least as unhonored and illegitimate in the world community as it is within each national community."

Anyone could apply, so long as they were at least eighteen years old. Sessions, limited to a maximum of twenty-six participants, would be held for six-, four-, and two-week periods, and over weekends. By early July 1965, half a dozen students had signed up, and Joan herself had set the Institute for the Study of Nonviolence as her new focus. "I will go on singing four months out of the year, and devote the rest of my time to the school," Joan said in the *Monterey Peninsula Herald* on July 6, 1965.

That same month Joan urged her sister Mimi and Mimi's husband, Richard Fariña, to come to Carmel and escape Cambridge, Massachusetts, where they were going through a rough patch. Fariña's first book, *Been Down So Long Looks Like Up to Me,* was on the path to publication, and they could use a change of neighborhood. Subsidized by Joan, Mimi and Fariña moved into a small, former photographic studio next to Joan's house. Ira didn't think much of Fariña. He thought the younger man seemed vulpine, out for the main chance, even, perhaps, his eye more on Joan than on Mimi. But then, Ira was always protective of his own relationship with the Baez women (Hajdu 2001, 265).

Joan eventually took to Fariña. She could see his blatant ambition, his raw hunger, and his trickiness, but he was also smart and rampant with a rogue's charm (Baez 1966, 129). He never got much involved with the peace school, but Mimi would become the Institute's dancer, shepherding students through daily exercises. Holly, in time, would move in as well, taking up residence in an old horse shed. In early July the Institute's first six-week session began in Joan's Carmel Valley home on Miramonte Road. Fifteen students were in the inaugural class. Ira had prepared a five-page, single-spaced, annotated reading list for the students. Ira's suggestions echoed the recommendations he would offer Kepler's browsers, ranging from Ovid's *Metamorphosis* and Flaubert's *Madame Bovary* to the *Autobiography of Malcolm X.* For every book, Ira offered his own brief critique. Of theoretician Herbert Marcuse, he declared that "the prose is thick but the ideas are good."

Joan's neighbors preferred their own peace and quiet. Some feared Beatniks and pacifists would besmirch their country club life. They certainly thought that residential neighborhoods were not designed for schools. By October, Monterey County authorities informed Joan that she could not run the institute from her own Carmel Valley house. The business needed to move. Joan and her team cast about, finally finding a one-acre site about one mile east of Carmel Valley village. Joan bought for $40,000 a tile-roofed former one-room county school, out among the scrub oaks and only ten minutes from her own home. The former Tularcitos School had everything: a kitchen, a seminar room, and, for Ira, a cozy shack in the back to live in. While the Institute was in session, he could leave Menlo Park behind and become the full-time sage.

The building's renter, a Mr. Russell M. Craton, was described locally as a "ballistician and gun manufacturer." Perfect: The peace school would evict the maker of guns. Mr. Craton, though, didn't appreciate poetic justice. He didn't like losing his place, and he definitely didn't trust Ira.

"Maybe they're non-violent," Craton said, as the *Monterey Peninsula Herald* reported on October 20, 1965, "but I think they're out to see just how far they can go and how much they can get away with."

When neighbors raised similar alarms, Holly the peacemaker sought to pacify them. The students weren't aimless Beatniks and they wouldn't be studying the art of picketing, she assured everyone. They were engaged in serious and disciplined study. The tuition requirement would deter rootless Beatniks. But nervous neighbors knew all too well what would be going on at this peace school, this Baez U. By the time the county planning commission convened the night of Wednesday, October 27, emotions were high and the chambers were crowded. One neighbor, Elizabeth Bair, declared that "the title [of the school] alone brings great questions to our minds as to just what will be taught in this so-called school." Neighbor Thomas Verga warned ominously that the Institute would be teaching people to "tear up your draft card."

Joan handled the crowd perfectly. Though only twenty-four, she had sung for large crowds; she knew the art of working strangers to her will. Even as she judged her neighbors as being content in their little valley, she publicly struck the right tone. She was becomingly modest when she told the planning commissioners that her school was simply her response to the world of conflict. "I think there must be a better way," Joan said, the *Monterey Peninsula Herald* reported on October 28, 1965. "I'm not saying I know the better way. That's why I have the school."

The weight of the presentation was left to her attorney, William K. Stewart, a gray-haired Harvard Law School graduate who offset the rambunctious youngsters with adult gravitas. The number of students would be limited, he reassured the commissioners. None would live at the school, and meals would not be served. Commissioner Willard Branson pressed him on what would be taught. Aldous Huxley, Leo Tolstoy, and Gandhi, Stewart replied. Branson asked whether the teachings of Jesus Christ would be included.

"Yes," Ira piped up, "specifically, the Sermon on the Mount."

"Are you going to have the Bible?" Branson pressed.

"That is the Bible, sir," Ira reminded him, as the *Monterey Peninsula Herald* recounted on October 28, 1965. "The Book of Matthew."

A divided planning commission approved the Institute's land-use proposal. With the county giving the green light, for the moment, eleven students began arriving for the next six-week session that started the first week of November. Most were from California, but one hailed from Georgia and another from Boston. Other hurdles, though, soon popped up. An unhappy neighbor had appealed the planning commission's approval to the county board of supervisors. Even before the board had a chance to meet, the county's building inspector showed up on Thursday, November 4, and declared the forty-year-old building structurally inadequate.

Joan was given a week to close the school while she awaited full county approval and had the necessary repairs done. The eleven young men and women who had shown up for their session continued right up until the last day, Thursday, November 11. In the inviting fall air of the Carmel Valley, they sat outside whenever they could. Ira, described by one visitor as "friendly, open, almost effusive," dominated the discussions. Joan, often, was silent, attentive, as Ira held forth.

"When you kill, what you're really saying is you know more than God or nature," Ira said in one of the final sessions before the school's November 11 shutdown, the *Monterey Peninsula Herald* reported on November 15, 1965.

On November 30, the Monterey County Board of Supervisors convened in Salinas to consider whether the peace school violated the section of the Monterey County Zoning Code that prohibited land use "detrimental to the peace, morals, or general welfare of Monterey County." Certainly the region's peace had been disturbed. Some three hundred people crowded into the Board of Supervisors' chambers. On one side Joan, Ira, and their attorney William K. Stewart sat with the Institute's supporters. On the other side of the aisle sat opponents of the Institute.

"We wonder what kind of people would go to a school like this," neighbor Sue Petkus asked. "Why aren't they out working and making money?"

Mrs. Petkus knew, of course, precisely what kind of people would attend the Institute. She could see them on the other side of the aisle, where the bearded young rebels in sandals and turtleneck sweaters groaned, mugged, and laughed throughout the neighbors' anxious presentations. The board of supervisors, too, presented a tough audience. Military honor meant something to them. Supervisor Beauford Anderson, a generation earlier, had been a young army technical sergeant in the 96th Infantry Division when he won the Medal of Honor on Okinawa in April 1945. Anderson was not very sympathetic to young antimilitary punks. But it was fretful Mrs. Petkus, among others, who caught the gimlet eye of a writer in the audience.

Joan Didion was in town, on assignment for the *New York Times Sunday Magazine*. Didion was only thirty, but her words could pierce all the world's folly. Didion mercilessly detected Mrs. Petkus's fretful eyes and quivering chin. Didion saw into Ira, too; she had his number: The Guru. In Joan Baez, Didion saw impressive depths.

Ira, who couldn't help himself from flirting, was in Joan Baez's eyes "appealing to the forbidden fantasies of the twittering, supposedly hostile, clubby wives." *Of course:* the uptight Carmel Valley clubwomen, outwardly decorous but inside imagining Ira's universal love. He was perfectly capable of it too. With a hint of pride, Ira would describe how a mother and daughter had once both thought themselves in love with him, so much so that the distraught mother threatened to kill him. Instead, she ended up killing herself (Sandperl 1974, 21). So Ira, his beard neatly groomed, his hair shorn close, with his black suit and tie and his sterling silver peace button affixed to his left lapel, was the rebel in the garden party, the dangerous man among the ladies of the club. Oh, *yes.*

"I think the peace of the valley is obviously very disturbed," Ira said, as the *Monterey Peninsula Herald* reported on December 1, 1965. "The peace of the world is obviously very disturbed. The purpose of this institute is to end this violence."

It was Joan, though, whom everyone waited to hear. A natural performer, she hit her marks perfectly.

"Everybody's talking about their forty- and fifty-thousand-dollar houses and their property values going down," Joan stated. "I'd just like to say one thing. I have more than one hundred thousand dollars invested in the Carmel Valley, and I'm interested in protecting my property, too."

It was a winning move, funny and finding the common ground. Joan didn't speak much longer, nor did she have to. Finally the board of supervisors by a 3–2 vote approved the Institute's continued operations. The supervisors did impose rules. The classes would have to be held indoors, and only between the weekday hours of 8 a.m. and 6 p.m. No more than two people could live or sleep on the premises. No more than twenty students could attend at a time, and no classes could be conducted outside of the building. The Institute had won.

The very next day Joan and Ira declared they had no intention of abiding by the county's restrictions.

"We feel we made a mistake in referring to ourselves as a school," Ira explained, as the *San Francisco Chronicle* reported on December 2, 1965. "The Institute isn't a school at all, legally speaking, and we don't believe we need a use permit."

Attorney William Stewart elaborated that the existing limited industrial zoning permitted seminars. The Institute for the Study of Nonviolence, he said, qualified as a research laboratory. The fact that the Institute attracted students and charged tuition was simply irrelevant. The argument seemed disingenuous and after the fact, given the debates that had taken place over the past several months. Typical peacenik trickery, some county officials thought.

↓

The Institute now had the green light. What it did not yet have was a permanent space. The school site was still undergoing the renovations. For the next class of ten students, who were arriving for a session previously scheduled to begin December 18, Joan subleased from a friend a small home in the nearby town of Pacific Grove, about fifteen miles away from her Carmel Valley place. The wandering Institute managed several days of meetings inside the Pacific Grove house before the afternoon of December 22, when one neighbor telephoned the police. Ira next met with students beneath a tall pine tree in Pacific Grove's Greenwood Park, where Joan arrived for a round of calisthenics that would close out the year for the Institute for the Study of Nonviolence.

In January 1966, as U.S. forces inaugurated widespread search-and-destroy missions in South Vietnam, the Institute for the Study of Nonviolence finally had a chance to open in its formal quarters. The Tularcitos School renovations were done, county approvals were in hand, and the new students were ready.

Sessions would start with ten or twenty minutes of silence. Students might then warm up with ballet exercises conducted to Beatles records; Joan's sister Mimi sometimes would lead them. Following silence and movement, the students would discuss their readings. When it was time for words, Ira typically spoke first. He was the theoretician, the articulator of the nonviolent philosophy that he and Roy had lived with for years. They had boiled down the key concepts. Nonviolence was not passive; a practitioner would never simply stand by while another was hurt. Instead of physical retaliation, choose restraint and creative alternatives. Simple courtesy was essential in social interactions: smile at one another, not as a slave but as one dispelling fear. Be punctual, a form of courtesy.

Ira might begin a seminar with a quote asserting that war has sometimes been considered an agent of progress. He would ask: What do you think of this notion? Does war prompt social progress? The students sat silently, dutifully awaiting the answer. They expected Ira

to tell them. Well, Ira would say finally, if no one was going to inter-
rupt, he would just keeping talking for the next week or two and *that,*
he would say, is a nonviolent threat.

Laughter loosened tongues. Slowly the students would begin feeling their way. Progress, they agreed, meant the movement toward
gentleness and love, away from war. Ira elaborated. Talk to people as
individuals, not as objects, not as things. It was a matter of I and thou,
as Martin Buber put it; I and *thou,* not I and *it.* You live your life as
an example. You march, you demonstrate, you embody your values.

Yes, another student interjected, that sounds fine in theory but in
practice might it not become utterly impractical? One after another,
the students warmed up, venturing their notions. Ira knew this
dynamic, from the Youth for Peace sessions he led in Palo Alto, the
Peninsula School classes he had taught since the 1950s, the informal
seminars he convened at the Kepler's cashier counter.

Ira and his first wife, Merle, had divorced in the early 1960s, an
awful, unsettled time for their children, Nicole and Mark. Nicole
didn't think much of Ira's second wife, a younger woman named
Susan, but Susan was for a time Ira's partner in activism. The couple
would travel with Joan and the Rev. Martin Luther King Jr. in September 1966 to Grenada, Mississippi, where white mobs were threatening black schoolchildren. In Carmel, sitting in on the Institute's
seminars, Susan would tease Ira with the hardest of questions. A killer
is trying to murder me, she would tell Ira; what would the pacifist do
then? Stop him without violence, Ira would say. But no, Susan would
not let her husband off that easily. If it was really a choice between
deploying violent self-defense or letting the stranger kill her, what
would Ira's choice be then?

"It would have to be you, baby," Ira would say, the *Monterey Peninsula Herald* would report on December 24, 1965. "It would have
to be you."

Ira had his favorite borrowed aphorisms. One must be tender as a
lotus and hard as granite, he would say, quoting Gandhi. He had, as
well, his favorite stories. One time, he would tell students, a would-be
robber stuck a gun in his ribs and demanded all his money. Unshaken,

8. Jesse Jackson, Joan Baez, Ira Sandperl, and Martin Luther King Jr. at a demonstration, undated. Photographer unknown, courtesy of the Kepler family.

Ira offered the robber half of his money instead. Turned around, the robber didn't know what to say, and Ira would tell his delighted students that he and the robber ended up going out to dinner together. It was such a perfect story, and he told it many times. Ira was made for the stage, though the attention could also be irksome.

A CBS television crew showed up for a feature on the peace school. The students calmed and quieted themselves, while a hefty cameraman stomped about as he maneuvered a microphone into position. He kept moving around, rattling the wooden floor, until Ira could not abide it any longer.

"You're ruining the goddamn purpose of the thing," Ira snapped.

The cameraman went outside for a cigarette, the *Berkeley Barb* subsequently reported.

Joan would tease Ira, call him Sandperl. Easy for you, Sandperl, to urge students to know themselves, she would tell him; you're a nice guy, easy to know, but I am Joan Baez, the girl singer, gifted with the voice and saddled with the neediness, such a bitch beneath it all. Ira laughed and lapped it all up: the debates, the confrontation with ideas, the *attention*.

"They all want Joan," Ira told a 1966 visitor, writer Peter S. Beagle. "They want her voice, that is, and her name, and her presence. But if they take Joan, they have to take me. I'm the free bonus. I'm the word from our sponsor" (Beagle 1966).

Joan was not confined to the Institute. Musically, she was branching out. Under Richard Fariña's enthusiastic tutelage, Joan was trying her first rock-and-roll-inflected album. Joan and Fariña had a certain rapport. He had loads of promise, the world opening up to him.

On April 30, 1966, after a book-signing party at Carmel's Thunderbird bookstore, Mimi and Fariña had joined in a party at the Carmel Valley home of Pauline Baez and her husband. Triumphant, Fariña and a newfound acquaintance had gone zooming off on a motorcycle just as the evening fog rolled in, Fariña riding in the back. On a sharp turn, moving about ninety miles per hour, driver and rider apparently failing to coordinate, one leaning in one direction and one leading in the other, the motorcycle failed to negotiate the road's turning. Fariña flew off, smashing his unprotected head and dying in an instant.

Fariña's death cast Mimi upon the rocks. She needed help, and Roy was close by. Already handling Joan's finances, Roy took on for a time Mimi's money as well.

"Roy oversaw what money came in and gave me advice and played a sort of fatherly role in my life," Mimi told *Peninsula Magazine* two decades later.

The FBI was watching at least as early as January 1966. Citing an informant described as a "highly sensitive source with respect to the racial situation in Atlanta," the FBI that month advised headquarters that Joan was probably going to invite Martin Luther King Jr. to participate in her Institute. Joan and Ira certainly were keen on the notion. Both, in their own way, had been cultivating a relationship with the civil rights leader. Ira habitually provided King books that he thought might be of interest: Arnold Toynbee's *Change and Habit*, or Frederick Wertham's study of violence called *A Sign for Cain*. Joan merely had to be her own winning self and King would be enchanted. King was a natural fit for the Institute, and this seemed to alarm the FBI. A January 1966 memo, obtained under the Freedom of Information Act, stated that Atlanta agents should "immediately" notify San Francisco agents if King were to receive an invitation from Joan since the Institute "is an extremely controversial issue on the Monterey Peninsula."

Joan, Ira, and King did meet in Chicago one day to discuss the peace school and its potential. Perhaps, Joan and Ira suggested, the Institute for the Study of Nonviolence could bring its seminars to the South. The region was, after all, in need of a peaceful and calming hand. The trio continued their discussion in a motel room, with Joan and Ira making the pitch. King assured Joan and Ira that God meant them to do great and good things together, but commitments were left open-ended and as it happened the Nobel Peace Prize winner would never make an appearance at the Institute for the Study of Nonviolence (Sandperl 1974, 19).

Poor Sue Petkus, meanwhile, was being driven to distraction by the peaceniks and the Beatniks. They were an abomination to her. She was receiving anonymous phone calls, she said, and strange people were ringing her doorbell, asking for directions. She had to go under a doctor's care, she was so upset, and sometimes she had to fight back. During some of the Institute's outdoor sessions, she put loudspeakers outside and blasted her music: Barbra Streisand and bossa nova.

"The sound of children squalling was really pleasant compared to that," Joan said in the *Monterey Peninsula Herald* of May 26, 1966.

Joan and Ira, having won the county's approval, felt themselves on the move. They also had a new legal champion. Attorney William Stewart was replaced by Francis Heisler, whom Roy had first gotten to know a generation earlier during his Germfask days. Heisler adopted different tactics, pressing for revisions to the Institute's use restrictions. By a 6–1 vote in late May, the planning commission agreed that weekend classes could be offered, and more people could stay at the school. Throughout the remainder of 1966, the county board and county planners would periodically return to questions about the Institute's governance. Use restrictions would be added and removed. Neighbors would be given another chance to complain. Mrs. Petkus, following one unsatisfactory session later in the year, burst into tears.

The Institute for the Study of Nonviolence began attracting students from around the world. Sometimes they were exotic, like a visiting Buddhist monk from South Vietnam. Sometimes they came from close to home. On occasion Joan's father, Al, would show up for weekend seminars (Baez 1966, 60). Holly might drive to the Monterey bus station to pick up the students. Joan's mom and aunt, living nearby, would at times provide sandwiches and meals.

Roy was not often a physical presence around the Institute and, as a teacher, he couldn't hold a candle to Ira. One Institute student confided that "people would fall asleep" when Roy came to speak. He could drone on abstractly. As a manager and designated adult, though, Roy stood out. When a Northwestern University professor wrote soliciting advice about setting up a peace center similar to the Institute, it was Roy who responded. It was Roy, too, who took the reins for a possible expansion of the peace school. In late 1967 Roy was communicating with sociologist Theodore Roszak about the possibility of Roszak's assuming leadership of a new, Santa Barbara–based wing of the Institute. Roszak had earlier landed his job with the London office of *Peace News* in part due to Roy's influence, and he was interested in knowing more about the Santa Barbara plans. He felt it had promise, but he also needed more details, as he had faculty possibilities at Hayward State University in the East Bay. In November Roy expressed hope the Institute's new branch could open in a year, but he cautioned that there was no certainty.

"Its future," he said, "is a function of our work and our ingenuity." Roy went as far as contacting his old ally Henry Geiger, publisher of *MANAS,* about the Santa Barbara real estate market.

"We don't pretend that the Institute is a turning point in education," Roy advised Roszak in January 1968. "We are simply growing from one experience to the next."

Roszak had confidence in Roy's organizational and administrative abilities. Unlike some others in the peace movement, he had his feet firmly on the ground. In the end, though, the Santa Barbara venture fizzled. Roszak would land at Hayward State, a school later renamed

California State University, East Bay, and in 1968 he would make his name with publication of *The Making of a Counterculture.*

The Institute for the Study of Nonviolence students were, by and large, young, white, and searching. Mandy Carter was young, searching, and black. Her race aside, Carter's experiences more or less typified life at Joan and Ira's peace school, with all its intentions and chance encounters.

Raised in two orphanages and a foster home for her first eighteen years, Carter was attending high school in Schenectady, New York, in 1965 when a representative of the American Friends Service Committee gave a presentation to her junior social studies class. Inspired by what she heard about the Quakers, Carter ended up attending an AFSC work camp in the Pocono Mountains. There a young folk-singing couple from the Highlander Center in Tennessee, Guy and Candie Carawan, told the students about Joan Baez's peace institute.

The seed was planted. After Carter graduated from high school in 1966 she attended community college for one semester before dropping out and moving to New York City. Then she hitchhiked across the country with two friends. Shortly after arriving in San Francisco, she heard on KFPA radio about a free downtown concert in tribute to folk singer Woody Guthrie. Joan Baez would be one of the performers. Carter went to the concert and saw Joan, accompanied by her sister Mimi Fariña. After the concert Carter walked around the backside of the theater, where she ran into Joan and her party leaving the theater. She introduced herself to Joan and told her that she had heard about her Institute. Joan conversed with Mandy and invited her to apply.

Once accepted, for a session in the summer of 1968, Carter received a reading list prepared by Ira. It was heavily concentrated on Mahatma Gandhi and Gandhian principles and practices of nonviolence. Arriving in Carmel, she and the other students settled into a building they called The Bunkhouse. They could walk to the schoolhouse and they could feel, Carter recalled, the eeriness of knowing that they were living close to the site where Mimi's beloved Richard Fariña had died two years before.

On the first day Carter and the others received the books they would be using. They would read and then, under Ira's tutelage, they would discuss. He would ask: What was it you just read? What did you think about it? Was it right? Have you considered this alternative? Slowly the students would warm up. An hour daily was committed to silence. One morning everyone drove the roughly forty miles to Big Sur and spent the day in silent coastal reflection, returning later to the Carmel Valley to report on their experiences. Throughout, Ira was the impresario. Joan would attend sessions and she would speak, about her own experiences as a performer and her adherence to pacifism, though she would purposely not dominate the room.

"Joan Baez was the thing that got you there, but it was Ira who held it together with his scholarly knowledge and teachings," Carter said.

As it happened, Carter's session in the summer of 1968 was the last Institute for the Study of Nonviolence program to take place in the Carmel Valley. The seaside valley had been a perfect haven for Joan, the necessary silence amid her harried public life, but she had also met another Kepler's-connected activist who was luring her away. Joan's new beau, David Harris, of whom more later, wanted not a retreat but a place to advance from. He needed proximity to the places where draft resistance was put into practice.

"I said, 'I can't live down here; I can't work down here,'" Harris recalled in an interview.

Joan relented. In August 1968, shortly after Mandy Carter's session ended, the Institute for the Study of Nonviolence packed up for the San Francisco Bay Area. Roy made the official announcement, explaining that the peace activists wanted to relocate closer to the action. Joan and Harris moved to a place in the foothills above Palo Alto, a Page Mill Road retreat they would call Struggle Mountain.

Struggle Mountain was quite a different trip from Carmel, which notwithstanding Joan's ministrations remained a Republican country clubber's paradise. The Palo Alto foothills were more a frontier, folds and oak hollows inviting casual habitation. Tents, teepees, and tree houses were sprouting, not one of them with any kind of license or authorization. The Institute's programs continued now with more of a communal, foothills outlaw flavor. A U.C. Berkeley student named Steve Ladd arrived for an Institute session in the summer of 1969 and found himself camping outside near an ex-con and an under-age runaway. One day Ira led everyone north to Point Lobos for the Institute's traditional day of silence on the coast. The discussions and reading lists followed the same pattern as at Carmel, though some of the institute's original touches were absent.

"Everybody hoped Joan would show up," Ladd recalled in an interview, "but she rarely did."

The Institute was also spreading beyond California, after a fashion. A Golden, Colorado, branch opened in 1969, established by Institute alumnus Burt Wallrich and partner Anne Guilfoile. Guilfoile and allies undertook efforts like protests outside the Rocky Flats nuclear weapons complex, but in 1971 the Institute for the Study of Nonviolence and its Colorado offspring would sever their legal and administrative ties.

The Institute for the Study of Nonviolence lived on in its Palo Alto home for a few more years, but it had lost something in the trans-lation to the Bay Area. Holly Chenery, the indispensable woman, had moved on. Committed in all her heart, she had converted to Catholi-cism in the mid-1960s and joined the Missionary Sisters of the Holy Rosary in 1970. Holly had been growing disillusioned with the egos and the personal dramas entangling the Institute. She had, as well, long pictured herself as a missionary in a foreign land. As it developed, Holly moved to Brazil in 1974 and would stay there for decades.

By 1970 what remained of the Institute had moved downhill from Struggle Mountain to Lytton Street in downtown Palo Alto. That June yet another Kepler's-connected pacifist, Lee Swenson, was appointed director. Swenson, who had once built bookshelves for Kepler's, had energy and ideas as well as practical experience. As the Institute's new director, he convened joint seminars with luminaries including author Wendell Berry and poet Robert Bly. Swenson worked with sponsor-ship of the Big Sur Folk Festivals that resulted in two records and a documentary movie.

Joan kept her hand in, to a degree. To a group of Stanford faculty spouses in April 1970, Joan spoke of the Institute and her own efforts to follow a nonviolent path even when the world intruded. She told the intrigued spouses how a speed freak had once come knocking on the door of her foothills home. Joan told the wild-eyed character that he should not act too weird; he would scare her baby. The speed freak left, but then returned. When she tried to bustle him away, they ended up in clinch in the doorway: the pacifist folk singer and the agitated young man.

"I really didn't want to hurt him," Joan said, the *Palo Alto Times* reported on April 9, 1970. "I couldn't even knee him like you're supposed to, so I ended up screaming for help just like a woman."

The anecdote was pure Joan, charming and funny and self-knowing. Whenever she spoke on the Institute's behalf, she was a reckonable force, and people listened. In June 1972, as FBI special agents watched, Joan helped lead some eight hundred demonstrators in an Institute-sponsored walk encircling the Capitol, after which she and speakers including actress Candice Bergen and Senator Fred Harris of Oklahoma urged Congress to cut off Vietnam War funding.

The Institute, endowed by Joan, spread its influence in other ways. In the summer of 1971 FBI special agents recorded in a memo obtained under the Freedom of Information Act that individuals sharing the same Palo Alto address as the Institute had bought some eighty acres of farmland near David Harris's hometown of Fresno. Their plan was to establish a cooperative farm, a place for radicals to grow. In a memo, FBI special agents subsequently reported that "six to eight young people representing themselves to be from the Institute for the Study of Nonviolence . . . dressed in the 'hippie fashion'" had shown up at a Fresno dealership to buy a tractor, manure-spreader, and other farm equipment.

But with the passing years, and particularly after the Vietnam War finally ended, Joan had less time to offer the Institute. Holly's absence, too, was keenly felt. Roy and Ira began finding the Institute's planning sessions chaotic and fruitless. In-fighting became the school sport, and Joan recalled attending horrible meetings at which hideous behavior among the peace-lovers became commonplace. The Institute, Roy warned Joan in February 1973, was showing dangerous signs of "in-groupism that keeps others out . . . accreting staff not so much through direct interest and competency, but rather through preferred sleeping partners, hangers-on, disciples interested in persons rather than shared ideas [and] careless handling of bookkeeping and finances."

Through the early and mid-1970s, the Institute in its Palo Alto incarnation supported some virtuous work. Its library was useful. Everyone meant well. Somehow, though, the engine was sputtering. Joan was both in and out; she was essential to the Institute, but also a complication for it. She was, after all, *Joan*. Her maturing fame commanded respect and brought the Institute continued status-by-affiliation, for which some newcomers seemed both grateful and resentful. She was the one who could not be ignored. Personalities and power trips began dominating decision-making; peace sometimes seemed secondary. A distinctly feminist-oriented coalition, known as "the collective," came to the fore. Roy, War Resisters League staffer Scott Ullman recalled, was too much the peace patriarch to feel comfortable with the new orientation. He was not the only one. Ira was unhappy. He thought of the Institute's early days in the Carmel Valley as an Eden; if only there could be a return. This did not sit well with everyone; enough, some thought, with the past. Some collective members were denouncing the Institute's organizational structure as a typical male patriarchy, an adversary to be overcome. Scott Kennedy, an idealistic new staff member come up from Santa Barbara, reported being dismayed at the collective's harsh rhetoric and us-versus-them mentality.

Finally, in 1976, the internal struggles grew too much. Ira, Roy, and Joan agreed to resign as Institute board members, giving over to "the collective" the remaining assets including use of the building at 667 Lytton Street near downtown Palo Alto. In return, they wanted to end use of the Institute's name. They were putting the Institute for the Study of Nonviolence to sleep, literally washing their hands of it.

"The many ambiguities and mixed history and reputation of the Institute, and the fact of Joan's and others' names and reputations being tied up with it, suggest to us the importance of ceasing to use its name," Joan and Ira stated in a May 11, 1976, note. And just to put a fine point on it, the departing activists stressed that "Joan will in no case publicly demean or criticize the work of the projects still based at 667 [Lytton Street]."

The Institute didn't exactly disappear. It evolved. In time a new organization arose in Santa Cruz called the Resource Center for Nonviolence. As one of their last acts on the Institute's board, Joan, Ira, and Lee Swenson signed the royalties from Joan's album *Come from the Shadows* over to the Resource Center. Remarkably, the money just kept flowing, a deep spring. In 2010, a generation after the Institute for the Study of Nonviolence formally went out of business, the Resource Center for Nonviolence was still receiving about $3,000 a year from Joan's album sales. Scott Kennedy, who went from the Institute's staff to the Resource Center, called the royalty payments crucial for the center's ongoing work.

The Institute's progeny retained other connections to Roy and his circle. As he grew sicker in later years, Roy approached Kennedy about the prospect of delivering his accumulated papers to the Resource Center. He started sending selected materials, and after he passed away Roy's wife, Patricia, continued to convey documents. The Resource Center's library in Santa Cruz was named in honor of Roy, although the document storage proved to be a temporary arrangement. Scott Kennedy eventually realized the boxes of letters, newspaper clippings, and manuscripts would be better stored at the Swarthmore College Peace Collection in Pennsylvania.

The shipment of Roy's papers from Santa Cruz to Swarthmore closed off one of the last physical connections between Roy and what began as the Institute for the Study of Nonviolence. What remained was the memory, of a love affair that was touching, precious, and passing. The Institute for the Study of Nonviolence did not last, save in the minds of those who lived it, but neither, in its time, was it alone. It would have brethren, new schools of a companionable nature.

13

The Free U

Roy had done his homework.

The Phi Beta Kappa man and former Fulbright scholar had excelled in conventional schools, but he didn't like what he had seen. University of Colorado administrators and professors had submitted to the state's loyalty oath mandates. A fussy one-time dean of the University of California–Berkeley's School of Education had filed a formal complaint against KPFA. Even the Parent-Teacher Association disappointed him. In March 1960 Roy and Patricia had joined with four other Palo Alto couples in voicing their distaste for having to accept what he called the "uncritical, good-fellow role" of the usual PTA meeting.

There had to be something better. The Institute for the Study of Nonviolence offered one alternative, but it was limited in subject matter and, during its heyday, geographically remote in the Carmel Valley. Other innovative educational outposts existed in the Bay Area, like the Peninsula School where Ira had been teaching off and on for several years, but Roy wanted an adult place. He was not alone. Roy and other radicals would redo the education establishment, with the creation of the Midpeninsula Free University.

The Free U, as many knew it, was one of the first of its kind in the country. In 1965, when Roy helped the Free U get started, fewer than a dozen free universities existed nationwide. By 1969 there were some 450. They had names like the University for Man, Everybody's School, and the University of Thought. They were nestled in warehouses, barracks, and abandoned churches. They offered classes and published magazines. They were the asylums, skeptics thought, taken over by inmates.

The Free U, in its own brief life, was a remarkably fruitful institution. At its enrollment height, the Free U's Winter 1969 catalog listed 278 "courses" serving 1,275 students. The radicals and freethinkers had created a school the same size as Reed or Swarthmore. The course catalog itself became a magazine, *The Free You*, showcasing the youthful works of Wendell Berry, Robert Stone, and poet Thom Gunn. The Free U attracted an intellectually restless crew who would drive Silicon Valley's personal computer revolution. It helped inspire city recreation departments and conventional universities to loosen up.

The Free U had a vivid few years before being turned so inside out that Roy and the other founders could hardly recognize it. This neither surprised nor saddened the straight world. The convention-makers at *Time* magazine on June 16, 1969, would smugly observe how "self-indulgence could turn free universities into a travesty of education, where rapping replaces research and reason gives way to sensitivity." And that was true enough, so far as it went, but the glib assessment overlooked the poignant facts, of how in the course of just a few years a new school could be born, grow, and finally break into shards.

Mega-universities were impersonally stamping out graduates like widgets. The human element was missing. Meeting in Port Huron, Michigan, in June 1962, the nascent Students for a Democratic Society (SDS) declared that the new generation must wrest control of the learning process from "the cumbersome academic bureaucracy extending throughout the academic as well as extracurricular structures." Instead of rendering students cogs in the social machine, the Port Huron Statement's chief author, twenty-one-year-old Tom Hayden, envisioned that "the university could serve as a significant source of social criticism and an initiator of new modes and molders of attitudes."

The SDS Port Huron Statement foreshadowed the coming revolt on U.S. college campuses, as students started to take into their own hands the universities to which they felt consigned. In December 1964, amid the Free Speech Movement at U.C. Berkeley, protesting students occupied the school's Sproul Hall. During the extended stay, demonstrators engaged in impromptu seminars, workshops, and discussion groups. The nonschool school was a revelation, and the Sproul Hall experience inspired those who founded in 1965 the Free University of Berkeley. They were rejecting, they said, "the educational establishment which produces proud cynicism but sustains neither enthusiasm nor integrity" (Draves 1980, 81).

At about the same time, San Francisco State University students began with the blessing of their school's faculty the Experimental College. Roy and other leaders of War Resisters League/West encouraged their field man, Bert Kanegson, to engage with the San Francisco State effort, where he helped found the ambitious-sounding Institute for Social Change. Ira would contribute to San Francisco State's Experimental College by leading a seminar entitled "Nonviolence in a Violent World" (Draves 1980, 80).

On the Peninsula too, new ideas were sprouting.

Stanford biologists Lee and Leonard Herzenberg had been frequenting Kepler's since they arrived in the Bay Area in 1959. "Where else," Lee Herzenberg asked rhetorically in a 2010 interview, "would you go for books?" The appeal, though, went beyond books. While at the California Institute of Technology for Leonard's graduate studies in the mid-1950s, the Herzenbergs had gotten to know Linus Pauling, and once at Stanford they allied themselves with Roy and Ira's Peninsula Committee for the Abolition of Nuclear Tests. Geneticists, they deployed their scientific expertise to challenge the utility of nuclear fallout shelters during the shelter craze of the early 1960s.

The Herzenbergs straddled several camps. From their Stanford laboratory, they were producing technical research papers typified by a 1964 piece in *Nature* entitled "Presence of Donor Specific Gammaglobulins in Sera of Allogeneic Mouse Radiation Chimeras." That was not Roy's cup of tea. But outside of the lab, the Herzenbergs were also politically and socially active. Put another way, they were hip scientists. They liked interesting music and stimulating conversations. They didn't like loyalty oaths and stultifying convention. In late 1964, about the time of the *Nature* magazine piece, the Herzenbergs opened their campus home for a little meeting of the like-minded.

Stanford graduate students Keith Lowe and Ken Mills, Lee Herzenberg recalled, "were really irritated that they could not get courses on Marxism." They, and a few others, wanted more options. In the Herzenberg's home, they batted around some ideas for taking more control of their education. From the conversation and others like it, the students established what they called the Graduate Coordinating Committee, and they came up with some offerings they spelled out on a mimeographed page that amounted to a rudimentary course catalog.

"It started," Lee Herzenberg said, "as a serious academic exercise."

Modest as it was, the Graduate Coordinating Committee captured something in the air. Through 1965, Mills, Lowe, graduate students Charles Li and Mike Pincus, and others talked informally about broadening the experiment. The activists had a notion of what they wanted. The distinction between students and teachers would be blurred, or erased altogether. Decisions would be democratic. The organization would be loose. Participants would enjoy freedom from prerequisites, grades, and competition. They would be free from the onerous restraints of the big academic institutions. They wanted something more than simply a counter-university. They wanted a vital, ongoing community—a way of life. A free university is what they wanted.

Roy could help. The graduate students, book lovers, and freethinkers were Roy's kind of people, Kepler's customers. Early on, Roy was asked if he was interested in helping organize. Of course he was. This new university idea was arriving at an opportune time. Roy was already engaged in preliminary discussions about the Institute for the Study of Nonviolence. The new university idea could fit in with the career reconsiderations that had him putting the stores up for sale in the late summer of 1965. Kepler's Books & Magazines itself was a de facto living room where friends could rap about this new school.

"It is an old American custom to build counter-institutions that claim to be more free than their predecessors," Roy would note in the *Stanford Daily* on February 11, 1966.

Multiple yearnings were coming together. Susan Bass, recently moved back to Palo Alto from New York City, had a notion of establishing a coffeehouse. Her friend and neighbor Eva Vincent was keen

on the new school idea. Presto: They became the housing committee, setting out in October 1965 to find quarters for the new venture. They lacked the money to buy, so they would have to rent. The
problem, Bass recounted in the April 1969 *The Free You* magazine,
was that "no one was too eager to rent his property to a bunch of
long-haired radicals and foreign-looking types." They finally found a
weedy, roach-infested, two-story house at 991 Runnymeade Street in
East Palo Alto.

Talk about alternatives. East Palo Alto was separated from Palo
Alto proper, very proper, by the Bayshore Freeway. It might have been
the Berlin Wall. East Palo Alto wasn't even a town, but a benighted
and unincorporated swath of San Mateo County. The population was
everything Palo Alto's was not: poor, black, and hungry. It had a reputation as a dangerous place. To get there, travelers would pass by the
evocatively named Whiskey Gulch, a commercial block whose moni-
ker said it all. East Palo Alto had its advantages, though. It was both
fiscally prudent and a gesture at racial and socioeconomic solidarity. The location demonstrated that the new educational experiment
would serve the People, not the Ivory Tower. It was a radical message,
though Mike Pincus assured a *Palo Alto Times* reporter in a December 9, 1965, article that none of the Free U planners were members
of the Communist Party. The reporter dutifully checked with a "U.S.
government spokesman," who confirmed that the Free U folk weren't
Communists. They were, he said, simply "peace marchers."

In January 1966 the organizers of what was then called the Free
University of Palo Alto sent out handwritten invitations to an audience Bass described as "the town's most wealthy and/or influential
left-wingers." On the weekend of January 15–16, at the East Palo Alto
Women's Club, the new university conducted its first public meeting
and class registration session following a presentation by journalist
Felix Greene, one of the few Westerners to visit North Vietnam. It
was a modest start, as some thirty students enrolled in various classes.
Keith Lowe, a Stanford graduate student in English recently returned
from two years in Africa, offered "Neo-African Literature." Psychologist Vic Lovell, forever to be known as the man who turned Ken Kesey

onto the federal government's LSD experiments, offered a Wednesday evening course on "American Youth in Revolt." Sunday afternoon current events forums were envisioned, with specialists available on different topics and global regions.

The rehabilitated Runnymeade place in East Palo Alto was cast as both coffeehouse and classroom. Volunteers set out candles, chairs, and tables. They made the coffee and brought homemade pastries and goodies. It was sweet, but even with the decorations the house felt exposed in the East Palo Alto ghetto. It never became the center that organizers hoped for; classes, in any event, were being held as well in scattered locations.

At his Los Altos home, Roy began teaching a Monday evening seminar entitled "Non-violence and Its Social Organization." He explained that the class would delve into the relationship between nonviolent resistance and "peace, freedom and social justice, [and] its use as a revolutionary world model." His syllabus included Leo Tolstoy's "The Kingdom of God Is Within You," Louis Fischer's *The Life of Mahatma Gandhi,* and *The Quiet Battle* by Mulford Q. Sibley. Sibley's name meant something special to Bay Area activists. He was a pacifist professor of political science whose bid for a teaching job at Stanford had been turned down in the late 1950s under suspect political circumstances.

Ever the organizer, Roy that spring also agreed to chair the Free U's curriculum committee. He was one of the designated adults in the room, for a free-form university whose classes ranged from jazz, piano, and improvisational drama to neocolonialism and the Chinese Revolution. Roy knew flaky when he saw it, but the curricular reach was liberating and he kept soliciting more class offerings. The content, style, and circumstance of a course were entirely up to the teacher. The new university was revolt in action, even in its sports, which included, for a time, Zen basketball.

"You do not play to win," Free U activist Robb Crist would explain to the squares in a *Sports Illustrated* article. "You play to get calm, to keep track of yourself, to keep your consciousness. It's like taking acid."

Roy knew nothing of acid, personally, though people around Kepler's Books & Magazines certainly did. Roy was about sobriety, not ecstasy. In Robb Crist and Roy Kepler, the new Free U had its dual visions. The two men followed different stars. Sardonically dubbed "Stanford's aging guru" by the *Stanford Daily,* but known by Free U colleagues like future journalist Phil Trounstine as an "incredibly bright" man, Crist was a one-time political science student who had, by his mid-thirties, wandered far from the academic path. A self-described veteran of sixty or so LSD trips, Crist considered straight political activism a potential cop-out, a way to avoid looking within and changing that which really matters.

Roy was not indifferent to personal transformation, which had been a central tenet of the Peacemakers movement he had helped found a generation before. Mostly, though, he inhabited the world where politics mattered. This divide between hippies and politicos, between change-your-life and change-the-world, split the Free U from the start. There were other divisions. Cofounder Mike Pincus, in the mimeographed *Free University News,* warned on April 12, 1966, that "there has been considerable dispute as to the ultimate goals of the school." Some considered the Free U simply a shaggier version of the Adult Ed offerings down at the local community center. Others had more ambitious notions.

The straight world, and even some of its more avant-garde elements, sometimes made it harder for Roy and the other organizers. In August 1966, as Roy was actively soliciting more teachers for more courses, Peninsula School leaders declined the Free U's request for use of the facilities. The rejection pained those Free U organizers who thought the school where Ira once taught and Jerry Garcia once performed might be more sympathetic. In the end, the *Free University News* reported on September 19, 1966, the Palo Alto Unitarian Church agreed to rent the Free U three classrooms for $150 a month.

Joint enthusiasm sometimes trumped the various dichotomies for the Free U's first year. It was great just to break free, try new things. Roy, with the occasional guest appearance by Ira, continued offering his nonviolence seminars, and the number of other classes continued to grow. Joan and Ira together helped kick off the Fall 1966 term with an October 2 forum on "The Myth and Fallacy of Violent Revolution." Longtime Kepler's employee Nick Simon gave a talk about "The Death of God and the Death of Capitalism."

But by the spring of 1967, the counterculture tension between the heads and the activists had also become too big to paper over. In April 1967 Free University course coordinator Georgia Kelly stepped down, charging, the *Stanford Daily* reported, that "the course offerings were becoming too mystical, too psychedelic and that the organization's original purpose of promoting radical political action had largely been lost." Each side thought the other was avoiding what was important.

The constant identity crisis came to a head in a marathon May 1967 Free U session. Some wanted to change the name to the "Open University," as being more reflective of the mission. That was voted down. A majority voted to subsidize an experiment in communal living, but opted not to formally endorse "poly-sexual and poly-perverse sex experiments" as a backbone of the commune. It would be wrong, psychologist Vic Lovell told the activists, to impose this vision on others "if it wasn't their thing." At meeting's end, the *Stanford Daily* reported, about a dozen self-professed Marxists and Maoists declared they would withdraw from the free university experiment.

The street revolutionaries' withdrawal was only temporary, though the gun-toters would eventually come raging back. Until then, though, Roy and his allies held the Free U together as a space in which different ideas could be planted. Roy was offering his evening nonviolence seminar. Stanford student body president David Harris, who had started working part-time as a Kepler's clerk, was likewise leading about ten Free U students through a weekly war-and-peace seminar at an East Palo Alto house dubbed the Peace and Liberation Commune.

The political activists and the ecstasy seekers could even still dance together at times. In the spring of 1967, the Free U convened a Be-In at El Camino Park, a compact, twelve-acre oasis sandwiched between El Camino Real and the Southern Pacific railroad tracks. It would be one of several similar events that would be convened at the park, bits of communal whimsy adorned with names like "Registration Be-In and Mary Poppins Umbrella Festival." Palo Alto city officials balked at the El Camino Park gatherings, demanding that the organizers carry expensive liability insurance. It seemed a transparent ploy to fend off the longhairs, and Roy stepped in. He didn't really know much about the liberating power of rock-and-roll music, but he knew political oppression when he saw it. He contacted the Northern California ACLU, and the city backed down.

Nor was the Free U's revolution limited to the classrooms, streets, and parks. Bedrooms and kitchens, too, were going to be liberated.

Les Earnest was the executive officer at the Stanford Artificial Intelligence Laboratory. At the California Institute of Technology in the late 1940s, his freshman chemistry professor had been Linus Pauling, then still known more for science than for activism. Earnest had subsequently worked on air defense systems and the like, but since coming to Stanford in 1965 he had been branching out. Earnest was perusing a Free U catalog one day and noticed a class entitled "Beginning Group Loving." Intriguing, Earnest thought. In the next catalog, Earnest noticed a class entitled "Advanced Group Loving," with the Beginning Group Loving class as a prerequisite.

"The Advanced course kept appearing thereafter with the same prerequisite, so they evidently all enjoyed it," Earnest said. "However there were no more Beginning courses offered, so clearly timing was everything."

On another luscious spring day, eleven Free U students gathered in a sunny kitchen overseen by Elisabeth "Babette" Wills. The French-born Wills was then in her late fifties, a true cosmopolitan whose first husband had died in World War II while serving with the Office of Strategic Services. She had since remarried and made her hand-built Bay Area home into a warm, welcoming place in which she would entertain the likes of Linus Pauling and Cesar Chávez. On this May day, a charmed *San Francisco Chronicle* reporter showed up with the Free U students and observed revolutionary education in action. Wills waved a spoon at the wine, chicken, mushrooms, and herbs heaped on the table as she expounded upon her intentions.

"You see, *mes enfants*," Wills told her Free U class, "today we are making *poulet marenge*."

At Kepler's, Roy was distributing the magazine-cum-catalog called *The Free You*. It was a trip, jammed with art, poetry, hipster history, and the occasional wild-eyed polemic.

"I formulated our editorial policy, which was we weren't going to turn down anything," *Free You* coeditor and former Stegner Writing Fellow Ed McClanahan said.

McClanahan had quickly discovered Kepler's upon his first arrival at Stanford in the late 1950s. It was his kind of joint, liberated and literary. A bit of a prankster as well as a talented writer, from whom peers kept expecting greater things, McClanahan by the mid-1960s was clinging to a teaching gig at Stanford even as he delved more deeply into the Free U. Along with fellow Kentuckian and former Stegner Fellow Gurney Norman, McClanahan became one of four editors of *The Free You* during its creative heyday. Together, *The Free You* contributor Judith Rascoe said, Norman and McClanahan were the "Kentucky Mafia." They were hip, and they were country, and all in all they were "extremely entertaining guys," Rascoe recalled in a 2010 interview. They were also highly talented editors who turned a slapdash catalog into a real piece of work. A Kepler's customer since her own Stanford undergraduate days in the late 1950s, Rascoe called Norman a "nurturing mentor of younger writers as well as a writer's pal, the sort of guy you'd take your new manuscript to for a first reading."

Under this leadership, *The Free You* was a remarkably juicy publication. McClanahan said he considered it his "responsibility to make sure good things got into print," and he spent considerable time hustling copy from anyone with something to say. Roy, who always kept his typewriter busy, wrote sober-minded essays on nonviolence. Robert Stone, the Kepler's aficionado and one-time Stegner Fellow who had since authored his first novel, *A Hall of Mirrors,* published a story about Ken Kesey going on the lam in Mexico. Rascoe would likewise be published in *The Free You* and then proceed to write the screenplay for the movie version of Stone's book *Dog Soldiers*, as well as other movies including Robert Redford's *Havana*. Susan MacDonald, a young single mother of two who had started working at Kepler's in 1968, found *The Free You* an outlet for her own poems. Hip psychologist Vic Lovell published in the magazine a multipart history of Perry Lane, the small Stanford-area neighborhood where the early LSD experimenters had congregated.

Distractions arose, naturally. Overseers of the Free U's print shop, which in time dedicated half of its profits to the antiwar group The Resistance, had to remind editors to make their deadlines. Free U classes, too, could veer off course. It could be hard to stay on the straight and narrow. Les Earnest was attending a Free U yoga class on the Stanford campus one night, a nice little break from his mind trips at the Stanford Artificial Intelligence Laboratory. Earnest and the other students tried their hands at some levitation exercises and the like, with mixed success, until loud music broke in from the class next door. The yoga students tried ignoring the interruption, but could not sustain their focus. Maybe there was the lesson: the world could not be simply shut out. Finally, at the instructor's suggestion, the yoga students en masse arose from their mats and went next door to present themselves.

"It turned out to be a course titled 'Sexual Freedom Now!'" Earnest recalled, "and the movie they were showing was sufficiently interesting that most of the yoga class stayed."

Roy knew: Peace is practice.

For the individual, meditation worked. Joan and Ira had enfolded meditation into the daily life of the Institute for the Study of Nonviolence. But for the violent world beyond one's own breath, peacemaking required other practice as well. In August 1964, at the Grindstone Institute training sessions, Roy had learned how role-playing could be used to practice peace. Roy, along with Ira, had returned to Grindstone for another training session in July 1968. There students could practice their roles physically, working out the kinks and trying their lines.

Role-playing, moreover, had become commonplace among the Free U heads. Psychologist Vic Lovell led psychodrama sessions and there was, amid the myriad late-night raps, a growing awareness of how people play roles all the time. It was enlightening to open the cage and let the inner selves out. Be a soldier, and then switch and be a victim, and then switch into some other part altogether. Sometimes the role-playing could get a little too vivid, but political activists and psychological argonauts alike appreciated the benefits. Roy did, and for the weekend of August 23–25, 1968, he announced his latest Free U seminar. The Peace Games were coming.

Roy rooted his Peace Games in concepts long discussed by pacifist theoreticians. War Resisters League founder Jessie Hughan had conjured, in a pre–World War II pamphlet entitled *If We Should Be Invaded: Facing a Fantastic Hypothesis,* images of citizens repudiating arms while remaining true to their nonviolent principles. Subjects would neither cooperate with the invaders nor demonize them. Roy's own reading of history further suggested the potential for nonviolent resistance. One prime example came in Norway during World War II. After Nazi invaders suppressed armed resistance in two months of active fighting, civilians began expressing themselves peacefully but willfully. Students, for a time, wore paper clips as a sign of unity. When the Quisling government clamped down, red caps flourished as the next symbol, then flowers. Norway's Supreme Court justices resigned. Athletic club members abandoned their teams.

Roy loved the Norway story, evidence of the viability of nonviolent resistance. Who would have thought paper clips and flowers could be nonviolent tools? A role-playing exercise could mother the invention of similar tools for peacemaking. Based on his Grindstone experience, Roy helped script the late summer exercise for the Free U. Certainly the moment was ripe. Richard Nixon had just been selected as the Republican presidential nominee. The Democrats were going to start convening in Chicago on Monday, August 26. And to really hammer home what the world faced, Soviet forces had invaded Czechoslovakia on August 20.

Roy's Peace Games participants filled out an introductory questionnaire. He did one too, identifying himself as politically radical, clarifying that this meant "one who seeks the roots of problems." He reported he had been arrested more than three times. The participants then convened several times at Roy's Los Altos home. They discussed what was expected of them and what roles they were to play. Once prepared, everyone headed over the Santa Cruz Mountains to the shaded little town of Ben Lomond.

What happened next was recounted in a ninety-four-page report prepared by activist and Peace Games participant Tom Coats. Coats donated his report to Roy, and it is now stored as part of the Kepler Papers at the Swarthmore College Peace Collection (Coats n.d.).

Roy divided the Peace Games players into two groups. Six uniformed participants, armed with toy guns, comprised the invading army. Twenty-one men and women would be the defenders. Roy was the chief umpire. He would observe, intervening only if essential. He had crafted the scenario for what was to come. He had prepared the script, though it was but an outline.

The participants gathered late Friday afternoon at the Ben Lomond Quaker Center, an eighty-acre retreat shaded by redwood trees. The defenders knew only that they would soon be confronted with an invading force, known as the Eurasians, against whom they would have to resist. But resist how? The defenders did a dry run, with some playing the role of stick-wielding invaders. In a flash the putative invaders had brushed past the defenders, marched into the building known as the Hostel, dragged away the defenders, and cleared out the building. The defenders agreed that it was not practicable to defend buildings or territory nonviolently.

But what was the alternative? The defenders finally settled on rights, those enumerated in the Constitution, as their precious territory. The rights to speak, to worship, and to be free were no longer simply inchoate principles. They were property itself. Unified, the defenders convened in a circle. Wordlessly, they passed a hand-squeeze around, faster and faster. Energy pulsed from one to another until they all felt connected. The evening wore on, the defenders gathered about singing folk songs until about midnight. They felt good. They felt ready.

In the morning, the defenders prepared twenty carbon copies of a principled statement entitled "To All Men." Anticipating life under occupation, one of the defenders hid their typewriter in the woods.

At 10:30 a.m., the invaders arrived.

There were six, representing the People's Liberation Army. They appeared brisk and efficient, searching the dining hall, removing the distributor caps from cars. No one was going anywhere. The invaders appropriated the Hostel, setting up interrogation tables beneath a poster of Chairman Mao. The soldiers would not converse until their captain, Crystal by name, summoned the defender Peter Bergel to the Hostel. Bergel was a twenty-four-year-old Reed College alumnus, an experienced antiwar organizer. The captain spoke peremptorily to Bergel and then asked for a typewriter. Bergel retrieved it from the bushes. He advised the soldiers to be careful, for it might be contaminated with poison oak. The soldiers eyed the typewriter suspiciously, wondering whether this was an act of resistance, a booby trap. Or, was this an act of friendship, to offer this warning? Exactly what kind of game was this peace-lover playing, anyway?

One by one the soldiers summoned defenders inside the Hostel and presented them with forms to sign. One was a cooperation agreement, pledging allegiance to the Peoples Democratic Republic and promising not to support subversives. Defender Diane Weinberg decided she couldn't sign such a loyalty oath, and began composing a point-by-point explanation.

"The other defenders got bored waiting for her to finish, so they started a volleyball game with a human net," Coats reported.

Crystal began questioning the defenders. He wanted to know how they were organized, what they were training for, whether they had weapons. Did they have a trainer sent by the government? The People's Liberation Army, he assured the defenders, had assumed control of the United States.

"Any enemies will be eliminated," Crystal warned. "Is there any confusion on these points?"

"No," defender Steve Morris said. "I think you might have to shoot 80 percent of the population, though."

Through the day, as Roy circulated silently, Capt. Crystal brought in pairs of defenders and questioned them. They were speaking different languages. The captain would ask about weapons. The defenders would say that only nonviolent weapons would be utilized. Ahh, the captain would say, so there *were* weapons after all.

The day wore on into night. Some defenders thought that they could fraternize with the invaders, human to human, get to know each other. They tried with Bob Cullenbine, who was sitting down with a bottle of wine. Cully might talk.

Cullenbine had been raised in the wealthy San Francisco suburb of Hillsborough, earning an economics degree from Stanford in 1962. Well before the Free University, he had gotten involved with the St. Michael's Alley crowd and then with Ken Kesey's La Honda parties. Cullenbine was a lively, inconsistent man. Some moments, he was the most responsible guy in the room, the Daddy in other people's psychodramas. Other moments, he might chuck it all and go cast sand candles at the beach.

Christine Wynne, a pretty young defender, made eye contact and beamed pure love at him. Love, her eyes radiated; love, and peace.

"The only immediate effect," Coats reported, "was that Pfc. Cullenbine started wearing dark glasses in an attempt to avoid her eyes."

The invaders posted a new statement, declaring that defender Karl Schonborn had been temporarily detained for examination. Schonborn's wife, Milli, grew upset. Her husband was under armed guard somewhere, and she did not know if he was safe. Christine Wynne, trusting in the look of love, sat with her back to the fire and her pure, smiling face turned to the guards. Cullenbine kept his dark glasses on.

One by one the defenders fell asleep, to be awoken at seven on Sunday morning by shrill whistle blasts and orders shouted by guards.

Crystal brought a new loyalty oath. Sign the oath, he said, and Schonborn would be released. The defenders would not be so compliant. They pledged they would not commit any violent acts, they condemned fascist elements, and they welcomed the presence of the

People's representatives. The oath they would sign, however, was not the oath the authorities had presented them. Captain Crystal called this treason.

Crystal summoned two guards, who hustled a defender into the Hostel. With the door left open, the other defenders could hear what happened next. "This is a treasonous statement," Crystal shouted. "You *will* sign the real statement." Outside, the defenders were comforting themselves with song. At 11:19 a.m. they stopped for a moment, pausing for breath. That's when they heard the machine gun sounds from inside the Hostel.

Stunned, some defenders began crying. They hugged each other. They linked arms. Peter Bergel stood up.

"We have lost a brother," Bergel declared, "but we have not lost the war."

Crystal went outside to order the defenders back away from the building. They refused to move. He ordered the guards to bring the defender outside. He had not been killed after all. It had been a ruse. Crystal looked at the defenders. Had they learned their lesson? They had not. Then they would learn, now, for real.

The captain ordered one of his soldiers to shoot the prisoner. The soldier aimed and fired, and the prisoner toppled over.

The soldiers dragged the prisoner's body back inside. Some defenders cried again. Others began pleading with the guards. Crystal sent out a written message, expressing regret for having to kill one of the defenders but urging the others to be reasonable.

It was 1:08 in the afternoon.

"The exercise," Roy called out, "is over."

14

Resistance

The Peace Games reinforced Roy. He was no longer alone on the pacifist fringe; trained cadres were joining him.

The war helped too. Whereas Roy's tax resistance was simply eccentric in the placid 1950s, the escalating Vietnam War brought him more allies. On March 3, 1966, Joan told the *San Francisco Chronicle* that she too would not volunteer her tax money for the armaments that "we can see tragically demonstrated day after day in this fearful world." With a customary patronizing swoon, the *Chronicle* reporter added that Joan was "sweet and charming as ever." The next night Ira and Joan brought their tax protest gospel to San Francisco's street-wise Glide Memorial Church. With 235,000 U.S. troops in South Vietnam, and their numbers fatefully climbing, every aspect of war resistance was drawing more attention.

Roy followed up on April 15, 1966, leading an antitax rally in front of San Francisco's Federal Building. He also expanded the reach of his own tax protests, advising the IRS he would not pay a 10 percent telephone excise tax imposed by Congress. The IRS, in turn, advised Roy he owed $19.14. Tax collectors, punctilious to the end, placed a lien on Roy's Wells Fargo account for the required amount. Roy couldn't fight that, but he protested when Wells Fargo sought to assess an additional service charge. Wells Fargo finally relented and withdrew the service charge.

Specific war tools incited other acts of resistance. Napalm, in particular, repulsed activists. Extraordinarily flammable, the sticky jelly blended aviation gas and aluminum naphthenates into a perfect little hell. In early January 1966 Stanford associate professor of English

H. Bruce Franklin and other members of the small Stanford Committee for Peace in Vietnam began a season of antinapalm protests after learning that United Technology in nearby Redwood City had received an $11 million contract from Dow Chemical to develop a new, improved product dubbed Napalm-B. Roy opened his own front in the same campaign. In July 1966 he penned a handwritten note to the Dow Chemical Company, informing the company that he was stopping use of all Dow products until the company stopped making napalm. The multibillion-dollar company ignored Roy's letter. It must have seemed a squeak from the fringe, but it was really the avant-garde of a coming national protest. Protests grew. By November 1969 Dow would be announcing that it was removing itself from the napalm business (Zaroulis and Sullivan 1984, 107).

Still, napalm was only an implement. It was not the crux of the matter. By resisting conscription, Roy was confronting more directly systemic war. In April 1966 Roy joined with Quaker activist Ben Seaver to form the small Committee for Draft Resistance. Though well past draft age themselves, they intended to support and encourage young men still vulnerable to conscription. Along with Ira, former KPFA fundraiser Denny Wilcher, and Alan Strain, the middle-aged protestors were articulating a position that would have gotten them clapped into irons during past wars.

"We explicitly encourage, aid and abet civil disobedience and thus place ourselves in equal legal jeopardy with draft refusers," the Committee for Draft Resistance members avowed in a four-page brochure. "We cannot leave them to take the risks alone for what is the basic act of conscience for our time."

The commitment to peaceful civil disobedience mirrored an earlier "Declaration of Conscience Against the War in Vietnam," circulated in 1965 by Roy's old allies David Dellinger, Bayard Rustin, and Linus Pauling. The Committee for Draft Resistance's 1966 declaration, though, went beyond the expression of conscience. It deliberately called for violation of the 1948 Selective Service law, which made it a criminal offense for a person to counsel, aid, or abet someone in refusing or evading draft registration. Some eight hundred people would sign the Committee for Draft Resistance's declaration, each potentially risking up to five years in prison and a $10,000 fine.

Prosecutors let the Committee for Draft Resistance slide by. Others wouldn't be as lucky. In 1967 authors including Marcus Raskin of the Institute for Policy Studies began circulating "A Call to Resist Illegitimate Authority." The statement declared that "open resistance to the war and the draft is the course of action most likely to strengthen the moral resolve with which all of us can oppose the war." Roy signed on to this national declaration, as did antinapalm activist H. Bruce Franklin, Beat poet Allen Ginsburg, essayist Susan Sontag, pediatrician Benjamin Spock, Yale chaplain William Sloan Coffin, and others. On October 12, 1967, the eight- hundred-word statement and array of signatures appeared on a full page of the *New York Review of Books,* opposite a review of the latest philosophical tome by Claude Lévi-Strauss.

This rang a bell that would not be ignored. Federal officials targeted Spock, Coffin, and three others, eventually citing their public affirmation of the "Call to Resist Illegitimate Authority" as one of several elements of a "conspiracy" to counsel resistance to the draft law. Mitch Goodman, a World War II army veteran who had been in touch with Roy about the possibility of coordinating the various resistance statements, would be found guilty along with Spock and other defendants and sentenced to two years in prison. Roy, for a while, thought he and his California colleagues might be next.

"A number of us may soon join them on similar indictments and so be faced with potential sentences of up to five years," Roy advised sociologist Theodore Roszak in January 1968.

In the end, federal prosecutors left Roy alone, while an appeals court, citing prejudicial missteps by the trial judge, later reversed the convictions of Goodman, Spock, and their colleagues.

Unindicted, Roy was traveling, meeting with young professors and other activists, collecting signatures, spreading the word. Ira, too, was traveling, usually in the company of Joan. They were a team, Ira taking time off from his Kepler's Books & Magazines duties and Joan taking time away from her singing career.

In early December 1966 Joan and Ira had made a quiet pilgrimage to the Gethsemane Monastery in Kentucky to meet with the Trappist monk and author Thomas Merton. Merton's poems and essays were required reading at the Institute for the Study of Nonviolence. Ira and Joan considered him a true embodiment of holiness. Merton, in turn, had reached out to Joan in the summer of 1965, sending her a copy of one of his own books. Eventually, over the initial resistance of monastery leaders, the meeting was arranged. Joan, Ira, and Merton walked the grounds, Joan's hair fetched this way and that by the Kentucky wind. After a worldly meal of cheeseburgers and fries, they brought the stroll back to Merton's small cottage. The trio put Joan's new record "Noel" on the small turntable while Merton and Ira proceeded to savor Irish whiskey. Merton regarded Joan, and like others before and since he fell under her charms. She was an epiphany.

"Joan sat on the rug eating goat-milk cheese and bread and honey . . . in front of the fire," Merton recounted. "She is an indescribably sweet girl, and I love her" (Merton 1995, 167).

Joan and Ira spoke to Merton about the Institute for the Study of Nonviolence. Merton, infatuated, was under Joan's spell; his heart opened to the possible. Ira, the intoxicated missionary of love, insisted the monk must *surely* have a lady somewhere. Ira knew about such things. Love was to be given and not withheld.

Well, Merton allowed, there was a special woman . . .

Yes! Ira knew exactly what must happen next. Obviously the monk must be smuggled out of seclusion and delivered unto passion. It was time to live! Merton was up for it. They could escape the monastery and arrive just in time for the beloved's getting off work. If they drove ninety miles per hour they could just make it.

But wait. There would be consequences. Responsibilities hung heavy. Maybe delay was best. The rampant moment subsided. Morning sobered the two middle-aged men up, and Joan began second-guessing the wisdom of shepherding the holy man out of the monastery for a physical assignation. The carnal plot was called off and Thomas Merton remained behind, hung over with monastic guilt (Baez 1987, 132).

Their various trips together bound Joan and Ira more closely: the pupil with the transcending voice and the teacher with the shining eyes. But their relationship was also transforming, as Joan grew up. There had been, of course, young men in her life, none of them yet threatening to displace Ira. And then along came David Harris.

↓

"David Harris," the *Palo Alto Times'* resident Establishment curmudgeon, Alexander Bodi, stated on December 15, 1967, "probably learned more at Kepler's bookstore than he did at Stanford."

Bodi meant it as a putdown. He always sketched Roy with a drop of acid, describing him once as one "whose prosperous bookstores apparently leave . . . enough time to indulge his conscientious scruples against military service." But Bodi also came by his skepticism toward peaceniks honestly, having served behind Japanese lines with the Office of Strategic Services in World War II. His crack about David Harris, moreover, had some element of truth. Before becoming Joan Baez's Sir Galahad and one of the Vietnam War's most prominent draft resisters, David Harris was a Kepler's loyalist. He took counsel from Roy, and he took a paycheck from Roy's store. Roy hired Harris to sell books, and then again to rally West Coast draft resisters. Roy even played matchmaker, albeit with imperfect results.

A native of California's Central Valley, Harris had grown up in sun-baked Fresno with traditional notions of achievement. The son of a lawyer, he aspired, at various times, to attend West Point or become an FBI agent. He had entered Stanford in the fall of 1963, where he had embarked on the standard curriculum. But in 1964, learning there was a seat available in a car heading to segregated Mississippi, Harris packed a bag and left on a two-week trip that opened his eyes. He started attending antiwar rallies back in the Bay Area, where he stood out: tall and slender, casually clad in blue jeans and tan moccasins, wireless glasses. Out of nowhere he ran for Stanford student body president in the spring of 1966, calling for legalization of marijuana and ending Stanford's cooperation with the Pentagon. More parochially, he declared that "fraternities are a crock of shit." Later there would be a reckoning for this effrontery; but, at the time, Harris got away with his lip.

"Against all odds," Harris later recounted, "I was a hit" (Harris 1982, 134).

Harris won the election, instantly becoming the most famous student body president in the country. He was also a working man. In the midst of his presidency, Harris took a job at Kepler's. The pay was only a buck-something per hour, but the scene was congenial and Roy and Ira always had something interesting to say. For the rest of the spring, Harris would juggle his studies, his student body obligations, and his part-time work at Kepler's Books & Magazines.

By the summer of 1966, Harris and three friends moved into a house on Cooley Street in East Palo Alto, the grim neighborhood that had been an early home to the Free U. The compadres had a group name, the Peace and Liberation Commune, and they had plans. They pooled their money to buy two presses and install them at the house. There would be a magazine called *Resist,* which would include poetry by Harris and his friend Jeff Shurtleff as well as essays and reporting. The newly established Peace and Liberation Commune Press produced two small booklets that might be picked up at Kepler's: *Beyond Prayers to an Unjust King* and *Six Statements for Peace in America.*

The pale-green Cooley Street house began attracting hangers-on. Inside the living room, the walls adorned with a Charlie Chaplin poster, joints would go round and round and notions would be conjured in the haze. Shurtleff, classified as a conscientious objector by his draft board, shared Harris's interests in Nietzsche and in motorcycles. They traded existential thoughts, and then took off into the Bay Area's hills: Shurtleff on his Triumph 650 and Harris on his Royal Enfield, neither wearing helmets (Ferber and Lynd 1971, 81).

Philosophically, Harris was allied with Roy and the Bay Area's older pacifist crowd, the old-line Quakers and Committee for Nonviolent Action, but he embodied a different spirit. The older pacifists were stern moralists, *abstinent.* That was not Harris's thing. He was more about freedom, the cowboy activist. The deed was all. Explanations were bullshit. Courage would be called upon.

On the night of October 20, 1966, Harris was walking across the seemingly placid Stanford campus. Twenty or so members of Delta Tau Delta fraternity, vexed over the student body president's radical pronunciations, confronted him. Some were Stanford football players, the beefy protectors of American tradition. They escorted Harris to an empty lot, plugged clippers into a dorm outlet with a long extension cord, pinned Harris down, and shaved his unruly hair. Harris did not physically resist, perhaps disappointing some of his fired-up assailants, but when the frat rats had finished his scalp and were preparing to go after his chin he spoke up.

"Look," Harris said. "I've cooperated with you so far, so let's make a deal that you spare my beard."

Impressed, the frat boys assented and, man to man, offered Harris a cigarette, the *Stanford Daily* reported on October 24, 1966.

The head-shaving brought more attention to Harris, who was telling his Fresno draft board that in good conscience he could no longer accept the student deferment. He would shoulder the consequences of his decision not to fight, rather than seek protection. His was an existentialist's stance, the act of a stand-up guy, but he still needed support. Harris and his housemate Jeff Shurtleff wanted to learn what they could from Roy and the older generation. Roy had endured the Civilian Public Service system as well as assorted short-term jail stints. He could teach them a thing or two, as could Stanford professor Paul Seaver, whose activist rap sheet dated back to the Korean War.

Seaver's father, Ben, had been the longtime peace education secretary for the San Francisco office of the American Friends Service Committee and cofounder with Roy of the Committee for Draft Resistance. His sons followed in his path. In 1950 Paul Seaver and his twin brother were sentenced to eighteen months in federal prison for refusing to register with the draft. Paul Seaver went on to earn his doctorate from Harvard, and by the mid-1960s he was immersed in Stanford's Western Civilization program. On the side, this expert in Puritan thought and the English Reformation counseled the Bay Area's potential conscientious objectors.

One extended evening that Seaver could still recall decades later, the Stanford professor sat with Harris and Shurtleff and told them all he could of Danbury and prison life. In hindsight, Seaver said in a 2010 interview, he wasn't sure how relevant his Eisenhower-era experiences could possibly be to the young men facing prison in the tumultuous 1960s. Harris, though, recalled that Seaver's words rang true despite the generational differences. Roy and Seaver both helped Harris ready himself for the joint, the place toward which he was irrevocably heading.

In February 1967, while still working for a pittance at Kepler's, Harris resigned as Stanford student body president. He would now devote himself nearly full time to dealing with the draft. In early March Harris convened in his East Palo Alto house with one-time Stanford student Dennis Sweeney and Berkeley activists Lenny Heller and Steve Hamilton. They rapped for hours, smoking dope and getting into each other's heads. They wanted to figure out ways to upend conscription, and they thought they had it. They would set a date for everyone to return draft cards. They agreed: October 16 would be the day for a massive turn-in of draft cards.

"We all dug each other," Harris said, "and we said, 'well, we're going to do it'" (Ferber and Lynd 1971, 89).

Shortly, Harris and his partners wrote up a one-page declaration: "We Refuse to Serve." Identifying themselves as the Bay Area Organizing Committee for Draft Resistance, the activists struck an absolute posture. They would not submit to the conscription system. They would renounce all deferments and refuse to cooperate with the draft in any manner, at any level. They summoned others to practice civil disobedience on a massive scale. The statement circulated at Kepler's.

Roy and Ira were gratified by the war-resistance reinforcements, but they were frustrated, too, by other developments. At the War Resisters League/West, based in San Francisco, Roy was becoming vexed by Bert Kanegson, who had arrived about a year earlier. Kanegson, Roy thought, focused on the few campaigns that interested him, while ignoring others.

"He fails as a leader, as an administrator, and as a person who can inspire confidence," Roy wrote David McReynolds on March 27, 1967.

Kanegson, though, saw well beyond the strictures of the War Resisters League. He could see the new world opening up, and he was involved in more than the straitlaced older generation of radicals. One weekend night, former Kepler's aficionado Jerry Garcia and his band the Grateful Dead agreed to play for a benefit helping the War Resisters League and the Central Committee for Conscientious Objectors. The two peace groups would split the take. Hank Maiden, from the Peninsula office of the Central Committee for Conscientious Objectors, came up to help work the door. The experience blew his mind. By 10 p.m. the ballroom jammed and the coffers closed, Kanegson was into the groove of the evening and wanted to go with it. Maiden, though, came from a different scene. It was time to leave; it was time to leave *now*.

"I insisted, remembering stories from jazz musicians who were either held up or ripped off by club managers and thugs," Maiden recalled in an interview.

Maiden prevailed, and he and Kanegson hauled the cash about eight blocks to a Haight Street apartment. They counted the money and split it between the WRL/West and the CCCO. Maiden, still feeling insecure, scurried to his car and drove down the Bayshore Freeway to his Palo Alto home.

"Friends of Bert," Maiden admitted, "told me later that they thought me to be one uptight dude."

On March 31, 1967, diplomatically citing "fiscal inadequacy," War Resisters League/West formally accepted Kanegson's resignation. The young activist conceded mistakes, but questioned more broadly whether the very idea of a single leader fit the purposes of the pacifist movement. He would go on to find himself, working as a manager for the Grateful Dead and ultimately finding himself under a different name. As Sat Santokh he would travel the world teaching the practice of Kundalini yoga.

The WRL/West leadership board met several days after the resignation, but the poison hadn't yet drained away. Executive Committee members delivered speeches about everything that was going wrong, all the problems afflicting the pacifist organization. Meetings left a bad taste in everyone's mouth.

"Some were listened to," the recording secretary dutifully recorded for April 3, 1967, "[and] others dismissed as bullshit. Clifford Burke resigned from the Executive Committee, because in his view we are piddling around and are losers."

Faithful Holly Chenery agreed to serve voluntarily as administrative secretary for an interim period. She and Roy cast about for a leader to rescue the organization. Roy suggested his old KPFA friend and Minersville colleague John Lewis, but Lewis demurred. From national headquarters in New York, David McReynolds advised Roy that the complications in Northern California were causing concern.

Publicly, though, the united peace front appeared intact. On April 6, 1967, Joan and Ira headlined a rally at Stanford's packed Memorial Auditorium. Ira, calling himself "the original dropout," spoke of Gandhi while Joan denounced the United States as "the most aggressive nation in the world." America went into Vietnam unilaterally, Joan said, and so America could withdraw unilaterally. Ira was sardonic. Americans believed in individual freedom and Communists believed in social justice and everyone believed in self-defense. No one believed in violence, but that somehow always ended up being the result of everyone's self-justified self-defense. They urged tax resistance, though Joan, in the *Stanford Daily* of April 7, 1967, said that the government could always flex its unlimited powers of confiscation.

Futile as it seemed, tax resistance kept recurring as a tactic. From a meeting in San Francisco grew Taxpayers Against War, which was more statement than organization. It had no members, dues, or meetings. It was an idea, a twist on the standard tax resistance. Instead of refusing to pay taxes, as Roy had done for years, Taxpayers Against War represented a new concept. People who had already paid their taxes would apply for a refund on the grounds that the Vietnam War spending in particular or the military budget in general was improper. When refused, as they knew they would be, the activists would sue. At the least, the lawsuit would rivet public attention.

Roy sought $300 from a coordinating organization in Cambridge called Vietnam Summer, so that he might hire a college student for assistance with the latest taxpayer protest. He also filed his own refund claim, which the IRS quickly rejected with the explanation that "there is no provision of law under which the service is authorized to make refunds based on the grounds set forth in your claim."

The Taxpayers Against War lawsuit would be filed in October 1967 and dismissed in January 1968. It succeeded in attracting a little attention, which was the primary point, but not everyone was happy with the results. One activist complained that attorney Francis Heisler's fees of $22 an hour were excessive. Beneath the surface unity, moreover, there was other second-guessing going around.

On tax day, April 15, 1967, some 35,000 demonstrators marched the four miles from San Francisco's Market Street to Kezar Stadium, where football players usually engaged in mock battle. For three hours twenty-three separate speakers took the Kezar stage. Representing the newly formed Resistance came David Harris, casually dressed in his trademark workman's Levis. "This war," Harris declared, "will not be made in our names. This war will not be made with our hands."

Esquire magazine reporter Gina Berriault accompanied Harris when he marched and spoke. Her ensuing article in the magazine's September "Back to School" issue raised Harris's visibility, with the reporter noting that Harris "gathers disciples around him wherever he goes." It was accurate enough, and this worried the older generation of War Resisters League leaders. Some feared Harris was becoming too much the rock star. Executive Committee members quietly considered whether Roy and George Reeves might have a discrete word with the younger firebrand, restrain him a bit.

Harris was still sporadically working at Kepler's on the side, where customers were buying the likes of Eric Berne's *Games People Play, Quotations from Chairman Mao Tse-Tung,* or perhaps the New

American Library's influential *New American Review,* the first edition of a periodical in paperback book. The first issue's contributors included sociologist Theodore Roszak, the conscientious academic whose peace explorations Roy had helped inspire at the start of the sixties (Davis 1984, 323).

Roy liked Harris; he saw his talents and potential. With Bert Kanegson gone, Roy arranged for Harris to be hired as a West Coast organizer for the War Resisters League. For a small stipend and the title of regional secretary, Harris began traveling from campus to campus, rallying draft resisters. He would hook up with local activists, speak at a rally, urge students to reject the war machine and return their draft cards. Paperwork and regular reporting weren't part of his obligation to the War Resisters League, nor was attendance at the WRL/West's administrative meetings.

"I never had a great allegiance to WRL," Harris said in an interview, "but they were paying me to do what I was going to do anyway."

Years later, Harris would count the work as a success: some 30,000 draft cards were returned in protest during the Vietnam War. San Francisco Bay Area men, in particular, resisted the war with notable vigor. By 1970 the Selective Service would estimate that 38 percent of all draft resisters nationwide came from the Bay Area. The work had a more personal impact as well.

One day Roy and Harris got to talking about an Oakland demonstration planned for October 1967. Resources were needed. The War Resisters League couldn't offer much, but Roy had an idea. He was still handling Joan Baez's business affairs, cutting checks and making investment advice. He knew her bank accounts, and he knew the state of her mind. Roy told Harris he should meet with Joan and make the pitch. Harris agreed, and through Roy the arrangements were made.

Harris drove over the Santa Cruz mountains to Joan's custom-built Carmel Valley home. Theirs was not an immediate love connection. Harris was serious, scruffy, and smoked too much. Joan was five years older, and famous. She seemed a queen, her brand-new Jaguar gleaming in the driveway. Still, she wrote out a several-thousand-dollar check to The Resistance for planning the October demonstrations.

Harris brought the check back to the Peace and Liberation Commune, where the brethren gathered round in appreciation (Harris 1982, 191).

The original tension would evaporate, and Joan would take up with Harris. That did not please some. Ira, in particular, never cottoned to Harris. Ira had found Joan first, molded her mind, back when David Harris was still a Fresno schoolboy. Ira and Joan had been lovers in every respect but physically. They had an understanding, albeit not one that everyone appreciated.

"She used him as her intellectual substructure, and learned how to articulate what she was feeling," Harris said.

In turn, Ira had basked in the reflected glory. He was Joan Baez's mentor. She also financially subsidized him. Now, after all they had gone through, middle-aged Ira had to watch while his Joan went off to the hills with a cocky young hero on a motorcycle. It burned, in both directions. Though Harris had respected Ira in the early days, he had never become one of his acolytes, and over time he had come to think of the older man as a shameless suck-up.

"When Joan and I were [later] splitting up, he was bad-mouthing me to her, and good-mouthing me to me," Harris recalled in an interview. "I had no fucking use for that."

Still, for all the periodic personal tensions, the activists had common ground in their opposition to the Vietnam War. They were conceiving big plans, specific targets. They were going to shut down the Oakland Induction Center.

15

Oakland

The Oakland Induction Center was a dread portal. So was Santa Rita jail. Both initiated the young into a world of hurt.

Civilians entered the induction center, also known as the Armed Forces Examination Station, at the corner of Oakland's Clay and 15th streets. Many exited the other end, extruded into the Vietnam pipeline. By the spring of 1967, the center was processing about four hundred young men a day. Civilians of another cast would enter Santa Rita, sent there as punishment for protesting the draft. Some would be brutalized there; others would be transformed.

Radical action connected the jail and the induction center. At the dawn of the sixties, Roy had been confined in Santa Rita for several days following his arrest at the Livermore nuclear weapons lab. Now he would be returning in major company. Demonstrators would shut down the Oakland center and pay the price at Santa Rita. It was an idea that had been growing as more young men thought to interfere with the draft center's operations. A typical impediment had occurred on April 20, 1967, when Berkeley activist Ken Epstein arrived for his draft physical equipped with copies of an antidraft statement. He handed them out until induction center officials hustled him away.

"Lots of people come through here every day," an army major told Epstein, the *Berkeley Barb* reported in the April 21–27, 1967, edition. "If they all passed out their personal statements, this place would close down."

Exactly.

The goal of shutting down the Oakland Induction Center altogether soon captivated Bay Area activists from many ideological camps.

Strategically, they shared the same vision. Tactically, they were all over the map. Roy and his allies urged a strictly nonviolent approach. Members of a Berkeley faction were more kinetic. They figured the war was a moral evil that had to be stopped by any means necessary.

"They were talking all this smack about how they were going to go out and fight the police," David Harris recalled in an interview.

Harris and members of The Resistance believed the militant SDS radicals would simply provoke police assaults. The Students for a Democratic Society agitators thought that was fine. The bloody images would radicalize the People. In time, fed up, Harris and some of his Resistance crowd withdrew from the Oakland demonstration planning. Roy stayed with the organizing, though he was aghast at some of the thinking. Using violence to combat violence was nonsensical, not to mention a foolhardy option to consider in a public meeting inevitably infiltrated by police informers. But the oddball ideas kept coming.

Nude demonstrators! That, some thought, would really shake up the authorities. Most cops, organizer Perry Cannon explained in a *Berkeley Barb* account, have tremendous male hang-ups. It was pretty obvious, really: all those uptight little men waving their big nightsticks and long-barreled guns. By stripping naked, the demonstrators could mess with their heads. The organizers respectfully considered the nudity option and rejected it. Over time, too, they figured out the bigger plan, a compromise, of sorts. There would be a complete week of protests. Roy and the pacifists would operate on Monday. The street revolutionaries could command the rest of the week.

Roy and the other leaders planned carefully for their day. It would be both a demonstration *against* the war, and a demonstration *of* the power of nonviolence. Selected monitors would guide participants, endeavoring to keep everyone relaxed and respectful. Keep people singing, the monitors were told; it would help pass the time. Heckling and chanting would be actively discouraged. An atmosphere of fill-the-jails gaiety should prevail. Demonstrators would confront the authorities in truth and openness, calmly absorbing whatever violence might be visited upon them.

Tactically, the plan was simple. Demonstrators would come forward in groups of twenty and set themselves in the doors of the induction center. To enter the army, young men would have to step up and over the bodies of the peaceful. When police removed one group of demonstrators, another wave would take their place. On Wednesday, October 11, in a predemonstration confab at the Palo Alto Friends Meeting House, Roy discussed the tactics as well as administrative details such as legal representation for those arrested.

The Oakland planning was not the only work afoot. On October 12, while U.S. Navy jets bombed the North Vietnamese shipyards at Haiphong, Ira, Joan, and fifty-five others filed their formal Taxpayers Against War suit in U.S. District Court in San Francisco. Against all odds they sought refunds of those portions of their 1965 and 1966 income taxes that had been used for the military. Thanks to Joan's celebrity, the lawsuit summoned attention to the pacifist cause. Joan reported having paid $60,947.61 in taxes for 1965. Of this, she demanded that $36,528.37 be returned as the portion that was devoted to the military. Ira, the Kepler's bookstore clerk, didn't have nearly the same year. He sought the return of $653 in taxes paid in 1965.

By the weekend before the Oakland protests, assembly points were identified, communication plans established. Demonstration monitors knew their roles. In a festive, eve-of-battle atmosphere, some activists gathered in the wealthy foothills community of Woodside on Sunday for a predemonstration garden party.

Buses started rolling for Oakland early Monday morning, October 16. Joan, her mother, and her sister Mimi traveled in with an Institute for the Study of Nonviolence contingent. Other buses drew in from other departure points. By 6 a.m. the first protestors were positioning themselves near the Oakland center. All the major peace tribes were represented. There were seasoned Quakers, earnest students, stoned heads. As the morning wore on, the knowing could detect a slight marijuana tang in the air. Several older women poured coffee for demonstrators and police alike. The largest group held the Clay Street sidewalk across from the induction center. Other, smaller groups formed picket lines including in front of the garage where police mobilized. Joan's mom, imagining the assembled police attacking with Mace and tear gas, was shivering with cold but sweating with adrenalin when she reached out to hold hands. Demonstrators began softly singing "We Shall Overcome."

At 6:55 a.m. about fifty helmeted Oakland policemen carrying gas masks and clubs marched out of the Clay Street garage to the center's main entrance and established, shoulder-to-shoulder, a walkway. Police Capt. James J. McCarthy, speaking authoritatively in the name of the State of California, ordered the demonstrators to leave. They did not. One by one, they were then escorted to the paddy wagon nearby.

Busloads of draftees arrived at about 9 a.m. The war-bound young men dutifully worked their way through the crowd, most looking neither to the right nor the left, protected by the lines of blue-helmeted policemen. The future soldiers passed through the crowd amid cries of "don't go" and, plaintively, "you don't have to go, guys." Sometimes it seemed utterly quiet. Sometimes individual sounds were isolated: the creak of leather boots. Then it grew noisy again. Police orders were shouted and then swamped by rounds of "We Shall Overcome."

The police came for Joan and Ira, who quietly stood and entered the paddy wagon without resistance. Ira entered first; Joan followed with a red rose in her hand. Roy and about fifteen others stepped off the sidelines and sat down in the street. Psychologist Vic Lovell had been wondering how he would get involved until he saw Roy lead the way into the street. Now he knew what was expected of him in that moment. Lovell joined Roy there, sitting down on the street and in time linking arms. Everyone was polite. Half of the men wore ties, Roy included.

From the start Roy and the other demonstration organizers divided their forces into those who expected to be arrested and those who did not. James Ware, for one, was a young mathematician half-way toward his doctorate in statistics from Stanford. He had not planned on being arrested, until he saw police hauling away those sitting in the induction center doorways. Caught up in the feeling, he joined a group of marchers. Once seized by police, the consequences started hitting home. Prosecutors declared they would charge Ware and the others with the felony charge of obstructing a police officer. The first wave of doorway protestors faced only misdemeanor charges. Felony time was serious, a commitment beyond their planning. But to Ware's everlasting relief, Roy and the demonstrators' attorneys insisted that the proposed felony charges be downgraded. Prosecutors, perhaps having made their point, agreed.

"Roy's willingness to support those who had joined the demonstration made a huge difference for me," Ware, who would go on to serve as dean of the Harvard School of Public Health, recalled in an interview.

By the early afternoon, the Oakland crowds had thinned. Altogether, some 125 protestors had been arrested. They were a varied bunch. They included professors, students, gardeners, and yogis. The first night in Oakland jail proved, for some, an exhilarating experience—"a riot of laughter," one recalled. The Oakland protestors knew

9. Roy Kepler (in the middle, with cap) and other demonstrators sitting in at the Oakland Induction Center, October 16, 1967. Photographer unknown, courtesy of the Kepler family.

they were part of something bigger that day. In Boston, about 70 draft-age men burned their draft cards while 220 others presented the cards to clergymen. In Los Angeles, an estimated 300 protestors charged the federal building before being turned back by security guards.

Still, jail was jail, foreign territory for most. Joan Baez Sr. observed warily the open toilets, the exposed showers, the hostile guards. The demonstrators shivered through cold-water showers and dried themselves with flimsy towels the size of dish rags. They confronted the mass squat of toilets, open to the world. So uncouth, Joan's mother thought, so deliberately humiliating. But she was learning; they all were. With as much bravado as they could muster they treated the various humiliations as a game. The peace queens and princesses perched upon their new thrones.

The male demonstrators settled in as well. In the stale jail air, the inmates improvised. The *Stanford Daily Magazine* of December 3, 1967, reported how young activists found a corner in which to practice yoga. Some sang. Some rapped. Some tried to escape into sleep. Roy and Ira, on Monday night, coordinated what would become a series of discussions about the tactics and strategy of nonviolent revolution.

Tuesday morning, the protestors were brought into the municipal courtroom presided over by Judge Delmar Brobst. The elderly judge offered arrested students the option of serving their time on weekends so they would not miss school, and he dismissed charges of trespassing, creating a public nuisance, and refusing to disperse. He allowed, as well, six of the 125 sentenced protestors to make a statement. Roy, a leader, was one.

"I am the father of four children," Roy declared. "I am in business. I have a home and all of the usual responsibilities. Yet, I could do no other than to be here. I want to be able to look them in the face and to let them know that I, with others, sought to prevent our own country from its own militarism and from carrying on the monstrous, illegal, immoral and unjust war against the people of Vietnam."

The judge could not care less. Brobst heard Roy out and then began summoning the demonstrators. Each received ten days in jail. Having given the protestors a chance to expound on matters of conscience, the judge had exhausted his sympathy. Some women asked for extra time to arrange for child care. Brobst sternly told them they should have thought about those considerations before they broke the law. Joan smiled throughout. Jail was the price for taking a stand.

While Joan, Roy, and the other first-day protestors were being processed through court Tuesday morning, some 3,500 demonstrators had gathered before the Oakland Induction Center. The Tuesday protestors had disdained the nonviolent tactics practiced Monday. The police, too, were ready for action, as if Monday was a mere scrimmage. The moment was ripe for action.

Starting at 6:15 a.m. Tuesday, megaphone-wielding officers warned the demonstrators to disperse. Demonstrators sprayed aerosol shaving cream on the pavement in front of the officers, a cartoon tactic some imagined might slow a police charge. Undeterred, officers moved in with a flying wedge. They were unstoppable. Demonstrators ran, fell, and were bashed about. Overhead, a police helicopter rattled the air. Some policemen, their blood up, began mockingly singing "We Shall Overcome." Shortly before 9 a.m., buses filled with draftees rolled up to the induction center. Demonstrators rushed the buses, shouting slogans. The police, standing shoulder to shoulder, held them back. Sporadically, several demonstrators would try without success to break through the police lines, a weakening wave upon a rock. At day's end, at least twenty-six injured demonstrators had been taken to Oakland hospitals for treatment.

David Harris hadn't planned to participate in the Oakland demonstrations. By late Tuesday, though, he had heard of what had transpired in the streets. That night Harris agreed to come to Berkeley, where he found himself planning the next day's events (Ferber and Lynd 1971, 143). Wednesday, Harris joined the demonstrators in Oakland. While standing on the sidewalk with a bullhorn in his hand, Harris was arrested. He was Santa Rita bound.

Roy was among the relatively few arrested demonstrators with prior experience at Santa Rita, Alameda County's jail, tucked about thirty miles away in the Livermore Valley. The jail occupied a thousand-acre former military base, a wire fence wrapped around eight barracks collectively known as The Compound. Women occupied a horseshoe-shaped set of barracks, and an old navy brig had been converted into a maximum security facility known fearsomely as Greystone.

The arriving demonstrators were ushered into the jail's fluorescent-lit bullpen, the twenty-by-twenty room where they would await processing. A black-letter sign advised men they would be shaved and their hair cut. Roy's compatriots began debating whether to refuse compliance: when should resistance begin?

Roy's answer was: Right now.

Arrested protestor Randy Kehler stood behind Roy when the men were lined up for fingerprinting. To Kehler's astonishment, Roy refused to go along with the program. The guards ordered Roy to submit his hands. He declined. "I'm not going to cooperate," Roy told them quietly. Kehler watched as the guards manhandled Roy to get the imprint they needed. Roy did not fight them, but neither did he cooperate. Afterward, Kehler recalled in a 2009 interview, he asked Roy exactly what had gone down and why.

"I was just testing them," Roy explained to the younger activist.

Roy had been getting jailed for peace since the 1940s. He knew when to lead, what to say. At one point, two Santa Rita guards bracketed Dr. Leland Rather, a fifty-three-year-old Stanford medical professor. One on either side, the guards took Rather's arms and escorted him from the bullpen. More literally than he might ever have imagined, the learned professor was in the grips of the law. Rather's colleagues watched him go. They feared where this movie would end. When the guards returned, the *San Francisco Chronicle* later reported, Roy stepped in.

"We're *all* ready to go," Roy said. He pushed himself into the arms of the guards, who obliged by taking him away to the processing room.

In time, all of the Oakland protestors were processed and assigned to their barracks. They were being kept separate from the rest of Santa Rita, protecting the demonstrators' virtue and the hard-core inmates' political innocence.

"They tol' us you was all Comminists an' we ain't s'posed to ever talk to you," one young black girl told Joan's mother (Baez Sr. 1994, 37).

Another inmate, a black male with a long rap sheet, slipped a letter to the peace activists to say he wished he could talk but the guards "fear you would wake me up." The separation, though, also protected the activists from having to turn the other cheek. Santa Rita would not prove as forgiving for some. One draft protestor, a former Kepler's employee, would report being beat up several times during a later stay at Santa Rita when he was not in the protective confines of a group.

Isolated, the Oakland protestors fell back on their own resources. Roy could recall what Gandhi had said: Imprisonments were opportunities for purposeful thinking. Up sprang the Free University of Compound 7.

Activists convened an ad hoc seminar on the radically different street tactics employed in Oakland. Roy argued that violence had begat violence: The Tuesday street radicals had brought force down upon themselves. By Friday morning, the locked-down demonstrators were leading each other in yoga classes and sensory awareness sessions. Stanford professor John Grey Curley led a seminar on Asian economic development. Ira talked about the Institute for the Study of Nonviolence. Retired geologist Dr. Robert Wesley Brown, at seventy-seven years the oldest of the inmates, held forth on "The Bible as a Revolutionary Document." Even the jailers enrolled. A deputy sheriff's sergeant, jocularly dubbed the "Dean of Students," gave a talk on jailhouse rules (Baez Sr. 1994, 37).

The men were only partially aware of what was going on in the world outside the wire. Patricia Kepler was writing Roy every day, as were others. At one point, an average of fifteen letters a day arrived for Roy. Santa Rita officials, though, declared it policy that each inmate receive only one letter daily. The rest were simply returned, undelivered.

On their eighth day, the protestors gathered outside of their barracks. The winter sun beat down companionably, and a number of the men peeled off their shirts. Having survived the past week, the men felt they could do as they pleased. They would let the sun shine upon them.

"Hey, you guys!" a guard shouted. "Shirts on!"

More protestors began taking their own shirts off. The guard unlocked the gate and came closer.

"Put those shirts on, or off you go to Greystone," the guard warned.

Roy stood up.

"I guess we're all going to Greystone," Roy said, and began walking to the barracks.

The other protestors followed Roy's lead. The guard swore and went for reinforcements. Shortly, a captain returned and agreed they could keep their shirts off, but he insisted they keep their pants on.

Santa Rita's black inmates were skeptical, at first, of these white boys who wouldn't fight. But after a week of observing each other, the cons and the peaceniks seemed to reach an accommodation. The demonstrators weren't snitches, creeps, or weirdoes. They showed spine. On Saturday night the demonstrators received their jailhouse reward when they were escorted en masse into a big room for the showing of the weekly movie.

"Hundreds of men, black and white, rose to their feet and applauded as we took our seats," Roy reported on a later KPFA commentary.

Santa Rita changed some lives for good. Kehler, a 1967 Harvard graduate who had spent a year teaching in Africa, was one. Kehler had just started graduate school at Stanford that fall. Once in California, he discovered the Free U and signed up for a nonviolence seminar taught by Roy, Joan, and Ira. It soon became clear that this was meant to be active learning, and the Oakland demonstration would be its street lab (Appy 2003, 234).

"The whole thing was pretty new to me, and pretty frightening, so I went thinking I would just observe," Kehler recalled. "But it was so inspiring I decided to join hands with some people and sit down in the street."

Inside Santa Rita, Kehler found his future. Graduate school was over, he knew that already. He considered the Stanford education curriculum bogus. What he didn't know precisely was what would come next. He found himself, though, observing the older, learned pacifists. Kehler could now see it was possible to live a committed life. In particular, there were the three men that Kehler considered the real Santa Rita elders: Roy, Denny Wilcher, and George Reeves. They had known each other since the days of the Civilian Public Service Union and, later, KPFA. They had been around the cellblock, and yet remained as devoted as ever to the great cause. The older men, in turn, saw something they liked in the young Harvard graduate.

One Santa Rita day, out of the blue, Roy approached Kehler and asked if he would like to work for the War Resisters League. Roy told him he could help organize West Coast pacifists and draft resisters. Kehler had already turned in his draft card, but he hadn't yet committed himself to full-time peace work. Here was Roy, though, opening a door to his future. A group of Stanford physicians and professors said they would put up Kehler's $150-a-month salary. All Kehler had to do was say yes.

"My life, in very concrete terms, had taken a new direction," Kehler stated in the *Stanford Daily Magazine* of November 3, 1967.

Once he served his ten-day sentence, Kehler moved into Denny Wilcher's Berkeley home. Roy gave him a green Nash automobile for transportation, and Kehler went to work in the War Resisters League's San Francisco office. He was there until he departed in February 1970 to serve a twenty-two-month prison sentence for draft resistance. Kehler went on to a lifetime of activism that included coordinating the National Nuclear Weapons Freeze Campaign in the 1980s.

Stop the Draft Week protests would continue in Oakland for five days. The largest and angriest was Friday, October 20, when up to ten thousand demonstrators roamed downtown Oakland streets. Some overturned cars and erected ad hoc barricades. Demonstrators dragged steel beams into one intersection and piled garbage cans and metal newsstands into the center. Demonstrators shoved cars, deflated the tires, and ripped out engine wiring. It was all very kinetic but it was not, Roy thought, very effective. The rowdies were less successful in blocking the Oakland Induction Center than the well-disciplined and nonviolent protestors who initiated the whole affair.

Several weeks following his release from Santa Rita, Roy received a phone call from Oakland Police Sgt. Carl Dahl, a member of the department's intelligence unit. Dahl suggested that Roy keep him apprised of future demonstration plans. In fact, plans were already afoot for a repeat performance in December. Roy agreed to meet. He wanted as much as the police did to secure a peaceful event.

This communication was crucial. Gandhi had taught the lesson, as he defined the concept of *satyagraha*. This was nonviolent resistance, but it was not *passive* resistance. One communicated with the opponent, patiently and openly, seeking not to coerce but to convert. A practitioner of satyagraha, Roy was not trying to trick the police or even to thwart them. He would work with them, in the spirit of nonviolence.

Accompanied at times by Randy Kehler, Roy met three times with Oakland police prior to the December demonstration. The demonstration plans were described and a map was drawn showing the names, planned positions, and function of each of the march monitors. The idea, Kehler said, was to communicate openly and thereby lessen the likelihood of a violent police reaction.

Roy was going to be one of six head monitors for the December demonstration, wearing a blue vest to mark his status. In return, police officers told Roy he could use a stone bench across the street from the induction center as the demonstration command post.

Early on the morning of Monday, December 18, Roy and other demonstrators were gathering outside in the cold at Palo Alto's El Camino Park. At 5 a.m., beaten by rain, three buses left the park for the drive to Oakland. By about 6 a.m. the demonstrators were in Oakland and starting to clog the induction center's doorways. More than one thousand sympathizers ringed two sides of the building. The wind-driven rain punished them, but the atmosphere was noticeably calm. Instead of picket signs, some demonstrators carried flowers. Instead of antiwar chants, they sang Christmas carols.

Still, there were busts to be made.

Two police undercover agents named August Yanke and Jon Sparks mingled with the demonstrators, one wearing an armband that marked him as a monitor. Both men wore flowers. One of the Oakland officers later testified that, early on, he saw Roy approach the Clay Street entrance to the induction center along with several demonstrators. Roy directed them to occupy the doorway. He told others to monitor buses so the demonstrators could position themselves properly. Roy informed one of the demonstrators sitting in the doorway that he was needed to fill in another doorway, on the center's 15th Street side. The young man accompanied Roy around the corner, as did, discretely, one of the undercover agents. Roy wanted all of the doorways congested, leaving the draftees no choice but to step over the demonstrators on their way into the army. This was the point, to force a moment of reflection among those going to war. Roy wanted to give people pause for a moment: Do you really want to go to Vietnam?

Under generally civil conditions, police arrested some 207 demonstrators during the day. Roy's own arrest came rather unexpectedly. He was one block from the induction center, preparing to cross a street, when police seized him. He was not, at the time, actively interfering with the induction center's operations. It seemed strange to be taken at such a time, especially after he had worked so cooperatively with Oakland police.

The next day, demonstrations continued at the induction center and an additional sixty-seven protestors were seized. Bookseller and poet Lawrence Ferlinghetti showed up on the second day along with Joan and Joan's fifty-four-year-old mother. They squeezed together tightly in the doorway, Ira not far away. Joan sang, mixing the Beatles' "Good Day Sunshine" with some revised bars from "Kumbaya." Ira was struck by the shadowed, downcast appearance of the young draftees entering the Oakland center. The demonstrators were chattering away and cheerful (Sandperl 1974, 112). When the police arrived, Joan led her fellow protestors in a soft-voiced version of "Silent Night." Ferlinghetti, too, was in good spirits, nattily sporting a brown derby and red plaid scarf. The World War II veteran told reporters that he "tried to find my navy commission so I could burn it."

Judge Brobst, who had seen some of these demonstrators in October, dealt out stiffer sentences the second time around. Ira received ninety days, with forty-five days suspended; Joan and her mother likewise received a forty-five-day sentence. "It's nothing, when babies are dying every day," Joan said, the *San Francisco Chronicle* reported on December 21, 1967.

Once again, Santa Rita became a revolutionary hive. The men were told they would be shaven and given a haircut; if they refused, they would be reduced to two meals a day. Some men refused. Everyone coped as they were able. They entertained themselves with a deck of cards, torn in half in order to create two decks. They played shuffleboard using mop handles, and Scrabble with a board that one inmate constructed from memory. As before, officials kept them in separate barracks, apart from Oakland thugs. In the women's barracks, War Resisters League/West staffer Mandy Carter said, the peace demonstrators wore dresses that were a different shade of blue from that provided the conventional inmates.

One night young inmates erupted in wild chants and dancing, an exultation of animal spirits. Ira had been setting a more contemplative tone. Prison could be a holy place, enforcing isolation from the world. Through the walls, though, Ira heard the ruckus. It was an intrusion, more suitable to the Fillmore Auditorium than the inside of the monk's cell. Finally it was just too much, the *Palo Alto Times* would report on January 8, 1968.

"Let us not forget why we are here," Ira sternly counseled the rowdy, shaming some and irritating others.

On Sunday, January 14, Roy packed his four children into the family's station wagon and drove to the San Francisco airport to pick up the Rev. Martin Luther King Jr. and a weary looking Andrew Young. Huddled together, King and the Keplers headed east to Santa Rita, the place Roy knew so well.

"Tomorrow is my birthday," Roy's daughter Melody informed King.

"Really!" the Nobel Peace Prize winner exclaimed, as Dawn Kepler recalled years later, "Tomorrow is mine."

At Santa Rita, King and Young were ushered into the jail meeting room with Joan and her mother. King embraced Joan, who wiped joyful tears from her eyes; then they sat around a table and swapped stories. Ira and King talked of the upcoming Poor People's March in Washington, though Ira thought the visitors appeared apprehensive and eager to depart the jail. They did so, after four black inmates insinuated themselves into the room for a quick hug and blessing. Several hundred sympathizers showed up outside, lining the road to Santa Rita with antiwar signs and banners. On exiting, King stood in a car doorway and boomed out his message.

"Cowards will ask the question, 'is it safe?'" King preached, as the *Contra Costa Times* would recall in a January 16, 2005, retrospective. "Expedience will ask, 'is it politic?' Vanity asks the question, 'is it popular?' But conscience asks the question, 'is it right?'"

Eleven protestors from the December action, including Ferlinghetti and Roy, had pled not guilty, securing a trial. The charges against Roy included a new one, enacted by California legislators only one month before the December protest. It was now a criminal violation to obstruct a sidewalk. Roy's trial convened on Friday, January 19, in Oakland Municipal Court. The local prosecutor, Robert Brody, struck Roy as being an "angry young man." His case relied entirely on the testimony of the two undercover agents.

Roy himself was said by his attorneys to have been perfectly upfront with authorities. Roy's reward for candor was to be tracked and arrested, Roy's attorney Sherwood Sullivan complained. It smacked of a set-up. Besides, Sullivan argued, police could not prove that any of the young protestors Roy had supervised were themselves subsequently arrested, so how could prosecutors claim Roy had contributed to an unlawful obstruction? Roy, personally, had not blocked any sidewalk or sat in any doorway.

The defense failed. The jury of eight women and four men on January 19 took only thirty-three minutes to find Roy guilty of aiding and abetting in the obstruction of the induction center. He was sentenced to another ten days in Santa Rita.

Roy stayed out on bail while appealing, his attorney challenging the constitutionality of the criminal charge against him. Authorities nationwide had been adopting sidewalk obstruction statutes as a tool against political demonstrators. The statutes were thinly veiled crimps on political speech, Sullivan argued, and the First Amendment infringement was even worse when, as in Roy's case, the statute penalized someone who urged another to take a stand.

Roy lost his appeal and had to return to Santa Rita, where other connections were being made. Joan and David Harris, first brought together by Roy for fundraising purposes before Oakland, had common ground through Santa Rita. Joan found herself finally smitten with the younger activist. Within two months of their release, on March 26, they would be married. At the wedding, Al Baez would snap three rolls of photographs that all turned out forebodingly black (Baez 1987, 150).

On the morning of Monday, May 27, 1968, Harris walked into the courtroom on the nineteenth floor of the San Francisco Federal Building. By his side was attorney Francis Heisler, the veteran, white-haired counsel who had been with Roy on so many other causes dating back to Germfask. Joan and Ira, along with Harris's parents, were in the crowded courtroom. Heisler and Harris saw the courtroom as a stage to question the morality of the Selective Service system itself. Heisler's proposed witnesses included Ben Seaver, peace secretary of the regional American Friends Service Committee organization. Roy was set to testify about Harris's character.

"Dave Harris [is] obviously a young man of exceptional intelligence and awakened social concern," Roy wrote in his prepared remarks. "One reason he came to me for employment was that he knew something of my views and activities, and he knew we shared ideas in common. [He] is not willfully striking out in some nihilistic fashion."

Prosecutors insisted on a stricter focus. Harris had not submitted to induction. That was all the case was about, not the morality of Vietnam or the draft. U.S. District Judge Oliver J. Carter, a former Democratic state legislator then in his late fifties, sided with the prosecutors. Carter instructed jurors that the sole issue was whether Harris's draft refusal was done knowingly and willingly. The direction ensured Harris's fate. Vietnam and questions of personal conscience would remain offstage, ghosts without speaking parts. All Harris could do was explain that he felt the need to "affirm the brotherhood of man and make clear my aim in life."

"In the world of brotherhood, there is no such thing as an induction center," Harris testified, the *San Francisco Chronicle* reported on May 29, 1968.

Late Wednesday, May 30, the jury returned to the courtroom and declared Harris guilty. Carter immediately sentenced Harris to thirty months.

"You don't need to be rehabilitated," Carter told the draft resister, the *Stanford Daily* reported on May 31, 1968. "You don't want to be rehabilitated, and I see no reason for you to be rehabilitated."

Harris had some time before he reported to prison, and the various peace factions needed to take stock. In the early summer of 1969, the Institute for the Study of Nonviolence cadre convened for an all-day session. They were plotting strategy, figuring out next steps. In the midst of the commiseration, Ira announced that all this talk about The Resistance was futile. He, personally, was ready to do something truly radical. He was going, Ira declared, to go off and go to work at a shoe factory in St. Louis. That would be the truly revolutionary act.

"He was trying to be more radical than thou," activist Lee Swenson recalled in an interview. "We went outside for a walk afterward, David and Joanie and I, and we wondered, 'what the fuck was *that* all about?'"

But, in fact, Swenson said everyone knew *exactly* what was going down. Ira, the old mentor, couldn't stand to see the young tiger David

Harris get the spotlight and—here was the point—get *Joannie*. So maybe David Harris was going to prison, but Ira was ready for the next step, ready to go all the way back to St. Louis.

"Of course," Swenson added, "he never did."

On July 16, 1969, deputy sheriffs arrived to take Harris away. He was a hero to The Resistance, and much admired by Joan, but their marriage would not survive.

"We were public creatures," Harris later explained. "Sweet-voiced heroine of a generation joins with young knight advancing the battle for peace in our time. Without the intoxication of those roles and the image they fostered, I doubt whether the relationship would ever have come off" (Harris 1992, 224).

16

Roots and Branches

Stewart Brand started swinging by Kepler's around the time he graduated from Stanford in 1960. Here, he thought, was a bookstore run for something other than money.

Himself a venturesome soul, Brand did a turn as an airborne-qualified army officer following his college graduation. He started making other leaps. By December 1962 Brand had swallowed his first legal dose of LSD through the auspices of the International Federation for Advanced Study, a small Menlo Park outfit unassumingly located above a beauty shop not far from Kepler's. There, starting in 1960, hundreds of individuals had been provided still-legal LSD or mescaline. Thoroughly turned on, Brand would in time emerge from the psychedelic carnival realizing that the counterculture needed tools and provisioning (Turner 2006).

By the spring of 1968, flush with about $100,000 in inherited stock, Brand was delving through Kepler's and other bookstores, pulling together ideas. He was going to help people equip themselves. In July he printed the first, mimeographed list of items for sale. Around the corner from Kepler's Books & Magazines, Brand opened the Whole Earth Truck Store for the selling of necessities. The Menlo Park location was no coincidence. Brand considered himself within the orbit of Kepler's, the place that was both inspiration and provider. "Roy helped make that a cool part of town," Brand said.

The Whole Earth Truck Store would be relatively short lived, but in time Brand's inaugural six-page mimeographed *Whole Earth Catalog* would grow to a 448-page encyclopedia, winner of the 1972 National Book Award. It was a smash success, commercially and aesthetically, and while not precisely a child of Kepler's it did have a trace of Kepler's DNA in it. So did other places, other movements. Kepler's provided training, connections, and inspiration for several generations of activist organizations, charities, and, naturally, bookstores.

The summer after Brand opened his Whole Earth Truck Store, Kim Desenberg and other recent peace-minded Stanford graduates opened Plowshare Books on University Avenue in downtown Palo Alto. They were consciously following in Roy's footsteps, though placing a particularly strong emphasis on books about higher consciousness, mysticism, and Eastern religions. They set aside a back room for community gatherings. For some, Plowshare Books seemed to distill the pure essence of Kepler's; when the Stanford Students for a Democratic Society published its 1969 guide for new students, they recommended Plowshare over Kepler's.

Menlo Park native Walter Carr, too, had grown up impressed by Kepler's.

"It was this voluminous, high-ceiling place," Carr told the *Seattle Times* in a July 30, 1990, article, "and [Roy] always had these enormous hi-fi speakers playing classical music."

In 1972, at the age of twenty-nine, Carr relocated to Seattle. The Bay Area was congested with bookstores, but Carr figured Seattle was still open turf. In June 1973 he opened the Elliot Bay Book Company in Pioneer Square, and over time built it into one of the city's most beloved places. Kepler's, Carr made clear, directly influenced him, as it had influenced others. A Clean Well-Lighted Place for Books opened in the Bay Area city of Cupertino in 1975, later expanding to San Francisco. The store's owner, Neal Sofman, had gotten his start at Kepler's. Susan MacDonald, a budding poet who got her bookstore start in 1968 at Kepler's, would join with other Kepler's alumni in 1977, opening Palo Alto's hugely successful Printers Inc. bookstore. Each of the stores would have great runs before falling prey to the same commercial forces that undermined Kepler's, but the Kepler's progeny went well beyond paperback commerce.

⬇

In the spring of 1969, Roy and six friends convened in the Stanford Faculty Club. They wanted to advance a discussion that had reportedly started in Santa Rita jail following some peace demonstration arrests. The notion was a peace endowment, a nonprofit organization that could collect money and spread it among the worthy. The idea drifted a bit, until the Stanford Faculty Club get-together. Roy, San Jose attorney and activist Robert Weir, retired geologist and World War II veteran Robert Wesley Brown, and the others spoke of the need to raise funds and the difficulty in doing so without the benefit of tax deductions.

"The question asked of us was 'Did we think we should create a foundation based on nonviolence, which would raise funds to distribute 'seed money' for social change?'" activist Claire Bradley Feder recalled. "All of us were enthusiastic and agreed to help."

Feder's first husband was a pediatrician who had cared for Roy's four children. Feder offered her home in the shaded, wealthy enclave of Atherton for the next meeting. The activists each brought potential names for the new foundation, but none fit quite right until Weir suggested Agape. Bingo. The Greek word *agape* had been described by Martin Luther King Jr. as love in action, "an overflowing love which is purely spontaneous, unmotivated, groundless and creative . . . not set in motion by any quality or function of its object" (Lynd 1966, 393). Perfect; it was agreed. Feder volunteered to serve as treasurer of the new organization, and Roy made the first official contribution of $25.

At first Agape's paperwork was funneled through a Stanford post office box and its work handled entirely by volunteers. It was a casual operation, and no one had a firm grasp of some technicalities related to the running of a 501(c)(3) nonprofit corporation. As contributions increased, Roy and the other Agape volunteers realized they needed a full-time executive director. They found one in Christopher Jones.

Jones was a Bay Area native who had hung out for a time at David Harris's Peace and Liberation Commune in East Palo Alto, and who later went to prison as a draft resister. Once released, he was seeking virtuous work when he heard about Agape. In the early spring of 1971, he went to a job interview in Feder's Atherton home. There

Jones met Roy, though they had encountered each other at least once before. Jones recalled that once, while hitchhiking on El Camino Real, he had been picked up by Harris and Joan Baez in Joan's dark green Jaguar sedan. The golden couple made space for their guest amid the musical instruments in the backseat and explained they were on their way to Roy's Los Altos home to sign a lease for land in the Palo Alto foothills. In time the land would become known as Struggle Mountain. Roy was not a communal character, but on Joan's behalf he would sometimes handle the associated communal paperwork.

At Feder's Atherton home, everyone hit it off, and the Agape directors hired Jones as the foundation's first executive director. He would hold the job for seven years. Jones quickly came to appreciate Roy's multiple ambitions. Roy the pacifist organizer saw Agape as another tool for raising money to assist nonviolent organizing and educational projects. Roy the canny business manager saw the nonprofit organization as a way for Joan and other wealthy people to reduce the taxes they paid to a war-making government. Roy the old pro, whose service on various administrative boards by then went back three decades, proved the most influential director on the Agape board. Roy recruited some of his store alumni, including manager Ralph Kohn and book buyer Susan MacDonald, to serve on the Agape board. He would personally meet with Jones before formal board meetings, sometimes carrying half a dozen checkbooks, each bound in rubber bands.

"He would see through issues clearly," Jones said.

Agape would initially funnel money toward the War Resisters League/West as well as the WRL's *WIN* magazine. Over time, the reach grew. A $1,000 grant helped the Institute for the Study of Nonviolence publish in 1977 *The Power of the People,* a paperback history of nonviolence. Joan's sister Mimi Fariña conceived an idea for producing free music concerts for prisoners, students, and patients. With Agape's help, Mimi established the Bread and Roses Booking Agency. Agape helped raise Bread and Roses' initial $7,000. Agape would endure and grow, as would Bread and Roses for a good long while. By 2004 Agape would be making more than $1 million in annual grants. Bread and Roses, perhaps Agape's most well-known beneficiary, was able to wean itself from the original foundation support and produce hundreds of shows each year: comedians at a San Francisco homeless women's shelter, jazz pianists at a San Rafael convalescent hospital, African dancers at a Contra Costa County juvenile hall. The foundation was still going strong in 2008, making grants totaling $853,000.

But then, former Agape executive director and WRL/West activist Scott Ullman said in a 2010 interview, "the recession hit us like a bomb." Donations dried up, commitments couldn't be kept. The future seemed terminally iffy. Board members, Ullman said, grew "exhausted" by the demands and in March 2010 Agape shut down.

It was sad, of course. Though it lasted some three decades and touched innumerable lives, Agape proved transitory, painfully so for those who loved it. Roy himself, though, had a certain perspective toward impermanence. Once, when Agape was financially shaky in the late 1970s and its young existence seemed in doubt, Roy had an illuminating conversation with Ullman. Institutions don't necessarily last forever, Roy told Ullman. They arise to meet a circumstance, and when they have served their purpose they may fade away, not mourned but replaced.

The Free U wouldn't last either, at least not as an institution. The internal tensions were too great. Its influences, though, would linger.

Roy's first Free U Peace Games exercise had left participants with much to digest. The young men and women had faced some hard truths. One participant wrote Roy to say the exercise felt like a fall from innocence, a realization of just how ruthless people could be. For Roy, this meant success. The defenders had avoided strictly symbolic measures, seeking instead to confront the invaders where it counted. They had outdone the Grindstone exercises that had helped inspire the Peace Games in the first place.

"The August experiment was not definitive," Roy concluded in an assessment published in *The Free You*, "but only the first of what we hope will be a series of experiments testing many different aspects of the overall relevance of non-violence to all aspects of our life."

As always, some bystanders were skeptical when they heard Roy speak about how Peace Games showed the potential for nonviolent resistance. "Perhaps Mr. Kepler and his friends will eventually convert enough followers so that we, too, can have an invasion by Russian or Chinese communists which few or none will bother to resist," Paul H. Kocher suggested in an August 27, 1968, letter to the *Palo Alto Times*.

Nonetheless, one month later, Roy organized another Peace Games exercise. Several young women wanted to take the role of invaders. Roy, the peace patriarch, vetoed the idea as unrealistic; women, he believed, were simply not soldiers. Bob Cullenbine and the other Peace Games veterans would take on the familiar roles, using old U.S. Army fatigues abandoned by soldiers who had visited the War Resisters League offices in San Francisco. As before, the second Peace Games were conducted at the Ben Lomond Quaker Center. As before, the defenders used such tactics as they could.

At one point during the simulation, after the men were separated from the women, the women inexplicably began singing "Yellow Submarine." One female pacifist let it be known that, through her clairvoyant powers, she had divined the presence of a guerrilla amongst the invading force. No one knew what to make of that. Three off-script friends of one of the participants came whooping through the woods, crashing the scene and trying to get the party started. They were subdued. And, as before, the frustrated invaders eventually concluded they could scare the defenders into compliance by pretending to execute one of their members. With two minutes to go before the execution, Roy and the other umpires called an end to the exercise.

Six months later, the Peace Games paid off.

In the spring of 1969, activist energy in Berkeley coalesced around the corner of Telegraph Avenue and Haste Street. The University of California had bought the property, announcing plans for new student residences and a parking lot. Then the building stalled. The land was vacant, inviting, and on April 18, 1969, the *Berkeley Barb* urged readers to take back the property. Hundreds showed up, clearing ground, planting trees, and setting up playground equipment. This was now People's Park. On May 15, some 250 California Highway Patrol officers and Berkeley police swept across People's Park before dawn. They forced out the squatters and erected a chain-link fence. Word spread rapidly, and shortly six thousand protestors surged toward the site. Rocks and bottles began flying; police sent tear gas canisters. That's when some Peace Games lessons kicked in.

"I found myself out alone trying to keep people from throwing rocks at cops who had guns aimed at them, directing traffic away from tear-gassed areas, and helping tear-gassed people escape from the melee," Peace Games alumnus Peter Bergel recalled in an interview.

Later, protestors planned to summon fifty thousand marchers. They were going to reclaim the park. Violence was in the air; Governor Ronald Reagan had called out the National Guard. Bergel and bookseller Fred Cody appropriated a grade school and began summoning all the nonviolence trainers they could think of. Roy and other Peace Games veterans that night ran a quick session in nonviolence. Hundreds attended.

"The next day, we salted ourselves through the entire march . . . and managed to head off any violence," Bergel said. "It was a magnificent success."

So the Peace Games lived on, though not always in the ways that Roy wanted. He had envisioned a Peace Games book as a way to convey the lessons to a broader audience. The journals of participants, and the ninety-four-page report painstakingly put together by Tom Coats, provided considerable detail about what had gone down. Roy presented the material to *The Free You* editor Fred Nelson, then working at *Sunset* magazine. Nelson took a whack at it, but finally advised Roy that it was hopeless. He simply couldn't conjure a coherent, publishable narrative out of the Peace Games material.

Roy's Peace Games exercises had occurred at the Free U's summit, when the school claimed about 1,200 members and for a time was called the largest free university in the United States. A storefront office on El Camino Real, across the street from Kepler's, had subsequently been relocated to downtown Palo Alto and expanded into a coffee shop called The Tangent. The courses, too, were expanding. Stanford geneticist Leonard Herzenberg, whose campus home had hosted some of the Free U's foundational discussions, offered one he playfully entitled Domino Theory. The phrase resonated during the Vietnam War, but the course had nothing to do with national security strategies. It was all about a game played with black-and-white tiles, a game, Lee Herzenberg noted, that had some appeal to an African American population not always represented in the Free U.

Attorney Jim Wolpman, a friend of psychologist Vic Lovell's and a Kepler's customer since their Stanford undergraduate days, had left his straight law firm and become a full-time activist lawyer, starting with the Free U's own legal needs. Wolpman would challenge city noise ordinances that were used to ban outdoor rock concerts and Be-Ins. In June 1970 Wolpman would file suit against what was dubbed the "Red Squad" of the Palo Alto Police Department. The lawsuit claimed the squad photographically monitored activists, maintained political dossiers, intimidated activists. One review found Palo Alto police had accumulated files on between 125 and 150 individuals of potential interest, ranging across the political spectrum from Right to Left. Within a year the city settled the complaint with a new general order for police that tightened the rules for opening conspiracy files. The general order further stated that cameras and other recording devices could not be used to harass or chill activists engaging in constitutionally protected free speech. Wolpman described the settlement at the time as the first in the nation of its kind.

Educators, church groups, and students were coming by the Free U for inspiration. In January 1969 a Duke University student wrote Roy, asking for advice about establishing a free university. Later that year the local American Association of University Women approached the Free U's coordinators. The AAUW ladies wanted to know more about this free university business, preferably, it was said, from someone who didn't look too freaky. A University of Denver student came to the Bay Area in 1969, checked out the various free universities, and returned to start the Denver Free University that year in Roy's hometown (Draves 1980, 27).

Roy was still handling the Free U's administrative work, leading his seminars on nonviolence. The Free U's growth, though, had also exacerbated the initial tensions among different counterculture factions. In the beginning, a common interest in breaking educational conventions united radicals of every stripe. Over time, the underlying fissures cracked wider. There were shadows as well. While the Peace Games players were dressing up in discarded army uniforms to practice peace, others were dressing up for the forceful dismantling of the establishment, the true Revolution itself.

The Revolutionary Union began in the Bay Area around 1968. Its earliest Palo Alto–area members included Stanford professor H. Bruce Franklin, an unlikely revolutionary. Bruce Franklin was an air force veteran and Herman Melville specialist then in his mid-thirties. For the Free U, this conventionally successful academic offered a class called "Marxism-Leninism and the American Revolution." Franklin described his Tuesday night class in the Free U catalog as one for "those who want to help make the American Revolution," and promised it would "integrate practice with theory."

Franklin's home, a House Internal Security Committee report would note, "had walls of bookshelves filed with revolutionary and communist literature." Kepler's, of course, might have been one source for the Franklins' library, though an FBI informer told the House committee that a San Francisco store called China Books likely provided the most radically martial literature. Franklin's incendiary style was hard to ignore, and in November 1968 the FBI ordered an investigation into charges that the Free University and several other Bay Area groups were under the control of the Revolutionary Union. "Because of the violence-prone nature of the RU and the Peninsula Red Guards, all of the above organizations should be afforded imaginative and penetrative investigation," an FBI agent wrote in a November 14, 1968, memo.

In a follow-up January 8, 1969, memo, FBI headquarters added that "the militant nature" of the Revolutionary Union necessitated prompt action. The San Francisco field office assigned two additional agents to the job. Other spies were on the case. The 115th Military

Intelligence Group was noted in the FBI memos as likewise having an "interest in anti-draft and anti-Vietnam activities," while the Immigration and Naturalization Service was noted to have an "interest in the activities of aliens in the Midpeninsula Free University." Soon the Bureau's files were stuffed with Free U catalogs and clipped articles from the *Peninsula Observer* and the *Palo Alto Times*.

The Revolutionary Union's members were said to espouse the necessity of violent revolution through guerrilla warfare. New members were only admitted following background investigations. In theory, they repudiated drugs and excessive drinking. The revolution needed young men and women in top physical condition. The virtues of exercise were preached. *Quotations from Chairman Mao* was studied line by line. Members were bound in tight discipline, submitting to their revolutionary supervisors detailed schedules. Numerous meetings and study groups took up four or five nights a week, the House Internal Security Committee reported in 1972.

The Revolutionary Union, in turn, was tied in to the melodramatically named Peninsula Red Guard. The Peninsula Red Guard, an admiring writer had observed in a May 1968 *Berkeley Barb* article, had "sort of roving commissions to attack the power structure at points of opportunity and fade back into the obscurity of the middle-class milieu." This included, at one point, an attack on a Stanford ROTC building.

This kind of militaristic posturing repelled Roy. In late 1968, meeting with the Free U's coordinating committee, Roy had warned against the polarization of the community through belligerent confrontation. In the November 1968 issue of *The Free You,* he raised red flags about "the unverified assumption that released emotions in and of themselves are good and humane, and that violence and hostility are 'worked out' through surfacing rage and acting it out."

"Through the glorification of spontaneity, of group action together, of the existential nature of all acts, there is a tendency to accept disruption for its own sake," Roy warned.

The conflict over tactics, pitting Roy and the pacifists against the street revolutionaries, was set to be debated at an April 3, 1969, general meeting of the Free U. There was a problem, though. The publicly announced meeting drew a *Palo Alto Times* reporter. This worried some meeting participants, who feared even a theoretical discussion of political violence could put them in legal jeopardy. The *Times*, besides, had always seemed hostile to the Free U. Its editor, ex-OSS man Alexander Bodi, was especially nasty. "When we walk down the street, we're made out as Communist dupes, as freaks who are about to take over the entire society," Free U member Phil Trounstine said, according to a transcript published in the April 1969 *The Free You*.

Some urged keeping the meeting private. Roy characteristically sided with those who wanted to let the reporter stay, noting that the meeting itself was announced publicly.

"It would be a real threshold in the Free U if we can't have completely open discussions with anybody who comes," Roy said, adding that "we're going to have to take risks for our values."

The meeting participants voted 22–12 to let the *Times* reporter stay, after which dissidents walked out. The division presaged more to come. The Free U was fracturing. Or, more accurately, the fracture lines that had always been present were becoming more pronounced. Roy increasingly worried, as he put it at the April 3 meeting, that "we've played around with a lot of rhetoric" that led to violent action.

Nonetheless, by the spring of 1969 the FBI had concluded that the avowedly violent revolutionaries lacked control over the Free University. The revolutionary classes were only a handful among the 278 offered that fall. RU members were teaching classes, the FBI noted, but so were others. Officially, the investigation was dropped, but authorities were keeping their eyes open. The Free U was attracting some strange characters and, in the shadows off the midway, even some of the fun and games could turn gruesome.

In the late summer of 1969, following one of the Free U's Be-Ins at El Camino Park, a thirteen-year-old girl awoke in a nearby creek bed. She had taken LSD, blacked out, and then was raped. Some chastened Free U leaders acknowledged that, as one put it in the Free U's September 4, 1969, coordinating committee meeting, "the community should . . . take care of ourselves so that these bad scenes stop coming down." Roy believed the same, though he stressed another point as well. It would be useful, Roy noted at the September 4 meeting, to research the incidents of rape following football games and other mass events. Who was to say traditional sports were any more virtuous than the Free U counterculture? Roy's was an assertive posture, forcing Free U skeptics to look at their own behavior.

The same month, the Free U's coordinating council met to discuss other pressing business. North Vietnam's leader Ho Chi Minh had just died, and the Free U leaders decided to send a telegram offering condolences to the freedom-loving North Vietnamese people. One coordinator suggested including a Free U course catalog along with the telegram, so Hanoi's cadres could check out the course offerings in yoga, dance, and radical self-empowerment. The motion to send North Vietnam a Midpeninsula Free University catalog died for lack of a second.

The catalog offering had a prankish tinge to it, but mostly good humor seemed in short supply. Roy was getting shouted down in public meetings. Outside the Free U's administrative confines, as well, the revolutionary rhetoric was taking a violent turn. One night in mid-July 1969, a Kepler's employee was carrying the day's deposit of $582.99 to the bank. Two men stopped him, one brandishing a gun. The employee handed over the money and stood still while the men took off.

"Brother," one of the robbers said, the *Palo Alto Times* would report, "this is for the people's revolution."

Maybe it was a joke; maybe not. Undeniably, the street revolutionaries had become the only ones interested in running for Free U office. They worked harder, stayed longer, and argued more than anyone else. "Increasingly," Roy recalled, "those who had been involved just finally dropped out and didn't contest the forces that were moving in."

By January 1971 the Revolutionary Union's membership split, with about half going off to affiliate with Venceremos, a relatively new Chicano revolutionary group founded in Redwood City. Those staying with the Revolutionary Union believed that the time had not yet ripened for armed conflict. Violent revolutionary action might not be right for another fifteen or twenty years. Venceremos, which had no relationship to the Cuba-friendly Venceremos Brigade, was the brainchild of activists who were of the belief that, as a 1972 House Committee on Internal Security report entitled "American Maoists" put it, "the political consciousness of the masses was already sufficiently high to begin waging the 'military' or guerrilla warfare phase of the revolution at once" (House Committee on Internal Security 1972). Venceremos members also worked on far more civil affairs, including attempts to defeat at the polls plans for a new Bay Area expressway and new office building development in downtown Palo Alto.

Venceremos, Stanford geneticist and Free U veteran Lee Herzenberg recalled, "had a very rigid Stalinist ideology, which was totally inconsistent with what we stood for, and what Roy stood for." Roy withdrew from the Free U, as did the Herzenbergs and, increasingly, everyone not committed to the revolutionary struggle espoused by Venceremos. Free U membership fell. The organization owed thousands of dollars. Personal interactions were getting messy, complicated. When Stanford computer scientist John McCarthy stood up at a Free U meeting to propose that the Free U reaffirm a policy of non-violence, the motion died for want of a second. Then, adding injury to insult, a militant stood up and threatened to kill McCarthy (Markoff 2005, 114). By sometime in 1970, Roy withdrew altogether. He stopped running his nonviolence seminars, and he left the curricular and administrative hassles to others.

What had been *The Free You* magazine became, under Venceremos leadership, the bilingual *Pamoja Venceremos*, which organization leaders called a "damn good revolutionary newspaper vital to the street struggle." Its rhetoric turned nastily combative. The self-described White Panther Tribe of Palo Alto characteristically declared in the summer 1970 issue that "we must deal with the capitalist pigs who are trying to destroy our community [and] gain community control of the local Gestapo force." The tone and posturing further drove people away. Classes withered. The Free U had lost its original cadre, its inspiration, and its way. In July 1971, with only about seventy members still hanging around, the remaining Midpeninsula Free University leaders formally gave up the ghost.

In a generally sympathetic portrait of free universities, the American Association for Higher Education provided an epitaph for the Free U's rise and fall. "Community people who were pretty satisfied with their lot entered," the American Association for Higher Education concluded. "They created touchie-feelie-psychodrama-encounter type groups and grooved on the experience. When the leaders tried to reinstitute radical policies and courses, they lost most of the Free U's constituents" (Lichtman 1973).

In its heyday, the Midpeninsula Free University offered an incredibly rich menu. Through the Peace Games, his nonviolence seminars, and his administrative guidance, Roy expounded his lifelong message of peace. People learned from him. Some classes succeeded beyond anyone's wildest imagination. Some specific moments endured. And though the institution collapsed, the notion of a liberated education lived on. By 1976, even though some of the earliest experiments no longer operated, enrollment in the nation's various free universities and offspring had reached a high of nearly 200,000 (Draves 1980, 93).

Conventional universities, community colleges, and adult education programs all adopted features of the free university movement. At Stanford, in the fall of 1969, students with the assistance of faculty members began the Free U–tinged Stanford Workshops on Political and Social Issues. The SWOPSI workshops combined the Free U's insistence on real-world relevance with the conventional university's currency of academic credit. Students could progress toward their Stanford degrees while they prepared in-depth reports on topics from arms control to Bay Area transportation and farmworkers' pesticide exposure. With a small budget from the university, SWOPSI would live on until the early 1990s. Other like-minded programs endured.

In 2009 Free U veteran Phil Trounstine could look around and trace, distinctly, the Free U roots beneath the surface of twenty-first-century conventional education offerings. Trounstine had served as treasurer during the Free U's later years and was part of the Vencer-emos movement, the opposite end of the tactical spectrum from Roy. Trounstine went on to serve as *San Jose Mercury News* political editor, communications director for California Governor Gray Davis, direc-tor of San Jose State University's Survey and Policy Research Institute, and then founder of the influential Calbuzz political blog. He went straight, that is to say, but all the while carrying inside him his expe-riences with the Free U. He knew that once the classroom walls had been busted out, school would never be the same.

"All the universities tried to co-opt that movement," Trounstine said, "and they succeeded."

17

Counterattack

The war came home, as wars always will.

October 1968. Violence was manifest, sheet lightning across the skies. Nearly half a million American troops were enmeshed in South Vietnam. Constant tumult shook Berkeley's Telegraph Avenue. Space cases and speed freaks haunted the streets around Kepler's Books & Magazines, City Lights, and Cody's. Rhetoric ran hot and heavy, though Roy tried to dampen the powder. In late summer he joined Fred Cody in a joint KPFA show, musing about the nature of violence and the persistence of its arising. But Kepler's, too, was also adorning itself provocatively; or so some thought.

That October, Kepler's front window display facing El Camino Real featured books about China and an iconic poster of Mao Tse Tung. The display was not an endorsement, though some thought it might be. Roy and Ira were, in fact, as vocally opposed to the oppressions of Chinese communism as they were to the war policies of the U.S. government. But when Kepler's workers arrived the morning of October 16, they discovered a broken front window, a hatchet, and a note.

"First Chairman Mao," the note warned. "Then Kepler."

Several hours later, the mess cleaned up and the store open for business, three men entered and took note of the broken window. They seemed to shake their heads at the way of things; it was a shame such violence should happen. There was something about them, though. They seemed pent up. The three men wondered why the store lacked a picture of George Wallace. There's a picture of a Chinese Commie but not of a good American war hero like Wallace, a bona fide presidential candidate. It made no sense. Then the three men left, some unsaid message remaining behind them.

Roy had always excited opposition. He craved it even, as the sign that competing ideas were truly met. And he knew that sometimes promoting peaceful ideals could provoke violent opposition. But by 1968 Roy feared the Left by its own acting out had drawn upon itself a commensurately physical response. Everyone was angry at everyone else. First the rhetoric escalated and then, when words no longer sufficed, the fists started swinging. He could see it, all around him. The thrown hatchet was part of a pattern.

On the night of September 2, 1968, the Free U offices several blocks away from Kepler's had been broken into. The vandals trashed equipment and files and painted the words "Communist swine" on the walls. The next month brought the hatchet tossed through the Kepler's Menlo Park store window. The night of November 13, employees at the Los Altos store observed two suspicious men lurking nearby after closing. Later that same night, a brick was tossed through a window at the Menlo Park store. The following night, two five-gallon gasoline cans were found in the rear of the Los Altos store. About eleven o'clock at night on November 24, a pipe bomb blew out a four-foot hole in a window at the Los Altos Kepler's store. The next morning, store manager Betty Sumrall found shards of glass stuck in books on the other side of the store from the blown-out window.

"I suppose someone is mad at me for not being violent," Roy sardonically told the *Palo Alto Times.*

Nor was Kepler's the only target. On Sunday, December 1, a small bomb tossed through the back window of a house near downtown Palo Alto blew out windows and knocked a door off its hinges. The house was used by several peace groups allied with the Free U, The Resistance, and the Concerned Citizens of Palo Alto. The next night, a pipe bomb careened through the window of the Free University's office on El Camino Real. The blast shattered the windows and wrecked an estimated $1,000 worth of arts and crafts.

The police seemed powerless to stop the attacks. Perhaps, some activists thought, the police were willfully turning a blind eye. It was time for self-help. The Free U convened a December 8 meeting to discuss what could be done. Some suggested secret surveillance teams. Others worried secrecy undermined the Free U's commitment to open thought and action. So the meeting adjourned, but Bob Cullenbine and four others stayed afterward for a second meeting. They had to do something, while still honoring the Free U's code. They cut a deal: They would act, not as Free U leaders but as individuals. Nightly leaders were assigned, each to recruit between three and five helpers. They equipped themselves with radios and binoculars. Over the course of several weeks, they collected hundreds of "suspicious" license plate numbers as well as "other data," in the words of *The Free You.*

Roy was taking steps on his own. In a precautionary move, he and Patricia had already moved Clark, April, Dawn, and Melody out of the bedrooms in their Los Altos home that had windows facing the street. Roy also hired a San Jose–based private eye to poke around. Roy himself was undertaking his own inquiries. Some time around November 1968, Bruce and Ed Peddy, pacifists and occasional part-time clerks at the store, mentioned that their brother Walter might be wrapped up in some kind of political fringe group. Roy decided he would check it out, face to face, which is how he met Jim McGee and Jim McGee's crowd.

McGee was thirty-four in 1968. He was a broad-shouldered, good-looking man with sandy hair, and sideburns, writer Ed Mc-Clanahan said, that were "just long enough to lend an unexpected dash of verve." The hipster McClanahan and the Christian conservative McGee had met when McClanahan took Ken Kesey to the Palo Alto Health Club for a steam bath. The next time McClanahan went to the club to work out, McGee was there waiting, ready to debate. Over the course of a year, McClanahan recalled, he and McGee argued endlessly about politics and religion. McGee was a George Wallace fan. McClanahan favored Eldridge Cleaver. Nonetheless, the two men liked each other. Theirs became a running debate, a mental workout, through which McClanahan was able to learn a bit more about McGee's upbringing.

McGee's father, Gene, had written articles for a right-wing newspaper. His mother was deeply religious and good-hearted. McGee's Christianity was equally fervent, and principled. He and his wife, Donna Lee, started a Friday night Bible class; they wanted to rescue kids from the manifold temptations of the 1960s. McGee felt the Free U was destroying American youth with sex and drugs. Kepler's could be just as bad. If this Kepler fellow opposed violence as much as he claimed, McGee wondered, then why did his store carry so many books fomenting rebellion?

"We weren't the only ones to hate Kepler's; there were thousands of people on the Peninsula who did," McGee said in an April 1980 interview. "We were against the store for what was being sold there [and] we wanted to draw kids away from the sex and drugs and immorality of the free university."

But McGee, in the same interview, stressed that he had no personal animus toward Roy. The store was the problem. It was "very well stocked," McGee acknowledged, but it was carrying nasty books, some of which he thought promoted the very violence Roy so adamantly opposed. The opposition to Kepler's remained civil, McGee said. No one in his circle participated in store attacks, he said.

A dental technician by trade, McGee could work with his hands, and he loved to experiment. He got to know another munitions experimenter, a Bay Area gun dealer. Call this dealer, for the sake of privacy, JM From his basement the twenty-four-year-old JM ran a small munitions business. After Palo Alto rejected his application for a license to store dynamite, JM formed the Palo Alto Citizens to Uphold the Second Amendment. There he met other concerned citizens like Josh Cooney.

Cooney was a character, an Irish emigrant then in his late forties. He took great pride in being a naturalized American citizen, sometimes wearing multiple American flag pins on his lapel. Though evidently trained as a chemical engineer at the University of Dublin, his passion once in the United States was fighting communism. In early 1966 he opened his own bookstore, the Christian American Heritage Guild, on El Camino Real near Kepler's. The Bay Area market for John Birch Society literature, children's patriotic tomes, and American flags proved fatally limited, though, and Cooney closed his store that December. Still, he had a certain appreciation for Kepler's. He frequented the store and he respected the man, despite their vast differences.

"Roy Kepler, to my knowledge and belief, would not kill a fly," Cooney acknowledged in the *Palo Alto Times* on February 22, 1969. "I wish we had somebody with his dedication to work on our side. [But] a great deal of permissiveness has crept up in the community because of Kepler's."

Cooney admired George Wallace. Once Cooney had been kicked off the Menlo-Atherton High School campus for distributing Wallace literature. Cooney disliked, as well, the sexual license promoted by the Free U, the total disregard for the sacred institution of marriage or the dictates of morality. At the George Wallace Bay Area campaign head-quarters, Cooney had introduced McGee to JM and to Walt Peddy, another concerned citizen.

Peddy came from a distinctive family. His brother Bruce was on the other side of the fence, politically; Bruce had spent some time at the Institute for the Study of Nonviolence and was favorably known to the Kepler's crowd. Walt, a talented young man, seemed to swing in the other direction. He had more in common with Jim McGee and Josh Cooney and JM, patriots who wanted to defend America against radicals like Roy Kepler.

In early December Roy showed up at one of the Bible study sessions held at Jim McGee's Menlo Park house, Following a long Bible lesson, the study group members clustered around Roy and pressed him with questions. They wanted to know about the Free University and that other radical outfit, the United Nations. Politely but persistently, they asked for his thoughts on violence, and nonviolence. Nonviolence, Roy told them, had a long history going back to the first Christians, who he said would refuse to be soldiers or carry spears.

"I was an item of some curiosity," Roy said afterward, the *Palo Alto Times* reported on February 21, 1969, but "we had a rather interesting dialogue."

Two weeks later, over the objections of his wife, Patricia, Roy again showed up at the McGee's Menlo Park house. This time he was accompanied by Bob Cullenbine from the Free U as well as Tom Coats, the Quaker friend who had closely attended Roy's Peace Games exercise. Roy thought both appearances useful as a way to "let them see me as a human being." Still, whoever was responsible for the attacks did not relent. On Monday morning, January 20, workers at the Menlo Park and Los Altos Kepler's stores arrived to find windows broken in both locations. Roy estimated it would cost more than $1,200 to replace the windows. The violence was also diffusing. Police began hearing reports that shots had been fired at a Lucky's grocery store in Palo Alto, a Shell gas station, and a Chevrolet dealership.

The police seemed to be literally clueless, or worse. Free U activists were swapping rumors and speculations. A George Wallace for President button was spotted on a Palo Alto detective. A sheriff's deputy had supposedly confided that the store-bombers were on "our side." Anything seemed possible.

On January 24 Roy took his concerns to the FBI, the very agency that had long snooped around Roy's pacifist circle. Roy stressed that he was not complaining about the police; he simply thought it was time to bring some fresh eyes on the problem. He advised the FBI agents, an agency memo of February 6, 1969, would recount, that he believed the harassment came from individuals who also disliked the Free U. Roy further told agents about his meetings with Jim McGee's Bible study group, a potential target of interest.

The agents dutifully recorded what Roy told them. They were civil but they couldn't spare the manpower to watch the bookstores. Until more definitive clues were available, Roy would, like Cullenbine and the Free U, have to keep depending upon volunteer watchers.

Susan MacDonald, newly hired by Kepler's, helped administer the store watch program. A native of England, MacDonald had moved to the East Coast when she was twenty-one, seeking adventure. She found some as a stewardess, but quit after a year when she tired of being a high-altitude cocktail waitress. She married, had a son and daughter, and ended up divorced in Menlo Park. There she had chanced one day upon a poster advertising the Free U. She signed up for a class on Dante and in time her own poetry began burbling up, though that didn't pay the bills. A mutual friend introduced her to Roy, advising him that she needed a job. Roy, a traditionalist, asked if she could type and do secretarial work. She ended up doing more.

"I was writing home to my mother, telling her I was working in a bookstore," MacDonald recalled in an interview, "but what I couldn't tell her was that I was actually scheduling volunteers to stand in the store with walkie-talkies."

On Christmas Eve 1968, MacDonald stood watch. Equipped with sleeping bags and walkie-talkies, her crew gathered toward the middle of the bookstore so that they were safe from any shattering front windows, but still close enough to peer outside. At three in the morning, MacDonald and her cohorts listened to the radio crackle and wondered what would happen next. To MacDonald, it felt like the frontier, the very edge of the known world.

"This was America / the Wild West," MacDonald later write, poetically, of her Christmas Eve bookstore watch. "I sipped my thermos coffee / and fingered through *The Territorial Imperative*."

The watches took a toll. One potential store watcher, a self-described "Tolstoyan," confessed to Roy that he backed out of one Friday night store-watch assignment after he heard Roy was cooperating with the police. The young man subsequently assured Roy that he had no hang-ups about cops, but the cooperation just didn't seem to square with Tolstoy's skepticism toward the criminal justice system. He hoped Roy would understand.

Another night, a young computer scientist and Free U activist named Larry Tesler joined the store watch. Tesler, an observant man, noted the license plate on a suspicious Volkswagen. The car matched the description of one seen previously by other store watchers. Tesler passed the number along to the Menlo Park Police Department, where officials, Tesler recalled, dismissed the information. The car owner, police officials explained, was an upstanding citizen. Months later, it would come to pass that the same man was arrested. "If they had believed me, several bombings and many sleepless nights could have been avoided," Tesler said in an interview.

The store watches were thrilling for a while, an adventure on the front lines, but they became an exhausting bore, and it took a different kind of break to end the string of attacks. It took the help of an ex-con named Joseph Dobiss, a seemingly unsettled young man in his late twenties. One day in November, while being questioned by police on another matter, Dobiss apparently saw a way out of his latest problem. He knew certain things; maybe the detective would be interested in knowing them too. JM, Dobiss told the detective, had once tried to recruit him into something called the Society of Man. To join, prospective members had to show their commitment to the cause.

Dobiss was brought to meet Palo Alto Detective Howard E. Carlyle. Carlyle, according to Dobiss, told him to search out license plate numbers, names, and other particulars on the Society of Man. Dobiss prepared a lengthy, single-spaced document spelling out names, addresses, and personality sketches.

"There is a series of bombings planned which will start on or about January 12 [to] May 31," Dobiss warned, according to a *Palo Alto Times* account of February 15, 1969. "The bombings are designed not to perpetrate bodily injury, but to cause the victims to disperse their organizations . . . it will be determined between January 12 and May 31 whether the bombings have had a definite effect on the curtailment of these liberal and leftist organizations."

Carlyle apparently dismissed Dobiss's report and didn't bother giving it to the Menlo Park Police Department. Through other hands, though, the Dobiss dossier was delivered to a well-connected *Palo Alto Times* reporter named Jay Thorwaldson. Thorwaldson gave the Menlo Park police chief Victor Cizanckas a copy in exchange for being kept informed of developments. Cizanckas was only thirty-one years old, a progressive, PR-oriented cop who would later clothe his constables in slacks and blue blazers, civilized garb for a civilized town.

He was willing to play along with Thorwaldson if it would help stop the blasts that had shattered his town's decorum.

Investigators had already caught another break by identifying a 1958 blue Chevy leaving the scene of one of the attacks. A twenty-five-year-old Menlo Park policeman named Armand J. Lareau happened to know the driver. Here was just the opportunity investigators needed. If Lareau could insinuate himself into the driver's world, he might earn an introduction to the inner circle. It would be dicey work. But they had their man in Lareau, a self-confident air force veteran whose voice still cut with the edge of his native Massachusetts. Lareau could talk to anyone.

Officials concocted for Lareau an identity designed to lure right-wingers. Lareau would become cast as an angry cop, frustrated over his treatment by a mollycoddling department. He would become bait. Cizanckas prepared a fake letter of reprimand, purporting to chastise Lareau for mishandling the arrest of a black teenager. Cizanckas then staged Lareau along El Camino Real so he could patrol the area frequented by the kid driving the '58 blue Chevy. His target worked at a gas station. Lareau would show up, and the two would talk. They weren't that different, they discovered. Lareau could have been his older brother. And Lareau was angry, seething over his treatment by the police chief.

The young gas station attendant—call him, for privacy's sake, DN—seemed to like what he was hearing from Lareau. DN was just eighteen, the son of a World War II veteran who ran a small business in downtown Menlo Park. He invited Lareau to a Bible study class on the weekend of January 25–26 at Jim McGee's Menlo Park home. Lareau quietly reported the development, and then on the weekend he showed up with DN at the study group. At first, Lareau thought, it resembled a cocktail party, with the ladies mingling and the conversation benign. Lareau and his guide moved on, to the second room, where men were talking about the need to take back their country from the Communists.

Careful not to overplay his hand, Lareau let the others in on his story. His Commie-loving chief, that S.O.B. Cizanckas, was riding him too hard. The other men were skeptical, but seemed desirous. They imagined the possibilities if they actually managed to recruit a disaffected cop. They asked Lareau for proof. Lareau showed the prepared letter of chastisement. Walt Peddy reportedly still didn't trust the newcomer. He thought Lareau might be a cop on the make. Others weren't too keen on Lareau either. Lareau and McGee, though, hit it off, the *Palo Alto Times* would report on March 18, 1969. And McGee, for the moment, was who mattered most.

At 4 a.m. on the morning of January 26, a Sunday, a bomb loaded with buckshot and nails blew a hole in the front door of Palo Alto City Councilman Kirk Comstock's house. The blast also shattered a window. Comstock was not home at the time, but later that day he picked up the phone.

"How did you like the little package last night?" the male voice asked, the *San Jose Mercury* reported on January 27, 1969. "If you keep it up, you'll get more of the same."

Targets abounded. The Tangent was a University Avenue coffeehouse affiliated with Free U types. Shortly before midnight on February 5, a blast knocked out an eight-to-ten-inch hole in a stained glass window, throwing glass and bomb fragments about fifteen feet across the room. Two days later, a cherry bomb set off among the bookshelves rattled customers at the Kepler's Menlo Park store. And less than twenty-four hours later, an unexploded pipe bomb fizzled out near the Free U store, where twenty people were hanging out. It was the scariest attack yet.

On February 10 the Palo Alto Unitarian Church would be hosting a talk on Red China. Some thought this deserved an emphatic retort. Communists were openly meeting in the United States, a direct threat to the country. Years later, in an April 1980 interview, Jim McGee insisted it was Lareau himself, the undercover cop, who had first originated the idea of disrupting the Unitarian Church meeting. However it developed, men gathered for a strategy session on February 8. They would need equipment. Lareau was asked to obtain gas grenades from the Menlo Park Police Department supply room. Their plan was simplicity itself. They would infiltrate the Red China talk, roll the tear gas grenade down the aisle, toss out some firecrackers, and then bolt.

Deep down, some men thought the idea of tear-gassing the church was way out of line. Cooney declined to have anything to do with it. Others bit their tongues. The night of the church talk, Walter L. Peddy, DN, JM, and another man—call him DS—gathered at the McGee's house while Donna helped her husband paste on false sideburns and mustache. The McGees then helped dude up Lareau with his own false mustache and goatee. Lareau produced the single tear gas grenade he had procured from the Menlo Park Police Department, and the men drove in a van over to the church. Things didn't look good. Lareau's supervisors wanted him to get the crew into the church for the sake of future prosecutions, but they didn't want any untoward incident.

The men did get inside the church, but everyone was antsy. JM stuck close to Lareau, who, accidentally or not, knocked over some chairs, and the men scampered back to their van before any real disruption happened. Then, for what Lareau recalled as hours on end, they drove around with no seeming aim. In the back of the van there was a storage drum whose purpose Lareau could not really fathom. What, or who, might be stored in such a thing? It nagged at him, what might be stuffed in there. An unmarked police car was supposed to be following them, but Lareau soon realized the chase car had been left behind. He was on his own.

"It was the scariest goddamn night in the world," Lareau said.

Finally, nearing three in the morning, the men dropped Lareau off at his house. Lareau waited a safe interval, then hooked up with officers who had been growing increasingly alarmed over his absence. After Lareau had been debriefed, the conclusion was made that the investigation had gone far enough.

On the night of February 14, computer scientist Larry Tesler, a friend, and two female acquaintances were assigned to watch the Kepler's Menlo Park store and the nearby Free U store. Halfway through the shift, in the middle of the night, they decided it was

a waste of time. They abandoned their posts and took their social-
izing elsewhere. What they didn't know was that at the start of the
same evening, some forty police officers from Menlo Park, Palo Alto,
Redwood City, and Mountain View had gathered at the Menlo Park
Police Department headquarters.

For two-and-a-half hours, the police went over the myriad details
of a multipronged raid. About 9 p.m. that night, Los Altos Police
Chief Roland Renshaw knocked on the door of Roy's Los Altos house.
Renshaw had been chief of the small department since 1958, but had
never had an experience like this. Inside Roy's house, he advised the
couple that there were rumors of an assassination list. Probably it was
all just talk, but he advised the Keplers to take a vacation.

While Roy and Patricia were absorbing this news, officers were
fanning out in half a dozen raiding teams. Shortly after 10:30 p.m.,
JM heard a knock on his front door. Cooney and DS were downstairs. JM pushed the intercom button and asked who was at the door.

"Palo Alto PD," a man yelled. "Open up!"

At about the same time, police were storming into the McGees'
home. Donna clutched a Bible, while her daughters were awakened to
a horrible fright. All told, officers arrested seven suspects that night,
and another one the following morning. They seized a dozen rifles and
shotguns, two semiautomatic weapons, pistols, seventy-five pounds of
gunpowder, and Nazi emblems and flags.

"Nazi Terror Net," the *Palo Alto Times* screamed in its postarrest
headline. The lead photograph showed the Menlo Park police chief
crouching next to a carefully staged selection of swastika flags, guns,
and Adolph Hitler photographs. The suspects were variously charged
with illegal use, possession or transportation of explosives, conspiracy,
and criminal syndicalism.

The night after the arrests, the suspects began learning more
about the world they had entered into. About 11 p.m. that night,
deputies in the San Mateo County Jail heard screams and a man yell-
ing, "Oh God, help me!" Rushing to investigate, they found twenty-
two-year-old DS, his face bloodied, crouched on a mattress. DS told

the deputies that three inmates beat and kicked him after accusing him of being a Nazi. Two other suspects were likewise jumped in jail.

The following Monday, February 17, seven of the nine suspects pleaded not guilty in a crowded courtroom. The two others asked for more time to prepare their plea. The judge set bail at $6,250. Donna McGee asked that she be released on her own recognizance, reasoning that she was a woman.

"Women can be just as vicious as men," Judge Roy Seagraves replied, the *Palo Alto Times* reported on February 18, 1969.

Chained together, the suspects were marched back to the county jail. The Home Defense Association, an Oakland-based group, announced it was raising funds to pay for legal costs. The self-described "deputy commander of the American Nazi Party of Northern California" told reporters that the Nazi Party "gives its full support to these defenders of the white race." But another man wearing a khaki uniform, black boots, and swastika armband said that *he* was the real voice of Nazism in the Bay Area, and he had never heard of the accused conspirators.

"Our method of operation has always emphasized legality," the swastika-wearing gentleman assured one and all, the *San Francisco Chronicle* reported on February 17, 1969.

Cooney emphatically declared that he had never been a member of any Nazi organization and he had never engaged in terror tactics. He would end up hiring a liberal Democratic attorney, Boris Baranowski, who joined some civil libertarians in raising concerns about how police were tainting public perceptions. The Nazi flag photos were really hitting home. On February 19, during another preliminary court proceeding, Walter Peddy's brother Ed took to the streets. Ed Peddy was one of the men who had first alerted Roy to the Bible study group meeting at Jim McGee's house. Nonetheless, Ed Peddy had been shocked at how his brother was being handled. Police, he said, had wildly ransacked his father's attic and collected mementos from World War II. Free U activists also seemed to be leaping to erroneous conclusions about young Walter Peddy, his brothers Ed and Bruce thought.

Roy, too, was troubled by how the case was unfolding and, more fundamentally, by how the attacks had occurred in the first place. Chatting with *Palo Alto Times* reporter Jay Thorwaldson on February 20, Roy said violence was a spasm, which needed to pass. Perhaps the young radicals from Stanford and the Free U could now realize how they were themselves carriers of the virus of hate and violence.

"I personally hope that some people in the [Free University] see how they contributed to the bombings," Roy said in the *Palo Alto Times* of February 21, 1969.

The street rebels spouting Marxist rhetoric and waving the flag of revolution had met their inevitable shadows in the street counterrevolutionaries clutching the flag of the United States. Violence begat violence; it was the perennial lesson. Roy was equally unhappy with how police and city authorities had cut Joe Dobiss loose after the arrest. The young man deserved something for his willingness to blow the whistle on a dangerous crowd, Roy thought. On March 3, just a few days after the arrests, Roy appeared with Dobiss at the Sunnyvale City Council to plead for tangible support. "If I, who have not bothered to infiltrate anyone, am in danger, then Mr. Dobiss is certainly in far more danger," Roy told the city council, the *Palo Alto Times* reported the next day. Roy's plea was futile; no help was forthcoming for Mr. Dobiss.

On March 5 the grand jury returned additional counts against the suspects. Now they faced charges of possession of explosive devices, transportation of destructive devices, and conspiracy, among other crimes. In an aggressive twist, police charged criminal syndicalism, a rarely deployed tactic intended for left-wing organizations. Written in 1919 amid the postwar Red Scare, California's criminal syndicalism law made it a crime to advocate or belong to an organization that advocated breaking the law "as a means of accomplishing a change in industrial ownership or control, or effecting any political change." It was a reach, hard to square with what the alleged conspirators were specifically accused of doing. They weren't accused of attacking government offices, public officials, or big corporate concerns. They were, if prosecutors were correct, troubling a hippy coffeehouse and a struggling left-wing school. Kepler's wasn't even mentioned in the indictments.

Syndicalism seemed such a stretch that some radicals considered aloud the possibility that authorities were simply trying to exercise a weapon that would in the future be used against the Left. Nor was this the only concern raised by thoughtful people, Kepler's kind of people, about how the authorities were handling the accused. Norman Sleizer, an attorney with the American Civil Liberties Union, cautioned in the March 12 *Palo Alto Times* that "the defendants have been prejudicially portrayed as Nazi terrorist bombers," even though they had never been charged as such.

A change of venue was needed, attorney Boris Baranowski told Judge Conrad B. Reisch, "because of the prejudicial pretrial publicity issued by the Menlo Park Police Department, one Mr. Kepler and representatives of the Midpeninsula Free University." Reisch did not grant the change of venue, though in mid-March he did impose a gag order on attorneys.

Baranowski, moreover, was adamant in maintaining that the government was persecuting Cooney for his unconventional political views. Some of Cooney's grudging admirers on the Left agreed. Cooney would later be released after authorities determined he knew nothing of the attacks. Others would not be so lucky.

On Thursday, November 6, 1969, just a few days before the first trial was expected to start, the remaining defendants threw in the towel. Jim McGee, Walter L. Peddy, DN, DS, and JM each pleaded guilty to a single felony count of conspiring to disrupt a public meeting. This was the Palo Alto Unitarian Church meeting on Red China. Two other men pleaded guilty to misdemeanors, and all charges were dropped against Cooney and McGee's wife, Donna. Cooney's wife wept in relief, but his attorney had some harsh words for prosecutors.

"I feel Mr. Cooney was persecuted for his political views," Boris Baranowski said.

Arthur L. Damon Jr., the Palo Alto attorney for Walter Peddy, added in the *Palo Alto Times* on November 7, 1969, that the original charges were "blown clear out of proportion." Peddy's eighteen-year-old brother Ed, a draft resister and part of the Kepler's circle, joined the objections, claiming that police and the press were engaged in a witch hunt in which they utterly mischaracterized World War II memorabilia seized from the family's attic. One attorney stressed that the men were patriots who may have been caught up in an excess of zeal but who nonetheless loved their country and wanted to protect it. Another attorney said Leftists and street revolutionaries had done far more harm.

The sentences came down on December 10, and they were harsh. DN: one to three years. DS: nine months. Walter Peddy: one to three years. McGee: one to three years. McGee appeared visibly shaken when he heard the sentence pronounced. It was far more than he expected, and he tried to withdraw his guilty plea. It was too late, and he could only wave briefly at his family as he was led away.

Defense attorneys and family members thought the men had gotten a raw deal. Strictly speaking, they were probably right. When Reisch cited the "totality of the circumstances" surrounding the case, he was roping in far more than the single act to which the men pled guilty. They had been tarred by the American Nazi label; even Governor Ronald Reagan, when he commended Officer Lareau, cited his work exposing the underground American Nazi Party in the Menlo Park–Palo Alto area. Newspaper articles had referred McGee's home as "Nazi work center" or the site of "Nazi meetings." The most prominent newspaper photograph following the initial arrests had been staged to display weapons surrounding a picture of Adolph Hitler.

A probation officer's presentencing report aggravated the judge's retributive thrust. The report's author relied heavily on a confidential informant in citing twenty-nine separate attacks on various Bay Area entities; a majority were attacks on Kepler's Los Altos or Menlo Park stores. None of the attacks had been part of the plea agreement; no criminal charges or formal accusations were ever made regarding the series of attacks.

Family members feared for their loved ones, with good cause. They worried the assaults in San Mateo County jail while the men awaited trial foreshadowed prison nightmares to come. They also believed in their hearts that a gross injustice had been done. Walter Peddy's mother, Agnes, stated that her son was misled into taking a guilty bargain plea by the district attorney. Donna McGee likewise declared that her husband had been misled into taking a guilty plea on the promise he would only be given six months in county jail. She wrote the state's attorney general after the sentencing, voicing shock and dismay at what she believed to be an unconstitutional bending of the law. Prosecutors had coerced her husband's plea, she said; if he didn't capitulate, they would have gone after her.

Reisch told reporters he felt sorry for Donna McGee and the family, according to news accounts, but he said he didn't feel like he had much choice about sending her husband to prison. Court documents show he also later wrote the San Quentin warden in April 1970 and advised there was no evidence Jim McGee had ever been affiliated with Nazis.

In December 1969 Bob Cullenbine and other Free U leaders sued Josh Cooney, James and Donna McGee, JM, DS, and DN. Cullenbine and the Free U claimed $575,000 in damages for four separate attacks on the Free U's store. The attacks drove away participants and caused enrollment to drop by about five hundred students, the leaders claimed. Then there was the cost of self-defense, enumerated in the *Palo Alto Times* of December 4, 1969: $200 for walkie-talkie radios and batteries, and $10,680 to pay for the overnight watchers who had been on duty eight hours a night for three months.

McGee and the other defendants were hardly in a position to pay. The lawsuit fizzled out. The men served their time and went on with their lives. The multiple attacks on Kepler's themselves were, in a sense, never solved. No one was ever charged with them. The notion that hard-core Nazis instigated the attacks stuck in the public's mind; it made for a coherent and satisfying narrative, but it was, in fact, as overblown as the criminal syndicalism charges that were in time dropped.

Violence begets violence, Roy always taught. The Vietnam War begat an opposition that propounded the need for violent revolution. That, in turn, inspired counterrevolutionaries, militaristic defenders of the faith. Caught in the crossfire was Roy, the one man who had warned all along against the seductions of violent rhetoric and militaristic posturing.

"He who mounts the tiger," Roy had cautioned in a 1967 *Midpeninsula Observer* article, "goes where the tiger goes."

18

Farewell to the Sixties

Roy kept the books straight, in every sense.

Others indulged, amid the gaudy excess of the 1960s. He abstained. "He would have one glass of wine to my twelve," Ira said. Others would hug. The world, Kepler's manager Betty Sumrall said, was suddenly full of huggers. Roy would not join them. He could seem as stiff as an unworn suit. Ira, who knew Roy's emotional depths, observed how difficult the expression of feelings came to his friend. Once, driving back from a San Francisco event, Ira felt moved to kiss his old friend on the cheek.

"I love you, Roy," Ira said.

Roy responded in kind, but Ira could tell the demonstration taxed him. Sometimes it seemed Roy was locked up somewhere inside. Another former Kepler's clerk said she would tell Roy jokes simply so she could observe his excruciatingly rational response, the processing of the punch line followed by laughter one beat too late. His restraint could pain others, but it helped him survive the era intact. He stayed constant. Others caught in the era's tumult turned this way and that. Drug burnouts found Jesus. Foothills residents descended from their tree houses to attend law school. Oakland Induction Center demonstrators became college deans. Writers found the mainstream. Phil Trounstine, the one-time Free U Venceremos activist, became a highly regarded political journalist. Holly Chenery became a nun. Danya Veltfort changed her name and became a Sufi.

One day in 1972, Roy received a package containing some paperbacks, a $20 bill, and a note from a self-described "humble patron" who admitted that "as a revolutionary" he had stolen from Kepler's.

"Now, no longer opposed to society, I offer these books as a partial payment of debt and symbol of good will," the regretful former rebel wrote.

The package from the past arrived when Kepler's was bigger than ever. By the early 1970s, Kepler's Menlo Park store had sprawled into a former auto body shop. Once a cubbyhole, Kepler's Books & Magazines had become by decade's end an ad hoc community center and marketplace for every notion ever put to paper. Customers could buy, or browse, or simply drift along until it was time to check out with the Kepler's clerks, a distinctive cadre.

"They always seemed to be reading something I Ought To Be Reading, but probably never would," customer David Yarnold recalled in the *San Jose Mercury News* of December 26, 1982, remembering the "usually thin women with stringy, straight hair and flannel shirts shedding fuzzballs, [who] spoke slowly, softly, with meticulous enunciation."

The bookstore was more popular than ever. For Roy, though, bookselling had lost some of its savor. The hours were long and the work rote. Having built his business, Roy was again ready for a change. He had already considered selling the stores at least once before, during the start-up of the Institute for the Study of Nonviolence. In 1970 Roy was thinking seriously about it again, and he prepared a narrative for potential buyers.

"Over the years, our stores have maintained the reputation of being among the finest on the West Coast," Roy wrote in a two-page summary. "As a matter of fact, we enjoy a modest international reputation brought about chiefly through the world-wide peregrinations of some of our customers who tell people abroad 'where they can find it' in the U.S.A."

Gross sales from the Menlo Park and Los Altos stores totaled $553,194 in 1969, with net profit of $65,765. For the two stores, Roy anticipated an asking price of $475,000 plus the value of the book inventory, which he pegged at about $70,000. Roy once more sought the advice of his old Minersville and KPFA friend John Lewis. Lewis dug into the numbers and offered negotiating advice, cannily suggesting that only at an advanced stage of the negotiations should Roy tell a potential buyer about the store's ongoing problems with shoplifting and internal theft. The 1970 sales effort eventually petered out. It reflected in part, though, the growing gap between Roy Kepler the man and Kepler's Books & Magazines the place. The separation was becoming physical as well as emotional.

Patricia Kepler, son Clark recalled, had "always been trying to get us to move out of the city and into the country." The Bay Area was hectic, a place of endless demands. The store attacks of the late 1960s had spurred her more; the family needed to get away. Roy and Patricia cast about and found a place in Grass Valley, three hours away from the Bay Area in the Sierra Nevada foothills. Grass Valley was good for Patricia and the kids, a safe remove at 2,400 feet elevation. In theory, it was also a move that would permit Roy to put more balance in his life.

"It's no use trying to save the world if you lose contact with family and friends," Roy reasoned in the *San Jose Mercury* of October 30, 1978, sometime after the move.

The lesson was heartfelt, because it was coming so late in the day. Roy's various crusades had often taken him away from his family. He had demonstrations to plan, courses to teach, jail terms to serve. Even when Roy wasn't gone, he was about serious business. Patricia once likened him to a statue: a steadfastly unemotional man more easily admired than embraced. Patricia loved to dance, Ralph Kohn recalled; Roy did not. Roy was not a dancer. With the children, there were some painful fissures. Patricia also had different priorities. She was sympathetic to Roy's beliefs but for years she was too busy raising four kids to devote herself equally to his great causes. By the 1970s, Patricia had also developed her own independent career aspiration. She started law school in San Jose, eventually graduating from the University of the Pacific's McGeorge School of Law in Sacramento. Once in Grass Valley, she had her own legal practice.

The Grass Valley move complicated store management, accentuating the divide between Roy and his employees. Increasingly, longtime Kepler's employee John Daniel said, Roy was butting heads with those running the stores on a day-to-day basis. Things were falling through the cracks, and Roy needed help. He turned to an old friend from Civilian Public Service, Ralph Kohn.

Kohn had served with Roy at the Laurel Training Center in Maryland before they went their separate ways. Since being discharged in the fall of 1945, Kohn had bounced around. He had worked for the Red Cross in Philadelphia, and then served as a wrangler on a United Nations Relief and Rehabilitation ship carrying supplies to South Africa, Palestine, and Mozambique. His last trip brought him $600, with which he financed his way through Iowa's Cornell College. Kohn then tried graduate school for a time, driving a cab and selling water conditioning equipment to make money. By 1962 Kohn had gravitated toward the college town of Columbia, Missouri. Not far from the University of Missouri campus, he opened the Agora House, a place for coffee and community.

Like Roy, Kohn declined as a matter of principle to pay taxes. After two years of this, his accountant suggested that the philosophical point had been made. Kohn settled up with the IRS and went on to have a good run with the Agora. Eventually, though, the building owner sold the property for a Jack in the Box restaurant, and by the summer of 1970 Kohn was once more at loose ends. That's when Roy stepped in, suggesting that his friend consider coming out to California to manage Kepler's Books & Magazines. The timing of the offer was opportune, and seemed all the more fitting as Kohn discovered the Kepler's reach. Kohn's then-girlfriend, Irene, was visiting Puerto Vallarta, Mexico. Kohn wrote her to say he would probably be heading out to Menlo Park to run a bookstore owned by a friend of his. Irene, in turn, mentioned in casual conversation to a woman she met vacationing that her friend would be taking over a bookstore in this California town.

"Is it Kepler's?" the woman asked Irene.

The woman turned out to be one of Ira's ex-wives.

In February 1971 Kohn went west. He would run Kepler's, freeing Roy to spend time in Grass Valley. It wasn't just family that drew Roy away from the day-to-day management grind. Roy gave Kohn the impression he wanted more time to write a book about pacifism.

Kohn thought the idea made sense. Roy had been writing in different forms for many years. In the early 1960s Roy had hopes of finding a publisher for an essay entitled "A Case for Open-Minded Consideration of Alternatives to War." In the same spirit, in January 1963 Roy sent to the Santa Barbara–based Center for the Study of Democratic Institutions a mimeographed manuscript detailing his latest thoughts on pacifist strategy and tactics. He had submitted a similar manuscript the year before and never heard back, nor did he receive any encouragement for his 1963 proposal. When the various book possibilities didn't pan out, a friend suggested Roy try to place his essays in *Redbook* magazine, about which Roy was skeptical.

"*Redbook* is still, I believe, essentially a women's magazine," Roy had noted in a October 16, 1963, letter, "and [it] does not easily penetrate the intellectual community, where we might first hope to find an audience for such 'far out' ideas."

Roy would struggle for years to find an audience for his densely written essays. In 1962 he would send an eighteen-page piece entitled "The Hard Way to Peace" to *Liberation* magazine. The editors suggested he slice it into two separate pieces. In 1974 he would send a thirty-five-page essay on "Thinking the Unthinkable" to *MANAS* magazine. He may even have had notions of writing fiction. Without further elaboration, one file among Roy's personal papers is marked "three separate ideas for a novel." Long-form writing success would, however, elude him. Outside of a pamphlet, the world-class bookseller would never finish writing a book, either fiction or nonfiction. And Ralph, for one, would always think that was a great shame.

At first, Kohn recalled being "a little open-mouthed" at the Kepler's scene. The spirit of the sixties still lingered. Abbie Hoffman's *Steal This Book*, Charles Reich's *The Greening of America,* and the Bantam instant version of *The Pentagon Papers* were popular. Ira still held court at the front counter. Joan was sometimes around, in part because Roy had been handling her business affairs. When Joan advised the IRS in 1973 that she would not pay taxes because of "general corruption at government levels," it was Roy who explained publicly that the tax collectors were simply going to attach Joan's bank account and take the money owed. At other times Roy's management of Joan's money was more mundane. Once he invested in a ranching venture that did not prove wildly successful.

For the next decade Kohn managed Kepler's. Bearded and big-hearted, Kohn seemed just the seasoned idealist to carry Kepler's forward. There were some customers, over the years, who assumed that Ralph *was* Roy, or perhaps Ira: a bearded, middle-aged man with an aspect that might seem, at passing glance, rather beatific. For those in the know, this was pretty funny. Placid, Ralph was not. Ralph grew to be, in fact, rather cynical about Ira, though Ira was not always around.

Ira was married again. He had gone to the University of Texas in the early 1970s to speak on nonviolence, and a student named Molly Black volunteered to drive him around. Molly was from a well-to-do family, "oil rich" and conventional, as Ira would later put it, but she was also idealistic. Ira was taken with her, and she with him. By the end of his visit, Ira asked Molly to come out to California and join him. She did. Roy saw mutual attraction. He told Ira that Molly was the nicest young woman he had met in years. Molly, in turn, was impressed with Roy. There was, Molly thought, a "muscular solidity, a solid quality" to her husband's longtime friend. Roy always looked clean and straightforward, his blue eyes radiating honesty.

"He had a clean essence to him," Molly said in an interview.

Molly and Ira set themselves up in a studio apartment near downtown Palo Alto. Roy would stay with them during his visits from Grass Valley. They might see a movie together at night, though Ira would draw the line at some of Roy's choices. Once the old friends split over Roy's desire to see *Son of Dracula,* not Ira's cup of tea. Through Ira, Molly was also introduced into broader Bay Area circles. She met Joan, her husband's most famous pupil, though the relationship was ever more complicated. Ira still adored Joan, but he also preferred the relationship within certain bounds: He was the teacher, she was the student. Joan, though, was now in her early thirties, and she had been around the world. She didn't necessarily feel herself to be a student anymore.

With the War Resisters League writ large, Joan was still *simpatico,* but she was not always available. David McReynolds queried Roy in 1972 about the possibility of organizing a Hollywood cocktail party as a WRL fundraiser. The organization was in another financial bind, its latest in an endless series. Roy asked Manny Greenhill, Joan's manager, about whether she could do a WRL benefit concert. Greenhill said the scheduling appeared tight. Joan had her latest album scheduled to come out in May 1973, entitled *Where Are You Now, My Son?* and she would be touring in support of it.

Roy would continue pressing. He'd have to; money and motivation seemed scarcer than ever for the pacifists. Roy had advised McReynolds in October 1971 that War Resisters League/West had exhausted itself and was no longer doing work of any regional significance. Its newsletter appeared only once every six months or so. It had little if any contact with nonbelievers or people over the age of thirty. It was, for all intents and purposes, a nonentity. Roy and Ira would still drive up from Palo Alto to San Francisco for monthly War Resisters League/West meetings, but it would usually be the same eight or nine people gathered in a room talking to each other. The headquarters itself, at 1380 Howard Street, occupied one large room in a building otherwise given over to various hippies and artists. Scott Ullman, who started volunteering with WRL/West and then joined the staff in 1974, recalled an old couch and an overused crank mimeograph machine. Roy, Ullman said, "took the role of the patriarch." He would question staffers about their activities and keep a close eye on the organization's finances, such as they were.

In early February 1972, maverick Republican congressman Paul McCloskey was scheduled to speak at the Menlo Park Kepler's. A Korean War hero and staunch environmentalist, McCloskey was in the midst of a quixotic bid for the GOP presidential nomination, on which behalf he had written a book called *Truth and Untruth.* On the rainy afternoon of February 6, he was set to autograph copies of his book for a Kepler's crowd. An hour before McCloskey's scheduled appearance, an anonymous caller advised the *Menlo-Atherton Recorder* newspaper staff that a bomb would go off when McCloskey spoke. Police rushed to the Menlo Park store, ordered customers out, and searched the aisles. They found nothing. McCloskey kept to his schedule, and under a gray sky he signed books in the store's parking lot.

One month later, on March 7, McCloskey's protest presidential campaign reached its modest high water mark when he gained 11 percent of the vote in the New Hampshire Republican primary. At the GOP convention in Miami, he garnered one vote. Richard Nixon steamrollered on, while the Democrats nominated South Dakota Democratic Senator George McGovern. Roy, to his own surprise, ended up backing the conventional liberal.

For years Roy had urged his fellow activists away from the standard political scene, the "liberal"-versus-"conservative" electoral trap that excluded truly fresh ideals. Roy was more radical than could be contained in the traditional partisan box. He had summed up his long-time skepticism about the hackneyed theatricality of politics in 1964, when he had aligned himself with Ira's view that conventional politics offered only an illusory choice. In that year, Roy said, it would be best to write in a symbolic presidential candidate like Martin Luther King Jr. In 1968 Roy had declared that "war protests through conventional political channels are unavailing because they are tribal rituals rich in symbolism."

So it was somewhat out of character for Roy, in 1972, to be volunteering for the Democratic Party standard-bearer George McGovern, a member of the U.S. Senate establishment.

"I find myself locally actually working for McGovern; not with any great hope or illusion, but simply to get Nixon out," Roy advised McReynolds in a June 24, 1972, letter. "But I sense in McGovern yet another dimension that is not political, really; a gut feeling he would likely be on a life trip rather than a death trip."

The simply pragmatic political calculation seemed a little unlike Roy, and so did the language. "Life trip" and "death trip" sounded like the younger Kepler's generation talking. Roy would not often employ such shorthand, nor would he throw himself into other conventional political campaigns after McGovern's resounding 1972 general election loss to Nixon.

The month after Nixon's victory, Joan was in North Vietnam. She was traveling as the guest of a North Vietnamese group called the Committee for Solidarity with the American People, along with former Nuremberg Trial prosecutor Telford Taylor, Episcopalian minister Michael Allen, and Vietnam veteran Barry Romo. They brought with them a sack of mail for American POWs and some hopes for making human contact. Then the bombs started falling, as American B-52s plastered Hanoi and Haiphong during a twelve-day blitz that became known as the Christmas Bombing. Abruptly Joan was in the very middle of the war she had opposed from the beginning. Its essence hit her when she came upon a blown-apart neighborhood where a woman hobbled around the crater that once was her home, her family.

"That woman's boy," Joan wrote later, "lay somewhere under her feet packed into an instantaneous grave of mud and she, like a wounded old cat, could only tread back and forth over the place she'd last seen him, moaning her futile song: Where are you now, my son?" (Baez 1987, 218).

The latter haunting phrase became the title of Joan's 1973 album, released in May. She and Roy and other peace activists considered the bombing spurt immoral. Nixon considered it a tool, essential in bringing North Vietnamese negotiators to the final settlement formally signed in Paris on January 27, 1973. The 23,700 Americans remaining in South Vietnam were removed over the next two months, while the peace activists did their accounting. During the entire Vietnam War, 209,517 young men were formally accused of violating draft laws. Of these, 25,000 indictments were handed down, 8,750 were convicted, and somewhat fewer than 4,000 went to prison. An additional 172,000 men were granted conscientious objector status.

The Vietnam War's ending sapped energy from the peace movement. It was much as Roy had found in his postwar reconnaissance missions for the WRL in the 1940s: Most people just wanted a return to normalcy. The War Resisters League's membership roster, which had quadrupled to 14,000 by 1973, shrank once more. Only a relative few kept carrying the flame, like those on the War Resisters League's national committee: Roy and Ira, serving along with author Grace Paley and old-timers like Jim Peck. They did what they could.

When War Resisters International General Secretary Devi Prasad wanted to spread his gospel, Roy helped arrange it. Prasad felt called to travel to Europe, Northern Ireland, India, Ceylon, and East Africa. He had a world to save, but he didn't want to write reports and do paperwork or handle other administrative hassles. Roy, Joan, and Ira felt Prasad deserved continued financial support. They respected his abilities. Knowingly, they could also appreciate how Prasad's Indian pedigree could win over Americans. Prasad had been trained at Rabindranath Tagore's school and then worked as an art instructor with Mahatma Gandhi himself. He stood in the line of direct transmission. Roy formed an ad hoc committee to fund Prasad's globetrotting. In time, this formalized into the Committee on International Nonviolence, for whom Prasad was the "ambassador at large for peace." In keeping with the post-Vietnam malaise, though, Prasad's April 1973 tour of Northern California drew disappointingly small crowds.

Prasad's tour occurred as Roy worked on another, even more challenging public event. What passed for peace in Vietnam coincided, as it happened, with the fiftieth anniversary of the War Resisters League founding. It was a time to celebrate and reflect and try, if at all possible, to avoid tearing one another apart.

Asilomar seemed a perfect, pacific getaway.

Roy and his associates with War Resisters League/West thought the state park and convention center offered everything needed for a successful anniversary. Flanked by forests and Monterey Peninsula beaches, Asilomar was close to Joan's old Carmel Valley home and the original Institute for the Study of Nonviolence. Once a Young Women's Christian Association retreat, the 107-acre conference center offered a soulful meeting hall, plenty of lodging, and a simple, honest ambience. It seemed the soothing antithesis of the confrontational urban grit in which the War Resisters League had come of age. The War Resisters League's leaders selected Asilomar as the place and set the weekend of August 6–9, 1973, as the date for the anniversary conference. Then the trouble started.

WRL activists in the Southwest had planned, for that same weekend, to demonstrate outside the Los Alamos national nuclear weapons laboratory in New Mexico, in commemoration of the fiftieth anniversary of the Hiroshima and Nagasaki bombings. They thought it quite unreasonable that their plans had been stepped on without a by-your-leave. Where was the consensus decision-making in that? Conference organizers ventured a compromise, suggesting that a day could be set aside for the Asilomar participants to drive to Lawrence Livermore National Laboratory for an A-bomb demonstration.

Roy had to help soothe ruffled feathers and resolve the calendar conflict, as the lead West Coast conference organizer. Other hassles proliferated. The understaffed New York office was slow in getting out brochures about the conference. David McReynolds explained there was just no manpower. Jim Peck, for one, had decided he was needed at the Wounded Knee demonstration in South Dakota, where there was some real action going on. Once the brochures did get out, other activists complained about the conference cost, $36 plus transportation. McReynolds tried explaining that it would simply mean one less rock concert, one less stash of pot or vodka.

Roy handwrote invitations to every peace-minded luminary he could think of. Some he knew well, others had crossed his path, and still others he knew not at all. Roy had long since lost any inhibition about introducing himself and his cause. He wrote poet Kenneth Rexroth, the fellow Civilian Public Service alumnus who had been a compelling presence during KPFA's early years. He wrote New York City congresswoman Shirley Chisholm and civil rights icon Coretta Scott King. He wrote old allies, like one-time *Politics* editor Dwight MacDonald and sociologist Theodore Roszak. He wrote those whom he had not seen in decades, like World War II–era WRL chairman Evan Thomas, and the luminaries he had apparently met before, like National Book Award–winning poet Robert Bly, the founder in 1965 of the American Writers Against the Vietnam War. He wrote psychotherapist Jerome Frank, who had met Roy in the early 1960s when they attended the Grindstone Island peace camp together. Since then Frank had attained a worldwide reputation with books like *Persuasion and Healing*. Frank wrote back, assuring Roy he remembered his bookstore from years before but offering his regrets about not being able to attend the conference.

From poet and City Lights' owner Lawrence Ferlinghetti, Roy asked for help in financing the program. Ferlinghetti said he couldn't spare any cash contributions, as his own bookstore was not faring so well financially. New York City congresswoman Bella Abzug sent her regrets as well, saying she was taking a much-needed vacation. Even some WRL intimates, who had once devoted themselves fully to the organization, had other plans. Bayard Rustin, Roy's marching partner from many years back, sent his regrets in a sentence or two. Abe Kaufman, who had spent nineteen years as WRL executive secretary, begged off. Several decades' worth of personal histories, rivalries, and tangled relationships had to be negotiated, not only in the invitations but in the selection of speakers. Slowly, though, the positive RSVPs began coming in. Daniel Ellsberg could make it. So could Joan and her sister Mimi.

"All the letters Roy wrote made the difference," recalled Mandy Carter, who had begun working for War Resisters League/West in 1969.

McReynolds, from WRL headquarters, urged Roy to keep the program looking ahead and not gazing nostalgically back at marches of yore. McReynolds further urged Roy not to choose David Dellinger as the speaker on WRL's history, for fear the acerbic peace veteran would focus on the League's many failures. Even titles incited dispute. Roy suggested "Whither WRL?" Too stodgy, McReynolds thought; he countered with "2001 and Beyond."

McReynolds himself was of an in-between generation. Born in 1929, McReynolds had been too young to face the Civilian Public Service camps or federal prisons that had shaped World War II radical pacifists. He was a self-professed Marxist who had debated with Roy over whether the North Vietnamese should be given a pass for committing violence. After visiting Hanoi, McReynolds once insisted to Roy that the North Vietnamese had a certain existential integrity and a history of being victimized. Their violence could be excused. McReynolds, likewise, saw some justification in black Americans carrying weapons. After all, they had been subjected to so many years of racist violence. Roy thought McReynolds was turning a blind eye to brutal behavior; being a victim did not justify violence. The two men's debating, in person and in letters, reflected the broader debate over means, ends, and justifications that consumed the War Resisters League.

Still, for all the agonizing and second-guessing, some six hundred people signed up for the conference. Ellsberg, in particular, was a real coup. He was then at the height of his fame, having had the criminal charges involving purloining of the Pentagon Papers thrown out just a few months before. He drew precious media with a preliminary San Francisco news conference that preceded the main event.

On Monday night, August 6, Roy stood onstage at the stone-and-redwood Asilomar lodge and welcomed the audience. To kick it off, Roy introduced Joan and her sister Mimi. For a precious moment, their voices blended in song, souls convened in the name of peace.

After Igal Roodenko and Larry Gara spoke of the WRL's history, Roy returned to speak of what must come next. We find ourselves members of a still-tiny minority, Roy told the audience. We are isolated from the Left, the Right, and the Center. We must start, once again, from scratch. But look on the bright side, Roy offered: There is nowhere to go but up.

McReynolds, in his own opening speech, opined that just as power corrupts, so does powerlessness corrupt, and absolute powerlessness corrupt absolutely. The wording nagged at Roy, who left the conference still thinking about where McReynolds' reasoning fell down. It was a clever turn of phrase, Roy conceded, but he thought McReynolds offered no evidence in support of the sophistry.

Kepler's Books & Magazines was represented well at the conference. Ira joined Lee Swenson, who once had hammered together Kepler's bookshelves before going on to head the Institute for the Study of Nonviolence, in leading a morning session on what the next fifty years might hold for the WRL. Store manager Ralph Kohn sat in on other sessions. Joan herself spoke at a session about Amnesty International. There were talks of war tax resistance and gay liberation, an issue of particular interest to the openly gay McReynolds.

The day before the anniversary conference was scheduled to end, Joan told Roy and Mandy Carter that farmworker organizer César Chávez was in dire need of support for one of his demonstrations. Abruptly, Carter recalled, a number of activists hit the road in a caravan that included Joan and Ellsberg, aiming to reinforce Chávez in Fresno. It meant the anniversary over which Roy had spent so much time ended prematurely, though Roy himself took a philosophical attitude.

"Roy said, 'this is what nonviolence is all about: when things come up, you have to go do it,'" Carter said.

19

The New Revolution

Steve Wozniak knew Kepler's well before he was The Woz.

In the mid-1960s, young Wozniak went to Kepler's not for the counterculture but for the most conventional of reasons. He went for the books. The revolution Wozniak subsequently helped foment would, like others, have Kepler's roots though Roy himself never took the full measure of it.

Steve Wozniak was born in 1950 and grew up in Sunnyvale, a deceptively bland suburb south of Menlo Park. His Cal Tech–trained father, like many fathers in Sunnyvale and surrounding towns, was immersed in classified projects. The placid suburbs masked a world of secrets. At home there was much that could not be talked about. Wozniak's father, Jerry, worked for Lockheed. The giant aircraft, missiles, and space firm, and its military contracts, had long been a target of Roy's and the activists within War Resisters League/West, but Wozniak's dad didn't take the protests personally. Jerry Wozniak would still hit up Kepler's in search of science and engineering books, and he would take young Steve with him.

Kepler's might have been, The Woz figured later, the only store that could satisfy some of his father's intellectual and textual needs. Young Wozniak himself bought books about engineering and ham radio operations at Kepler's, including, he believes, an updated version of Stanford professor Frederick Terman's classic 1955 text *Electronic and Radio Engineering*, which he considered the best electrical engineering book ever.

"There was no bookstore like it," Wozniak said. "Kepler's was as important a source of good knowledge in my field as my college courses were."

↓

Drive a stake into the ground at Kepler's Menlo Park store.

Now, author John Markoff imagined in his book *What the Dormouse Said: How the 60s Counterculture Shaped the Personal Computer Industry*, draw a five-mile circle around the center point. This is Ground Zero for the personal computer revolution (Markoff 2005, xiv). Markoff's imagery underscored Kepler's central place in the Silicon Valley firmament. The store sold the books that propelled progress. The atmosphere nurtured young rebels. The whole neighborhood was a hothouse.

Stanford University, of course, loomed right next door, along with mainframe standbys like Hewlett-Packard. Half a mile east of Kepler's, the Stanford Research Institute, as it was originally known, employed the researchers who in the early 1960s developed the computer mouse and other elements of the human-computer interface. This same research center, in 1969, went online with ARPANET, the first computer network. Five miles to the west, in the rolling foothills framing the Stanford campus, the Stanford Artificial Intelligence Laboratory, started in 1963 by computer scientist John McCarthy, nourished pathfinding programmers. In the Stanford Research Park, established as an industrial park in 1951 under Professor Terman's nurturance, Xerox's Palo Alto Research Center arose in 1970. It was the home to Free U alumni, Kepler's customers, and freethinkers who came up with laser printing, graphical user interfaces, personal work stations, and more. Around the corner from Kepler's was a nimble nonprofit called the Portola Institute. This had helped seed Stewart Brand's *Whole Earth Catalog* as well as another radical joint called the People's Computer Center, likewise located just around the corner from Kepler's.

Even before it was dubbed Silicon Valley, in a felicitous headline accompanying writer Don Hoefler's 1971 series in *Electronic News*, the region was home to engineers whose crew cuts could camouflage a Kepleresque turn of mind.

Several founders of the first Stanford Industrial Park tenant, Varian Associates, embraced progressive politics and Socialist ideology even as they produced klystron tubes for the military (Lecuyer 2006, 94). Rebellion, rejection of the corporate status quo, drove growth. In October 1957, the same year Roy, Ira, and Al Baez started the Peninsula Committee for Nuclear Disarmament, bright young engineers dissatisfied with the heavy-handed management at Shockley Semiconductor declared their independence and celebrated their corporate freedom at Rickey's Hyatt House. As it happened, this was the same El Camino Real fixture where several years later Jerry Garcia and Sara Ruppenthal would hold a wedding reception following their meeting at Kepler's. No two cultures might seem farther apart than Jerry Garcia's bohemians and Robert Noyce's engineers, but they had something in common beyond Rickey's Hyatt House. They each determinedly went their own way, and others followed. Author Tom Wolfe, the chronicler of Ken Kesey et al., likewise recognized in his lesser-known work "Two Young Men Who Went West" how Noyce rejected social hierarchy and traditional status symbols at his new company, Fairchild Semiconductor. What mattered was the thing itself, the work and not the corporate trappings. In its own way, it was antiestablishment.

The region's scientists and engineers had several options for their book-buying needs. For pure utility, the efficient acquisition of technical books and magazines, other bookstores might surpass Kepler's. The Stanford University Bookstore served up texts. Stacey's in downtown Palo Alto, part of a small San Francisco–based chain founded by a physician in the 1920s, had an intelligently selected science and engineering collection. Roy himself had no particular inclination toward hardcore science, and his book buyers were liberal arts types through and through. When Roy bought his first computer to track book orders, no one seemed to know how to use it. But as a general proposition, if there were words to sell, Kepler's Books & Magazines would carry them. The store's expansive collection alone could draw the Bay Area's science and engineering crowd from the Stanford Artificial Intelligence Laboratory and beyond.

"Most of the people in SAIL used to go there," said engineer Les Earnest, one of the influential lab's early leaders.

Starting with the basics, then: Kepler's Books & Magazines sold the information that propelled the computing revolution. Personal computing cheerleader Bob Albrecht would tell the *Intelligent Machines Journal* of August 13, 1979, that Kepler's was one of the best-stocked sources of computer books in the region. Others shared his view. A reporter for *Interface Age,* a short-lived periodical, spelled the store's name wrong but nonetheless got the important idea right when he reported in June 1979 that Kepler's in "catering to computer aficionados [has] one of the most complete line[s] of computer books I have seen." Many Silicon Valley pioneers, like Steve Wozniak, gravitated toward Kepler's during their formative years.

"I bought hundreds of books at Kepler's that had deep effects on my life," Douglas Hofstadter, Pulitzer Prize–winning author and professor of cognitive science and comparative literature at Indiana University, recalled in an interview, citing his "very first calculus book, a ton of other math books, and many books on various languages, as well as books on art and philosophy and so forth and so on."

It helped that Roy was always finding ways to stock more. On August 1, 1974, Kepler's Menlo Park store had expanded into an adjoining 32,000-square-foot space, formerly occupied by an automobile body shop. The expansion more than doubled the store size, adding sixty new bookshelves. Store manager Ralph Kohn said the "open and airy" space, naturally lit with new skylights, would provide breathing room and a venue for public presentations by authors. The 1974 expansion broadened Kepler's reputation for comprehensiveness. *The Joy of Sex,* by World War II pacifist and former *Peace News* contributor Alex Comfort, sizzled off the shelves that year along with Erica Jong's *Fear of Flying.* Engineers could get their tingles along with their tech specs.

Alan Kay was one of the store's frequent denizens at the time. The intellectually adventurous computer scientist arrived in 1970 at the newly opened Xerox Palo Alto Research Center, several years out of an engineering doctorate program at the University of Utah. At Xerox, he brought the idea of the portable Dynabook, a conceptual precursor for the laptop computers to come. He drove the idea of networked work stations, developed what became known as object-oriented programming, and was the original designer of the now ubiquitous graphical user interface. For books, he might meander by Stewart Brand's Whole Earth Truck Store, the Stanford Bookstore, or Bell's Books, but mostly he went to Kepler's.

"Many other Xerox PARC folks were [there], also," Kay recalled in an interview. "It was pretty much the only reasonable place to go for many kinds of desirable books."

Beyond books, the Kepler's community and the personal computer revolutionaries shared a common DNA. Novelist and one-time Kepler's customer Robert Stone knew the score. Looking back at the Bay Area's transition from the sixties to the seventies, Stone recognized that "a certain bohemian style" informed both the "transistor-microchip postindustrial revolution" and the earlier, mindful drug experimentation (Stone 2007, 80). Theodore Roszak, the sociologist and former *Peace News* writer inspired by Roy, specifically traced the relationship in his 1986 book *From Satori to Silicon Valley*. Roszak recognized the connections between the rise of the personal computer and the eruption of the counterculture, itself a term Roszak was credited with coining in his 1968 classic *The Making of a Counterculture*. Books and computers both expanded the mind, sometimes beyond conventional boundaries.

"We were part of the late 1960s, hippies, anti-war, members of the Free Speech Movement, that was going to fix all the problems of the world, even if it took a year or two," Free U veteran and personal computer pioneer Jim Warren said (Kaplan 1999, 93).

Markoff elaborated on this connection in *What the Dormouse Said*. The spirit of the sixties, of liberation and self-empowerment, was made manifest with the personal computer. In the course of a decade, Markoff noted, computing "went from being dismissed as a tool of bureaucratic control to being embraced as a symbol of individual expression and liberation" (Markoff 2005, xii). And much of it happened, Markoff said, on the Midpeninsula, where there occurred "an epochal intersection of science, politics, art and commerce."

Kepler's country, in other words.

The intersection wasn't always congenial. Defense Department contracts drove much of the early Silicon Valley innovation, a wedding between technology and policy that activists wanted to disrupt. The ultimately unsuccessful Building Peace campaign of the War Resisters League/West from the mid-1960s was one approach, when young activists hoped to mess with the minds of military contractors. More kinetically, a gathering protest that in 1969 came to be known as the April 3rd Movement drove Stanford to shed the Stanford Research Institute, following a series of sit-ins, tear-gassed demonstrations, and graffiti-scrawling along the lines of "SRI Kills." SRI computers were considered tools of war, and the activists wanted no part of that.

But computers, per se, were not the enemy. They were tools, which could be useful.

The Free U offered early courses in Fortran programming under the category of "People's Technology." Alternatively, Free U students could study the abacus, which was dubbed "the poor man's adding machine." *The Free You* magazine, during its exuberant prime, published prescient articles about personal computing and artificial intelligence. A January 1968 article discussed the potential for computers to change lives. Several months later, computer scientist Larry Tesler, who was one of Kepler's volunteer store-watchers during the attacks, used *The Free You* to discuss Stanford's use of a new IBM computer system. Several pages away from Tesler's critique, the magazine published Roy's own "Testament of a Radical Pacifist." Pacifism and computer power were, literally, bound together in the pages of *The Free You.*

John McCarthy, coiner of the phrase "artificial intelligence" and founder in 1964 of the Stanford Artificial Intelligence Laboratory, wrote about "the thinking computer" in the magazine's August 1968 issue. About the same time, McCarthy donated a teletype terminal

so that Free U volunteers could more efficiently enter course catalog information. Stewart Brand, in *The Free You*'s June 1969 edition,
explored the possibilities of "using computer-generated symbols to
enhance mental functioning."

Kepler's and the Free U were attracting fresh thinkers. One, Marc
Porat, was a Palo Alto native who threw himself into Free U work that
eventually included organizing rock concerts at El Camino Park. In
time, holding a Stanford graduate degree in economics, Porat would
be credited with coining the term "information economy" as an Apple
Computer worker (Markoff 2005, 114). The word was also spreading
beyond the Bay Area. John McCarthy told a friend, air force veteran
and MIT professor Ed Fredkin, about *The Free You*. Fredkin was
intrigued. Here was something that allowed anyone to contribute,
freely. "John arranged for me to get a subscription to the catalogue
and I found that I agreed with him," Fredkin recalled in a 2010 interview. "The catalogue itself was interesting and had literary merit."

Fredkin ended up getting more involved than he planned, after
McCarthy told him *The Free You* needed money for an offset press
that would permit color printing. At McCarthy's urging, Fredkin said
he helped arrange for about $5,000 to be provided. The investment
soured. Fredkin said McCarthy subsequently reported that the Venceremos radicals who had taken over the Free U had converted the
once-colorful periodical into a militant propaganda organ. Fredkin
saw the direction of things when he received a Free U periodical that
included a headline about ten ways to Off a Pig. Kill a policeman, in
other words. Fredkin hadn't signed up for that.

Other, more peaceful, Free U cultural offerings could be found at
the Menlo Park home of Bob Albrecht. A former Control Data Corp.
worker, Albrecht spilled over with ideas, with everything. During the
evenings, Albrecht led a thriving Greek dancing class for the Free U.
During the days, he proselytized about how computing power would
change the world. In October 1972 Albrecht had come out with the
first issue of a tabloid newspaper called the *People's Computer Company*, proclaiming that "computers are mostly used against people

instead of for people. Used to control people instead of to free them. Time to change all that . . ." (Levy 2001, 172).

Inside a drab Menlo Park office complex around the corner from Kepler's, Albrecht's People's Computer Center was festooned with blinking Christmas tree lights, a Digital Equipment Corp. minicomputer, and terminals for all. The center offered classes, public computer access for fifty cents an hour, and Wednesday potluck dinners. Bookshelves offered a circulating selection of science fiction paperbacks that at one time might have been bought at Kepler's but were now, tattered but readable, in the public domain (Levy 2001, 173).

Larry Tesler embodied the overlap between Kepler's, computers, and the Free U.

Slender and somewhat shy, the Bronx High School of Science graduate had been delving into programming since he entered Stanford in the fall of 1961. One fine day, Tesler had heard Joan Baez sing at Stanford's White Plaza. She introduced Ira to the crowd, intriguing Tesler. Tesler made his way to Kepler's, where he became a regular, enjoying chats with Ira at the checkout counter. Tesler had just put himself on two tracks, computers and counterculture. By the spring of 1968 he had grown a beard and was active in the Free U. He and his friend Dorothy Bender once offered a class entitled "It's a Beautiful Day!" It was, the catalog explained, a "one day happening" and a chance to "enjoy and feel ourselves and each other" at San Gregorio Beach (Markoff 2005, 116–19).

Tesler and Bender shared other notions too. Through the Free U, Bender taught one of the area's first computer programming courses. Tesler was juggling his work at Stanford's Artificial Intelligence Laboratory with his Kepler's and Free U passions. In late 1968 he combined his interests by leading a class provocatively entitled "How to End the IBM Monopoly." A friend from the artificial intelligence lab, engineer Les Earnest, was among about eight people to show up for the first session at a house in East Palo Alto.

"It appeared to me that everyone other than Larry and I were from IBM, based on attire and conduct," Earnest said in an interview.

In fact, Earnest and Tesler later concluded, two of the Free U students were essentially spies for IBM, checking out the opposition. The Big Blue monitoring did not deter the Free U men, and in the next quarter beginning in January 1969 Tesler started leading another class targeting the IBM monopoly. But that January 17, the outgoing Johnson administration's Justice Department filed an antitrust lawsuit against IBM. Tesler recalled marveling at the similarities between the Justice Department's arguments and the case being built informally by the Free U class participants. The federal government having finally caught up with the Midpeninsula Free University, Tesler figured the course had become moot; he canceled it.

Another night, at the Free U's offices, not far from Kepler's on El Camino Real, Tesler and James Warren, a like-minded soul, were finishing the latest edition of a Free U publication. Warren had been teaching math to the polite young ladies of Notre Dame College until word spread of his growing predilection for nudist parties. It was time for him to go. That was fine, because Warren had alternatives. In the fluid world of the Free U, he naturally moved into leadership positions. So there they were, Warren and Tesler, cutting course descriptions out of typewritten pages and gluing them to print-ready sheets, and some new ideas popped to life.

"We have these big computer monitors at the [computer] lab," Tesler told Warren, "and we could really just display these pages up on the screen. You could just cut and paste right in the screen, and we wouldn't have to do this stuff anymore."

But how, Warren asked, would the computer text be transferred onto real paper? It won't be long, Tesler suggested, before technology had a solution for that problem (Markoff 2005, 129). Tesler and Warren would keep thinking about many similar problems, through the Free U years and beyond. Warren would go on to cofound, in 1977, the West Coast Computer Faire, which would become the largest personal computer convention of its kind. Tesler would join the Xerox Palo Alto Research Center and, later, serve as chief scientist for the upstart young computer company called Apple.

↓

Rolling Stone sold well. It was a Kepler's kind of magazine.

Founded in 1967 as a weekly journal for the rock-and-roll crowd, the magazine kept the counterculture in touch with what was happening. In the December 1972 issue, author Stewart Brand grabbed readers' lapels from the start. "Ready or not," Brand announced, "computers are coming to the people. That's the good news, maybe the best since psychedelics." Then, in an article entitled "Spacewar: Fanatic Life and Symbolic Death Among the Computer Bums," Brand steered readers through the Bay Area's artificial intelligence labs and think tanks where the future was apparently being born.

"These are heads, most of them," Brand observed approvingly. "Half or more of computer science is heads."

Heads meant the hip and the turned on, those who, like Brand himself, had been hanging out at Kepler's for years. Brand's *Rolling Stone* article, and the accompanying pictures by twenty-three-year-old photographer Annie Leibovitz, proved a coalescing moment. Another came in January 1975, when technically avid Kepler's browsers picked up a copy of *Popular Electronics* with a cover article about "the first minicomputer in a kit," called the Altair 8800. As had Brand's article before it, the *Popular Electronics* story was positively euphoric: "The era of the computer in every home, a favorite topic among science fiction writers, has arrived!" The article was a revelation, inspiring, among others, Harvard students Bill Gates and Steve Ballmer to go into the business of programming.

Fred Moore, too, found the words intoxicating. In 1959 Moore's solitary protest against U.C. Berkeley's ROTC mandate had inspired other young men like Lee Swenson, the one-time Kepler's bookshelf-builder who went on to head the Institute for the Study of Nonviolence during its final Palo Alto years. Moore himself was fully committed to righteous causes, serving seventeen months in prison for draft resistance. Once free, Moore held to his principles. He would shun bank accounts because banks make war. He considered money to be obsolete, anti-life. When he ended up with $15,000 given away by Stewart Brand in June 1971 following the expiration of the *Whole Earth Catalog,* Moore had ultimately handed over the money to San Francisco–based community activists whose efforts included time-share computing (Markoff 2005, 196).

Moore himself had started getting involved with computers, operating for a while from Brand's Whole Earth Truck Store around the corner from Kepler's and then working on the Stanford campus. Through the People's Computer Company he taught computing classes to kids. He saw computers' potential: Huge. In early 1975, following publication of the influential *Popular Electronics* Altair issue, Moore began posting signs through the Bay Area announcing a meeting for an "amateur computer users group." Or, as some preferred it, a "homebrew computer club." The signs invited one and all to a March 5 meeting at a Menlo Park home owned by Moore's friend Gordon French. On a rainy night, thirty-two participants including Bob Albrecht and Steve Wozniak gathered in French's jam-packed garage. Moore took notes (Levy 2001, 202).

By March 15 Moore had produced the first edition of the *Home-brew Computer Club Newsletter.* The club's second meeting convened at the Stanford Artificial Intelligence Laboratory in the foothills, courtesy of John McCarthy. The fourth meeting was held in the Peninsula School's old mansion, that freethinker's haven where Ira had once taught, the school itself founded by the mother of the pacifist who was with Roy when his brother died. The new revolutionaries were following in the footsteps of those who came before.

Many were strictly interested in computing. Others, including Moore, saw a bigger picture. The *Homebrew Computer Club Newsletter*'s June 1975 issue tellingly asked, "Why did the Big Companies miss this [personal computer] market? They were busy selling overpriced machines to each other and the government and the military."

The Kepler's magazine racks were thickening with journals tracking the new developments. Brand, who had seen the wave coming early, was selling the Summer 1975 issue of his new magazine *CoEvolution Quarterly,* with a special seventeen-page section on personal computers. *Byte* magazine arrived on the stands with its inaugural issue in September 1975, including coverage of the Homebrew Computer Club. By January 1976, alongside the more conventional fare, Kepler's customers could find the first edition of the dementedly titled *Dr. Dobb's Journal of Computer Calisthenics and Orthodontia*. This was the offspring of a small computer newsletter begun by Bob Albrecht's People's Computer Company. His editor was Free U alumnus Jim Warren.

The Homebrew Computer Club kept meeting, every two weeks. Into the role of moderator arrived Lee Felsenstein, an engineering dropout from Berkeley who had previously been anointed "military editor" of the *Berkeley Barb* during the late sixties' most combative chapters. Kepler's had always stocked the *Barb*, though Roy sometimes abhorred the paper's militant enthusiasms. One night in 1969, the Stanford navy ROTC shack had burned down in what was presumed to be an act of revolutionary violence. It was just the kind of militaristic spasm Roy detested, but others admired. "No one in the Red Guard seems to know who the arsonists might be," the *Barb* winked, "nor are they interested in inquiring too diligently." In the lead-up to the October 1967 Oakland Induction Center sit-ins, Felsenstein had trained demonstration monitors in the use of walkie-talkies and helped finger some police informants who had infiltrated the operation.

In time Felsenstein found his way to the same San Francisco community computing project whose benefactors included Fred Moore. Moore had performed his role admirably in the opening stages of the Homebrew Computer Club, taking notes and producing the biweekly newsletter that helped bind everyone together. Still, he was not an engineer or a technologist at heart. He fretted over the use of technology, while the hackers embraced it for its own sake. By the summer of 1975, the Homebrew Computer Club was humming along and Moore was confronting other issues. He had broken up with a girlfriend. He was unsettled. He needed to recommit himself to the cause of peace. He was ready to walk across the continental United States.

In 1961 the San Francisco to Moscow peace walk had riveted public attention. The audacity had elevated the stunt to the level of a statement.

People remembered it. Struggling for money, membership, and relevance in a post–Vietnam War world, the War Resisters League joined with the American Friends Service Committee, Fellowship of Reconciliation, and others in August 1975 with a call for a new transcontinental venture. The Continental Walk for Disarmament and Social Justice was self-consciously patterned after past ventures. It would be a relay of peace and justice groups, passing the torch from town to town. It would be a generational relay too, as marchers reached out to those who came before them (Leonard and MacLean 1977).

Fifteen or twenty hard-core activists planned to cross the entire country. Others would join for only a short distance. The War Resisters League/West headquarters in San Francisco produced flyers, mapped out routes, and obtained rally permits. Joan Baez and other peace celebrities like Benjamin Spock endorsed it. The first band of walkers stepped off on January 21, 1976, in the Northern California town of Ukiah. By January 31, a sunny, blue-sky day, some eight hundred marchers and supporters gathered in San Francisco's Union Square for a pep rally. Several dozen enthusiasts, filled with the spirit of the moment, announced their intention to walk the entire continent. Off they went, south again, down the Peninsula. Roy joined the march there, swelling the crowd as it streamed into Palo Alto.

Roy remembered from two decades earlier the San Francisco to Moscow peace walk. Publicly, that earlier peace walk had struck certain chords. It had flair. Internally, though, Roy knew it had been undermined by personality and strategy conflicts. He feared the same dangers threatened the 1976 Continental Walk. After participating during the day, Roy had a good talk with Bob Swann. Roy could trust Swann, a conscientious objector who had served two years in prison during World War II. Already, Swann advised Roy, early storm warnings were rising. Organizers lacked the capacity to handle a large crowd. Several would-be walkers seemed too literally footloose, mentally unbalanced even. Nobody seemed to have learned important lessons from the earlier transcontinental walk. Roy subsequently advised David McReynolds that he feared the Continental Walk would prove embarrassing, evidence of the pacifists' continuing ineptness.

The marchers moved on from the Bay Area and then stopped in Southern California while organizers tried to impose more order. The Walk's myriad internal dramas were absorbing so much energy that there was nothing left for the greater causes of nuclear disarmament and global peace. McReynolds and Joanne Sheehan from the War Resisters League flew out to California, and for three days in Thousand Oaks they talked through the problems. The Walk resumed, then halted again in Indio. Finally the organizers compiled a list and posted it, identifying twenty-four who could keep walking and twenty-seven who had to leave ("Report on the Continental Walk" 1976).

One of the disrupters was the painfully earnest Fred Moore, recently moved on from his Homebrew Computer Club activism. For some people, he was just too much to handle. Organizers, trying to regain control of the Walk, determined they would nonviolently but firmly escort Moore away if he tried to show his face again.

"Fred was a troublemaker, but he was a very sincere troublemaker," recalled former WRL/West staffer Scott Ullman, who worked on the Walk. Put another way, Ullman added, "he was an anarchist."

On the marchers finally went, safely un-Moored. In New Mexico they gathered outside the gates of Los Alamos National Laboratory, Lawrence Livermore's sister nuclear weapons lab. In the Midwest they convened with Roy's old compatriot David Dellinger. Eventually, taking various side trips, the walkers reached the Pentagon for a demonstration on the cold, cloudy morning of October 18. Publicly, organizers played up the successes. Privately, the Walk organizers recognized that serious problems had bedeviled them all along the way. Some felt the Continental Walk fell short because organizers placed too much faith in individuals to behave appropriately. Perhaps, McReynolds mused afterward, the New York leaders of the War Resisters League had trusted too much.

"Bullshit!" Roy exclaimed, in an April 20, 1976, letter to McReynolds. "This was not an error of trust, except that we could trust a significant percentage of our 'anarchist' brethren [and sisters?] to act as they did. We know the whole scenario, and have for many years.

"We know all about our eccentrics, our 'unstable contingent,' and our youthful, innocent fanatics and anarchists who move only to their own drummer," Roy went on. "Until we learn how to deal with them in advance and with forethought, our enterprises will be rocky."

But peace ventures weren't the only enterprises to face rocky times. Time had been taking a toll on the three great Bay Area bookstores, the triumvirate of City Lights, Cody's, and Kepler's.

20

Transitions

Kepler's and its Bay Area bookselling kin staged history, every business day.

They were Beatnik Central, Where the sixties began. Books could be bought anywhere. The Bay Area triumvirate of Kepler's, Cody's, and City Lights offered something more. They were living theater, for the reenactment of familiar scenes: Ira Holding Forth, the Poet amid the Stacks. They signified. When Robert Stone's end-of-the-sixties novel *Dog Soldiers* was being turned into a movie inexplicably retitled *Who'll Stop the Rain,* with the screenplay co-written by former Kepler's customers Stone and Judith Rascoe, the filmmakers wanted a place that conveyed the decade. So in January 1977 they dressed up Cody's Books with old antiwar posters for one atmosphere-setting scene. The setting projected verisimilitude, allowing clued-in viewers to nudge each other in recognition: That's Cody's, the real deal!

The true cognoscenti, though, were hip to a different fact. In Stone's even darker vision of a book, the *Dog Soldiers* character had worked not at an esteemed bookstore but at a mob-run porn theater (Cody and Cody 1992, 179).

Bay Area bookstore insiders knew other plot twists as well. By the time *Who'll Stop the Rain* was being filmed, some of the stores' proprietors were feeling, well, written-out or distracted. At City Lights, Lawrence Ferlinghetti was publishing his poetry and traveling widely, leaving the store's administration in the hands of manager Shig Murao. A veteran both of the army and of the Japanese-American internment camps, Murao was considered by San Francisco–based author Herb Gold and others as the true soul of City Lights. Over time, though, he had also become increasingly infirm. A Coca-Cola fiend, known to suck down a dozen or more Cokes a day, Murao suffered a stroke and developed diabetes in the mid-1970s. His misfortunes multiplied when he took a bad fall in the store's basement, and suffered another stroke. Hospitalized, Murao finally left City Lights in the late 1970s, embittered as were some of his writer allies over Ferlinghetti's unwillingness to take the ailing man back as manager.

Fred Cody was worn down too. Cody's Books had been caught in the Berkeley crossfire for years. When police shot tear gas during one demonstration or another, the panicked, choking demonstrators would crash into Cody's seeking respite. Fred and Pat would offer water, repair the shattered glass, and await the next round of incoming. Even when the demonstrations calmed, Berkeley was never perfectly calm. By 1974, utterly fatigued, Fred was letting it be known that Cody's Books was on the market. Roy said he might bid for the store, and the longtime friends talked about the potential sale. Ultimately, Roy concluded he did not want to take on such a large commitment (Cody and Cody 1992, 170).

The Codys would eventually sell their store in 1977 to a one-time graduate student named Andy Ross, previously the proprietor of a quiet Sonoma bookstore. It was a good sale, for buyer and seller alike. Ross, thirty-seven at the time, brought fresh energy to Cody's while retaining the seasoned spirit of the place. For a good long while, Ross kept Cody's alive.

Down the Peninsula, at Kepler's, Roy seemed to be falling out of touch.

In some ways it was a literal fact. Roy was spending much of his time in Grass Valley, 170 miles from Menlo Park. He would drive down to the Bay Area for a week or so every month, staying at Claire Feder's Atherton home or another friend's house, and then return to the foothills. His hands were off the tiller, even, at times, when he was physically present. He sometimes befuddled workers. He would order expensive books from the likes of Princeton University Press without noticing that the same titles were already two-deep on the shelves. Roy was losing it, some began to think.

"Ralph always used to say to me, 'you should have known him in the old days,'" one former Kepler's employee said.

Employee relations frayed. Book thefts epitomized the problem. Roy had, in fact, a longstanding conviction that his employees could not really be trusted. Once, clerk Falline Danforth was in the Menlo Park office when she overheard Roy talking about why he paid workers so little. Danforth, who started off in 1972 making about $1.85 an hour, heard Roy explain that he kept pay low on the assumption that the workers were making up the difference with theft. The constant petty thievery vexed Roy. Finally, in the late 1970s, he made his accusation known. At a general meeting of the store employees, Roy revealed that he had hired a private investigator to stop the bookstore stealing. It was a rational decision, Roy figured. He needed facts. Sometime, he knew, an investigator could get to the bottom of things. A decade before, in the late sixties, he had hired a San Jose private detective to help crack the store-bombing case.

But the employees felt affronted, former employee John Daniel recalled. *Roy Kepler*, of all people, had hired a private dick.

"Because of Roy's political integrity, some of the employees thought he was Jesus," said former Kepler's book buyer Susan MacDonald, "and they were miffed when, as a business owner he acted like an owner and not a comrade."

MacDonald's first job for Kepler's had been to organize the late-night store watches during the 1968 attacks. By the mid-1970s, when MacDonald was a buyer for the store, the attacks were the stuff of legend, invariably described as store "bombings." In the mythic conception, it was if American Nazis had been shouting "Heil Hitler" while tossing grenades through the windows. The reality had been rather different, but the attacks, however misremembered, had helped cement the store's reputation. That only made it harder for those who expected one thing and got another. Buff Bradley, another Kepler's book buyer during the 1970s, explained that "Kepler's was a place that felt to the workers like a community, like a collective, and they believed that it should be run like that. They were upset and hurt that Roy didn't feel the same way."

This was the thing. Roy might be a pacifist and tax resister, but he was also a money maker, a businessman. A tightwad, some thought. The cars he drove, Ira's wife Molly Black recalled, were invariably clunkers. The clothes he wore came straight off the rack, cheap and polyester. Roy was not a generous tipper. He was a Depression kid, hoarding his pennies. Extravagance disturbed him. While helping handle Joan Baez's finances, he watched her accounts so carefully, Ira said, that "she was afraid to ask him for her own money."

Joan eventually stopped using Roy as her business manager.

Roy's peers understood this. They knew where he had come from, his Great Depression roots. But among the younger Kepler's set, some disgruntlement set in. Roy, in a word, had become the Establishment. At one interminable Kepler's staff meeting during the 1970s, employee and longtime peace activist Hank Maiden recalled, Roy was "openly attacked for being oppressive, insufferable and dominating." Maiden, who had once managed the San Francisco office of the Central Committee for Conscientious Objectors, wasn't himself always simpatico with Roy but he cringed at the disrespectful confrontation. The conflicts kept recurring as the freethinkers attracted by the Kepler's reputation ran into Roy's insistence that they abide by his directives.

In the late 1970s one Menlo Park staffer drew a written rebuke from Roy for bringing his young son into the store and allowing him to play with the cash register. The staffer, Roy added, had also cost the store $24.50 by selling a copy of the *Random House Encyclopedia* at an inappropriate discount rate. Further transgressions could lead to termination, Roy warned sternly. Another frustrated Kepler's employee quit in the summer of 1979, went home, cried for a long time, and then wrote Roy a heartfelt letter. This young clerk told Roy of how he had come to the store with one notion of Kepler's Books & Magazines, only to find something altogether different. The clerk wanted love and hope, not endless crises, anger, and alienation.

Most vividly, Roy was clashing with a store clerk named John Chandler, whose appearance spuriously struck some as the very epitome of the Kepler's spirit.

Born in Indiana in 1929, Chandler had done an air force stint as a radar technician and eventually went into chain variety store management. He was living in San Jose in October 1967 when a mutual friend suggested he check out this Menlo Park hippie bookstore. Chandler wasn't a bibliophile, nor was he all that impressed by the layout of Kepler's Books & Magazines when he entered. It was dusty and dirty. It wasn't bright and shiny.

But the right vibe was there, and by the time Chandler had returned to his San Jose home, he'd gotten a telephone call offering him a job at Kepler's. Chandler would stay for more than a decade. With his beard and mountain man stylings, he could seem the quintessential Kepler's counterculture guy, though the real Establishment that John Chandler would end up fighting would be Roy Kepler himself.

Chandler would argue about anything. Tibby Simon, the widow of longtime Kepler's clerk Nick Simon, recalled Chandler as the sort of man who would inevitably take the opposite view in any dispute. He endlessly irked those who ostensibly supervised him.

"I would come home," store manager Ralph Kohn recalled, "and [wife] Irene would make me a martini."

The sore relations between Roy and Chandler were aggravated by discussions about a Kepler's store union. This was a real sore point. Kepler's employees were coming to feel underpaid, underappreciated, and disrespected. They needed better bargaining power to ensure their rights were protected. Like the Civilian Public Service men of an earlier generation, they felt used by the supposedly virtuous institution into which they had enlisted. Roy, though, took umbrage at the very notion. Ralph Kohn thought he was even a little hurt at the idea, for all he had done for the workers.

Cody's, too, had been confronted by newly militant workers who in the spring of 1970 wanted to form a union. The narrative was similar. Both stores were run by freethinkers. They attracted workers of similar bent, who inevitably wanted to break away from the employment patriarchy. This, in turn, prompted feelings of betrayal. When Pat and Fred Cody had been presented with the demands from their workers, Pat told a friend she became deeply depressed and, literally, sick to her stomach (Cody and Cody 1992, 151).

At Kepler's, the union tensions and the frayed relationship between Roy and Chandler came to a head. As Chandler recalls it, Roy called him toward the end of his 1977 summer vacation. Don't bother coming back to work when the vacation ended, he told Chandler; you are no longer working for my store. A slightly different version is told by another employee. In late July the Kepler's employees gathered for a staff party. As recalled by this former Kepler's worker, Roy told the forty-eight-year-old Chandler at the party that he was fired: don't bother coming to the store on Monday.

However it happened, Roy subsequently explained in the August 27, 1977, issue of the *Palo Alto Times* that he had fired Chandler upon recognizing after a series of run-ins that the two men were "psychologically incompatible." More bluntly, Roy told one of his lawyers, Paul Kelley, that he had fired Chandler for "bad work performance and for constantly challenging my authority as manager/owner."

In response, Chandler claimed Roy was retaliating against him for his labor organizing efforts. Chandler filed a complaint with the National Labor Relations Board (NLRB), alleging interference with his labor organizing rights, and he kept agitating. Within a month of his firing, Chandler claimed that more than half of the thirty-five Kepler's employees had signed the cards authorizing establishment of an independent union. Chandler's complaint spelled out seven alleged incidents, starting in May 1977, in which Roy or store manager Hal Holding had supposedly infringed on workers' rights.

In each case Roy could explain away what had happened. Each explanation, though, also revealed more of the tensions gripping the store. Roy acknowledged, for instance, that in early May he had discussed with Hank Maiden the possibility of returning to the store on a part-time basis. Hank had quit several months earlier; he had been a good worker, but also vocal in his assessments of Roy's management.

"I told him I didn't care to rehire him, since I didn't care to bring back a person who was so critical of my employment policies," Roy explained to attorney Paul Kelly on November 25, 1977. "I'm not masochist enough for such punishment."

Roy said he eventually relented, on the condition that Maiden remain aloof from store politics. It was a remarkable demand, one radical pacifist demanding self-censorship from another, but Maiden agreed and Roy took him back on as an occasional substitute worker. When Maiden decided he would not be silent after all, Roy let him go. Roy considered the dismissal as a straightforward matter of a breach of oral contract and not as suppression of federally protected labor rights.

About nine months after Chandler filed his NLRB complaint, federal investigators finally got around to listening to a tape Chandler had provided them of a Kepler's employees' meeting, at which Roy had spelled out his reasons for firing Hank Maiden back in May. Roy appeared to have implicated himself on the tape, conditioning a job offer on an employee agreeing to gag himself, and under pressure of the NLRB investigation he had little choice but to rehire Chandler and provide him back pay.

The resolution did not bring peace. At Kepler's, unbeknownst to many customers, the candle was flickering. Ira, for one, had left. He had taken Molly with him to Ireland, where they set up house on Dublin's Lower Mount Street, also known as Murder Mile.

Ira wanted to be both peacemaker and the man of letters. He had published in 1974 *A Little Kinder,* dedicated in part to Roy and written as a series of letters to a fictionalized young woman, always Ira's target audience. In Dublin, Ira was scribbling away at his next effort, which he described to Roy as a series of letters written to a fictionalized character based on Holly Chenery. By the early spring of 1978, having conceded the futility of his peacemaking efforts, Ira took Molly on to Paris. Molly was studying cooking and Ira was being Ira, savoring the city. He was the thoroughly civilized man, enjoying Montaigne and his Havana cigars while his wife handled household chores, apprenticed in a French restaurant, and studied for her Grand Diplôme de Cordon Bleu.

"He does occasionally look up to give friendly words of encouragement," Molly advised Roy in a February 1978 letter.

Ira finished his first draft of his new manuscript, about twice as long as the 163-page *A Little Kinder,* including within it some versions of his own boyhood and youth. He called his new manuscript *Leap Before You Look,* from a favorite poem by W. H. Auden that describes a man who's on a path that is both short and steep:

> However gradual it looks from here
> Look if you like, but you will have to leap.

"[It] ain't no more of a bestseller than the first, but I would like to see what would happen if it got properly distributed," Ira wrote Roy on March 7, 1978. "Spiritual intellectual that I am, I would like to make money."

Ira's book would not, in the end, find a publisher. It was philosophical and personal and pretty much precisely not what publishers were looking for. The paperback industry during the 1970s was increasingly relying on a relatively few major bestsellers. The likes of Colleen McCullough's *The Thorn Birds,* published in 1977, epitomized the consolidation trend. Avon had paid $1.9 million for the paperback rights to the sprawling Australian soap opera. The blockbuster's publisher then had to recoup its investment by investing still more in a single-minded marketing campaign that left less for other, smaller books. Paperback publishers were going for the one big score, to the exclusion of the many modest offerings.

Paperback publishers shoveled out five-figure, then six-figure advances, not reluctantly, but proudly, a sign of commercial seriousness of purpose. "Before the year is out," Howard Kaminsky of Warner Books said in 1972, "you can look for us to buy two or three books for over two hundred or three hundred thousand dollars" (Davis 1984, 371). Movie tie-ins, though not new, mattered more than ever. Warner Books paid $1 million for the paperback rights to *All the President's Men,* and got its money back and then some with the 1976 release of the movie. The size of the advance itself could be a marketing tool, a real attention-grabber, but then book prices had to rise. In 1976 E. L. Doctorow's *Ragtime* broke the $2 price barrier, and the prices kept rising (Davis 1984, 375).

↓

The Vietnam War was done but Vietnam itself was still lashed, now by the Communist rulers of Hanoi. Political prisoners jammed the country's jails. Injustice endured. Working through her newly formed Humanitas International Human Rights Committee, Joan published on May 30, 1979, an open letter to the Socialist Republic of Vietnam. Roy signed on, as did nearly one hundred others ranging from Lawrence Ferlinghetti to rock promoter Bill Graham. The full-page ad ran in the *Los Angeles Times, San Francisco Chronicle, New York Times,* and other papers.

"For many Americans," the open letter stated, "especially among those who actively opposed the [Vietnam] war, there is a reluctance to face or admit that wholesale travesties of human rights occur daily in Vietnam."

Militants rejected the missive. Roy's old WRL ally David Dellinger worried about how the ad might undermine Vietnam's international standing. Normalization of relations between the United States and Vietnam should be the top priority, agreed actress Jane Fonda. Besides, Fonda opined, the victorious North Vietnamese should be judged in a different light than the one applied by certain American idealists. "I don't know if we can expect the Vietnamese to turn free those millions of people overnight, people who were involved in a war much more hideous than any repression only five years ago," Fonda advised in an open letter of her own on May 30, 1979.

The notion was popular in some activist circles. McReynolds, for one, had insisted to Roy that revolutionary violence was to be judged more sympathetically than repressive violence. Roy didn't buy it, and neither did Joan. Violence was violence. Joan said the Hanoi regime seemed to have some members of the War Resisters League and American Friends Service Committee in its pocket.

Now it was getting personal. McReynolds pleaded with Roy to counsel Joan. Noting Roy's long relationship with Joan, McReynolds hoped Roy would help stop what McReynolds considered a terribly unfair criticism. McReynolds told Joan the same, bluntly. In England, he warned, her claim that the WRL seemed to be in Hanoi's pocket could subject her to one hell of a libel suit. Roy played peacemaker with a letter sent to both protagonists. It pained him to see his fellow pacifists devolve to nasty personal attacks. He told Joan she went too far in casting aspersions on organizations. He was even more direct with McReynolds, saying the War Resisters League head appeared consumed with rage.

"You have got to be willing to still talk, and listen, to each other, and to be willing to forgive one another," Roy advised Joan and McReynolds on March 28, 1980.

McReynolds did apologize, even before receiving Roy's letter, while still insisting that Joan likewise owed an apology for her own behavior. Roy himself received a form letter from the Joan Baez organization thanking him for his willingness to sign the Vietnam ad, to which was appended a handwritten note from one of Joan's assistants. Joan had hoped to send a personal note, the assistant noted, but time and a concert tour intervened.

It sounded a bit impersonal, but that was just Joan being busy. The real chill was between Joan and Ira. Ira, who had delighted in mentoring the teenage folksinger, now was telling friends about the shortcomings of this middle-aged celebrity. Joan was an egotist, said Ira. She loved the spotlight too much. She craved the attention of men, her many doting men. Joan was not a reader, Ira complained; she had never been a reader. Joan, in turn, surely wearied of the relationship in which she had somehow evolved from acolyte to patron. Ira always seemed to need tending, his rightful due as a teacher. He overly indulged himself, in more ways than one, including, as he once put it, in his "decade of false and wanton worship of . . . the evil barbiturate" (Sandperl 1974, 71).

"Ira was my mentor for years, and when someone is your mentor, you don't see their flaws," Joan said in an interview. But then, over time, "I began to see his impetuous behavior."

Caught in the middle of the growing Joan-versus-Ira rancor were mutual friends like Roy and Randy Kehler, who would periodically hear from one or the other about myriad shortcomings.

By about 1980 Joan had stopped subsidizing Ira. She had long paid his way to some extent or another. In the very early days, she had picked up the tab for their meals at St. Michael's Alley. Later she had hired him for the Institute for the Study of Nonviolence. She had found other ways to support him too, but that stopped as their relations soured. Ira and Molly returned from France in 1980, and Molly went to work at Stanford. There then ensued an uncomfortable set of negotiations in the early 1980s in which Joan, through the Humanitas Foundation, agreed to again put Ira on the payroll in exchange for assorted peace education efforts. Humanitas made it official in a February 1983 mailing, describing Ira as a "Gandhian scholar, anti-war and civil rights activist and friend of the late Martin Luther King and [Joan Baez]." Roy's copy of the mailing included a brief, sardonic note penned by Joan, suggesting the whole business seemed like a rerun.

Joan had no interest in being in stuck in reruns. As she told one reporter, she "[did] not wish to be relegated to obscurity, antiquity or somebody else's dewey-eyed nostalgia about days gone by" (Block 1987, 14). Part of this moving on was leaving Ira. The loving bond that had made Joan and Ira such a powerful team was finis. Their special moment had passed. As Joan put it in a March 28, 1983, Humanitas letter, "It is 1983. It is time to leave the '60s behind, which many people are reluctant to do." Time, too, to leave Ira behind, Joan might have been saying.

Still, Ira was being given the opportunity to teach again. He had a title, as director of the Humanitas Nonviolent Education Program. He led a seminar on the Stanford campus, and began informal nonviolence discussion groups on Sunday evenings. He would spin marvelous yarns and drop some names: first names, of course. "At a dinner party one time, someone asked Martin, 'Isn't there anytime that violence is justified?'" Ira recounted at one session. "I thought he hesitated too long, and I jumped in and said, 'No, absolutely never.'" Ira also traveled, visiting southern California for a series of talks in early 1984, but the money came only sporadically and he was obliged to resume some Kepler's work.

Ira and Molly had returned to California, as it happened, in the year Kepler's Books & Magazines celebrated its twenty-fifth anniversary. A quarter-century in business, and Roy could be proud of what he had done. His name was synonymous with Bay Area bookselling. His store was beloved, his pacifism a local legend. Still, like every anniversary, Kepler's twenty-fifth accommodated both loss and achievement. The Menlo Park store was bigger than ever, but the Los Altos store was no more.

The second Kepler's, though originally in south Palo Alto and then relocated to Los Altos, still had the Kepler's counterculture bloodline. Longtime Los Altos store manager Betty Sumrall recalled how *Soul on Ice* author and ex-con Eldridge Cleaver would wander in seeking book recommendations, the cross around his neck "big enough for the pope." The Los Altos store even had its ultimate initiation, when its windows were broken by radical antiradicals. Still, the store struggled for identity and for sales. It was sequestered in the Village Corners shopping center, where the neighboring Irish gift shop was selling Gaelic schmaltz like *The Mantovani Orchestra Plays Favorite Irish Folk Songs*. The Los Altos Kepler's was easy to miss from the street. The Los Altos employees, Sumrall among them, would gripe about being ignored, getting the short end of the stick. The Menlo Park store employees, in turn, thought the Los Altos crew a bunch of whiners.

A self-appointed Committee to Save Store 2 in the late 1970s recommended that the Los Altos outlet be rescued by a specially selected team of top-flight workers. The outdated and esoteric inventory should be overhauled with an infusion of hardcover and gift books. The Silicon Valley crowd should be attracted with batches of technical books. The shelves should be rearranged to open up more space. The sprawling philosophy, religion, and Eastern mysticism collection should be consolidated, and the drab social science section shrunk. Best-seller racks, humor books, and games should become more prominent.

The only way to save Kepler's Los Altos store, they seemed to be saying, would be to become B. Dalton's, with a better name. It did not avail. In the summer of 1979 Roy put his 2,479-square-foot Los Alto store up for sale. It had been a pretty good run for the store since Roy opened it in 1964. For the fiscal year ending February 8, 1979, Roy reported the Los Altos store rang up gross sales of $429,325. Of arguably equal value, for a potential buyer, was the Kepler's reputation itself.

"Our image in the community is that of a forerunner," Roy wrote in an August 22, 1979, summary. "Our store is contemporary and enjoys the patronage of thousands of young people. They come expecting to find the kind of books, periodicals and posters which the youth culture of today is creating."

In relatively short order the Los Altos store was sold in May 1980 to businessman Thomas Thorpe. For Roy, the sale offered several benefits. Already distracted, he could consolidate his interests in Menlo Park. He could also rid himself of another burden. The first time he had fired John Chandler, he acted illegally and was forced to rehire him. The men kept feuding. Roy's new opportunity came when he sold the Los Alto store, requiring him to lay off two workers. He selected John Chandler to go.

So Chandler, a longtime store fixture, was not around when Roy put out a handwritten press release announcing Kepler's twenty-fifth anniversary celebration. The Menlo Park Kepler's was different in other ways too. The store was vastly larger. The competition was much stiffer, and the man behind the estimable Kepler's name was absent much of the time. His peace-seeking contemporaries had moved on to other priorities. When Linus Pauling, Roy's old ally from the Livermore protest days, came to speak to an overflowing Kepler's crowd in February 1980, his topic was not disarmament but Vitamin C and cancer.

The store's anniversary celebration itself was a casual affair. Some three hundred people gathered in the Menlo Park store for bagels, balloons, and cheap champagne. Roy snacked on whole wheat bread and cherries as he sat at a small card table.

"I didn't think we'd make it," Roy told one visitor, the *San Jose Mercury* reported on June 15, 1980.

The store took on a different quality in the fall of 1981 when it relocated to a new Victorian-styled shopping center along El Camino Real. The previous location, with its concrete walls and raw wood book racks, had stressed function over form. The new building had been remolded to match an honest old Victorian building next door. The new Kepler's was clean and spacious, well-ordered. It still was stuffed with some 70,000 titles, and flavored with the familiar old red chairs and hand-lettered shelf labels listing categories. Old-timers thought the new store was a little too tidy, sterile even. Roy took a less sentimental view.

"I don't feel that the spirit of the bookstore rests in those walls," Roy told the *Palo Alto Times* in September 1981. "What rests in the walls depends on what we do."

The paperback industry had changed. There were more titles than ever before, but corporate consolidation had turned the paperback revolution in a different direction. Some familiar old publishing names that had been part of Kepler's Books & Magazines from the beginning were falling by the wayside. In 1955, as Roy was opening his first store, the magazine-publishing Fawcett family had added to its existing Gold Medal line a new fiction house called Crest. Through the Crest name, and a nouveau riche strategy of buying up quality, Fawcett had become a reckonable force with the paperback versions of Vladimar Nabokov's *Lolita* and William Shirer's massive *The Rise and Fall of the Third Reich,* among others. Corporate suitors enamored of the thrilling paperbacks came calling, and CBS bought Fawcett. But by 1981, Fawcett Books lost a reported $6.4 million in a year, and early the next year CBS flicked it off in a fire sale (Davis 1984, 376).

Fawcett's fate both mirrored and foreshadowed what was happening throughout the paperback industry. Storied old names were giving up the ghost or being absorbed by behemoths. Independence was exhausting. Roy felt it too. Even after selling off the Los Altos store, he did not feel it possible to continue in the business. He was tired, and the work was no longer so rewarding. The long drives back and forth from Grass Valley to Menlo Park were becoming harder, the hassles with the employees more irksome.

By August 1982 Roy formally put the Menlo Park store up for sale. He had done so before, but this time he seemed close to pulling the trigger.

"I've reached the point where I don't have the energy," Roy said, the *San Jose Mercury* reported on August 23, 1982.

Roy had been off his game for several years. Starting in the late 1970s, his friends, family, and coworkers noticed something was amiss. At first they attributed it to fatigue or travel or who knows what. Kepler's clerk Maureen Day recalled Roy's drinking cup after cup of coffee until he was buzzing like a bee. Maybe that would explain Roy's occasional twitching, she thought. Then Molly Black began noticing something else, a shuffle in Roy's walking. Roy, always fit through his life, knew something was slipping. He resisted Patricia's urgings to see a doctor, but he did submit, at one point, a clipping of his hair for laboratory analysis.

The final diagnosis came about through the persistence of Roy's family. After Patricia failed to persuade Roy to see a physician, Roy's daughter Dawn called store manager Ralph Kohn, who knew a doctor skilled in diagnostics. Kohn asked the doctor to come by the Menlo Park store and casually observe Roy. The doctor saw the rigidity with which Roy moved, the way he maneuvered his entire body rather than simply turn his head from side to side. The doctor asked Roy to walk up and down an aisle, and he discerned the ungainliness with which Roy moved. He asked Roy to visit him in his office, and there the sentence was pronounced.

Roy had Parkinson's disease.

The diagnosis both horrified and helped. The degenerative nervous system disorder meant Roy could expect tremors, physical rigidity, and the slowing of movement known as bradykinesia. Roy could anticipate cognition problems and, in time, a high probability of dementia. He knew there was no cure. It was a nightmare, arriving in slow motion. On the other hand, Roy and Patricia at least had a name for what they were facing. They also had an effective and ideologically sympathetic ally in Dr. Henry Mayer, a navy veteran of World War II who had traveled to Vietnam in 1967 with the Committee of Responsibility to Save War-Burned and War-Injured Children. They could now identify palliative therapies and medications, and could communicate with others who were living with the disease. Those minor solaces would disappear as the symptoms progressed, but at the time Roy put the Menlo Park store up for sale he was still coping relatively well.

Roy asked $850,000 for the 45,000-square-foot Menlo Park shop, but he made clear that a potential buyer should "forget the price idea." Instead, Roy said, bargaining should commence on the principle of "what I want to accomplish and what the other person wants to accomplish." He even publicly suggested he might donate any sales profit to the antiwar movement. Certainly, Roy made clear, he wanted to sell to someone who was "interested in books and committed to being involved in the community." Someone, that is, who understood that Kepler's was "more than just a dollar business." Some potential bidders began sniffing around, asking about the $5,159-a-month rent, the fifteen-year lease, the $1.1 million in gross annual sales.

None of Roy's children seemed, at first, particularly keen on taking over the family business. His daughter April had trained as a certified masseuse and delved into various metaphysical disciplines, but running a store was not for her. Melody wasn't interested. Dawn loved books, and was a 1977 graduate of U.C. Berkeley with an English major, but running the business didn't appeal to her. Clark, after graduating from high school in 1977, had started working in the store's receiving department in August 1979 and then had gone on to serve as a book buyer, but he didn't feel he was on a career track. There were other things he could do with his life.

Store manager Ralph Kohn and some other store loyalists contemplated putting together a bid. Kepler's Books & Magazines needed to retain its unique identity, they thought. Besides, they figured it would be a solid investment. Nothing came of this notion, though, and so Roy was receptive when Los Altos Hills businesswoman Evelyn Sluck expressed her interest. Sluck was a forty-five-year-old accountant who owned a donut shop in downtown Los Altos. The Donut Lady, as some Kepler's clerks began calling her, reportedly wanted to diversify her financial holdings. Sluck made her inquiries and commenced discussions, and by mid-December the deal was all but closed. The sale was final enough that Bay Area newspapers began running valedictories for Kepler's Books & Magazines, including one written by Roy himself and published December 26 in the *San Jose Mercury News*. Sluck herself sought to reassure Kepler's worried customers.

"I do not intend to change anything until I really know what the bookstore business is all about," Sluck told the *Peninsula Times-Tribune* on November 23, in a comment that might have been more revealing than she knew.

And then something changed.

Clark had been considering his own future, life beyond his father's bookstore. He'd been considering, too, what it was his father had wrought. In short order, Clark made a choice. The sale was off. He would step in for Roy, and Kepler's Books & Magazines would stay in the family. Clark's decision gratified those who loved Kepler's. The store was more than a simple name. It was its own personality, irreplaceable.

"I hadn't planned to go into the family business," Clark said. "But at that point, I realized I had an opportunity to help my family rather than chase after a bunch of idealistic dreams. I made that commitment, and I haven't looked back."

Several months after Clark's store-saving decision, his father's old bookselling compatriot Fred Cody was diagnosed with lung cancer. Discontented with traditional medicine, Fred and Pat Cody embarked for a Tijuana hospital, where a radical diet therapy was said to be working wonders. Amid violent winter storms lashing the coast, Fred began the so-called Gerson treatments. Returning home to Berkeley, he continued his regimen of organic vegetable and fruit juices. The family thought he was making progress, but on July 9, 1983, complaining of sudden nausea and shortness of breath, Fred suffered a heart attack and died.

21

Book Wars

Roy built the Kepler's brand over half a century, in some ways effortlessly. He simply went about his life, embodying his principles, and Kepler's Books & Magazines was the natural consequence. Roy was tolerant, curious, unconventional, and brave, and that is what his store became.

Once manifested, though, Kepler's Books & Magazines had a life of its own. After Clark took over, he had to sustain it while adapting to new circumstances. Cobwebs needed sweeping. Systems needed updating. The bookselling competition required attention, more than ever. Even the most loyal Kepler's customer could be tempted away by a chain store's killer prices.

Clark instituted regular catalogs mailed to customers. He expanded the store's lecture series and computerized the inventory system. He was not particularly active politically while growing up, as Patricia preferred to keep radical activism out of the home, but Clark sought to keep the store engaged. In February 1989 Iran's Ayatollah Khomeini condemned Salman Rushdie's novel *The Satanic Verses*. A multimillion-dollar bounty was placed on Rushdie's head. Some stores responded prudently by pulling Rushdie's book from their shelves. Kepler's responded defiantly, hosting a public reading of *The Satanic Verses*. More than one hundred people crowded into the store to hear Ira and, in a surprise appearance, a guitar-toting Joan Baez. Two plainclothes Menlo Park police officers stood watch, while Joan sang Bob Dylan's "With God on Our Side."

The Salman Rushdie event summoned the good old Kepler's spirits: courage, song, and protest. It was also one of the last big events held at the Victoria Lane store. With the big chains encroaching, the 5,200-square-foot store was no longer big enough to compete. Across El Camino Real, developer Russ Collier was creating what he called Menlo Center, a block-long project on the east side of the busy street. It included a 10,973-square foot location, where Kepler's could shelve its 70,000 titles and then some. Clark wanted a book-lover's maze with many tall, full shelves where customers could lose themselves amid the books. The new store would not provide coffee, but a congenial establishment called Café Borrone moved down from Redwood City and opened about a month after Kepler's moved in.

The latest Kepler's opened on September 1, 1989, in time for the store to celebrate its thirty-fifth anniversary the following May. It was the last big store celebration the store's founder would know. Roy had been in serious decline through the eighties. Randy Kehler, recruited by Roy inside Santa Rita jail in 1967 to work for the War Resisters League, recalled driving up to Grass Valley sometime early in the decade. He found Roy periodically frozen in mid-conversation, at an extended loss for words. It's aphasia, Roy was finally able to tell him, rather matter-of-factly. It came with the Parkinson's disease. This was his condition, and each year it got worse. The direction was irrevocable. Over time, Roy began shuffling. He lost the ability to button his shirts and trousers.

Roy's physical deterioration was all the more painful because so many knew him for his remarkable energy. Mandy Carter, who had first started working with Roy through War Resisters League/West in 1969, recalled seeing him sometime during the 1980s at a WRL event. Everyone was standing about chatting, allies from the common cause, old comrades to hug and reminisce with. Then Roy was ushered into the get-together in a wheelchair, barely able to speak.

"I didn't even recognize him," Carter said, "and I sort of wish I hadn't seen him that way."

By 1989 Roy's family had placed him in College Park Convalescent Hospital on Crane Avenue near downtown Menlo Park. It was close to the store and Bay Area physicians but far from the family's Grass Valley home where Patricia lived. The Bay Area location made it easier for friends to visit. Roy would want to talk in the worst way, but the words were incarcerated. Longtime Kepler's employee Betty Sumrall would attend Roy at the convalescent home, and sometimes translate his garbled speech for others in the room. Molly Black, though since separated from Ira, would visit both with Ira and by herself. When Roy could still communicate, he would plaintively ask Molly and Ira not to leave. Molly would sit with him, read the newspaper or sometimes just be there. Molly thought Roy seemed to enjoy the reading sessions, the words connecting him to the world that was going on without him. Ira would leave in tears, seeing what had become of his old friend.

Don't think of Roy the way he used to be, Molly would say; it's still Roy, there.

Confusion unsettled Roy's mind, scattered his thoughts. Once Agape cofounder Claire Feder came to visit and discovered that Roy had seized his medical records and was refusing to surrender them. These records will be used against me, Roy told Feder. Then, after a time, Roy lost even the capacity to act on his Parkinson's-driven anxieties. He was utterly enwrapped.

Some, like Ralph Kohn's wife, Irene, blamed the drugs even more than the disease. Roy seemed to be perpetually doped up. It was hard to know where he was, *who* he was. Irene would visit and hold Roy's hand. She would tell him to squeeze her hand, and he would, the limit of his capability. Roy lingered, though in time he was no longer himself.

"I would dream," his daughter Dawn recalled, "that it was the medicine that was making him unable to talk. I always dreamed that the meds had worn off, and he was fine."

Roy could not fight off what insisted on taking him. In December 1993 Roy contracted pneumonia. The nursing home administrators told the family he would die without an aggressive course of antibiotics, but Dawn said the family knew that defeating the pneumonia would only extend Roy's hopeless days. Perhaps, Dawn thought, it was time for Roy to join his mother and his father and his beloved brother Earl. Roy's physician, Dr. Craig J. Hoffman of Redwood City, visited on December 29 and Dawn visited on Friday, December 31. They could observe Roy's labored breathing, his barely hanging on. The moment ripened.

It's OK, Dawn told her father. Death is OK. You can go now.

The next day, New Year's Day 1994, Roy went into cardiac arrest as a natural consequence of his pneumonia. At 11:45 in the evening and at the age of seventy-three, Roy Kepler found everlasting peace.

Half a century before his death, Selective Service officials had asked Roy to identify his religious affiliation. He answered bluntly that he was unaffiliated, but Roy was not antagonistic toward God. Christian love, Agape, was at the heart of his pacifism. He simply didn't feel a part of any religious institution. For his brother Earl, a similar sentiment had had dire consequences. Earl went to prison, in part, because the draft board legionnaires hadn't accepted the notion that a man without religious affiliation could hold sincere pacifist beliefs. Roy was similarly unaffiliated but had been spared prison, he always believed, at least in part because of his brother's harsh fate.

As an old man, too, grossly insulted by Parkinson's, Roy had been asked for an affiliation. Again he offered none. He had no preference for the type of memorial service that might be conducted on his behalf. His one stated preference was that his remains be cremated. On January 6, Roy's ashes were scattered into the Pacific Ocean three miles off of the Marin County coast.

Operating without instructions from their late father, daughters April and Dawn put a service together. The room was crowded, filled with weathered faces and vivid memories. Everyone had a story about Roy. One man recalled a particular sit-in. He said that he and the other participants were nervous, knowing they could go to jail for what they were about to do. "Then, Roy stood up," the man recalled, Dawn later recounted, "and all he said was, 'now!' and we all felt it."

Ralph Kohn spoke. He had first gotten to know Roy half a century before in Civilian Public Service, back when he was a regular Brigham Young, afire with purpose. Sociologist Theodore Roszak, who had allied himself with Roy at the start of the sixties, described his old marching companion as a man who defined the word *citizen*.

A nondenominational minister spoke. Ira thought it a poor choice. Roy, he would note, was not fond of ministers as a general matter. Ira also thought it unseemly that Roy's children in their remembrances might hint at some paternal shortcomings due to their father's insistence on going out and saving the world. It was not a criticism, though, coming from children who loved their father dearly. It was an observation, a necessary truth-telling. Ira himself did not speak during the service, demurring even after Molly and Clark asked him to say some words. Ira had just gotten out of the hospital himself and was feeling shaky. It seemed, to some, an eccentric affront for Ira to stay silent at the service of his close friend, but Ira had his reasons. He felt if he spoke it would turn attention away from Roy.

It was a dicey time for Ira. Through 1993, as Roy was slipping away, Ira's own tenuous financial circumstances had brought him to the brink. Years of bookstore clerking and unpaid peace activism left Ira with no savings and unshakeable debts. He was getting by, barely, on a sporadic Kepler's salary and his Social Security payments. He owed money to a succession of banks. Finally, in September 1993, Ira filed for Chapter Seven bankruptcy protection. Thirty-five years of working at Kepler's, time frequently interrupted by various peace ventures, had left Ira with few material goods. Books, fittingly, accounted for nearly all of Ira's assets. He loved the endless fascinations found within the thirteen volumes of the *Unabridged Oxford English Dictionary* or the twenty-eight volumes of the 1911 edition of the *Encyclopedia Britannica* (Sandperl 1974, 87). Amassed over the years, carried by his acolytes from one bachelor's apartment to another, Ira's book collection was his treasure. Beyond that, Ira essentially had the clothes on his back.

Sobering as it was, the bankruptcy declaration cleared the decks. By early February 1994, debts resolved, Ira's Palo Alto–based attorney was able to file the papers discharging the Chapter Seven petition. Other matters, too, were resolved. Just about the time Ira was getting out of bankruptcy court, roughly a month after Roy's original memorial service, Ira helped organize another service at the Palo Alto Friends Meeting House, the place where nearly four decades prior Ira had first encountered a young Joan Baez. Roy and Ira had never been entirely aligned with the virtuous Friends. Still, the Friends Meeting House on Colorado Avenue was a suitable place for Roy's final memorial service.

The room was overflowing and the stories told there, former War Resisters League/West staffer Scott Ullman said, were utterly fascinating. Some, like Ullman, heard for the first time accounts of Roy's time in the Civilian Public Service camps, his stint with KPFA, his life's work undertaken before some of them were born. There, Ira finally stood, and he spoke of his closest ally, his brother in arms.

Roy's reputation was also brought to the attention of the congresswoman who represents Menlo Park, Representative Anna Eshoo, D–San Mateo, and in early March she placed into the March 10, 1994, *Congressional Record* high praise for the late pacifist.

"Roy opened his doors to young people, people of color, and young men escaping draft boards, and dedicated himself to their financial well-being by hiring them to do odd jobs," Eshoo's statement declared. "He was a warrior for peace."

At Kepler's Books & Magazines, the published comments were a bright note in a darkening time. Clark was carrying on against ever-stiffer competition. The chain stores were at Kepler's throat. Since the early 1980s, the mall-centered Waldenbooks had been opening up to ninety new stores annually. It became the first bookstore behemoth to have at least one store in all fifty states. Other chains were proliferating both in size and number. In May 1990 Crown Books had opened the first of its "Super Crown" extravaganzas in Alexandria, Virginia. With a collection three or four times larger than the chain's average location, the Super Crown seemed a harbinger. The future was about being big.

Kmart bought Waldenbooks in 1984, adding the Ann Arbor–based Borders and its nineteen stores in 1992. Barnes & Noble was even bigger. A firm founded as an Illinois used book outlet in 1874, Barnes & Noble had taken on its fully modern cast when it was sold in 1971 for a modest $1.2 million to bookseller Leonard Riggio. The one-time New York University bookstore clerk had ambitious plans. He had pioneered television ads in 1974, and a year later initiated 40 percent discounts on new books. With the 1987 acquisition of B. Dalton's 798 stores, Barnes & Noble became the country's largest bookstore chain. The company kept buying, adding Scribner's Bookstore in 1989 and Doubleday Book Shops in 1990 (Miller 2006, 2).

These chains were tough competition. They gave customers huge selections and excellent prices, and they weren't simply warehouses. They could be fun places to browse. Barnes & Noble, drawing lessons from independents, explained in one annual report how it conjured "a library-like atmosphere of wood fixtures, antique-style chairs and tables, and ample public space used for sitting and reading" (Miller 2006, 94). David Harris, more skeptical, called Border's "Kepler's on steroids, without the grounding in people and culture." Even so, it was a formula that worked well for a lot of people.

In the face of all this, some stores simply folded.

Shirley Cobb, who had been in the bookselling business before Roy, felt obliged in March 1985 to close her downtown Palo Alto shop. The chain stores were encircling Kepler's. In 1992 Barnes & Noble opened a store in San Mateo, eight miles from Menlo Park. The next year the chain opened another store in Redwood City, two miles away. It no longer mattered that one chain had withered away. Crown Books, whose early Bay Area thrust had intimidated the independents, unceremoniously shut down its Palo Alto store in February 1991. The Kepler's crowd thought it apt that the Crown boors slunk out of downtown Palo Alto with a misspelled window sign: "Closed Permenantly." The Crown chain collapsed amid family squabbles, finally descending into bankruptcy in 1998. Few missed Crown in the Bay Area, but that particular chain and its famously fractured family proved the least of Clark's problems.

Twice, during the 1990s, Clark hired a San Carlos firm to survey customers. The initial survey revealed that customers still favored Kepler's over the new chains. By the time of the second survey, though, customers were citing prices as an issue. They could get discounts at the chains that they couldn't at Kepler's. A bookstore's legacy and atmosphere no longer sufficed. Customers might browse at the independent store, praise its character, and even lament its loss, but they would buy their books at the cheapest price possible. For Kepler's, it was a familiar problem. In the late 1950s Roy had complained that Kepler's browsers would become the Stanford Bookstore's paying customers because of the latter's rebates. Roy's approach then had been to rally other independents and challenge the university bookstore's rebate policy. Now his son had to find his own answer to the competitive challenge. Kepler's began offering 30 percent discounts on New York Times' bestsellers, and 20 percent discounts on the "Buyer's Choice" books store workers selected. It seemed the only way to keep up.

"When the chains moved into the areas, and the impact of the chains up and down the Peninsula and the Bay Area started to occur in the mid-90s, that's when I started getting customers asking about 'what's the price, [and] what are you selling it for,'" Clark explained in a May 9, 2000, deposition.

But the discounts alone didn't work for Kepler's. Customers who only wanted the cheapest prices would still go elsewhere, to the chains where high volume could compensate for lower margins. It was happening everywhere. Independent bookstores accounted for 32.5 percent of adult books sold in 1991, while chain stores claimed 22 percent of the market. By 1997 chains were selling 25 percent of the books and independents accounted for only 17 percent of sales (Miller 2006, 52). Kepler's and the other independents looked to the courts, again, for help. They had done so once before, with mixed success.

In April 1982 the Northern California Booksellers Association had sued Avon Books. Kepler's and the other Northern California stores claimed Avon gave preferential treatment to B. Dalton, Waldenbooks, and other chain stores. Invoices showed publishers were giving chain discounts of up to 48 percent on trade paperbacks. Smaller independent stores were getting only a 43 percent discount. The Avon lawsuit was a test case for the independents. If they were successful, they could take on the other publishers.

Other booksellers outside of Northern California watched carefully, though the American Booksellers Association stayed neutral. It represented not just the aggrieved independent booksellers, the Kepler's and the Cody's of the world, but also chain bookstores and even, to a degree, the publishers themselves. Publishers accounted for 60 percent of the association's annual income. The association's outgoing president, Joan Ripley, said she didn't doubt that the mass market publishers were giving different terms to the large chain buyers, but she cautioned that the independents were casting everything in too simplistic terms. This was a business, not a simple morality tale.

The publishers added that incentive payments offered to chain stores made sense financially. The chains were buying books in much higher numbers than the independents, and every business followed the tradition of providing cost breaks for bulk purchases. The publishers further noted that federal law specifically permitted discounting that could be justified on a cost basis. The chain stores needed very little, if any, servicing, Avon's attorney Royce Schulz added. The independents might have an emotional argument, but legally, Schulz said, the chains should prevail. Nobody was forcing people to buy from the chain stores, which after all were the ones serving the mass public and not just the snooty few.

"Sure, they've got some pretty sharp guys at Cody's," one unnamed Crown Books manager told the *Christian Science Monitor* in an October 21, 1982, article. "But they're the kind of people that, if you ask them for *Gone with the Wind,* they'll laugh at you."

The independent booksellers found an empathetic listener in U.S. District Judge Thelton Henderson. Small world, this. In the mid-1960s Henderson had gotten to know the Rev. Martin Luther King Jr. while serving as the first African American attorney in the Justice Department's Civil Rights Division. Henderson then had started a legal clinic in an old East Palo Alto dental office. This was the same benighted neighborhood inhabited by Free U idealists, David Harris's Peace and Liberation Commune, and their ilk. Henderson was later named assistant dean of Stanford Law School, where he conducted minority outreach and had some passing acquaintance with Free U activists before being named to the court by President Jimmy Carter. A Berkeley resident, Henderson shopped at Cody's many a time, he recalled in a 2010 interview, He knew Roy, though not very well. In all, the independent booksellers couldn't have asked for a more independent-minded judge.

Ultimately Henderson ruled in favor of the Northern California independents, determining that Avon's chain discounts were anticompetitive. Shortly afterward, on one of his regular book-buying ventures, Henderson entered Cody's. The clerk somehow recognized him and rushed into the backroom. A manager came out to say he wanted to give the federal judge some free books.

"I told them," Henderson said in a 2010 interview, "that I couldn't do that."

The publishers took a different route. They appealed. They had the deeper pockets and the endurance, and in 1987 the seemingly exhausted Northern California booksellers and the publishers settled when Avon and Bantam said they would make it easier for independent stores to earn good discounts.

The settlement may have spurred the Federal Trade Commission, which in 1988 opened its own investigation. Regulators observed that the publishers were giving certain national bookstore chains price and promotional concessions that they did not offer to independents. The complaint named six of the nation's largest publishers, including Harper & Row, Random House, and Simon & Schuster, as well as three large chains: Waldenbooks, B. Dalton and Crown. It wasn't the first time the Federal Trade Commission had wagged its finger. In 1959 regulators had alleged that paperback heavyweights New American Library, Dell, Bantam Books, and Pocket Books gave certain chain retailers special allowances not granted to smaller independents. After three years of wrangling, the publishers signed a 1962 consent decree dutifully agreeing to end the practice (Davis 1984, 266).

The 1988 complaint differed in the particulars from the 1959 case, though it still involved the same generic cast of characters: publishers, chains, and independents. Regulators were still saying the chains were getting preferential discounts, albeit in new ways. For instance, publishers were allegedly giving a price break for a large order placed by the chains even though the book orders themselves would be broken up for distribution to individual stores. Regulators also believed the chains were getting secret, off-the-books discounts unavailable to the Kepler's of the world. The Federal Trade Commission eventually withdrew the complaint, citing both the rise of new superstores and self-help action renewed by the independents.

"The dynamics and structure of the book distribution industry have evolved in significant ways," the FTC explained on September 10, 1996, adding that further investigation would be "time consuming and resource intensive." Besides, the FTC's majority reasoned, the independents had already filed their own lawsuit through the American Booksellers Association. If there were problems, a lawsuit filed in 1995 should resolve them.

The lawsuit in question had been filed in 1995 by the American Booksellers Association against five major publishing companies, including Penguin USA, Houghton Mifflin, and St. Martin's Press. Representing independent stores including Kepler's and the Kepler's spin-off Printers Inc., the association claimed the publishers violated state and federal law by giving the big chains extra discounts and special terms. "We have to compete with them," Clark told the *San Jose Mercury News*. "We just want the competition to be fair."

The publishers, at first, brushed off the complaints, saying the independents were indulging in a nostalgic longing for less competitive times. In time, settlement once again proved cheaper for all. Penguin agreed in 1998 to pay $25 million, with the stores receiving half. Out of this, Kepler's got $59,717. The money, Clark said, was used to buy more books. It evaporated quickly, as did any notion of lasting peace among the booksellers. Twenty-six members of the American Booksellers Association filed suit yet again on March 17, 1998, accusing Barnes & Noble and Borders of violating the 1936 Robinson-Patman Act requiring sellers to offer the same price to everyone. The law is supposed to block large businesses from exploiting their purchasing power. Once more the independent booksellers claimed the big chains struck secret deals with publishers in order to secure better arrangements like complete refunds on unsold books. The unfair deals were taking a fatal toll on independent booksellers. In just the four years prior to the filing of the lawsuit, an estimated 150 independent bookstores folded nationwide. The chains, in turn, were certainly growing. In 1997 Barnes & Noble opened 65 of its superstores, increasing to 483 stores nationwide. It had sales of about $2.8 billion. Borders opened 46 stores that same year, increasing its national total to 203. The Michigan-based firm had sales of about $2.3 billion.

"There are rules in business just like in sports," Squirrel Hill Bookstore owner Sherry Bloom told the *Pittsburgh Post-Gazette* in a March 19, 1998, article, "and right now those rules aren't being followed."

Across the country the renewed legal fight incited a David-and-Goliath narrative. Every city boasted of its own independent bookstores, and every local reporter seemed to be rooting for them, the likes of Denver's Tattered Cover, Omaha's Old Market Bookstore, Tampa's Inkwood Books, Boise's Book Shop, Missoula's Feed and Read and, in Ira's hometown of St. Louis, Left Bank Books. The plucky independents, without a doubt, were winning the PR front, though the chains had their arguments too.

"Barnes & Noble," the company declared in a corporate statement, "follows accepted industry practices in all of its business dealings. Programs that are available to us are made available to booksellers across America."

In March 2001 the judge ruled that the independent booksellers couldn't obtain damages from the chains. That took the wind out of the independents' sails, removing as it did the prospect of meaningful financial pain for the chains. There was really nothing left to fight for, and in the second week of the trial, the independents settled. As part of the settlement, the big chains each paid $2.35 million to partially cover attorneys' fees. The settlement, though, did not give the independents what they really wanted: an agreement that they could get the same prices as the big chains. The American Booksellers Association, moreover, agreed as part of the settlement not to file another lawsuit for at least three years. The settlement, Barnes & Noble CEO Leonard Riggio declared, was "nothing short of a total vindication for Barnes & Noble."

Practically speaking, Riggio seemed to be correct. The settlement ended, for at least several years, the round of lawsuits by which Kepler's and other independents challenged the chains and the publishers. Nor did the chain stores have to significantly alter their way of conducting business. The fat cats had won again, Lawrence Ferlinghetti concluded.

But the chain stores, in some ways, were no longer even the biggest problem for Kepler's and other independent booksellers. The bricks-and-mortar chains had simply won the biggest dinosaur contest. The online merchant Amazon.com, since its formal launch in 1995, had been dominating more of the market. The company didn't even expect to make money in its first four or five years. Over time, though, cheap prices, the infinitely vast virtual shelves, and the growing public comfort with transacting business online combined to make Amazon.com and its ilk the true competition. When Kepler's offspring Printers Inc. finally closed in 1999, the Internet and not the big chains took the blame.

Printers Inc. co-owner Gerry Masteller, a Kepler's alumnus, noted in news accounts that the store had survived the intrusion of chain stores but could not face the new combination of the Internet competition along with a rent increase.

Clark tried moving Kepler's cautiously into online sales. Kepler's had established its first Internet site around 1997, using an outside firm to help set it up. Clark did not invest a great deal in it at first; he recalls spending about $10,000 for getting the site up and running in the first year. He intended to have it grow slowly. A year later Clark would report that he was selling only about $3,000 worth of books a month through the Internet site. By 1999 Clark estimated the store was selling about $20,000 a year through the Internet site. For a store with total sales exceeding $2.5 million, it was a pittance. Kepler's, anyway, was always about the place, as much as it was about the books. Some things could not be duplicated online.

In public, for all the competitive turmoil, Kepler's Books & Magazines appeared to be enduring, especially as Clark and the family celebrated the store's fiftieth anniversary in May 2005. The place looked festive, with banners hanging and the bookshelves ripe with volumes. Clark invited the Kepler's circle, the old-timers who had made the place what it was. Neither Joan nor Ira appeared, but Joan's mom showed up and so did Ralph Kohn, in a wheelchair following a stroke. Roy's widow Patricia, though ill, mingled with old friends.

Ten weeks later, on the morning of August 31, 2005, the doors remained shut when they were supposed to be open. Customers began gathering on the plaza, peering through the windows, casting anew Leo Tolstoy's timeless question: What, then, must we do?

Epilogue

Love and moxie resurrected Kepler's Books & Magazines.

But tears came first.

Menlo Park City Councilwoman Kelly Fergusson could not believe her ears on August 31, 2005. As a Stanford undergraduate studying applied earth sciences in the mid-1980s, and then as a doctoral student in civil engineering, Fergusson had often escaped to Kepler's for her favorite fantasy and science fiction books. The store was a festive getaway, a place like no other. Once she saw Grateful Dead drummer Mickey Hart. Three decades after Jerry Garcia noodled folk songs in Kepler's backroom, Hart showed up to discuss his new book on anthropology and percussion. Where else but Kepler's could that happen?

Now, hearing the store had closed, Fergusson showed up to see for herself. The evidence was unassailable. On the plaza, people wept.

"It looked so forlorn, with the door chained shut and paper covering up the windows," Fergusson recalled in a 2010 interview. "Then and there I resolved myself that Menlo Park could not lose this community treasure, that was so much a part of, and inseparable from, our city's heritage and identity."

Fergusson tried without success to reach Clark by phone and e-mail, finally resorting to leaving a note at his Menlo Park home. Until then, she had known him only slightly. Others too were reaching out. Daniel Mendez had been eating breakfast at Café Borrone the day Kepler's closed. The cofounder of Visto Corp., a mobile e-mail business, Mendez had made a habit of bicycling with his children to the Kepler's and Café Borrone complex on weekends. He was one of the dispossessed in the plaza that morning, wondering what had happened, but the Harvard graduate and holder of several computer science–related patents was accustomed to confronting problems. He began talking, casually at first and then with more focus, about what might be done. He knew Fergusson slightly from her city council campaign, and they conversed. Then Mendez managed to get in touch with Clark with an e-mail that cut straight to the point.

"I have talked to a number of my friends and neighbors in Atherton and Menlo Park," Mendez wrote, as *Inc.* magazine reported in 2006, "and I can in short order put together a syndicate to purchase all or a portion of the operation from you . . ."

Clark agreed to meet, though he perhaps was a little conflicted. Clark had been living with the numbers for weeks, months, years. Net pretax profit margins, once livable at 2 percent, had been getting sliced ever thinner. The swell of chain and Internet competitors was driving publishers to press for quicker turnaround and payments. Kepler's annual revenue had been declining precipitously by 25 percent a year since 2001. Clark might count his own errors, but Kepler's clearly had been caught in a whirlpool not of its own making. Maybe Kepler's time had simply passed.

But Kepler's also had unique advantages. People would be willing to fight for it; they *wanted* to fight for it. It was a cause. The public sentiment became publicly apparent on September 6, a week after the store's closing. Fergusson and others had organized a pro-Kepler's rally on the plaza outside the closed store. Menlo Park city staff provided logistical support, a sympathizer cut a check to pay for sign supplies, and some 250 people convened. They brandished signs: "Read Globally, Shop Locally" and "Menlo Park is not Menlo Park without Kepler's." Some brandished specific ideas. Fergusson urged the demonstrators to pull together, and for God's sake to stop buying at Amazon. Seeing the support, Clark confessed to feeling a glimmer of hope.

"We are not dead yet," Clark told the crowd. "I hope to bring you good news sometime soon."

Many demonstrators then walked the quarter-mile to the Menlo Park City Hall for a special council meeting. Speaker after speaker claimed the microphone and had their say. There were "lots of heartfelt expressions of love for the business, its history and legacy," Fergusson recalled. Some thought the airing of sentiments sweet but a bit long-winded; it was time to get down to the nitty-gritty. This would have been a familiar scene for Roy, who had spent a lifetime in do-gooder meetings where, as he once wrote, activists "wore people out" with their talk. Still, the council meeting confirmed a reservoir of energy. Outside the council chambers, Mendez talked with Anne Banta, a former Intel marketing executive who had worked for numerous Silicon Valley firms. They might have been frustrated over the public meeting's inchoate rambling, but they appreciated the common resolve that was being expressed in many different ways.

Rick Opaterny, a Google employee in his mid-twenties who had been coming to Kepler's since high school, had started a Web site, savekeplers.com. Within the first week the site had drawn 20,000 Internet visitors. The same online capacities that had undermined Kepler's commercial potential were now enabling the Kepler's community to stay informed. Virtually and in person, Kepler's aficionados were floating ideas. The store could charge membership fees. It could charge for book readings. There was talk of establishing a fee-based research service, akin to what Roy himself had once proposed in the pre-Kepler's months after he left KPFA in 1954. Maybe money could be raised from tech-enriched Kepler's loyalists, the lease could be renegotiated, and new fundraising schemes adopted. Let the reading public literally invest in Kepler's.

It was an unusual idea, but not unheard of. Ruminator Books in St. Paul, Chapters Literary Bookstore in Washington, DC, and Black Images Book Bazaar of Dallas had all benefited from customer donations and charitable events. In San Francisco, Cover to Cover Bookstore had survived a threatened closing in 2003 after more than five hundred Cover to Cover fans pledged to spend at least $25 a month at the store. Roy himself had once toyed with securing community investment, telling a friend in 1973 that he had tried raising money for his store through private parties. He would approach people who liked the store and what it offered the community, and offer them slightly better interest than they might get parking their money in a bank.

Roy had only limited success with the venture and did not pursue it aggressively.

Mendez and Banta had many contacts and the power of a good cause. Over the course of several weeks an inner circle of seventeen investors pledged a total of $500,000 toward reopening Kepler's. The money wasn't conceived of as a charitable contribution, but it was a complicated investment. The Kepler's investors believed in the marketplace. No one was naïve enough to imagine a twenty-first-century bookstore was a surefire way to make money. Mendez made sure everyone was cognizant of the odds. This was trying to do the virtuous thing, rationally. The estimable law firm of Orrick, Herrington & Sutcliffe volunteered to represent a new investment group pro bono.

Roy would have loved it.

The new board members included Geoff Ralston, the chief product officer at Internet search innovator Yahoo, and Bruce Dunlevie, general partner of the Menlo Park–based Benchmark Capital investment firm. Dunlevie typified the board. He was a well-to-do man who had formed an intense loyalty to the store. The venture capitalist and father of three had been going to Kepler's for twenty-three years, since his days as a Stanford business school student. Mitch Slomiak, a Menlo Park consultant, came on to offer advice on a new business plan. John Doerr, perhaps Silicon Valley's most prominent venture capitalist, put in $25,000. Banta came on as chief marketing officer. In return for their dollars, the investors would own 70 percent of the store's stock, while Clark would own the remaining 30 percent.

The new team examined Kepler's operations top to bottom. Clark had been operating from a small, remote office in Belmont, several miles north of the Menlo Park store. That should close, consolidating management in the bookstore itself. The store environment should be reordered, the mazes of bookshelves rearranged after the fashion of other stores. No more getting lost in the stacks. Authors' readings and public gatherings could be marketed more effectively, remaking Kepler's as a destination. The store could offer fresh enticements: a new Kepler's Literary Circle, where for $20 members could get discounts, author invitations, and more.

"I see it as a whole community of booklovers, people who are passionate about their literary pursuits and who are volunteers in the store," Mendez told the *Palo Alto Weekly* in the October 5, 2005, issue. "They may not be able to run the cash register, but they can help people with recommendations."

The new Kepler's circle didn't want charity. They wanted to build something sustainable, part of the market economy. Roy would have appreciated that. Those who didn't know better had always been surprised by Roy's insistence on making a buck, but he was a businessman through and through. The bottom line needed tending, consistent with one's ideals. Clark, Mendez, and the new inner circle of potential Kepler's investors had to settle new terms with book vendors and other creditors. That was a snap, compared to the task of renegotiating terms with the landlords at the Tan Group, owners of the Menlo Park property. Mendez couldn't seem to get his phone calls returned. Letters went unanswered.

Fergusson said she realized she needed to meet face to face with the Tan Group executives and drive home just what a jewel they had in Kepler's. She showed up, unannounced, at the Tan Group's Palo Alto headquarters, where she finally found a staff member who seemed to listen indifferently as she laid out the picture.

"I just want you to know that the eyes of the community are upon you. The community will be very grateful for anything you can do," Fergusson said, as *Inc.* magazine subsequently reported in a detailed account of the Kepler's resurrection (Burlingham 2006).

Everyone was working their individual networks. Going all the way to the top, Fergusson said in an interview that she went to the gated Atherton home of Faber Tan, the privacy-loving patriarch of the Tan Group, and left a personal letter. The heat was felt. The Tan Group finally broke its silence by declaring that "contrary to the impression given by the media," the bookstore was considered a "unique asset to and irreplaceable part" of the overall Menlo Park business center. Negotiations commenced. This was business, not sentiment. If the Tan Group was going to loosen the strictures of Kepler's ten-year lease, it would insist on concessions in return. Time was passing; each week another lost revenue opportunity. Fergusson finally reached the Tan Group's president at home as he was on his way to a San Francisco Giants baseball game, and that seemed to cinch it. On Monday, October 3, the negotiators reached agreement on a new lease. That freed investors to sign their own agreement on Friday, the day before the store was set to reopen.

Five weeks before, on August 31, 2005, a stunned and grieving crowd had gathered on the plaza as word spread about Kepler's closing. Now it was Saturday, October 8, and the sun was shining just as it should. Upwards of eight hundred people mingled outside. The celebrants sipped coffee from Café Borrone, shook hands, swapped yarns. Cars slowed along El Camino Real as drivers checked out this latest scene. Another protest perhaps?

Clark sported a black T-shirt, one not seen before. Friends and perfect strangers admired the back message: "Follow me to Kepler's. It's our bookstore." *Our* bookstore. It was a statement not just of ownership, but of joint venture. Shortly after 11 a.m., Fergusson took the microphone.

"We refused to accept that faceless economic forces could steal the heart and soul of our community," Fergusson declared, the *Country Almanac* reported on October 12, 2005.

The mayor of Menlo Park spoke, and the local state assemblyman. They were cheerleaders, celebrating the hometown team made good. Daniel Mendez told the crowd that "it's a thing of beauty, to see the community come together." Anne Banta urged the crowd to put their passion into practice. Then it was Clark's turn.

"I've worked harder the last thirty-five or forty days than I have my entire life," Clark told the crowd.

And with that, Clark led the customer parade back into Kepler's, once his father's store but now his own.

Like every good thing in life, the reopening of Kepler's was a close call. It would have only taken one missed message, one mixed signal, and the whole improbable venture might have failed. As it was, the rush of good feeling that accompanied the store's triumphant reopening inevitably faded. Business more or less as usual returned. By early 2009, with thin ice cracking all around, Kepler's was reducing its weekend hours in an effort to save money. Longer term, of course, there could be no guarantee that Kepler's Books & Magazines would survive at all. Happily ever after didn't always happen. Cody's Books, in its own way as beloved as Kepler's, hung on until the summer of 2006 before owner Andy Ross closed the famed Berkeley store. A year later, Ross closed Cody's San Francisco outlet. In 2012, Clark retired and the store was sold to former business consultant Praveen Madan.

There were no guarantees. Roy knew that. His brother Earl's death had seared in him the recognition of life's indifferent give-and-take. Blossoms seemed always to decay. A public radio alliance would fracture. A free university would rise and fall. A nonviolent institute would come and go. Lovers would divorce, a peaceful moment pass.

One could never be certain, of either outcome or direction. In a February 5, 1951, letter, Roy advised his college newspaper that "the pacifist does not *know* that his course is right." Rather, Roy reasoned, the pacifist acts as he does "because insofar as he thinks he can see a part of the truth . . . this is what it tells him to do."

A part of the truth is as good as it gets. Surely Roy Kepler saw at least that much. He followed the truth as he was able. He spoke it as he could. He fell short, and then he resumed his labors, working toward what his life was about, that which he sought.

Said simply, now:

Peace.

References

Index

References

Interviews and Correspondence

Ken Babbs, Joan Baez, Valerie Bell, Dorothy Bender, Ron Bevirt, Molly Black, Buff Bradley, Stewart Brand, Mandy Carter, Holly Chenery, Melinda Clarke, Lola Edwards Clay, Falline Danforth, Maureen Day, Winter Dellenbach, Dan Dingman, Les Earnest, Claire Feder, Kelly Fergusson, Ed Fredkin, Vernon Gates, David Harris, Hank Harrison, Thelton Henderson, Lee Herzenberg, Douglas Hofstadter, Robert Hunter, Christopher Jones, Denise Kaufmann, Alan Kay, Randy Kehler, Scott Kennedy, Clark Kepler, Dawn Kepler, Patricia Kepler, Roy Kepler, Irene Kohn, Ralph Kohn, Steve Ladd, Armand Lareau, Willy Legate, Susan MacDonald, Gerry Masteller, Ed McClanahan, Boyd McDonald, Jim McGee, Dennis McNally, Barbara (Brigid) Meier, Judith Rascoe, Ira Sandperl, Nicole Sandperl, Sat Santokh, Roy Seburn, Christie Siegel, Tibby Simon, Robert Stone, Betty Sumrall, Melinda Sumrall, Lee Swenson, Larry Tesler, Alan Trist, Phil Trounstine, Scott Ullman, Ruhama Veltfort, James Ware, James Wolpman.

Books, Dissertations, Reports, and Magazines

Appy, Christian. 2003. *Patriots: The Vietnam War Remembered from All Sides*. New York: Viking.

Baez, Joan. 1987. *And a Voice to Sing With*. New York: New American Library.

———. 1966. *Daybreak: An Autobiography*. New York: Avon Books.

Baez Sr., Joan. 1994. *Inside Santa Rita: The Prison Memoir of a War Protester*. Santa Barbara, CA: John Daniel & Co.

Beagle, Peter. 1966. "Joan Baez: A Voice of Nonviolence." *Los Angeles Times Magazine*, Oct. 23.

Bennett, Scott H. 1998. "Pacifism Not Passivism: The War Resisters League and Radical Pacifism, Nonviolent Direct Action, and the Americanization of Gandhi, 1915–1963." PhD diss., Rutgers Univ.

————. 2003. *Radical Pacifism: The War Resisters League and Gandhian Nonviolence in America, 1915–1963.* Syracuse, NY: Syracuse Univ. Press.

Block, Adam. 1987. "Baez Means Business: On the Comeback Trail with the Other Madonna." *San Francisco Examiner Image Magazine,* Aug. 2.

Bonn, Thomas L. 1982. *Undercover: An Illustrated History of American Mass Market Paperbacks.* Middlesex, England: Penguin Books.

Burlingham, Bo. 2006. "Rewriting the Ending: The Unfortunate Demise and Surprising Rebirth of a Very Special Business." *Inc.,* Apr. 1. http://www.inc.com/magazine/20060401/kepler.html.

Coats, Tom. N.d. "Draft Narrative of Midpeninsula Free University Peace Games." Kepler Papers, Swarthmore College Peace Collection, Swarthmore, PA (SCPC).

Cody, Fred, and Pat Cody. 1992. *Cody's Books: The Life and Times of a Berkeley Bookstore, 1955–1977.* San Francisco: Chronicle Books.

Cooney, Robert, and Helen Michalowski, eds. 1977. *The Power of the People: Active Nonviolence in the United States.* Culver City, CA: Peace Press.

Davis, Kenneth C. 1984. *Two-Bit Culture: The Paperbacking of America.* Boston: Houghton-Mifflin Co.

Dellinger, David. 1993. *From Yale to Jail.* New York: Pantheon Books.

D'Emilio, John. 2004. *Lost Prophet: The Life and Times of Bayard Rustin.* Chicago: Univ. of Chicago Press.

Dempsey, David. 1953. "The Revolution in Books." *Atlantic Monthly,* Jan.

DeVoto, Bernard. 1954. "The Easy Chair: Culture at Two Bits." *Harper's,* Oct.

Didion, Joan. 1990. "Where the Kissing Never Stops." In *Slouching Toward Bethlehem.* New York: Farrar, Straus & Giroux.

Dingman, Dan. N.d. "My Life as a Conscientious Objector (Pacifist)." Swarthmore, PA: SCPC.

Draves, Bill. 1980. *The Free University: A Model for Lifelong Learning.* Chicago: Association Press.

Duveneck, Josephine. 1978. *Life on Two Levels: An Autobiography.* Los Altos, CA: William Kaufmann.

Eisan, Lesli. 1948. *Pathways of Peace: A History of the Civilian Public Service Program.* Elgin, IL: Brethren Publishing House.

Engelman, Ralph. 1996. *Public Radio and Television in America: A Political History.* Thousand Oaks, CA: Sage Publications.

Ferber, Michael, and Staughton Lynd. 1971. *The Resistance*. Boston: Beacon Press.

Fisher, Louis. 1962. *The Essential Gandhi: An Anthology*. New York: Random House.

Frazer, Heather, and John O'Sullivan. 1996. *We Have Just Begun Not to Fight*. New York: Twayne Publishers.

Gandhi, Mohandas K. 1993. *An Autobiography: The Story of My Experiments with Truth*. Boston: Beacon Press.

Gara, Larry, and Lenna Mae Gara. 1999. *A Few Small Candles: War Resisters of World War II Tell Their Stories*. Kent, OH: Kent State Univ. Press.

Goines, David Lance. 1993. *The Free Speech Movement: Coming of Age in the 1960s*. Berkeley: Ten Speed Press.

Greenfield, Robert. 1996. *Dark Star: An Oral Biography of Jerry Garcia*. New York: William Morrow and Co.

Gross, Sidney, and Phyllis B. Steckler. 1963. *How to Run a Paperback Bookshop*. New York: R. R. Bowker Co.

Hafer, Harold E., and Dudley I. Hutchinson. 1951. "Report to the Board of Regents of the University of Colorado." May 29. Boulder, CO.

Hajdu, David. 2001. *Positively 4th Street: The Lives and Times of Joan Baez, Bob Dylan, Mimi Baez Fariña and Richard Fariña*. New York: Farrar, Straus and Giroux.

Harris, David. 1982. *Dreams Die Hard: Three Men's Journey through the Sixties*. New York: St. Martin's Press.

Hill, Lewis. 1958. *Voluntary Listener-Sponsorship: A Report to Educational Broadcasters on the Experiment at KPFA, Berkeley, California*. Berkeley: Pacifica Foundation.

House Committee on Internal Security. 1972. "America's Maoists: The Revolutionary Union (and) The Venceremos Organization." Washington, DC: House Committee on Internal Security.

Hughan, Jessie Wallace. 1942. *Three Decades of War Resistance*. New York: War Resisters League.

Jackson, Blair. 1999. *Garcia: An American Life*. New York: Viking Press.

Johnson, C.S. 1945. "Summary of CPS 135." SCPC.

Kaplan, David A. 1999. *Silicon Boys and Their Valley of Dreams*. New York: William Morrow.

Katz, Milton Steven. 1973. "Peace, Politics and Protest: SANE and the American Peace Movement, 1957–1972." PhD diss., Saint Louis Univ.

Katz, Neil H. 1974. "Radical Pacifism and the Contemporary American Peace Movement: The Committee for Nonviolent Action, 1957–1967." PhD diss., Univ. of Maryland.

Kaufman, Abraham. N.d. "Outline of WRL History." Abraham Kaufman Papers, SCPC.

Keim, Alfred N. 1990. *The CPS Story: An Illustrated History of Civilian Public Service.* Intercourse, PA: Good Books.

Kepler, Roy. N.d. Diary. Kepler Papers, SCPC.

———. 1951. "The Function of the Terror in the French Revolution." Aug. 20. SCPC.

———. 1964. "Nonviolent Defense." Sept. 24. SCPC.

———. 1949. "Report on Country-Wide Trip: March 4–May 30, 1949." SCPC.

———. N.d. "The Terror During the KPFA Revolution: A Chronicle of Division and Dissent." SCPC.

Land, Jeff. 1999. *Active Radio: Pacifica's Brash Experiment.* Minneapolis: Univ. of Minnesota Press.

Lasar, Matthew. 1999. *Pacifica Radio: The Rise of an Alternative Network.* Philadelphia: Temple Univ. Press.

Lecuyer, Christopher. 2006. *Making Silicon Valley: Innovation and the Growth of High Technology, 1930–1970.* Cambridge, MA: MIT Press.

Leonard, Vicki, and Tom MacLean, eds. 1977. *The Continental Walk for Disarmament and Social Justice.* New York: Continental Walk for Disarmament and Social Justice.

Levy, Steven. 2001. *Hackers: Heroes of the Computer Revolution.* New York: Penguin Books.

Lichtman, Jane. 1973. *Bring Your Own Bag: A Report on Free Universities.* Washington, DC: American Association for Higher Education.

Lipton, Lawrence. 1959. *The Holy Barbarians.* New York: Julian Messner.

Lyman, Richard W. 2009. *Stanford in Turmoil: Campus Unrest, 1966–1972.* Stanford, CA: Stanford General Books.

Lynd, Staughton, ed. 1966. *Nonviolence in America: A Documentary History.* New York: Bobbs-Merrill.

Markoff, John. 2005. *What the Dormouse Said: How the '60s Counterculture Shaped the Personal Computer Industry.* New York: Viking.

McKinney, Eleanor, ed. 1966. *The Exacting Ear.* New York: Pantheon Books.

McNally, Dennis. 2002. *A Long Strange Trip: The Inside History of the Grateful Dead*. New York: Broadway Books.

Merton, Thomas. 1995. *Run to the Mountain: The Story of a Vocation*. New York: HarperCollins.

Miller, Laura J. 2006. *Reluctant Capitalists: Bookselling and the Culture of Consumption*. Chicago: Univ. of Chicago Press.

Moroi, Yuichi. 2008. "Ethics of Conviction and Civic Responsibility: Conscientious War Resisters in America During the World Wars." PhD diss., Boston Univ.

Olmstead, Frank. 1946. "The Minersville Liberty Men." SCPC.

Ong, Mark Stuart, and John Walker. 1991. "The Roy Kepler Story." Final draft, copyright Mark Stuart Ong.

Peck, Jim. 1958. *We Who Would Not Kill*. New York: Lyle Stuart.

Perry, Paul. 1990. *On the Bus: The Complete Guide to the Legendary Trip of Ken Kesey and the Merry Pranksters and the Birth of the Counterculture*. New York: Thunder's Mouth Press.

"Report on the Continental Walk." 1976. SCPC, Apr. 7.

Robinson, Mitchell Lee. 1990. "Civilian Public Service During World War II: The Dilemmas of Conscience and Conscription in a Free Society." PhD diss., Cornell Univ.

Sandperl, Ira. 1974. *A Little Kinder*. Palo Alto, CA: Science and Behavior Books.

Sareyan, Alex. 1994. *The Turning Point: How Men of Conscience Brought About Major Change in the Care of America's Mentally Ill*. Washington, DC: American Psychiatric Press.

Schlissel, Lillian. 1968. *Conscience in America: A Documentary History of Objection in America, 1757–1967*. New York: E. P. Dutton.

Selective Service System. 1950. "Conscientious Objection." Special Monograph no. 11, vol. 1, SCPC.

Server, Lee. 1994. *Over my Dead Body: The Sensational Age of the American Paperback, 1945–1955*. San Francisco: Chronicle Books.

Sileski, Bernard. 1990. *Ferlinghetti: The Artist in His Time*. New York: Warner Books.

Stone, Robert. 2007. *Prime Green: Remembering the Sixties*. New York: HarperCollins.

Tebbell, John. 1987. *Between Covers: The Rise and Transformation of Book Publishing in America*. New York: Oxford Univ. Press.

Tracy, James Russell. 1993. "Forging Dissent in an Age of Consensus: Radical Pacifism in America, 1940 to 1970." PhD diss., Stanford Univ.

Turner, Fred. 2006. *From Counterculture to Cyberculture: Stewart Brand, the Whole Earth Network, and the Rise of Digital Utopianism*. Chicago: Univ. of Chicago Press.

Tyson, Samuel. 1960. "Non-violent Action at Livermore." Aug. 9. SCPC.

U.S. House Committee on Armed Services. 1950. *Selective Service Act Extension: Hearing*. 81st Cong., 1st sess.

U.S. House Committee on Un-American Activities. 1960. *The Northern California District of the Communist Party: Hearing*. 86th Congress, 2nd sess.

Veltfort, Ruhama. 2010. *The Things We Do for Love*. Petaluma, CA: Wordrunner Press.

"The Wartime Service and Treatment of Conscientious Objectors in the United States." 1945. American Friends Service Committee, reprinted in *Congressional Record*, July 21.

Whiting, John. 1992. "The Lengthening Shadow: Lewis Hill and the Origins of Listener-Sponsored Broadcasting in America." http://www .whitings-writings.com/lengthening_shadow.htm.

Wittner, Lawrence S. 1984. *Rebels Against War: The American Peace Movement*. Philadelphia: Temple Univ. Press.

Zaroulis, Nancy, and Gerald Sullivan, eds. 1984. *Who Spoke Up: American Protest Against the War in Vietnam 1963–1975*. Garden City: Doubleday and Co.

Index

Italic page numbers denote illustrations.